Mel Brooks FAQ

Mel Brooks FAQ

All That's Left to Know About the Outrageous Genius of Comedy

Dale Sherman

APPLAUSE
THEATRE & CINEMA BOOKS
An Imprint of Hal Leonard LLC

Published in 2018 by Applause Theatre & Cinema Books
An Imprint of Hal Leonard LLC
7777 West Bluemound Road
Milwaukee, WI 53213

Trade Book Division Editorial Offices
33 Plymouth St., Montclair, NJ 07042

The FAQ series was conceived by Robert Rodriguez and developed with Stuart Shea.

All images are from the author's collection unless otherwise noted.

Printed in the United States of America

Book design by Snow Creative

Library of Congress Cataloging-in-Publication Data
Names: Sherman, Dale, author.
Title: Mel Brooks FAQ : all that's left to know about the outrageous genius of
    comedy / Dale Sherman.
Other titles: Mel Brooks frequently asked questions
Description: Milwaukee, WI : Applause Theatre & Cinema Books, an Imprint of
    Hal Leonard, LLC, 2018. | Includes bibliographical references and index.
Identifiers: LCCN 2017052707 | ISBN 9781495025136 (pbk.)
Subjects: LCSH: Brooks, Mel, 1926—Criticism and interpretation.
Classification: LCC PN1998.3.B7596 S54 2018 | DDC 791.4302/33092—dc23
LC record available at https://lccn.loc.gov/2017052707

www.applausebooks.com

Dedicated to Brian Schnau, Mike DeGeorge, Jill Sherman, and Maddie Sherman (age eight), for their dedication to me.

Contents

Introduction   ix

1   We're Unrehearsed: The Early History of Mel Brooks
in Ten Easy Lessons   1
2   Far Enough Out for You? The Beginning Caesar Years   17
3   Too Simple, Too Pure: Television Writing—the Freelance Years   38
4   And Loving It: *Get Smart*   49
5   The Difference Between Comedy and Tragedy: The Long
Journey of the 2000-Year-Old Man   54
6   All American: Early Broadway Attempts   65
7   I'm Going There, Too: Anne Bancroft   77
8   Where Did I Go Right? *The Producers*   88
9   Tito Has the Car: *The Twelve Chairs*   116
10   You'd Do It for Randolph Scott: *Blazing Saddles*   128
11   Quiet Dignity and Grace: *Young Frankenstein*   157
12   Which One of You Is Funn? *Silent Movie*   187
13   I Got It: *High Anxiety*   207
14   They Stink on Ice! *History of the World: Part I*   223
15   And Nobody Saw It: *To Be or Not to Be*   239
16   Just Plain Yogurt: *Spaceballs*   254
17   A Bunch of Moments: *Life Stinks*   270
18   It Worked in *Blazing Saddles*: *Robin Hood: Men in Tights*   282
19   Would an Enema Help? *Dracula: Dead and Loving It*   299
20   They're All Oddballs: The Films of Brooksfilms   310
21   Talking in a Closet Under a Naked Lightbulb: The Later
Television Series   323
22   You Be What's-His-Face: Guest Appearances   330
23   King of Broadway: Staging *The Producers* and *Young Frankenstein*   335
24   To Be or Not to Be: Projects Abandoned   348

Appendix: The Awards   361
Bibliography   363
Index   373

Introduction

Mel Brooks has entertained more than four generations of people in his lifetime.

That's almost enough for an introduction right there.

Let that sink in a bit. Mel Brooks began working in the Catskills in the 1930s, entertaining audiences as a young teenager. He not only lived through World War II, he was a soldier who saw action in the final days of the war in Europe. He struggled finding his niche as a writer on Broadway during the grand days of the musical comedy through the 1950s and 1960s, only to finally create a Broadway show forty years later that would win twelve Tony Awards. Speaking of which, he is one of the few recipients of all four major entertainment awards in America: the Emmy, the Grammy, the Oscar, and the Tony. He also participated in live television in its infancy, while his audio work with Carl Reiner has led to the success of comedy albums that few have surpassed. As for the movies, he has been a writer, director, and actor—talents even his worst critics have begrudgingly admitted he could do quite well.

The movies he directed are what many remember the most about Mel Brooks, as they set the standard for movie comedies ever since. With certain risk to his career as well. There may have been other entertainers willing to lampoon conservative values and even Hitler before the daring ventures of Brooks, but most of them were people working in smoky venues on dimly lit stages. Brooks with *The Producers* was screaming from the rooftops, with the wide arc lights aimed directly at him for all the world to see. He followed this up a few years later by convincing a major studio to release *Blazing Saddles*, where he tore up racism and the N-word together. Just as risky was the chance to make more personal comedies over this career, with films such as *The Twelve Chairs*, *To Be or Not to Be*, and *Life Stinks*.

How much of an impact did his movies have? Consider this—he only directed eleven movies in his entire career. Yet a good number of them are considered classics. Many writers, directors, and actors who grew up enjoying his movies were inspired to make comedies, and in various ways push the envelope even further once Brooks showed them that it was possible. Without him, we may never have seen such films as *Animal House*, *Airplane!*, *American Pie*, or *The 40-Year-Old Virgin*. Even the films Brooks made that did not perform as well at the box office, such as *Spaceballs* or *Robin Hood: Men in Tights*, are now considered cult movies and performed well on video (Brooks has claimed that *Spaceballs* is still his biggest seller on video in comparison with his more "artistic" endeavors). No doubt, grown-ups who were kids when they first saw such films loved them and have turned their children on to the films, thus furthering the generational aspect of Brooks's work. Further, there is also Brooks's headstrong involvement in producing high-quality dramatic movies through Brooksfilms between 1980 and 1992, giving early national exposure to exceptional directors such as David Lynch (*The Elephant Man*) and David Cronenberg (*The Fly*), amongst others.

Mel Brooks has stated many times over the years that the purpose of life, or at least *his* life, has been to "make a noise"—rattle things, shake up the people, upset the status quo—and get everyone to notice and perhaps give something of yourself to make others happy, or at least entertain them in some manner. In pursuing that lofty goal, Brooks has wandered through various corners of the entertainment world over a period of seventy-five years and earned his role as a living encyclopedia of events that have shaped our current world, both good and bad.

In the following pages of *Mel Brooks FAQ* are examinations of his early career, his various television years, each of his movies, Brooksfilms, and more. Many times, Brooks hit a home run, while other times there were setbacks, and through this examination perhaps we'll see how what Brooks has gone through has affected his world and ours as well.

We're Unrehearsed

The Early History of Mel Brooks in Ten Easy Lessons

You want to know where my comedy comes from? It comes from not being kissed by a girl until you're sixteen. It comes from the feeling that, as a Jew and as a person, you don't fit into the mainstream of American society. It comes from the realization that even though you're better and smarter, you'll never belong.

—Mel Brooks to Paul Zimmerman, Newsweek, 1975

One thing certainly can be said for Mel Brooks—he isn't much for being a man of mystery. Some writers wish to let their work speak for them and seldom allow for interviews; others may only talk about their projects, but nothing about their past or personal lives. That has never been the method to Brooks's madness. This man lives to speak and is the proverbial "open the refrigerator door and he does ten minutes" showman.

In other words, Brooks loves the spotlight and will tell stories about himself, his past, his movies, his future, his clothes, your future, your dog's past, the future of imaginary creatures—anything and everything, and as often as asked. The upside is that he has told the stories so many times there is a consistency to them. Better yet, as a storyteller, such tales are constructed to deliver a windup to set up a home run as a finisher. On the downside, he is a master writer, and therefore tends to clean up his anecdotes in order to give them more punch. This is particularly true about his past from before he settled into his film career. If a remembrance works better being told with aspects changed slightly (not so much nixed completely, but altered just a smidge) to enhance the story, so be it.

Not to downplay anything Brooks has said over the years, but it does somewhat jumble the timeline of Brooks's history, which has been reported differently in various official and nonofficial sources. And while it may be spoiling a punch line or two to annotate the stories here, the greater purpose is to help focus on what led Mel Brooks to develop his career the way he did over the years.

King of France

Mel Brooks was born Melvin James Kaminsky on June 28, 1926, in his family home—Brooks has said he was born on the kitchen table—in Brownsville, a section of Brooklyn in New York that then and now has a large Jewish population. His father was Maximilian Kaminsky, a process server known to have served summonses to famous people often enough to be given the nickname "at the courthouse as 'Process Server to the Stars.'" Maximilian had come to America as a boy from Poland, a country that Brooks would return to for his remake of *To Be or Not to Be*. Brooks also used his father's first name for the seedy—but father-figure-like—producer in his first movie, *The Producers*, as well as naming his son with Anne Bancroft Maximilian. His mother was Kitty Kaminsky, whose maiden name was Brookman, and had come from Kiev, the capital of Ukraine. The two had married young and had their first child by the age of twenty.

Melvin was the fourth and final child, all boys, for the proud parents. His oldest brother, Irving, was born in 1916, followed by Leonard in 1917, and then Bernard (Bernie) in 1922. The family seemed to be adequately surviving on his father's salary until Max passed away from tuberculosis of the kidney when Mel was two and a half. It was a death in the family that shook the young Mel and helped formed some of the aspects of his creativity later in life. He reflected upon this in 1975 to *Playboy*: "All I know is what they've told me. He was lively, peppy, sang well. Isn't it sad that that's all a son should know about his father? If only I could look at him, touch his face, see if he had eyebrows! Maybe in having the male characters in my movies find each other, I'm expressing the longing I feel to find my father and be close to him."

With his father's passing, the family had to shuffle financial responsibilities. As each son reached the age of twelve, they went out after school to find work, while—with some additional cash coming from both sides of the family at times—Brooks's mother began to work as a seamstress, taking in additional work to do at home at night to help cover the rent. Although it was a struggle to keep all four boys in school, fed, and clothed, Kitty Kaminsky did exactly that, which Mel would always be proud to point out in interviews, such as, again, for *Playboy* in 1975. "Worked the normal ten-hour day and then brought work home. Turned out bathing suit sashes until daylight, grabbed a few hours of sleep, got us up and off to school and then went to work again. . . . All night she would sit up sewing, pressing rhinestones, going blind. Wonderful woman."

Besides his immediate family, Mel was constantly the source of amusement for many of his relatives who would come by to check on Kitty and the boys. "I was always being tossed in the air, kissed, adored and punched. As early as I can remember, I was expected to perform." As he often did, Brooks referred to this period in his 1975 *Playboy* interview as being moved from the happy arms of one relative to another so often that "my feet didn't touch the ground until I was 6 years old." It also developed his personality in the sense that he thought he would always someday be "the King of France" because everyone treated him as royalty.

Amongst the relatives who came to see the family, one of two he saw the most was his grandmother, who would tell jokes—even dirty ones sometimes—in a mixture of English and Yiddish, and helped influence Brooks's interest in comedy. The other relative he saw was Uncle Joe, who was a cab driver so short that he drove sitting on phone books and had a special adapter for the pedals on his taxi. Uncle Joe, sensing his sister's son was missing a father figure, tried his best to do what he could to give young Mel an adult male to look up to in the family, coming by often to play with the boy and give him treats. These two family members, along with the love Mel felt for his mother and her temperament and humor, would later pour forth into one of Brooks's greatest works: "The 2000 Year Old Man is a pastiche of everyone around me," Brooks told David Susskind, "my mother, my Uncle Joe, my grandmother. When I became him, I could hear 5,000 years of Jews pouring through me."

It was this attention and care he got from his family that would also lead Brooks to consistently criticize the common belief that comedians want laughs because of having harsh family lives growing up. "The notion," he told *Newsweek* in 1975, "that we get into the business of making people laugh because we didn't get enough love as kids—that's all bullshit. I knew what love was, so I wanted more of it. And I realized early on that if you truly entertain people, they'll love you for it."

Education In and Out of School

While Brooks felt this love at home, he did have to deal with the world outside of the front door. Being a poor kid, public school was his natural first real step into the world, going to PS 19 (now PS 414 Brooklyn Arbor) in Williamsburg, a school largely made up of the children of immigrants. When Mel was thirteen and a half, the family moved to Brighton Beach and he continued his education at Abraham Lincoln High School. The school would later become known for having educated three Nobel Prize winners, but Mel only attended a year before the family moved back to Williamsburg, as his mother missed the closeness of friends and family. At first, Kitty thought Mel should go to trade school, but his brothers wanted him to attend the same school they had, Eastern District High School. Mel also "for forty-five minutes" attended Shul, the synagogue, for Hebrew School. "We were the children of immigrants. They told us religious life was important, so we bought what they told us. We faced it, nodded like we were praying. Learned enough Hebrew to get through a bar mitzvah," Brooks remembered to *Playboy*.

Mel had little use for school besides the opportunity to perform in front of the other kids. "When I had to read a composition, I would turn into a wild-eyed maniac, fling out my arms and announce in a ringing soprano, 'My Day at Camp!'" Although his brothers would excel, "I wasn't a big reader. Couldn't sit still long enough." While Brooks tends to downplay his accomplishments in school, he did achieve some distinctions by being active in the student council, a member of the school's fencing team, and even working for a time as the dean's assistant.

Mainly, however, it was the hard-knock world outside of school that Mel remembers—or wants others to remember—of his youth. "We couldn't wait to get away from school. We hung out in the street—and on the corner." And that was where the humor and music built up inside of him helped him survive in a world that was corroded with anti-Semitism coming from kids in the street and on up. Even in a neighborhood full of Jews, he still had to watch his step, and kids went in groups to avoid being preyed upon by others. "Only place to swim was McCarren Park, which was in a gentile region of Brooklyn. We could only go there if there were six to twelve of us. Otherwise, we'd be attacked. Like, we'd be in the locker room and a gang of Irish or Polish or Italian kids would be there and they'd inspect you. They'd see you were circumcised, so they knew who was what."

Outside of his family, Mel soon found his gift for comedy when he was seven, by imitating the counselors at the Sussex Camp for Underprivileged Children he attended; barking out inane orders and making the other kids laugh. It would typically end with him being slapped by the counselors, but the beatings were worth it if he got laughs and the respect of the other children. From there, Brooks saw an outlet for his lack of physical attributes—being "short, scrawny and the last one they picked to be on the team"—and the anger he felt over the anti-Semitism he sometimes saw in the neighborhood. "I'm sure a lot of my comedy is based on anger and hostility," Brooks told John Wakeman for his book *World Film Directors*. "Growing up in Williamsburg, I learned to clothe it in comedy to spare myself problems—like a punch in the face."

Thus, he concentrated on using his intelligence and his ability to make people laugh, allowing him to circumvent the barriers that were supposed to keep him in place by society. "But I was smarter than most kids my age, so I hung around with guys two years older. Why should they let this puny kid hang out with them? I gave them a reason. I became their jester." It would be a role that would not only get him through this school years, but later in his professional career as well.

An Early Taste for Broadway

One thing that Brooks remembers was the music he heard everywhere while growing up, "Not Vivaldi, or Verdi, but the popular music of the day," Brooks wrote in an article for the *New York Times* in 2001. He went on to reminisce about hearing a variety of music, not only on the radio in his family walk-up in Brooklyn, but from the open windows of apartments and stores down the street. By 1935, he proudly knew all the biggest hits and would perform them at get-togethers: "I was a pretty good singer, on pitch, and usually able to hit all of the top notes. I always got 'em at family parties with my imitations of Jolson singing 'Toot, Toot, Tootsie' and Eddie Cantor doing 'If You Knew Susie.'"

Things would crystallize soon for Mel when he was only nine years old. One day in June 1935, Brooks's Uncle Joe came by with the news that a doorman had traded Joe a ride in his cab for two free tickets to *Anything Goes* at the Alvin Theatre on Broadway. Knowing many of the Cole Porter songs from the musical, Mel was keen to go and was happy even when it turned out that the seats were in a row second from the back of the balcony. He listened and watched in amazement as he heard musical star Ethel Merman clearly sing "I Get a Kick Out of You" (a song he would satirically employ at the beginning of *Blazing Saddles*) without the use of a microphone all the way to where he was sitting, making it a memorable experience that would last him a lifetime. He stated in his *New York Times* reminiscences

A youthful Ethel Merman with Bing Crosby in the 1936 Paramount production of *Anything Goes*. In 1935, a nine-year-old Mel Brooks would be blown away by Merman in the Broadway production of the show and decide to go into show business.

that, as he laid awake in bed that night after the show, "Being a Broadway songwriter, I decided, would be even better than playing shortstop for the Brooklyn Dodgers, which up until then had been my most fantastic dream." It should be noted that Brooks sometimes will tell this story with himself being a ten-year-old, but the Broadway production of *Anything Goes* ended in November 1935, long before his tenth birthday.

As the years went by, Brooks would be put to the test trying to reach the goal he gave himself as a nine-year-old. First, in wanting to perform as a musician, then later obtaining a chance to work on Broadway . . . and when that fell through, a chance to try again . . . and when that didn't work, a chance to try again. And again.

But more on that topic in later chapters.

Growing Up on Movies

As one would expect, Brooks spent a good amount of time going to the movies as a child. Being born in 1926, the sound era of talkies would be pushing out the silent movies by the time he was old enough to even care about such things, but it wasn't completely unusual to see a few silent films still playing somewhere, especially in his frequent haunt of Coney Island, as he told Dan Lybarger for *The Keaton Chronicle*: "We'd go there, and we'd get a frankfurter, a root beer, and a boiled-to-death ear of corn at Feldman's. In the back, they had a silent movie theater. The screen was just a white sheet. They had this flickering machine . . . I never cared about religion, but I prayed to silent movies. It was my contact with things soulful. I'd go there as often as I could."

It is no wonder that Brooks would have a certain amount of love for the old silent movies, especially those featuring comedians of the period like Charlie Chaplin, Harold Lloyd, and Buster Keaton. Intermingled with those silents were the sound movies aimed at the younger viewers in the audience: action films, horror films, slapstick comedies, and westerns—all of which tie into the type of films he would later parody in his career.

Brooks's First Brush with a Celebrity

Brooks also saw his share of serials, which were typically a collection of two-reelers—short films on two ten- to twelve-minute reels—done in twelve to fifteen parts called chapters. Each week, a new chapter played before the main feature, so kids would have to come back each week for at least a dozen weeks to see the complete story. One of the best remembered of the period is *Flash Gordon*, which featured Olympic gold-medalist Larry "Buster" Crabbe. Crabbe had also played Tarzan in a serial in 1933 called *Tarzan the Fearless*, and would later play Flash Gordon again in *Flash Gordon's Trip to Mars* in 1938. All of which young Mel would have seen.

It was common for studios to send out their stars on tour at theaters across the country to appear during such portions of the program to promote themselves, their films, and the studio. It was at one such event in 1938 at the Loew's in Brooklyn that Mel Brooks got to meet Buster Crabbe—his first celebrity.

"I waited at the stage door," he reminisced to Will Harris in 2011.

Buster Crabbe as Flash Gordon in the truncated film version of the thirteen-part *Flash Gordon* serial. Crabbe would be the first celebrity Mel Brooks would meet in person.

"I screamed, 'Larry "Buster" Crabbe, you're the best thing since sliced bread!' And he really laughed. He got such a kick. He said, 'How old are you?' I said, 'I'm 12, and I loved the show. Can I please have your autograph? I know it's a bother.' And that was the first autograph I ever got. Larry 'Buster' Crabbe! Flash Gordon! I couldn't believe I saw him in person. 'That's the guy who saved everybody on planet Earth!'"

Learning to Become a Musician from a Pro

Brooks's love for music grew more serious as the family moved from the Williamsburg area to Brighton Beach when Mel was thirteen. Mel joined the school band as a drummer and became friends with another band member named Mickey Rich, who lived only a few buildings down from Brooks's family. As it turns out, Mickey's brother was none other than Buddy Rich, who by that time was already known as a drummer for Artie Shaw. As Brooks told *Film Score Monthly* in 1997: "One afternoon I said to Mickey, 'Could I sit at Buddy's drums?' He said, 'Sure!' So I picked up Buddy's sticks and sat at the drums, put on a record, and I played along with it, remembering a couple of Buddy Rich solos. I was trying to imitate them. Then I heard from the back, 'Not bad. Not good.' And that was Buddy."

Buddy Rich offered to teach Mel and another friend the drums when he wasn't on the road with Artie Shaw, which he did over a period of about six months. Evidently Mel was good enough that Rich invited him to come along and watch the Artie Shaw orchestra record an album, which led to Mel becoming friends with Shaw. "We've been friends," Brooks told *Film Score Monthly*, "and every couple of months we have lunch and talk about music and philosophy. He wants to talk about Nietzsche, and I want to talk about Jelly Roll Morton."

The drumming lessons would eventually pay off, blending in with his other ambitions as time went on.

Starting in the Catskills

Soon after picking up drumming, Brooks was introduced by his brother Lenny to Don Appell (1919–1990), an actor who was just getting his foot in the door on Broadway, and later would write and direct; his biggest Broadway hit being *Milk and Honey*, which ran for over a year. Appell, who also lived in Williamsburg, would regale Brooks with tales of the limelight, which only fortified Brooks in his career goals. Pleading for some way to get into the business, Brooks convinced Appell to help him, as he remembered to Lew Harris for *The Wrap*. "He finally said, 'OK. They're auditioning for people who can be busboys and waiters and be a part of the social staff at a place called the Butler Lodge in the Catskills. The resident director at that time was a guy by the name of Joseph Dolphin.' So I auditioned for this guy." With Dolphin's okay, Brooks would take on a job as a *tummler* in the Catskills, an area in New York defined by entertainers as the Borscht Belt.

Which, for anyone younger than the age of fifty from anywhere outside of the state of New York *and* doesn't know show business, I might as well be saying that

Buddy Rich
PLAYS
Rogers

enough said!

For 8x10" glossy print of this Buddy Rich photo, send 10¢

Oh, yes, the big news is the new
BUDDY RICH QUINTET
featuring
MIKE MAINIERI on Vibraharp
A great group that's really going places
—paced by a Rogers Dyna-Sonic drum!

dyna-sonic

It's Dyna-Sonic... metal or pearl   *ROGERS DRUMS*   740 Bolivar Road · Cleveland 15, Ohio

An ad with Buddy Rich. Rich would not only turn out to be a neighbor of the young Mel Brooks, but would give lessons to the teenage Mel back in the 1930s, which would benefit Mel as he later gained work as a drummer in the Catskills.

Mel Brooks raised cattle on the Moon. So here's a brief history: The Catskills refers to the Catskill Mountains, located a hundred miles north of New York City. This scenic area began to be settled by immigrants—particularly Jews—at the beginning of the twentieth century. Many initially tried to farm there, but the area quickly became popular with vacationers wanting to get away from the cities, and the farmers found they could make more money building bungalows, hotels, restaurants, and other forms of entertainment for those out-of-towners than they could trying to grow crops. Moreover, with so many immigrant Jews being the ones doing the building of such properties, the Catskills offered New York Jews a haven where they could have a chance to assimilate into the American Dream without worries of anti-Semitism. It is due to this influx of Jews into the area that the Catskills would sometimes be referred to as the Borscht Belt, which was a parody of the term "Bible Belt"—a somewhat vague area in the southern U.S. populated by Protestants (especially Baptists). Instead, the Catskills became the Borscht Belt, by substituting Bible for the name of a soup from Eastern Europe called borscht, made of beets.

By the 1920s, the area was seeing a boom in business, naturally leading to competition between the former farmers/now entrepreneurs. Unsurprisingly, this meant building more conveniences for the vacationers to encourage them to come back, like hotels, restaurants, swimming pools, tennis courts, golf courses, and theater halls for entertaining. Anything to keep the customers happy. For such resorts, performers would be needed: singers, dancers, acrobats, and lots and lots of comedians.

Mel Brooks would make his start in entertainment by being something else, however: a tummler. Also spelled as toomler, tumler, and tumulter, a tummler was a person at a hotel or resort who entertained the tourists. However, rather than performing on-stage, they would be out amongst the guests during the day, smiling, making jokes, helping, and by the evening—if handsome enough—dancing with the female guests who were without a companion. Their objective: do anything and everything to make people glad to be there. Of course, it was a kind gesture, but more importantly, it was to keep people at the resort instead of wandering off to spend their money elsewhere. If they're content at the resort, why go anywhere else?

"You're a kid," said Brooks to *Playboy* back in 1975, "You work in the mountains. For eight bucks a week and all you can eat, you do dishes, rent out rowboats, clean up the tennis courts, and, if you beg hard enough, they let you try to be funny around the pool." He went to the Catskills at the age of fourteen and eventually got the chance to do a regular routine at the pool. He would dress in a black derby and alpaca overcoat, hauling two suitcases filled with rocks. Screaming about how business was terrible and he was going to "end it all," he would then jump with his suitcases into the pool from the diving board, sinking straight to the bottom and to the laughter of the crowd at poolside. Also to the annoyance of the lifeguard, Oliver, who each day would have to pull non-swimmer Brooks out of the pool and then go after his cardboard suitcases of rocks before they disintegrated in the water.

It was also where Brooks performed in a play for the first time in his life, although the results were not what he expected. As Brooks tells the story, the play being performed was *Uncle Harry*, a hit Broadway psychological crime drama written by Thomas Job. In the play is a small role for an old district attorney, who pours a glass of water for the lead character and hands it to him, saying, "There, there, Harry. Sit down. Here, have a glass of water, and tell me in your own words what exactly happened on Tuesday night the 15th."

One night, the actor who was to play District Attorney got sick and young Brooks was told he would play the part, even though there was about a forty to fifty-year age difference between the boy and the character. With a wig, fake beard, and heavy makeup to age him, Brooks was pushed out on the stage. In picking up the glass pitcher to pour water into a glass, Brooks's hand slipped and the glass container crashed on to the table onstage, shattering into pieces and sending water on the actors and the stage.

"There's silence on stage," Brooks told Michele Wojclechowski in 2013. "Shocked silence everywhere. We don't know what to do. I walk down to the [end of the stage]. I take off my wig and my beard, and I say, 'I'm 14. I've never done this before.'" It would lead to Brooks's first big onstage laugh; not that he got to hear much of it, as he was soon chased off by the angry, knife-wielding director.

While the story is great, the timeline is a bit iffy as to Brooks's age at the time, as *Uncle Henry* wasn't on Broadway until 1942 (it ran from 1942 to 1943), and even a curtailed version probably would not have been performed anywhere until 1943. That would make Brooks sixteen years old, probably closer to seventeen, rather than the fourteen- or fifteen-year-old he commonly depicts himself in the story (but, admittedly, "fourteen years old" is funnier than seventeen). It should also be noted that Brooks did let slip during an interview with Eric Estrin in 2009 that he never worked at the Butler's Lodge again after the incident, thus pushing the timeline to when he was seventeen anyway, as Brooks's career in show business was about to be put on hiatus when he returned from the Catskills for his final year of high school.

Going to War

Even though Brooks had a lot on his mind in his late teens, one thing that everyone was talking about was the ongoing war. World War II was still going strong as Brooks approached his eighteenth birthday, and the frenzy for young men to prove themselves by helping the country led many to enlist, including the seventeen-year-old Brooks. This may seem as if he had jumped the gun, but the army had at that time recently started something called the Army Specialized Training Program (ASTP). The program was set up so that seventeen-year-olds could apply ahead of their graduation, if those who signed up passed an IQ test with a minimum of 115, which Brooks did easily. He recalled several years later: "These Army recruiters came around and said, 'You can go to college at 17 and a half; we can accelerate your high school graduation and you can go to college, so take the test.'"

One benefit of the program was that, if you hadn't taken ROTC in high school to be automatically commissioned as an officer upon joining the military, the ASTP gave you a chance to do so through its training program. As for the army's objective, the ASTP trained young men for specific technical jobs rather than for standard combat roles.

Upon graduating high school, Brooks immediately joined the ASTP. He had the option of going to Harvard, MIT, or Princeton, but instead chose to attend the Virginia Military Institute in Lexington, Virginia, where he began learning military engineering, as well as handling a saber while riding on horseback in the soon-to-be-retired (in 1947) Cavalry division. "They had us ride horses and cut down flags on bamboo poles," Brooks told *Newsweek* in 1975. "I was trained to become a Confederate officer." The training would last for twelve weeks in Virginia, where Brooks suddenly found himself in a strange new land that seemed nearly out of a fairy tale. "I learned how to ride a horse. Learned to eat a cheeseburger. Learned to drink a Southern drink called Dr. Pepper, which became popular later. Learned to dance the waltz with beautiful Southern belles at Washington and Lee College, adjacent to VMI. It was oh so different from living on the asphalt and cement all my life." He would later lament that it was one of the best times in his life, while noting that it was his emerging talents that gained him the attention of the women he began to meet. "I was just this Jew from New York and not so good-looking," Brooks told *The Virginia-Pilot* in 2015. "It was right there and then that I decided to go into show business—and into comedy. That was the only way I'd ever get these girls to notice me."

However, the ASTP was rapidly changing in 1944 when Brooks entered—the program had been around long enough to show the military they were sending much-needed men for combat "off to college" instead, and it was decided to trim the program. Thus, at the age of eighteen, Brooks was shipped to Fort Sill, Oklahoma, for normal basic training, where he was assigned to the Field Artillery Replacement Training. Yes, those initials did not bypass Brooks's sensibilities, as he remembered in a Yahoo Movies interview in 2014: "It was all over the place. You saw F.A.R.T. written everywhere at Fort Sill, and I said, 'Don't they know this? Can't they see this?' I said, 'Well, that's the military mind. I mean, they overlook that or something.'"

After the pageantry of VMI, Fort Sill delivered a different type of shock. Even though both were military, VMI carried on like a traditional military college, aiming to create officers. Fort Sill was there to keep men from getting their heads blown off while fighting the enemy hand-to-hand. It was the typical grind of early marches, miles-long hikes, eating bad food, and other elements that typically washed away the fantasy of soldier life most of the kids had when entering. On a darker side, in a *60 Minutes* interview from 2001, Brooks also remembered facing anti-Semitism face-on when at Fort Sill, especially one instance when a fellow soldier began to heckle him. "'Jewboy! Out of my way, out of my face, Jewboy!' I took his helmet off. I said, 'I don't want to hurt your helmet 'cause it's G.I. issue.' And I smashed him in the head with my mess kit." It would lead to a stay in the stockade, but Brooks never regretted allowing a momentary flash of anger get the best of him.

By the time Brooks was ready to enter the fields of combat, it was early 1945 and less than a handful of months shy of the end of the war in Europe. Even so, soon after arriving in Le Havre in France, however, Brooks knew he was in a war zone. "One day they put us all in trucks, drove us to the railroad station, put us in a locked train with the windows blacked out. We get off the train, we get on a boat. We get off the boat, we get into trucks, we get out of the trucks. We start walking. Suddenly, all around us, Waauhwaauhwaauh! Sirens! Tiger tanks! We're surrounded by Germans! Hands up! 'Wait!' I say. 'We just left Oklahoma! We're Americans! We're supposed to win!' Very scary, but we escaped," as he told *Playboy* in 1975.

Having studied field artillery, Brooks was first assigned to be a forward artillery observer, which involved mapping coordinates for shelling, but he found himself unable to discipline himself for the duty. "I'd say, 'No, no! You're missing it! You're going over, dummy! You're not even near! Aim for the big tree by the church! Say, listen, did the chow come up yet?' Very unmilitary." Soon after, he was moved to the 1104th Engineer Combat Group of the 78th Division, near the front line in Belgium, which led to Brooks participating in the Battle of the Bulge. Brooks would frequently downplay such involvement, however, stating that he only saw some scrimmages around the edges rather than being smack in the middle of the action. The group's main pursuit was to construct bridges for those advancing behind them, while dealing with the enemy shooting artillery and firing mortar at them, not to mention the snipers who were both the enemy and local civilians. The group also cleared roads for the safety of those to come after them, and Brooks's main job with the group was to deactivate land mines along the way. "We would throw up bridges in advance of the infantry, but mainly we would just throw up," he recalled.

When Brooks has discussed World War II, his memories of the war were certainly not of anything like the heroics found in the movies. "'Incoming mail!' Bullshit. Only Burt Lancaster says that. We said, 'Oh, God! Oh, Christ!' Who knows, he might help. He was Jewish, too. 'Mother!'" Brooks found that most of the time was spent trying to survive enemy fire in whatever kind of hole you could dig, and keep whatever sanity you had left while watching your friends die around you. As the Nazis withdrew, Brooks saw the horror of watching the refugees struggle in the ruins of their home villages; at one point he almost shot a civilian when his battle instincts nearly took over. "When we were transporting away a few prisoners of war in a train," Brooks told *Spiegel* magazine in 2016. "I discovered an old man who looked like my grandfather. He suddenly leaped out of the carriage. I took my rifle and aimed at him. He called, 'Don't shoot, I have to shit.' Most of the Germans who survived the war were just poor simple people."

Brooks did try to bring some humor to the situation, including a famous incident involving singing to the Germans, although the story has been told in two different forms by Brooks over the years. The version most often told is one where there was a lull in a battle and Brooks heard a group of Germans over the river singing a song. In response, he picked up a megaphone and began singing Al Jolson's "Toot, Toot, Tootsie," which was then followed by a round of applause by the Germans. Brooks has also told another version of the story, both in an interview with *Newsweek* in 1975 and with *CBS News* in December 2009, where the Germans had been using a loudspeaker system across the river to deliver propaganda messages to the Allied forces, whereupon Brooks got on a loud-speaker system on his side to sing the song to the Germans. Either way, applause was accepted.

A very early ad for the Red Banks Players, with whom Brooks worked for many months after coming back from World War II. Ironically, one of the first plays produced by the Red Banks Players would be directed by Joseph Dolphin, the man who chased Brooks with a knife through the Catskills before the war.

It was four months before the war ended for him, whereupon he was sent to work as a Noncom in Charge of Special Services in the newly liberated Germany. What "Noncom in Charge of Special Services" meant is that he provided entertainment for the forces—whether just a few (admittedly) stolen jokes to help cheer up a handful of soldiers or putting on complete shows for the troops. "I did Army shows. First for the Germans, then at Fort Dix. We all rolled up our pants and were the Andrews Sisters," Brooks would remember later in *Playboy*. By June 1946, Brooks would be discharged from the Army as a Corporal; although a newspaper clipping from Fort Dix that appears in the book included in the Shout! Factory DVD collection *The Incredible Mel Brooks: An Irresistible Collection of Unhinged Comedy* gives his rank as private, just a few weeks before he was discharged. He was then sent back to Williamsburg, and back to his family, with a military career behind him and a loose future still ahead at the age of twenty.

College or the Next Best Thing

Although several bios on Brooks make mention of his abruptly having to leave college to go to war, this was not the case. Instead, it would be after the war that Brooks would finally attend college—Brooklyn College, which his older brother Irving had attended—under the G.I. Bill. Brooks would study psychology sporadically over a ten-month period before reluctantly dropping out due to not being able to concentrate on his studies.

His continuing interest in show business certainly was a hindrance with his schooling. Army life, especially having spent more time entertaining troops than dodging bullets, only enhanced the dream he had as a kid of making it to Broadway someday. For a time, a job at the Abilene Blouse and Dress Company helped with expenses and pleased his family, who expected nothing less from him. "Everybody in my building aimed at some position: salesman, maybe a cutter, maybe a pattern maker, something in the garment center," Brooks told NPR. "I mean, we all aimed for Seventh Avenue. We never thought we were gonna go by or past Seventh Avenue." Even so, Brooks was still looking to get back on the stage and had enrolled for a time at The New School for Social Research to study diction and other dramatic arts. Then, in the summer of 1947, he heard about a group starting in Red Bank, New Jersey, that would be an "Equity A" theatrical group. This meant the theatrical group would be unionized and thus be able to bring in bigger names in support of the shows performed. In other words, not just a bunch of kids putting on a show; it would be the legit theater, even if it did turn out to be pretty much a bunch of kids putting on a show.

The group, called the Red Bank Players, was produced and managed by Benjamin Kutcher, commonly referred to in the trades as B. F. Kutcher. Enthusiasm was high in June 1947 when the local paper, *The Red Bank Register*, began running stories about the classes to be done and the promises of bringing such big names as Luise Rainer (star of such films as *The Good Earth* and *The Great Ziegfeld*) and Dorothy Gish (famed silent movie star and sister to Lillian Gish) to perform with the "new kids." Whether such talent knew about their supposed appearances is hard to say, however, as Kutcher was known for hyping productions in ways that were not completely truthful. Ironically, one of the first plays put on by the Players, *Three Cornered Moon*, was directed by Joseph Dolphin, the man who chased Brooks out of the theater back in the Catskills before going into the Army. Brooks got a job as a stagehand, as well as doing any number of odd jobs for the company, such as putting up posters in barbershops for upcoming performances.

The first play, *Hell-Bent for Heaven*, was performed on June 24, 1947, at the Mechanic St. School Auditorium in Red Bank. Brooks sometimes would report this period as being from before he went into the Army and/or at the age of sixteen, but newspaper reports and even a photo of a theater program seen in the PBS special about Brooks, *Make a Noise*, clearly show it was after the war in 1947. As it turned out, enthusiasm would soon wane on both sides of the curtain due to a lack of interest from the public as well as its producer. By August, the Red Bank Players resorted to "2 for 1" ticket sales, and cutting prices in half to attract customers to the shows. Members of the troupe were finding themselves pep-talked into foregoing most of their salaries, sometimes taking home $6 or less a week.

Before the summer was over, manager/producer B. F. Kutcher would leave the company as well. This was not that unusual of an ending for Kutcher, who had earlier in 1946 cancelled a production of Don Appell's short-lived Broadway play

This, Too, Shall Pass "when a newcomer's bankroll was apparently used up" (according to *Billboard* magazine at the time), and would later be sued by actress Janice Kingslow for promoting a production of *Anna Lucasta* in the fall of 1949 with her name and photo, though she had left the company beforehand. By 1950 he was running a theatrical company with the pretentious title of Manhattan Opera and Guide . . . out of Red Bank, New Jersey.

Brooks would remember Kutcher to *Written By* magazine as a character who would live in his office to save money. "He would wash his shorts and hang them out over the desk. He wasn't supposed to live there, but he lived in his office and he'd clean up everything by 5:30 because at 6:00, in case the janitors came by, they'd see him behind his desk working." He also would help raise money for productions—and possibly himself—in a dubious manner: "He would make love to old ladies on the way to the cemetery. He would nail them, and they would give him money." It was from Kutcher that Brooks heard something that would eventually make its way into one of his movies, *The Producers*: When one of his benefactors asked how to make out a check, Kutcher had told her to make it out to "Cash." When she mentioned that it sounded like a funny name for a play, Kutcher replied, "Well, so is *The Iceman Cometh*," shrugging off the enquiry. There was even the matter of raising more cash than needed—usually about $2,500—and Kutcher pocketing the funds. When Brooks asked him why, Kutcher felt he deserved it as a bonus for his hard work. When Brooks asked why he didn't try to get more than just a little, Kutcher shook his head: $2,500 could be a mistake and easily returned if spotted; more and you were setting yourself up for trouble. Brooks understood, but the discussion and his time with Kutcher would percolate in his mind for years to come before being released as his first movie (see chapter 8 for more details).

Even though Kutcher left, the company struggled onward for a time and even enjoyed the newfound freedom in everyone involved being young and able to do any type of show they wish. Brooks pushed his way up through the ranks, going so far as to direct some plays for the group, including *Separate Tables* in December 1947, in which he also starred as one of the characters. "I played a character named Scoop David," Brooks told Mike Sacks, "and I had one line, the opening line. I ran out on the stage and screamed, 'We made it! It's a hit! It's the greatest thing since pay toilets!' That was my opening." He would also begin to write skits and little dramatic pieces for the company. However, by the end of the year, the company had folded; and, besides becoming friends with his Red Bank roommate and later famous stand-up comedian Will Jordan, the golden promises that came with the early days of the Red Bank Players did not pan out. Instead, Brooks had to consider other options, including a return to the mountains.

Back to the Catskills . . . and About That Name

This is where things really get confusing. As mentioned earlier, Brooks tends to condense his timeline in interviews, and sometimes will even rework a bit of his history if he thinks he can find a better punch line to the story. Overall, everything and every event that made Mel Brooks "the" Mel Brooks is pushed to his teenage years. The drumming, the Catskills, the stabs at theater, his first attempts at comedy, and even his name are elements that came out of his growing years. Then Brooks goes to war and returns with determination and readiness to become the writer and later director and producer that came down the road.

Yet, as is the case with most of us, it isn't quite that simple. As seen already, Brooks came out of the Army looking for work and struggling to find himself, be it through school, work, or in show business. And yet, two years out of the Army now and heading toward the age of twenty-two, he was looking to find work back in the Catskills, the same place he started when he was a teen, so many years before. No doubt, it felt a bit like drifting, even though it was still a potential source of finding his way at the same time. With that in mind, it is no wonder that he may want to merge details a bit and get to the real meat of his stories without having to go through the whole process of mentioning that his aspirations were interrupted by the war.

And in all fairness, the inkling of future success was there for Brooks before going into the Army; it is just that it was only upon his return to the mountains in 1948 that things began to fall into place for him. Although many biographies list Brooks as playing drums in the Catskills when he was a teenager, his career as a musician didn't blossom until after the war, where he began to work in a four-man ensemble. "I started on the Borscht Belt in the late 1940s as a drummer and pianist," Brooks told *Tablet* magazine in 2016. "We did three or four items a week in a musical review. A play, then amateur night. I was always busy onstage doing something."

It was during this period that Brooks actively took to using the stage name of Mel Brooks. Although he had come up with the name years before—an article from his military days mentions his stage name as "Melvyn Brooks," and the program for his Red Bank Players directorial job on *Separate Tables* has him as "Mel Brooks"—it was not until his return to the Catskills that the name became dominant. Drawing from his mother's maiden name of Brookman, Brooks would frequently state that he changed his name to Brooks because "the name Kaminsky didn't fit on a drumhead very well."

However, in an interview with *Rolling Stone* in 1978 and the famous *David Susskind Show* interview from 1970, Brooks revealed that he decided to stick with the stage name due to an incident where he had gotten a musician gig at a hotel for $200, four times what he was used to getting. It turns out the hotel staff thought they were hiring Jazz trumpeter Max Kaminsky (there's that name Max again) and were "not amused by the mix-up." Brooks decided he didn't want to risk trouble over the name, so he went for Brookman, and then later Brooks, foreseeing it as a temporary situation. "I thought if I ever did anything important, I'd change it back to Kaminsky. No wonder Woody Allen and I are great. We are not Brooks and Allen, we are not some department store. We are Konigsberg and Kaminsky. Now those are names, like Tolstoy and Dostoevski."

Just as Brooks found himself playing a character in a play due to an actor getting sick, his next foray into the limelight came when a comic that was to perform one night called in sick. Now it should be mentioned that Brooks usually tells this story as if it occurred when he was fifteen, possibly sixteen, and thus before the war. Yet the setup of the story has him playing drums for the comics as part of an ensemble, which indicates it occurred after the war. His interview with *Playboy* in 1975 about the incident also begins with the words, "When I went back to the mountains after the war, I played drums and sang . . . ," while the timeline featured on the PBS *American Masters* website for the documentary produced about Brooks, *Make a Noise*, also lists him performing drums in the Catskills after the war. Therefore, although Brooks himself usually paints himself as being younger when telling the tale, all indications are that it happened when he was in his twenties and a bit more confident of himself as a performer.

Whatever the timetable, Brooks was performing with the ensemble when the "standard mountain comedian" couldn't make it to do the show due to being ill. The manager of the lodge, Pincus Cantor, needed someone to talk to the audience and zeroed in on Brooks. "He says, "I've watched you doing rehearsals. I can tell you're a funny guy." Brooks, who now had a history of performing in front of an audience, and with no glass pitchers to shatter, was up on the idea. The thing was, however, "I didn't want to do those ancient jokes, so I decided to go out there and make up stuff. I figured, I'll just talk about things we all know and see if they turn out funny."

Back on that day, an incident at the lodge had found one of the maids getting locked in a closet and repeatedly screaming "Los mir arois!" so loudly that everyone in the hotel could hear her. It had been the event of the day, and obviously a ripe moment to refer to in the show. "So when I went on stage, I stood there with my knees knocking and said, 'Good evening ladies and gentlemen . . . LOS MIR AROIS!' They tore the house down." Brooks would also do impressions in the show, but of staff familiar to those staying at the hotel, like the manager, Pincus Cantor. More effectively, however, Brooks invested time in talking directly to the audience, engaging them, and putting them at ease. He eventually came up with a theme song to do when appearing onstage, deliberating stating that he was a ham but that he would grow on everyone: "Won't you be kind? And please . . . love . . . Melvin Brooks!"

Not all of Brooks's ideas worked. A gag where he would claim to have "1,000 faces"—which typically would mean several impersonations of famous stars—and then do various facial contortions instead—went over like a lead balloon. "They kept waiting for me to do all 1,000." When asking for reactions later from the people in the tearoom about his shows, the responses would be advice on going into another career or telling him he stunk . . . but with a hint of a smile to mean they were kidding. "You could never get a kind word out of the Jews," Brooks reflected years later to *Playboy* with a smile. "Anyway, I wanted to entertain so badly that I kept at it until I was good. I just browbeat my way into show business."

Soon, Brooks's determination paid off, and he became the social director at one of the best-known resorts in the Catskills, Grossinger's Catskill Resort Hotel. He was still throwing together fresh jokes and trying to put smiles on faces of people that were his mother's age or older, but it was still a step up on the ladder by the nine-year-old boy who dreamed of Broadway. Now he had music; he had laughs; he had the spotlight. And that was all about to change.

2

Far Enough Out for You?

The Beginning Caesar Years

T he first mention of Mel Brooks in the pages of *Variety* came on May 5, 1926, when Mel Brooks purchased the Rainbow Nuntre, in Sulphur, Oklahoma. Which points out two things: one, I have no idea what a Rainbow Nuntre is, and two, that this is the wrong Mel Brooks and I need to find a better researcher, as the Mel Brooks under discussion here wasn't born until June 28, 1926. Instead, our Mel Brooks first became worthy of *Variety* in 1952, when he was listed as having written a sketch for a review called *Curtain Going Up*. At that point, Brooks was already gaining momentum working in television as a writer, thanks to a former mentor introducing him to a future one. Thus, while his introduction in *Variety* may have come in 1952, it would be ten years before that when Brooks's future as a professional writer for television began to fall into place.

Meeting Sid Caesar

Brooks had started working in the Catskill Mountains when he was fourteen, thanks to the help of a man named Don Appell, who was gaining success on Broadway. Before that, Appell was working as the social director of the Vacationland Hotel in the Catskills, a job that included scheduling the entertainment for the summer season and hiring musicians, actors, and comics. In the summer of 1939, Appell was approached by the seventeen-year-old saxophone player in the hotel band who wanted to contribute to the comedy bits done in the show.

The kid asking was Sid Caesar, who was born September 8, 1922, in Yonkers, New York, and had begun playing the saxophone at the age of eleven. Much like Brooks, Caesar would begin working in the Catskills by the age of fourteen, strictly as a musician. On rare occasions, however, he had been given a chance to make the audience laugh and he was anxious to continue to do so. Appell, seeing that Caesar was not asking for any additional pay, seized the opportunity to have two performers for the price of one and agreed to hiring Caesar. Appell was a tad hesitant with Caesar's insistence that original material be incorporated into the show, but finally relented when Caesar agreed to go back to the old material if it didn't work out.

Thanks to Appell's trust in the young man's ability, Caesar would be allowed to develop his comedic chops, including something that would be a cornerstone of his act through the rest of his career: mimicking foreign languages while clearly speaking gibberish—a talent that is much harder to pull off than it sounds.

In 1942, Sid worked one final season as a comic with some occasional saxophone solos for Appell at the Avon Lodge, where Appell had become the social director. Various sources state that it was at the Avon Lodge that Brooks met Caesar for the first time, but if so, Caesar entered the Coast Guard in November 1942, and thus their relationship would be stalled for the time being. While stuck guarding the docks in Brooklyn, Caesar began performing in revues, including some with Vernon Duke, a songwriter-composer (1903–1969 and best remembered today for cowriting "Taking a Chance on Love" and "I Can't Get Started"). Duke had Caesar reassigned to Palm Beach, Florida, in order to use him as a musician and comic in a musical revue called *Tars and Spars*.

Tars and Spars was to be the Coast Guard's answer to the Army having the hit musical *This Is the Army* by Irving Berlin that played on Broadway in 1942. The show featured fellow Coast Guard officers, such as Victor Mature, who was already appearing in movies by 1942, and was choreographed by Gower Champion (1919–1980, and who will pop up many more times in later chapters). More importantly to Caesar's career, it was directed by Max Liebman (1902–1981), known as the "Ziegfeld of the Borscht Belt." Liebman had broken through while working as the social director in the 1930s for Camp Tamiment in the Poconos Mountains of Pennsylvania, sometimes referred to as "a progressive version of the Catskills." His first big star was Danny Kaye, who came out of Camp Tamiment and became a sensation when featured in Liebman's first Broadway revue, *The Straw Hat Revue*, in late 1939. Kaye would move on to stage and screen, leaving Liebman in search of a new protégé.

Caesar so impressed Liebman that the producer suggested Caesar contact him after the war to work together. Sid would continue with the show until it eventually moved to Hollywood for a film version with the same title done in the summer of 1945 for Columbia Pictures. By the time the film was out in January 1946, however, the war was over, and response to the film was lukewarm, except for Caesar, who was seen as a major talent on his way up.

Caesar left the Coast Guard after making the picture in hopes of doing more films, but he found the parts being offered were either not right for him, such as the lead in *The Al Jolson Story*, or were that of the "amusing sidekick" to the star, which he didn't want to play as he wanted to be the lead. Yet *Tars and Spars* did help land Caesar a two-month engagement at the famous Copacabana nightclub in New York. Caesar was eager to work, but still had limited material, so he contacted Max Liebman, who was happy to help him put together a half-hour act. The association with Liebman directly led him to casting Caesar in the Broadway show *Make Mine Manhattan*, which ran through 1948 and featured Caesar in a variety of roles, including a sketch where he played a variety of diplomats that allowed him to fall into his now patented foreign gibberish act.

After leaving the Broadway show in January 1949, Caesar was asked by Liebman to meet with him and the executives at the National Broadcasting Network (NBC) about doing a weekly live show every Friday night. After agreeing to do an hour-long program, Liebman and Caesar were apprehensive, but as Caesar would reflect years later in his autobiography, *Caesar's Hours*, "If it flopped, who would know? Neither of us knew anyone who owned a television." Which was true—television was still a growing industry. By 1949 there were a little over four million television sets in the country, and most major cities had at least one television station, but reception was poor and sets were expensive. Radio was still the big way for broadcasters to go, and it wasn't until the mid-1950s that television really became something many people could afford to have and wanted.

Which is where Mel Brooks comes back into the story. Renewing his friendship with Don Appell after the war, Brooks accompanied Appell to see Caesar perform at the Copa in early 1947 and meet with him after the show. Impressed with Caesar's act, Brooks repeatedly turned up to see him perform during his 1947 engagement at the Roxy Theater, as well as becoming friends with Sid's brothers, Abe and Dave, who were Caesar's entourage, before moving on to work with the Red Bank Players and a stint as the social director at Grossinger's in the Catskills in 1948.

By the time they met up again in late 1948, Brooks had grown as a performer and writer. He also knew how to make Caesar laugh, stating in a Charlie Rose interview that a routine he did about old Jews dying from eating too much sour cream and trying to sing Crosby in the wrong key—a bit Brooks replicates in the Norman Lear 2016 documentary *Just Another Version of You*—clinched their friendship and business relationship from that point forward. Feeling his oats, and seeing that Caesar had made the leap to the Broadway stage, Brooks kept in contact during Caesar's run in the Broadway show *Make Mine Manhattan*. Which was fine with Caesar, as he enjoyed the company during the hours before and after the shows.

Those around Caesar were somewhat less impressed with the short loudmouth, whom many referred to (when being polite) as "the kid." When Caesar first introduced Brooks to Max Liebman during rehearsals for *Make Mine Manhattan*,

Poster for *Tars and Spars*, the movie that would help gain Sid Caesar a national audience.

Caesar joyfully told Brooks, "Do for Max what you just did for me." Whereupon Brooks leapt onto the stage and began singing his intro song from his Catskills days, which he has sung many times since.

By the time Brooks begged everyone to love him, got on down on one knee, and threw out his arms to feel the warmth from his captive audience in return, Liebman had already grown to dislike him. "Who is this meshuggener?" Liebman said, before huffily walking away from the experience. Even so, or maybe because of Liebman's reaction, Caesar kept Brooks around, leading to Brooks's introduction to writing for television.

Admiral Broadway Revue (1949)

The series that Caesar and Liebman agreed to do was an extension of an earlier series called *Admiral Presents the Five Star Revue—Welcome Aboard*, which was a half-hour variety series hosted by various celebrities, including Jerry Lewis and Dean Martin in its first two episodes. The series ran on Sunday nights from October 3, 1948, until February 20, 1949, and was sponsored by Admiral, an electronics company that had begun selling television sets. Liebman and Caesar agreed to do their show live on Friday evenings at 8:00 p.m. Eastern Standard Time for an hour each week starting January 28, 1949, and which ran until June 3, 1949. The program was simulcast on both the NBC and the Dumont networks, which may seem odd today to have the same variety show on two different networks, but at a time when there was only a limited number of programs, and where stations sometimes ran more than one network's programming, it was not that unusual.

Amongst the performers starring alongside Caesar were Imogene Coca (1908–2001), who had costarred on Broadway with Danny Kaye in Liebman's *The Straw Hat Revue* in 1939; dancer Gower Champion; and his wife Marge Champion (born 1919). Liebman's main goal in the series was to emphasize the concept of variety, much like that of his previous revues, making sure that the comedy did not overwhelm the chance to bring more cultured entertainment such as ballet and opera to the masses. Live music, dance, comedy, and special guest stars were thrown together into each of its nineteen episodes with a central theme for each week. All for $15,000 per episode, which was considered a sizeable cost for a weekly television show at the time.

Both Caesar and Coca would throw in occasional ideas for each episode, but most of the writing was done by Liebman with two writers, who would be Brooks's constant companions and influences for the next few years:

- Mel Tolkin (1913–2007) was born Sam Tolchinsky and immigrated from the Ukraine when he was thirteen. After finishing high school, he began writing and performing left-wing musical revues in Montreal, Canada, under the stage name of Mel Tolkin to distance his family from his politics. In the 1930s, he worked summers at Camp Tamiment, where he met up with Lucille Kallen; and they would become a writing team, working under Max Liebman there. Tolkin continued to work for Caesar as his head writer into the 1960s. He later

Sid Caesar and Max Liebman, who together would create one of the first unique comedy showcases of early television, *Your Show of Shows*. Caesar would keep Brooks on as a personal writer, while Liebman would attempt to fire Brooks at every opportunity.

wrote for shows like *I'm Dickens, He's Fenster, Make Room for Daddy*, several Bob Hope specials, and was a scripter and story editor for *All in the Family* in the late 1970s. With his musical background, Tolkin also wrote the theme song to the later Liebman series *Your Show of Shows*, "Stars over Broadway."

• Lucille Kallen (1922–1999) was born in Los Angeles and moved to Toronto at the age of three. Studying to be a concert pianist, Kallen went to Julliard School at the age of sixteen, but found that her small hands and dislike for practice limited the pursuit of her dream. Instead, she began to write, putting together a revue that Liebman had seen, which led to being invited to start writing for Liebman's revues at Camp Tamiment, teaming up with Tolkin in the process. She would become known as one of the few writers on Caesar's various shows who could physically write on paper while arguing over jokes and sketch ideas—an ability that many of the others did not share or avoided. As the only female writer on the program and for *Your Show of Shows*, Kallen usually voiced the female characters in sketches. A small woman—just over five feet tall—she found the best way to get the attention of the bickering group of men in the later series was to stand on the sofa in the writers' room and wave a red scarf or her sweater. She would break away from Caesar after *Your Show of Shows*, writing several episodes of *The Bell Telephone Hour* in the 1960s before finally leaving television writing behind. She may have retired from television, but was never far away from writing, and between 1981 and 1986, she wrote five mystery novels.

As the series began, Caesar, Coca, and the Champions were performing, Liebman was producing, Tolkin and Kallen were writing . . . and Mel Brooks was standing outside the International Theater, where the filming took place, disturbing the peace. Early in rehearsals for the series, Brooks arrived one day to meet up with Caesar at the theater; perhaps uninvited, although Brooks would claim in *Where Have I Been?*, "Sid had invited me to come by because he was interested in my mind and maybe I could help him [with some ideas for the show]." Caesar's manager, Leo Pillot, saw Mel Brooks inside the stage door and immediately sent two burly ushers to physically toss him from the theater. "I said, 'You're crazy! You

Newspaper ad for the very first episode of *The Admiral Broadway Revue*. This would transform into *Your Show of Shows* the following year, with most of the cast in place. Brooks, however, was forced to wait in the hall or outside, hoping to pitch jokes when possible.

can't do this to Mel Brooks! *I'm potentially very important!*'" When Pillot walked away, Brooks began to cause a ruckus, long and loud enough that Sid heard the noise and went to investigate. Once Caesar saw who it was, he told the ushers that Brooks was his guest and could come into the building.

The invitation did the trick—Brooks was on the inside, and Pillot backed off from trying to cause any trouble between him and Caesar. Brooks would later suggest that Pillot was just looking out for his client over this "punk" who was trying to ride Caesar's coattails. Yet, although Brooks was allowed on the premises, he wasn't allowed to contribute, especially as Liebman didn't care for him and only hoped that Brooks would eventually get tired of being ignored and leave. "The only animosity I got from the beginning was from Max Liebman, who saw me as some kind of adventurer and didn't think I was very talented," remembered Mel years later in *Where Have I Been?* "I was a street kid and didn't have any sophistication. Max was a classy guy who wanted to do a real Broadway revue every week."

Then in the fourth episode, a problem came up with a sketch. The sketch itself was not unusual as it involved Caesar in one of his staple concepts, the "airport sketch," which involved a character, usually called the Professor, being interviewed about his experiences in some type of oddball activity as he either was arriving or leaving from a plane at the airport. In this case, the sketch was a Jungle Boy, and while the premise was solid, the writers were having problems coming up with gags that punched up the script. Frustrated, Sid eventually pulled Brooks into the office, who was "hanging around, hanging around" (as Sid called it) and put him to work, saying, "Do something. Write."

Brooks took the idea and came up with several gags for the sketch, leading to Caesar, Tolkin, and Kellan agreeing Brooks could help with the writing. Not that often, of course; after all, he was just this punk kid who was a hanger-on from what they saw, but it couldn't be denied that when gags or punch-ups in scripts were needed in a flash, Brooks got the job done. Perhaps just as well; Liebman had already run into trouble for reusing material from a couple of his Broadway revues that resulted in a lawsuit by writer Devery Freeman, who saw his material being used without permission. New material was needed for the program, and no matter how much of a powerhouse Kallen and Tolkin were at writing, it was a lot of time to fill on a weekly basis.

Caesar was convinced Brooks should be hired as one of the writers. Max Liebman, however, nixed the idea. From his mindset, there was no way Brooks was going to be sponging off his show. Finally, Caesar said that he'd pay it out of his own pocket and asked Brooks how much he wanted. Brooks asked for $50 a week, which Caesar thought was a bit much. He offered to pay Brooks $45 if Max would pay the other $5, but Liebman still refused. It was finally agreed to pay Brooks $40 a week, only for Caesar to bump it up to $50 (approximately $500 in 2018 U.S. currency) when he saw that Brooks was living in a cellar a few blocks away.

Although never listed as a writer on *The Admiral Broadway Revue* in an official capacity, Brooks would contribute off and on to the final sixteen episodes in the series, which ended on June 3, 1949. Even so, he was strictly being paid as Caesar's personal writer instead of a credited writer on the program. This explains why, in January 1950, an ad in *Billboard* magazine for a company offering "comedy writers of special material" for hire, Brooks is listed as simply "writer for Sid Caesar," instead of anything mentioning the series.

After one season, Admiral announced that they were withdrawing sponsorship and cancelling the show. Caesar was initially stunned by the news; however, he was later told by the president of the company, Ross Siragusa, that the program had done too good a job promoting sales of television sets. Admiral at the time could produce about one hundred television sets a week; suddenly the demand had increased where they were asking to produce 5,000 sets a day. Although the company was making money with the show, the program, along with general interest in television itself, was increasing demand for television sets to the point where Admiral had to decide whether to keep putting money into the series or into building a factory to meet demand. It was decided to meet demand, and so Admiral pulled out.

There was a bright side to Admiral's departure, however: NBC saw that there was interest in the show and that such a variety program could be a success. The only question was how they were going to bring back the format from the dead.

Your Show of Shows, Season One (February 25, 1950–May 1950)

Sylvester "Pat" Weaver, Jr. (1908–2002) was the vice president of NBC who had greenlit *The Admiral Broadway Revue*. He was happy with the success of the show and determined to keep such a series in the lineup for the network, especially as it featured some "culture" amongst all the shenanigans. Thus, in a bit of irony, Liebman may have annoyed Caesar and the comedy writers with the emphasis on ballet and opera breaking up the comedy sketches in the program, but it probably was the main reason Weaver wanted to keep them around after Admiral pulled out. Not only did Weaver want the show to return, he wanted to expand upon it by making the program *three hours long* every Saturday night.

Liebman choked at the thought of creating three hours of live programming for the nation every week, and after some negotiations, Weaver finally agreed to the program being ninety minutes, with the eye on placing another hour-long variety show at 8:00 p.m. EST and then follow with Liebman's show at 9:00 p.m. EST. In the first season, the 8:00 program was *The Jack Carter Show*, hosted by comic Jack Carter (1922–2015), another comedian out of the Borscht Belt who had just come off a successful season hosting a similar variety show for the Dumont Network, *Cavalcade of Stars*, later the launching pad for Jackie Gleason's career. The 9:00 program from Liebman would turn out to be the iconic *Your Show of Shows*, and both shows together would be given the wrap-around title of *NBC Saturday Night Revue*. This in replacement of game shows and political talk shows—including *Meet the Press*—that had aired the previous season on Saturday nights for NBC.

As for the framework of *Your Show of Shows*, initial thoughts were of showcasing the first act of a current Broadway show, with some various musical interludes to fill out the time. Ultimately, however, the ninety-minute program would fall back on what had worked so well on the Admiral program: a mixed page of music, dance, and comedy, although scrapping the previous show's premise of each episode being based around one topic.

Guest hosts would appear each week with a cast of regulars, beginning with Burgess Meredith as the host for the premiere episode on February 25, 1950. Of the regulars, Caesar and Imogene Coca returned along with Howard Morris (1919–2005), an actor who had appeared occasionally on *The Admiral Broadway Revue*. Morris is probably best remembered today as Ernest T. Bass on *The Andy Griffith Show*, but he also directed films and television shows, including *Who's Minding the Mint?* (1967), *With Six You Get Eggroll* (1968), episodes of *The Dick Van Dyke Show* (produced by fellow *Your Show of Shows* costar Carl Reiner), *Hogan's Heroes*, and the pilot episode of *Get Smart* (1965).

1950 *Billboard* ad promoting Brooks as a writer at large. Although he could truthfully say he was a writer for Sid Caesar, he was still not considered a writer on Caesar's television show.

When Morris joined the *Admiral* show, the writing staff had been introduced to him as Mel Tolkin, Lucille Kallen, and "Monsieur Bri," a funny short man who spoke only in poor French and Yiddish. This turned out to be Mel Brooks, of course, and he would make it his campaign to pull pranks on Morris. The most noted event occurred soon after the start of *Your Show of Shows*: Brooks was walking down a street with Morris when he suddenly threw Morris upside a Studebaker and told him "This is a stick-up!" Morris at first thought Brooks was joking, but Brooks refused to drop his guard and Morris finally handed over his wallet, watch, and wedding ring in fear of what Brooks might do to him. After Brooks ran off with Morris's personal items, Morris called Sid, to which Sid only replied (as per Brooks in the 1975 *Playboy* interview, "Oh, he's started that again, has he? Whatever you do, don't call him up or go to his house, he'll kill ya."

After Caesar told Morris to wait until Brooks snapped out of it, Brooks stretched out the joke for as long as possible. "Well, for three weeks," Brooks remembered. "Howie waited. No wallet, no watch. Had to buy another wedding ring. I'd say hello to him every morning like nothing had happened." Finally, Brooks acted as if he had suddenly come to his senses and apologized, giving Morris everything back as a Christmas present, since it was the holidays. Then, three years later, as the pair were rowing in a boat on the lake in Central Park, Brooks pulled the same stunt again, eventually forcing Morris to swim ashore. But this time he only waited a few days before handing Morris his wallet and watch back.

And it was the start of a beautiful friendship. Besides being recommended to direct the *Get Smart* pilot by Brooks in 1965, Morris later contributed by acting in three of Mel Brooks's films—most prominently as Dr. Lilloman ("Little old man!") in *High Anxiety* (1977).

When the series started in February 1950, the writing arrangement didn't change; the official writers credited in the show and in reviews were Max Liebman, Mel Tolkin, and Lucille Kallen. In fact, Liebman would go out of his way to tell the press that the other two were all that was needed to write a ninety-minute show every week. Of course, Mel Brooks was around, although still unofficial and still being paid out of pocket by Caesar.

People on the show may have seen Brooks as Caesar's jester, but they also saw that Brooks had a calming effect on Caesar when very much needed. Yet, even with this ability and his useful additions to the scripts, Liebman was still not sold on having Brooks on the payroll. He wasn't even that crazy about having him in the building. "The truth was," Brooks commented in a 1996 interview at the Writers Guild Theater in Los Angeles with fellow former Caesar writers, "Max Liebman was not exactly thrilled to have me around. When he saw me, he assessed my character and personality immediately, and he was absolutely right. He saw a very arrogant, obnoxious little shithead, who thought he knew everything and had patience for nothing but his own thoughts." As the first season of *Your Show of Shows* began, Caesar was still paying Brooks out of his own pocket fifty dollars a week, with Caesar, Tolkin, and Kallen (along with Coca occasionally offering ideas) writing together, while Brooks was kept outside in the hall or even left pacing the sidewalk outside the theater, waiting to be able to throw a gag or two into the mix. "I'd wait in the hallway outside where Sid and Max and Mel [Tolkin] and Lucille were writing the show. After a while, Sid would stick his head out and say, 'We need three jokes.' So, I'd give him three jokes, but Max wouldn't let me in" (*Playboy*, 1975). If that didn't work, Brooks would wait for the writers to leave the building to go to lunch and then join them, trying to stake his claim as one of them.

Then in early April, Brooks wrote a sketch that was too good for even Liebman to pass up. The sketch, about a Russian actor, was obviously written to Caesar's strengths; it even featured Caesar imitating a pinball machine, such as in his early revue act, and was probably written by Brooks with Sid's assistance. Even so, Liebman knew when he was licked, especially as Tolkin, Kallen,

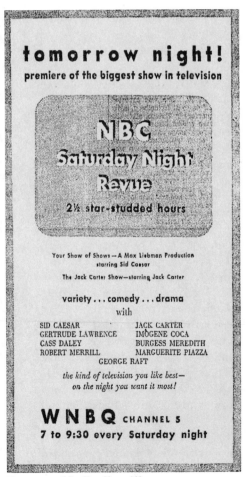

tomorrow night!
premiere of the biggest show in television

NBC
Saturday Night
Revue

2½ star-studded hours

Your Show of Shows—A Max Liebman Production
starring Sid Caesar

The Jack Carter Show—starring Jack Carter

variety . . . comedy . . . drama
with

SID CAESAR   JACK CARTER
GERTRUDE LAWRENCE   IMOGENE COCA
CASS DALEY   BURGESS MEREDITH
ROBERT MERRILL   MARGUERITE PIAZZA
         GEORGE RAFT

*the kind of television you like best—
on the night you want it most!*

WNBQ CHANNEL 5
7 to 9:30 every Saturday night

Newspaper ad for *Your Show of Shows.*

and Caesar all agreed that Brooks was contributing enough to the scripts to get some type of mention in the program. The seventh episode of *Your Show of Shows* would feature an on-screen credit for him, saying "Additional Dialogue by Mel Brooks." He was still making fifty dollars a week from Caesar, but at least his name was appearing on television.

The first season was only thirteen episodes, running until May 20, 1950, and was a success, ranking #4 for the year while going up against Roller Derby on ABC and various variety shows on CBS (*The Ken Murray Show* and *The Frank Sinatra Show* at times during that year). There was no doubt that a second season would commence in September 1950 for a full thirty-nine episodes.

Pushing Caesar (Sometimes Too Far)

Caesar always exhibited a tendency for volatile behavior if he felt he was frustrated or being pushed around. He also had almost unworldly strength when angered—there are stories by the writers on his show of him literally picking office desks off the floor, supposedly by one hand, and dropping them when he was furious. There was one famous event that even led directly to a gag in *Blazing Saddles*: when a horse nipped at his wife, Caesar in blind fury punched the horse in the head. Many discussed an incident where Caesar became so incensed with a man sitting in a car that Caesar told him he was about to reexperience birth; whereupon Caesar attempted to pull the man out of his car through the tiny driver's side window of the car.

Brooks's impish nature and "always-on" humor, however, helped calm Sid at times when he would start to go nuclear. This is one reason why Brooks was with his friend when Caesar went to Chicago the summer of 1949. Caesar had agreed to do a show at the Empire Room in the Palmer House—a popular hotel in Chicago—for two weeks and brought his brother David and Brooks with him to keep him company. The show also featured the dance team Bob Fosse and Mary Ann Niles, the Merriel Abbott Dancers, and Ted Straeter and his Orchestra, but Caesar was the core of the show. He performed a solo act he had created with Liebman, along with some additional gags from Brooks.

Caesar would state in his book *Caesar's Hours*, he and Brooks were at the hotel in June 1950 where he was appearing as a single act at the Chicago Theater, while James Robert Parish's excellent bio on Brooks, *It's Good to Be the King*, says it was actually in June 1951. Yet Caesar did not play the Chicago Theater in 1950, and his appearance there in 1951 was with Coca and many others from *Your Show of Shows*, and only for a week. Brooks, on the other hand, has frequently mentioned the Palmer House—the hotel where the Empire Room was located—as being where the following event occurred, and the Empire Room shows he did in 1949 lasted a total of five weeks that summer, matching closely the tale Caesar has told in his autobiographies. Thus, it was most probably in June 1949 when the following incident occurred.

Having a habit of not eating until done performing for the evening, Caesar arrived back at his hotel room after a disastrous show hungry, tired, angry, and heavily drinking. It depends on which version of the story one hears, but in the hotel room either Brooks wanted to get away from Caesar's nasty cigar smoke (Brooks's version) or Brooks was needling Caesar to go out because he was afraid to venture out into Chicago on his own. Either way, Caesar was just settling down to dinner when Brooks said he "wanted air." Without another word, Caesar came at Brooks, grabbed him by the belt and the collar of his shirt, and held Brooks halfway out the eighteenth-story window of the hotel room. As Caesar remembered in his book *Caesar's Hours,* he then asked the petrified Brooks, "How far out do you want to go? Is that far enough?" Brooks, looking down at the traffic below, replied, "Oh, no, I don't want to go out. I'm out far enough." By then, Sid's brother Dave—a big man and one of the few who could hold Caesar down—pulled them both out of the window and back into the room.

Brooks and Caesar quickly made up, and truth be told, Caesar acknowledged that Brooks could convince him to do things that others would not have even attempted for fear of what he could do to them. Once, when walking down the street, Brooks had a joke for a "professor" sketch that he thought would bring the house down. Caesar wasn't buying what Brooks was trying to sell. Brooks finally got mad enough that he stopped in front of Caesar and poked him in the chest with a finger saying, "You've got to do this joke."

Nobody did that to Caesar. Typically, it would have been the type of stunt that drove him into a dark rage. But it was "the kid," and he could see that even Brooks knew he had gone too far by getting physical. After pointing out Brooks's mistake, Caesar half-jokingly told him, "I will let you live." He then went on to tell Brooks that if he fought that hard for the joke, then perhaps there was something to it, and he agreed to do the gag.

The joke was about a snake in a zoo. The snake wants to get out of the reptile house and is asking the Professor to help him. "Why," the Professor would ask. The snake fearfully replies, "They're all snakes in here." "What do you expect," the Professor replies. "You're a snake."

It's a joke that went past its natural punch line, and isn't that strong to begin with. "I did the joke on the show," Caesar remembered later. "Nothing—no laughs. Not a single one. Complete silence." Completely dropping character, Caesar called out Brooks in his own voice at that moment. "'Mel,' I said, 'I will see you after the show.'" After that, whenever any of the writers fought for a gag that no one thought would work, the others would reply, "You want to do the snake joke again?" (*Caesar's Hours*).

Your Show of Shows, Season Two (September 9, 1950–June 2, 1951)

A second season began with the show in good shape. Caesar, Coca, and Morris were back along with most of the musicians and dancers from the previous season. There was one more costar added to the show, however; a man who was hired thanks to his size as well as his talent, and one that would go on to play a very important role in Brooks's career: Carl Reiner.

Carl Reiner was born March 20, 1922, in the Bronx, New York, to Jewish immigrant parents. At the age of twenty-one, Reiner was drafted into the Army Air Corps, and did jobs pertaining to voice and language; namely training to become a French interpreter and even directing for the first time with a Moliere play done all in French in 1944. Eventually he joined the Special Services as an entertainer for the troops and trained under actor Maurice Evans (then a major), who had performed as a lead in several Shakespeare plays on Broadway in the 1930s (and would go on to do an adaptation of *Hamlet* on Broadway in 1945). Evans is probably best remembered today, ironically, for being covered in makeup as Dr. Zeus in *The Planet of the Apes* and *Beneath the Planet of the Apes.*

While Brooks was in Europe during the last days of the war, Reiner was performing with the Special Services in the Pacific Theater ("Securing our country's freedom by touring the Pacific in an army musical entitled *Shape Ahoy*," Reiner would recall in his 2003 book *My Anecdotal Life: A Memoir*), and be honorably discharged as a corporal in 1946. After a year-long road tour in the musical *Call Me Mister*—which included Howard Morris and future stars Buddy Hackett and Bob Fosse—Reiner landed a role in another revue, only this time on Broadway itself, *Inside U.S.A.* (April 1948–February 1949). The Broadway show ended just as Reiner landed his first weekly role on television in the revue series called *54th Street Revue*, which ran on CBS opposite *The Admiral Broadway Revue* on NBC/Dumont in 1949.

The series would only last until the beginning of January 1950, and although Reiner was coming across as the top banana on the program, he wanted out soon after starting. "I left, saying 'Let me out of this television shit,'" Reiner stated in *Where Have I Been?* but he didn't leave the revue format of sketches and songs behind for long. In January 1950, Reiner landed a role in a Broadway revue called *Alive and Kicking*, which was having some writing issues with the book. Max Liebman was asked by the producers to help, which he did with the support of Lucille Kallen. It did little to save the show, however, but it did allow Liebman and Reiner to meet. As it turns out, Liebman was looking to add a second banana to *Your Show of Shows* who could play bigger men against the tall Caesar.

After being interviewed by Caesar, Reiner was asked if he wanted to join the program when it returned in September 1950 for its second season. Reiner was thrilled—he had seen Caesar in *Tars and Spars* and proclaimed at the time, "Who is this guy? . . . That's Danny

Newspaper ad for the Empire Room shows for Caesar in June 1949, where Brooks tagged along and nearly got thrown out of a window for pestering Caesar once too often.

Kaye, with talent!" Later, when doing *54th Street Revue*, Reiner recalled watching Caesar on *The Admiral Broadway Revue* and telling his wife, "I belong on that show." Now, it looked like he was going to get that chance, and being a supporting cast member instead of the star was not an issue. "(Sid) was very nice about it. He knew I had credentials as a Top Banana. I said, 'I'd love it. I belong there. With you, I'd be very happy to be a Second Banana'" (*Where Have I Been?*) With Reiner in place, the series would go with the core group of comedic actors—Sid Caesar, Imogene Coca, Howard Morris, and Carl Reiner—until the series ended in 1954. As time went on he would become close friends with Brooks as well.

Meanwhile, Brooks made the jump to being an official writer on the show in Season Two and began being listed in the credits as such. This meant he finally began being paid by the production instead of Caesar, and at $250 a week. Also that season, Brooks met Broadway dancer Florence Baum, who at the time was appearing in the original Broadway production of *Gentlemen Prefer Blondes* and would eventually work on *Your Show of Shows* as one of the dancers. They dated and eventually married in 1953, although some sources state 1951, and had three children together—Stephanie, Nicky, and Eddie—before divorcing in 1962. For the moment, however, things were looking to be on the rise for Brooks, as he continued to work with "Big Mel" (Mel Tolkin, while Brooks was "Little Mel" to those on staff) and Lucille Kallen every week.

Liebman still didn't think much of Brooks, and became known for throwing lit cigars at Brooks for infuriating him at times. Brooks even once charged that Liebman would blow on the end of the cigar to get a good red glow going before throwing it at him. Liebman would also occasionally shout at Brooks, "You're nothing," only for Brooks to reply "And you're the king of nothing." Not taking a hint, Brooks also had a habit of disrupting rehearsals just to disrupt them, including sliding across the rehearsal room floor as if stealing a base in baseball. "I yelled, 'Pepper Martin sliding into second! Watch your ass!' and I ran straight at him at full speed and then threw myself into a headfirst slide. Slid right between his legs, sent him flying in the air, scared the shit out of him" (*Playboy*, 1975).

He was also notorious for once bursting unannounced into a conference with General David Sarnoff (1891–1971), the chairman of the board of RCA, in attendance. Liebman, Pat Weaver, Caesar, and Sarnoff were having a meeting to decide the fate of the series. "I wanted to know what they were planning. Would there be a new show? Should I buy a new car?" Brooks found a white duster and straw hat and then crashed into the room, jumped on the conference table, and shouted, "Hurray! Hurray! Lindy has landed at Le Bourget," and threw the hat into the air. "Skimmed it across the room and it sailed right out the window and has never been seen since." Caesar was in convulsions, but everyone else just stared. When Liebman finally croaked, "And now, if you will kindly leave us, Mr. Brooks." Brooks could only reply, crestfallen, "Don't you understand? Lindy made it!" (*Playboy*, 1975). Yet, to be fair to Liebman, even with such incidents occurring, he knew Brooks was contributing to the show and even agreed to allow Brooks to be listed in the credits as a writer alongside Tolkin and Kallen, instead of just as with an "additional dialogue" credit as in the previous season.

Critical reviews, which were somewhat positive the first season, got even better in the second, as the program began to be seen in more areas of the country. The public and the critics took note that Caesar was a completely different type of comedian in comparison to the at-the-time well-loved Milton Berle—prone to not mug at the camera to get laughs, and with a writing staff that favored original concepts rather than age-old vaudevillian gags. More specifically, people noted that the show demonstrated a New York intellectualism somewhat unique for national programming that even other shows out of the New York area did not promote at the time. Kallen and Tolkin (especially Tolkin) were both culturally aware, and it was not unusual for them to attend showings of foreign movies in the Manhattan area at a time when foreign films were just beginning to blossom as "must see" engagements in the big city. Tolkin also pressed Brooks to read the classics and move beyond the education he had. "When I met him, I had read nothing—nothing!" Brooks remembered to *Playboy* about Tolkin in 1975. "He said, 'Mel, you should read Tolstoy, Dostoievsky, Turgenev, Gogol.' He was big on the Russians."

The program was slated against Roller Derby (the quintessential study of the inner-aggressions that hide within us—okay, actually just women knocking each other down while rolling around on skates) on ABC and *The Frank Sinatra Show* on CBS, and ended the season at #4 in the ratings. Midway through the second season came the annual Emmy Awards, with *Your Show of Shows*, Caesar, and Coca all nominated in their respective categories. The program lost to *The Alan Young Show* for Best Variety Series, while Caesar lost to Alan Young for Best Actor (Young is probably best remembered today as Wilbur in the talking-horse series *Mr. Ed*), and to Groucho Marx as Most Outstanding Personality. Coca lost to Gertrude Berg, who played Molly Goldberg in *The Goldbergs*). It was a disappointment, but there were still years to come in which to achieve such goals as winning Emmy Awards.

Going AWOL, Part I—Texaco Star Theatre

Looking for work in the period between seasons for *Your Show of Shows*, Brooks asked his agent for more opportunities. As it was, the *Texaco Star Theatre*, with regular host Milton Berle, was looking to hire someone to play a stooge to Sid Stone in a short sketch on that program. Stone was an actor who appeared on the program to pitch products as a commercial, but also in a type of parody of the loud street salesmen of yesteryear; and as time went on, his routines went more toward comedy than selling various products

Brooks auditioned for the job as the stooge and got it, playing a dimwitted window washer with a black eye. As Brooks later stated in *The Incredible Mel Brooks* DVD boxset, it got him noticed among a handful of people, but would also be his last television appearance until the time of the *2000 Year Old Man* (see chapter 5). Soon after, he would return to the fold to assist with the one-week appearance at the Chicago Theatre for many in the cast from *Your Show of Shows* (as mentioned earlier), and then back to work on Season Three of the series.

Brooks would finally get a chance to do a part on *Your Show of Shows* in an episode from 1952, although it was only a voice-over. The sketch was a parody of the Joan Crawford movie *Sudden Fear* (1952), and it required the sound of a cat screeching in pain early on. Brooks knew how to do such a ruckus and demonstrated so in the writers' room, thus getting the chance to do it in the show. However, perhaps due to having to perform in front of his peers rather than an unknown audience, Brooks went dry during the run-through of the show and completely missed his cue. After a profuse apology and a lecture from one of the cast that "you wanted this job, don't screw it up for us," Brooks pulled himself together and managed to do the cat howl during the live broadcast without fail. Brooks would later produce a cat yowl in his 1974 film *Young Frankenstein* as well as in the 2005 film of *The Producers*, proving a skill never leaves you.

Your Show of Shows, Season Three (September 8, 1951–May 31, 1952)

Brooks's salary was now at $1,000 a week as a writer on the program.

That was the biggest change Brooks saw that season, as the program continued to coast without any drastic changes. It was still a core writing team of "Big Mel," Lucille, "Little Mel," Sid, and Max at this point, while cast and crew pretty much stayed the same. Another thirty-nine episodes were done, and while ratings fell a bit—from #4 to #8 for the season—it was not a surprise that the show continued to perform strongly when one saw what it was up against: CBS had *Faye Emerson's Wonderful Town* (a variety series set in various towns around the United States) and *The Show Goes On* (a talent contest series). Meanwhile, ABC pretty much gave up after the attempt to excite people with Roller Derby, going instead with *Lesson in Safety* and *America's Health* . . . and essentially allowing local stations to air their own programming instead if they wish.

The Emmy Awards in February 1952 saw the series win for Best Variety Show, Caesar for Best Actor, and Coca for Best Actress. Sid and Imogene both did lose out on Best Comedian or Comedienne, however, which went to Red Skelton and Lucille Ball that year. After the awards show, there would be a short diversion to Europe in July for Caesar, his wife, and some other cast and crew, including Brooks. Not surprisingly, both Caesar and Brooks were disappointed that no one recognized them and returned quicker than planned to get ready for the next season.

Your Show of Shows, Season Four (September 6, 1952–May 23, 1953)

There were only thirty-eight episodes in the fourth season of the show, which saw some changes to the core of the program. NBC was now looking for the show to rely less on the musical numbers and more on comedy, which put a deeper strain on the writers.

Although the series was still doing well against its competition at 9:00 p.m.—a movie on ABC, and CBS with the variety series *U.S.A. Canteen* (with singer Jane Froman), *Meet Millie* (a sitcom about a secretary in Manhattan), and *Balance Your Budget* (a game show featuring housewives trying to score enough money to balance their yearly household budget)—*Your Show of Shows* was beginning to sink in the ratings, reaching only #19 that year. At the Emmy Awards in 1953, the series won for Best Variety Program, but although Caesar and Coca were nominated as Best Comedian and Best Comedienne, both lost again, this time Sid to Jimmy Durante and Imogene to Lucille Ball. Reviews of the program were also starting to get nastier, pointing out some repetitive aspects of the program. A review in *Variety* on May 13, 1953, pointed out that three sketches "were reprises" and Liebman was obviously "finding it tough to sustain the high quality of diamond polish he has sought for 90 minutes, week after week." It was becoming increasingly clear that something was going to have to change, from the perspective of the network.

And Brooks was now making $2,500 a week, and starting to see the writing on the wall.

Going AWOL, Part II—Hollywood Calling

Variety announced on July 13, 1953, that Mel Brooks had been signed by Columbia to write a script for a movie to be called *The Pleasure Is All Mine*. The film was to be a musical version of an earlier comedy called *Too Many Husbands* (1940), about a widow who remarries only to find that her missing husband has been found and returns into her life. For Brooks, it was a surprising break away from New York, Sid Caesar, and all that he had done on the East Coast up to that time. Brooks, nonetheless, was determined to strike while the iron was hot. He had been billed as a writer on the well-known *Your Show of Shows*, and had some achievements to back him up as a good choice for writing a screenplay for the studio. With a good run in New York behind him, he struck out to Hollywood in July 1953, ready to start the next phrase of his career.

Brooks's first exposure to the studio system was much different than what he had grown accustomed to in television. In New York, he could fly into the room, jump on a table, and make merry—or manic—without causing any problems. In California, he arrived right as the president of the studio, Harry Cohn (1891–1958) was in the studio's barbershop getting a shave and yelling at a bunch of yes-men. Stretched out flat in the barber's chair, as Brooks remembered in a Dick Cavett interview, Cohn was twirled around by the barber "like mobile artillery" to face each executive and ask details on latest projects. Finally, spotting Brooks, Cohn shouted, "Who's the kid?" Brooks meekly replied, "I'm not here. I'm—I'm not here." Cohn replied, "Good. I like that boy," and moved on.

Later, Brooks was taken to his office in the four-story studio building. He watched as the nameplate of the previous tenant was removed from the door and Brooks's name was slid in. It rattled Brooks to see how quickly the fate of someone's life could change. "I didn't want to go in there. It was like death was behind the door." But then "the kid" took over and Brooks would play a practical joke on everyone in the building based on the fear he felt when watching the names change. Grabbing tiles from the top floor, he moved those names to the first, and the first to the third and the third to the fourth. By the time he was two-thirds of the way through, he had been caught and brought in front of Harry Cohn in his office. "What are you doing?" Cohn asked. "I have agents and lawyers calling for the people in the building. You know how quickly people get fired here. You gave everyone a heart attack" (*The Dick Cavett Show*). Brooks replied that it was just a joke. Cohn told him he was fired, but was eventually coaxed to only reduce his salary. Eventually, even that wasn't enough and Brooks was sent back East to the final season of *Your Show of Shows*, realizing that sometimes his jokes could backfire on him in a big way.

The *Pleasure is All Mine* was eventually made, but more than a year later and starring Betty Grable and Jack Lemmon, along with Gower and Marge Champion performing dance numbers in the film. The movie, now titled *Three for the Show*, was released in February 1955; it used a final script by Leonard Stern and Edward Hope, without any input from Brooks. Stern would continue to work in Hollywood and eventually return to another project involving Brooks in 1964, *Get Smart* (see chapter 4 for more details).

Your Show of Shows, Season Five (September 12, 1953–June 5, 1954)

Big changes came in the final season of the program. With the drop in the ratings, Liebman was having less pull than in previous years, and NBC began dictating more of the feel and look of the show. Although there would still be thirty-nine weeks in the season, *Your Show of Shows* would only have twenty-four episodes that year, with *All-Star Revue* taking over the ninety-minute spot every fourth week, ending the original concept of *The Saturday Night Revue*. (In January 1954, *All-Star Revue* would become *The Martha Raye Show*, which starred the then-frequent host of *All-Star Revue*, Martha Raye.)

Musical guests were given more airtime than in previous years, while new writers were finally hired to help the "Mels" and Lucille:

- Joe Stein (1912–2010) had worked on the first season of *The Red Buttons Show* in 1953 before moving on to *Your Show of Shows*. He would go on to write the book for *Fiddler on the Roof* (1964), which would help to revitalize the career of Zero Mostel. He also would later adapt Carl Reiner's semiautobiographical novel *Enter Laughing* in 1963 as a Broadway comedy starring Alan Arkin.
- Tony Webster (1922–1987), jokingly referred to as the one "non-Jew" in the room. Webster had been brought over after working with the comedy radio team of Bob and Ray and would write two Broadway plays—*The Greatest Man Alive* and *God Almighty*—as well as write for programs like *The Phil Silvers Show*, *Car 54, Where Are You?*, and stories for *The Love Boat*.
- Hannah Grad Goodman, a writer for *General Electric Theater* who was brought in to be a female voice once Lucille Kallen found out she was pregnant and went on maternity leave. Goodman would go on to become an art critic and write several nonfiction books on history, especially Jewish history, for school teaching.
- Danny Simon (1918–2005) had done previous work on *The Colgate Comedy Hour* (1950), briefly worked on both *The Jackie Gleason Show* and *The Red Button Show* (neither experience of which was good), and had spent time writing skits at

Camp Tamiment—Liebman's old stomping grounds—in 1952, all with his brother Neil. Danny Simon would become one of the head writers on Caesar's subsequent shows and a teacher of comedy writing in his later years (Woody Allen once stated that everything he learned about comedy writing came from working under Danny Simon, and Neil agreed with that assessment for his education in comedy as well).

• Neil Simon (born 1927) would break out from the pack after his Caesar years with the success of his Broadway comedy *Come Blow Your Horn* in 1961. He would follow that up with *Barefoot in the Park* (1963) and *The Odd Couple* (1965)—all three of which would be made into successful movies. He would write many movies and Broadway shows over the years beyond the ones listed, including his own interpretation of his Sid Caesar years, *Laughter on the 23rd Floor* (1993).

While the writing was perked up with the additional help, the scheduling and other changes to the program did little to help. *Your Show of Shows* was falling dramatically down the ratings well. It wasn't that the competition was becoming fierce either: ABC had boxing as competition, while CBS ran *Two for the Money* (a game show), the television version of radio favorite *My Favorite Wife*, and *Medallion Theatre* (a thirty-minute anthology dramatic series). None of which were rating hits, although it could be said that the highly rated *The Jackie Gleason Show* at 8:00 p.m. on CBS probably kept viewers around for the remainder of the evening. Yet some reviews referred to the attempts to change the show's format as driving away viewers who were watching to see Caesar, Coca, Reiner, and Morris go at it. Even the Emmys did little to help support the show, as although the program, Sid, and Imogene were all nominated again—along with Carl Reiner in the new category of Best Series Supporting Actor—none won. It was as if the show had to be nominated due to longevity rather than being something worth being nominated.

It was clear that *Your Show of Shows* as a ninety-minute experiment in variety programming had run its course. It was time to move on, and it was announced in February 1954 that the series was coming to an end that June. The cast and production team downplayed any concerns people had about the show being cancelled, feeling everyone had grown beyond it in some fashion. The creative team were getting opportunities to do other things and taking those offers up. Besides, Caesar was feeling the pressure of doing the ninety-minute show for thirty-nine weeks a year and was getting offers from other networks as well as Hollywood; with the star looking elsewhere, it probably was time to wrap things up.

NBC may have wanted a change as well, but didn't want to lose their star performers. Max Liebman was given the chance to do what he did best, a variety show revue, once a month, allowing him to focus on presentation rather than "getting it ready by next Saturday." The monthly broadcasts, entitled *Max Liebman Presents* and *Max Liebman Spectacular*, began on September 12, 1954, and ran until June 9, 1956, airing every fourth Sunday from 7:30 until 9:00. NBC also offered Imogene Coca her own series, a situation comedy, with Lucille Kallen on board to be the head writer. This became *The Imogene Coca Show*, which would air on Saturday nights at 9:00 for a half hour starting in October 1954. As for Sid, although enticed by the offers from Hollywood, NBC offered him a lucrative ten-year deal. He also had a hard time abandoning the format of working in front of an audience instead of a film crew. It was a move that Brooks felt held Caesar back, and kept him from becoming more remembered than if he had gone to Hollywood and did movies. By the time his next series, *Caesar's Hour*, came to an end, "Hollywood wasn't that interested," Brooks remembered with regret to Alan Sepinwall. "They had more or less had him. He was used up. There wasn't an easy segue after doing so many shows to go to the big screen."

As for Brooks?

By the time *Your Show of Shows* was in its final season, Brooks was making $5,000 per episode. He had proven himself with a high-paying job, and a beautiful wife; yet he was vomiting between cars on the way into work each day. "I figured any day now they'd find me out and fire me. It was like I was stealing and I was going to get caught," Brooks recalled later to *Playboy*. The anxiousness of wanting to prove himself had now led him to the anxiety of having to prove himself on a weekly basis, which was leading to physical issues such as low blood sugar, an underactive thyroid, and insomnia. He also began having bouts of melancholia and phantom illnesses that convinced many on the show he was a hypochondriac and making him perpetually late for writing meetings; which only helped propel the psychological issues onward in a cycle. Finally, Mel Tolkin suggested Brooks see an analyst, which he would do for a six-year period, sometimes going as often as four times a week. This was treatment that was relatively new for many in the 1950s and typically mocked in comedy, but for Brooks it was a godsend to allow him to adjust to becoming an adult. Failure was no longer a mistake of a kid who needed to wise up, but a professional man who didn't know what he was doing, which was hard to accept for someone who felt he could light up the world just by being there. "I was grieving about the death of childhood. . . . Now I really had to accept the mantle of adulthood" (*Playboy*).

A climactic moment of realization for Brooks can be found in every interview he has done since: all the work he did up to and including the Caesar years categorized him as "the kid," which skewed with the reality. For example, the theatrical incident in the Catskills became when he was fourteen instead of seventeen, as seen in chapter 1, and in the famous David Susskind interview from 1970, Brooks talks of making $5,000 when he was twenty-three or twenty-four, when he was twenty-seven in the final year of the program. The separation of the child from the adult occurred in those sessions, and Brooks always refers to himself as "the kid" up until that point. Now he saw he was drifting along as Caesar's jester, and the career for himself—a career that his ego and talent demanded of him—had been stalled by not attempting to break away from Caesar. When Brooks stated in 1975, "I would have been a successful comic on my own ten years earlier if I hadn't met Sid. But he was a great vehicle for my stuff," he wasn't blaming Caesar for what happened, but himself for possibly taking the easy road by hanging on to his role under Caesar. It was time to be an adult.

It had taken him years to finally see that it was what had to be, although others saw Brooks beginning to mature earlier, even Max Liebman. Years later, Liebman would reflect on a time near the end of the first season where Brooks was not flying around, trying too hard to make others laugh, or doing outlandish things, but rather sitting at a piano in the rehearsal hall, playing a song in all seriousness. Liebman realized that the kid he had seen years before was maturing, whether he wanted to or not.

Ironically, Caesar and several others would manage to stay stagnant and comfortable for the foreseeable future. But the kid was nowhere to be found.

3

Too Simple, Too Pure

Television Writing—the Freelance Years

Caesar's Hour was a go for that fall in 1954, heading to Monday nights from 8:00 to 9:00. Joining Mel Tolkin, Tony Webster, Joe Stein, Carl Reiner, and Sid Caesar in the writers' room was Aaron Ruben (1914–2010). He previously wrote for Milton Berle, George Burns and Gracie Allen, and Dinah Shore. He would leave after the first year of the series to concentrate on directing and producing, including creating *Gomer Pyle, U.S.M.C.* and working on shows such as *The Andy Griffith Show*, *Sanford and Son*, and *The Phil Silvers Show*.

As for Brooks, he had an incredible offer waiting for him that would allow him to direct as well as write for a big entertainer who had a massive hit show on his hands. And it lasted two weeks.

The Red Buttons Show (1954)

Brooks probably knew what he was in for before he got there. *The Red Buttons Show* had debuted in 1952 to high critical praise and ratings, but had almost immediately fallen upon rough waters when Buttons began questioning every action about the program, especially those of the writers. After a time, the show became known for "having more writers than scripts," with writers either fired or (more frequently) quitting after short stints with Buttons; including several people who had already proven themselves or would quickly prove themselves as some of the best writers in the business. As mentioned in the previous chapter, Joe Stein had come from the program to work on *Your Show of Shows*, as did Danny and Neil Simon. Future Caesar writer Larry Gelbart had been known as the glue that was holding the writing together in its first year, but left after "one year and three fights" and moved to work on Caesar's new show.

The second year of the program saw it still going strong, thanks to following *I Love Lucy* on CBS, but the network soon tired of the headaches and cancelled the program. NBC then dove in and gave Buttons a last-minute reprieve. With the change of network came a new creative time for the program, with Brooks joining to write the opening episode and, per *Variety* in September 1954, to direct the second episode. Instead, friction between the star and Brooks appeared with issues on the first script and Brooks bailed before the new season even started on NBC. It was the final season of the program before being cancelled for good.

The Imogene Coca Show (1954)

Out of a job, Brooks was looking for work. As it turns out, some of his old acquaintances from *Your Show of Shows* were looking for help on a new program. *The Imogene Coca Show* had started on NBC on October 2, 1954, as a situation comedy with Coca, and ratings were poor the first two weeks. Brooks was brought in to shake things up, but he quickly began to terrorize the writers' room instead. What came across at *Your Show of Shows* as "the kid" pulling pranks and trying to liven things up looked to the writers on the sitcom as a bully with no interest in helping anyone but himself.

Brooks was not intimidated when it came to telling others that he thought a joke didn't work, but his brashness, coupled with his inability to come up with better material himself, left everyone angry or in fear of dealing with him. When Lucille Kallen, the head writer and former head writer to Brooks on *Your Show of Shows*, told him in a group meeting that a joke was good but not right for the script, he lashed out. "Don't tell me what's funny, you just type." It was the breaking point for the writers, resulting in a meeting between Kallen and the producers, with the writers being told to just submit material and not work together anymore. After attempting to rework the show as a half-hour variety series, and then again as a situation comedy about a variety series, the doors closed on the series after one season. Brooks was out of work once again.

Newspaper ad for *The Imogene Coca Show*, a troubled series that Brooks joined for a short time, only to add further problems as a writer.

Caesar's Hour (1955–1957)

To be fair, no one could blame Brooks for what happened on *The Red Buttons Show*—the battlegrounds were too littered with the bodies of fellow writers to think otherwise. Likewise, many felt the issues with *The Imogene Coca Show* had to do with the concept of the show itself, rather than the star or those trying to make it work. So, when the offer was made for him to return to "the womb" in a sense with Sid Caesar, Mel Tolkin, and the rest, it may not have been the exciting new direction for Brooks that he craved, but at least it was a steady paycheck with creative opportunities that were hard for him to pass up.

As to Caesar's view about losing and regaining his prodigal son? He would write later, in *Where Have I Been?*, "Mel had lost his way. He needed the guys around to give him competition and a kick in the ass. I gave him that." It was never much discussed, and the attempt was there to go back to what they had before, but their roles had somewhat changed with Brooks's departure and return. Caesar was never quite as ready to protect Brooks as he had been in the past, while Brooks came back feeling a bit of an elder statesman in the room, even with Mel Tolkin—as head writer—and Sid in charge. Caesar would be the first to joke to the press about their relationship being master/slave in nature now—grabbing Brooks by the head and proclaiming, "This is mine!" When this occurred, however, Brooks grabbed Caesar's wallet and held it up saying, "And this is mine!" It was behavior they would not have been so ready to show earlier, but now seemed normal to two men that had "grown up together."

The program was much more comedy-driven than in *Your Show of Shows*, not only because it was only sixty minutes rather than ninety, and with less musical breaks between sketches, but because Max Liebman, who demanded such diversions, was no longer involved. Caesar wanted comedy and that's what he got, with the show stumbling a bit in its first season, and never earning the ratings that the initial years of *Your Show of Shows* had gotten; but eventually keeping a steady viewership and winning Emmy Awards over the course of the three years it was on.

Brooks came back in its second season, working in a writers' room that was familiar yet alien at the same time. Tony Webster, Joe Stein, and Aaron Ruben had all moved on, but in their places came others:

- Larry Gelbart (1928–2009) had bought his comedy badge by working for Bob Hope, both in specials and on the road overseas (including writing for Hope while visiting troops during the Korean War). Gelbart had received wide notices in the business for his work in the first year of *The Red Buttons Show* (see earlier entry this chapter) and was a catch for Caesar when added in 1955, alongside Brooks. He would go on to help conceive, write, and produce the television version of *MASH* in the 1970s, while also scripting such movies as *Oh, God* (directed by Carl Reiner and discussed in further detail in chapter 24) and *Tootsie*.

- Sheldon Keller (1923–2008) had worked a bit with Allan Sherman (best remembered today for the comedy song "Hello Muddah, Hello Fadduh") before taking part in World War II. He was just getting his comedy writing career off the ground when he was hired to write for *Caesar's Hour* in 1955, and would later write for several shows, including both *The Dick Van Dyke Show* (created by Carl Reiner) and *MASH*.

- Selma Diamond (1920–1985) had been writing for *The New Yorker* before moving to scriptwriting in the 1940s, when she worked for a few different shows, both situation comedies and variety packages. She and Lucille Kallen would be the inspirations for the Sally Rogers role on *The Dick Van Dyke Show* that Reiner would do after moving on from working with Caesar. She also appeared in the first two seasons of *Night Court*, an NBC sitcom, as bailiff Selma Hacker, which was essentially an extension of her own persona. She was in this role when she passed away in 1985 from lung cancer.

Caesar's Hour would be nominated for several Emmy awards in 1956, with the program losing out to *The Phil Silvers Show*. Carl Reiner once again lost to Art

Carney (*The Honeymooners*), and the writing team lost to the writers from *The Phil Silvers Show*. However, Nanette Fabray (born 1920), who replaced Imogene Coca as Caesar's foil when *Caesar's Hour* began, won for Best Actress in a Supporting Role. Fabray had already made a name for herself on Broadway in musical theater and had appeared on numerous variety shows before *Caesar's Hour*, both singing and dancing before she got the job on *Caesar's Hour*.

The writers' room changed a bit in the final season of the program. Diamond was gone, but Gelbart and Keller stayed on with Brooks, Tolkin, Caesar, and Reiner. Joining them in the final season were a returning Neil Simon (who had been working without his brother for a while by this point) and two new faces:

- Gary Belkin (1927–2005), like Diamond before him, had started his humor career working for *The New Yorker* before moving to television and eventually becoming a full-time writer on *Caesar's Hour*. He would go on to cowrite an episode of *Get Smart* with Brooks in 1965, work on several episodes of *The Carol Burnett Show* between 1973 and 1978, spend a year as a writer on *The Tonight Show with Johnny Carson*, and write the classic *Newhart* episode "Pirate Pete" in 1985.
- Michael Stewart (1924–1987) had been writing sketches for various revues around Broadway when enlisted to write for *Caesar's Hour*. Stewart, whom Brooks tended to refer to in retrospect as "the typist" for the writers in the room, later worked with former Caesar associate Gower Champion (along with Charles Strouse and Lee Adams) to create the Broadway musical *Bye Bye Birdie* (1960) and on the 1964 musical *Hello, Dolly!* He also worked on *Barnum* and *42nd Street* (the latter with Champion again, and Champion's last before his death), both hits from 1980.

It was during this period that Brooks's tendency to be late to work caught up with him. Knowing he was always late wore on the other writers, mainly due to his habit of ordering a bagel and coffee be delivered to the writers' room before he arrived, and, subsequently, needing someone else to pay for it because Brooks wasn't there yet. Finally, Caesar took matters into his own hands by paying the delivery boy twenty dollars and telling him to keep the change. Thus, when Brooks arrived, with fifty cents to pass on to whomever paid for the order, Caesar told him that it was $20. When Brooks argued, Caesar replied, "Mel, if you don't want to come on time, it's going to cost you $20 a day. And I may raise it to $50 if I like the delivery guy." As Caesar pointed out years later, Brooks was still late, but only by a half-hour after that incident.

As annoying as Brooks was in not arriving on time, the other writers excused him because he could not only make them laugh when he showed up, but he usually could look at someone's work and add to it to make it even better; becoming known as a "comedy writer's comedy writer." "[Mel] didn't need the eight hours we put in," Neil Simon reflected in 1992. "He needed four hours. He is, maybe, the most uniquely funny man I've ever met."

The Emmy Awards came around once again, and *Caesar's Hour* would finally have its moment of glory. The series won for Best Series, One Hour or More;

Caesar won for Best Continuing Performance by a Comedian in a Series; Nanette Fabray (although no longer on the show, the award was for the previous season) as Best Continuing Performance by a Comedienne in a Series; Carl Reiner at long last won against Art Carney for Best Supporting Performance by an Actor, Pat Carroll for Best Supporting Performance by an Actress. The only category that the program was nominated for and did not win was Best Writing, Variety or Situation Comedy, with the award once again going to the writers of *The Phil Silvers Show*. When this was announced, Brooks leapt up on the table in the NBC Studios in Burbank, where the ceremony was occurring, and shouted, "Coleman Jacoby and Arnie Rosen won an Emmy and Mel Brooks didn't! That bullshit writers can win the award and geniuses like us would be denied! Nietzsche was right! There is no God! There is no God!" (*Caesar's Hours*) Fortunately, by this point, people in the industry knew enough about Brooks to take it as the joke it was meant, instead of the words of a crazy person (or perhaps both).

In the first two seasons, *Caesar's Hour* ran into problems with ratings due to being slated against *The Burns & Allen Show* and *Talent Scout* on CBS—both top ten shows in the ratings. To counteract this for the third season, NBC moved *Caesar's Hour* to the old *Your Show of Shows* hour of 9:00 p.m. on Saturdays in hopes of knocking out the lethargic *Lawrence Welk's Dodge Dancing Party* on ABC. It was a massive mistake, with *Caesar's Hour* tanking in the ratings against the *Welk* juggernaut. (Okay "juggernaut" is a bit much, but let's just say that people wanted to watch *Welk* rather than *Caesar*.) It was clear to NBC that the show did not meet ratings expectations. Considering their long and successful history with Caesar, NBC offered him a chance to do several specials for them, but he turned it down. What he wanted to do was exactly what he had been doing, and nothing else.

In May 1957, *Caesar's Hour* came to an end, as did Caesar's nine-year run on NBC. The program and everyone who had been nominated previously for the Emmys were nominated again for the final season, but only Carl Reiner won. By that time, anyway, people were moving on, and Brooks was once again looking for work.

The Polly Bergen Show (1957)

Brooks was hired to temporarily produce this show from October 19, 1957, through November 30, 1957, after its original producer, Bill Colleran, asked to step down so he could concentrate on directing. Brooks would produce a total of four episodes out of the eighteen done for the series before being replaced that December by Irvin Mansfield, who retooled the program for the final episodes aired.

Polly Bergen was a singer and actress who had fought to play singer Helen Morgan in *The Helen Morgan Story* (airing May 16, 1957), for which she won an Emmy in 1958 and that led to her obtaining her own variety show that fall. The show was troubled, however, as it was in competition with *Lawrence Welk* on ABC and two hits programs on CBS—*The Gale Storm Show* and *Have Gun—Will Travel*. The show was cancelled and last aired on May 31, 1958.

Sid Caesar Invites You (1958)

In the July 24, 1957, edition of *Variety*, it was announced that Sid Caesar was returning to television "this fall" in a half-hour show with Imogene Coca for ABC. By October 30, it was announced that Carl Reiner would be returning as well. In January 1958, *Variety* reported that several of the writers from the past for Caesar would be returning, including Mel Brooks, along with Michael Stewart, Neil Simon, Mel Tolkin, Larry Gelbart, and Danny Simon. The first episode aired January 26, 1958, at 9:00 p.m. EST on ABC.

The ratings were strong the first week, doing better than both *General Electric Theater* on CBS and *The Dinah Shore Chevy Show* on NBC. Yet critics were harsh, stating viewers would be "only moderately entertained," and work was needed by the writers to keep its audience. There were also criticisms that the sketches ran too long for a half-hour show and needed to be punchier. Slowly, the show began to sink in the ratings, and by March, it was clear that it would be cancelled after thirteen episodes, ending on May 25, 1958.

Sid was already looking forward to another program by March 1958, having signed a deal with the BBC to do a half-hour program that summer on Tuesday nights at 8:00 p.m. The show featured Imogene Coca once again, but that's where the likeness ended besides the writing, which was made up of sketches by Mel Tolkin, Mel Brooks, and Michael Stewart that had been done in one of Caesar's previous series. The British version—also called *Sid Caesar Invites You*—ran from July 1 through September 16, 1958, before being cancelled after thirteen weeks.

Newspaper ad for *The Polly Bergen Show*, which Brooks wrote and produced for a time.

The Jerry Lewis Show (1958)

Brooks soon bounced back with a new show, working with Danny Simon and Harry Crane on two Jerry Lewis specials that aired on NBC in late 1958 for Timex. The first aired on October 18 at 9:00–10:00 p.m. EST, and the second aired December 10. *Variety* reviewed the first special as "a complete shambles," while the second was criticized for "having top writers" but not using them well, going on to say, "It's up to Lewis himself to get more mileage out of his scripting staff and to rely less on his own improvisations; also, to do less strictly solo stuff and more bits where he can play against someone other than the director or the audience."

Nevertheless, something obviously clicked between Lewis and Brooks, as Brooks would be hired in June 1960 to write the screenplay for Lewis's new movie, *Lady's Man*, which was soon changed to and released as *The Ladies Man* in 1961. Brooks began working on the script when he was joined by a friend of Jerry Lewis, Bill Richmond (1921–2016). Richmond knew Brooks from their Catskill days where they were both drummers, with Richmond working with Les Brown and Nelson Riddle amongst others before actively pursuing a writing career. Richmond had the temperament to work with Lewis, who was known for being a bit egocentric, driven, and sometimes hard to track down long enough to listen to ideas. "Mel and I only worked together on the script for *The Ladies Man* for about two weeks," Richmond remembered years later to Justin Bazung for TV Store Online Blog. As Variety reported in early August, Brooks was no longer working on the script due to frustrations in working with Jerry Lewis, with most biographies placing Brooks as working on the script for thirteen weeks. But the time frame appears to be closer to six to eight weeks. "Once we had a good idea, Mel would say, 'Let's run it by Jerry and see if he likes it.' So, we'd call Jerry, and Jerry would say, 'I can't talk right now, but let me get back to you.' Now if anybody had a bigger ego than Jerry Lewis, it was Mel Brooks. Jerry did this to Mel about four times. So, finally, Mel said, 'Fuck this, I quit.'"

Richmond, however, would go on to write seven movies with Lewis, including *The Nutty Professor* (1963), and write for several programs on his own, including a bit in the television special *Peeping Times* (1978), which was directed by Brooks's cowriters Rudy De Luca and Barry Levinson and featured Brooks in a short film (see chapter 22 for more details). Brooks would take

The Ladies' Man (1961) starring Jerry Lewis. Brooks was originally hired to cowrite the script, only to quit when frustrated with Lewis's methods.

his salary of $46,000 for writing on the picture, which would turn out to be over half of his earnings in 1960.

The Specials (1959–1967)

Without the steady paycheck from *Your Show of Shows* waiting for him, Brooks had to take work where he could get it after his work on the two Jerry Lewis specials ended.

The first came at the beginning of January 1959, with Brooks working on an episode of *Pontiac Star Parade*, usually referred to as simply *Star Parade*; an occasional special airing on NBC and sponsored by Pontiac, with the episode Brooks worked on airing on February 28, 1959. The special was hosted by Louis Jordan, but advertised with special guest star Ginger Rogers. Included in the cast was old Brooks crony Ronny Graham (discussed more in later chapters), along with Elaine May and Mike Nichols, who later directed Brooks's second wife, Anne Bancroft, in *The Graduate* (1967). *Variety*, in reviewing the special, entitled "Accent on Love," stated it was directed by Joe Cates and written by Brooks with Mel Tolkin. Reviews for the program were rather tepid, emphasizing how good the commercials were between the sketches and musical numbers, although Gower Champion was given solid praise for his work on the show.

Brooks again worked with Mel Tolkin on an NBC special that aired May 3, 1959, entitled *At the Movies*. The special was sponsored by Rexall, a drugstore chain, and featured Audrey Meadows with Sid Caesar, along with Art Carney and Jaye P. Morgan. Also writing on the special was Woody Allen, who would be one of a handful of writers that would break out to become a public figure, much like Brooks, and the two were commonly linked together in articles of the 1970s. This was especially true in the early 1970s, when Woody Allen was constantly promoted as "the next Mel Brooks" after *The Producers* and later *Blazing Saddles* were released. Allen would later say of their times together, "I love Mel Brooks, and I've had wonderful times working with him. But I don't see any similarities between Mel and myself except, you know, we're both short Jews." Brooks would agree, stating, "Woody and I don't get in each other's way—we do different things. His comedy takes a more cerebral tack than mine does." Even so, it is perhaps because of this very comparison that many biographies have linked Allen to the golden years of Caesar and his writers from *Your Show of Shows* and *Caesar's Hour*.

Brooks and Tolkin continued to work together after the *At the Movies* special, and for a short time they worked on a pilot script for a possible series to star Caesar with Audrey Meadows that was to air on the *Alcon-Goodyear Theatre*. When that fell through, the two wrote an episode of *The Kraft Music Hall* with Sid C. Green and Dick M. Hills for British actor/comedian David King that aired on May 20, 1959. This was followed by the two working with Sydney Zelinka (1906–1981) on two episodes of *The United States Steel Hour* featuring Sid Caesar and Audrey Meadows: "Holiday on Wheels" on October 21, 1959, and "Marriage . . . Handle with Care" on December 2, 1959. The trio also worked on two episodes of *The Revlon Revue*, both of which also starred Caesar and Meadows: "Tiptoe Through TV" on May 5, 1960, and "The World of Show Biz" on June 2, 1960. Zelinka had worked previously on various Jackie Gleason programs, including several episodes of *The Honeymooners*, episodes of *Car 54, Where Are You?*, and even an episode of *Get Smart*.

Brooks, however, was no more joined at the waist with Tolkin than he was with Caesar at this point. Brooks had been writing some material on his own, such as for an episode of the *Pontiac Star Parade* that aired on NBC on April 16, 1960, entitled "The Man in the Moon," which featured host Andy Williams, Tony Randall, Diahann Carroll, and a young Cloris Leachman (who, of course, will be cropping back up in Brooks's history later).

Brooks also worked on a special for ABC on September 13, 1961, *The Connie Francis Show*, which was sponsored by Beecham Products. The special was produced and directed by former *Your Show of Shows* director Greg Garrison and featured Art Carney and Bea Arthur. Brooks was one of five writers for the show, which included Jack Wohl, Jim Haines, Chick Green, and Gwen Davis.

In 1963, Brooks was enticed back to Caesar territory for the third episode in a monthly series of half-hour specials on ABC for Sid called *As Caesar Sees It*. The program found Brooks working with Terry Ryan (1922–2001), who had worked on *The Phil Silvers Show* and *Car 54, Where Are You?*, amongst others, and Ernest Chambers (born 1928), who would write and produce a number of shows, in particular *The Smothers Brothers Comedy Hour* (1967–1968). *Variety* would review the series as uneven, but stated that this particular episode gave Sid "plenty of fodder for the proper display of his varied talents."

Brooks then worked on *The Sid Caesar Imogene Coca Carl Reiner Howard Morris Special*, which aired at 8:30 p.m. EST on April 5, 1967. The special was announced in August 1966, with the press release stating the four main cast members of *Your Show of Shows* would get back together for a one-hour special on CBS. The final writing credits for the program had Brooks with Mel Tolkin, Carl Reiner, and the writing team of Sam Denoff (1928–2011) and Bill Persky (born 1931). The pair had written several well-remembered episodes of the Carl Reiner–created series *The Dick Van Dyke Show*, and created both *That Girl* for Marlo Thomas and *Lotsa Luck* for Dom DeLuise. The special also included an adaptation of an earlier *Caesar's Hour* sketch that had been written by that show's writing staff and I. A. L. Diamond. The special would win an Emmy for Outstanding Variety Special and—more importantly for Brooks in association with Caesar—an Emmy for Outstanding Writing Achievement in Variety.

The special would not exactly be the end for Brooks's association with the Caesar years. In 1973, kinescopes of *Your Show of Shows* were edited together to create a theatrical "best of" presentation called *Ten from Your Show of Shows*, which did well in theaters and create a resurgence of interest in the program and Caesar and Coca. In 2004, many segments from episodes of *Your Show of Shows*, *Caesar's Hour*, and even the old *Admiral Broadway Revue* were edited together to create a series of DVD collections, although they are a bit hard to find these days.

One final writing project for Brooks, just as filming was about to begin on his first film, *The Producers* (1967), was for Zero Mostel. The Tony-winning performer had a one-hour special on ABC on May 1, 1967, featuring Mostel in a variety of sketches. Brooks wrote one sketch for the program, alongside such writers as Ian Hunter (who was then working on a script with Mostel that would be *The Producers* equivalent on movie studios), Pat McCormick, Jack Burns, and Avery Schreiber, who would appear briefly in Brooks's last two films.

Between all these specials came two bigger projects for Brooks, however. Both pilots, with one close to Brooks's heart and another that was just a chance to make up a funny show. Of the two, only the later one would succeed.

Inside Danny Baker (1963)

William Steig is an artist best remembered today for created the character Shrek, an ogre that would become the basis for a series of movies from DreamWorks Studios beginning in 1991. His later years saw him doing a series of children's books that have remained popular, such as *Sylvester and the Magic Pebble* (1969) and *The Amazing Bone* (1976), but before that he did cartoons for *The New Yorker* and had various collections published over the years.

One of his collections was *Dreams of Glory and Other Drawings* in 1953, which featured one-panel pictures showing a young boy performing amazing feats of valor and derring-do (such as stopping robbers in his house with his expert knifing skills, or single-handedly saving damsels from burning buildings). The cartoons were typically referred to as a boy's version of James Thurber's story "The Secret Life of Walter Mitty" (about a man who daydreams about various feats he wishes he could be doing). Not that Thurber's writing was the first or last place such daydreaming had made it into popular culture; it was simply one of the more memorable ones.

Mel Brooks teamed with producer Stanley Chase (1927–2014)—an off-Broadway producer who at the time was best known for producing the Tony Award–winning musical *The Threepenny Opera* in 1958—in developing the property in early 1962. *Variety* reported in May 1962 that the pilot would be named after the book and that Brooks and Chase were trying to line up "west coast writers to go to New York to script" what was obviously hoped to be a series bought by one of the networks. By November 1962, *Variety* stated the pilot was to be called *My Name Is Danny Baker* and would be a joint venture of United Artists and ABC, with Arthur Hiller (1923–2016) being added as the director. Hiller soon moved on from television assignments after this to motion pictures, including *Love Story* (1970); two Neil Simon–written films, *The Out-of-Towners* (1970) and *Plaza Suite* (1971); two Gene Wilder/Richard Pryor films, *Silver Streak* (1976) and *See No Evil, Hear No Evil* (1989); and *The In-Laws* (1979), which was penned by Andrew Bergman, who wrote the story on which *Blazing Saddles* was based.

The pilot follows the adventures of a twelve-year-old boy named Danny Baker, who lives with his mother and dentist father in New York. The premise for the show would be that each week, Danny's daydreams would lead to some type of wacky adventure. The name Danny Baker came from Brooks, who chose it because "it was the most gentile name I could ever conceive of," and it is this need to homogenize his humor for Middle America that tends to let down fans who view the pilot today. The show was also hurt by its main premise—the outlandish daydreams of the boy—which was used only once in the episode when Danny dreams of becoming a famous painter. With that premise shifted to only a short one-off segment in the show, the pilot remained pretty much a *Leave It to Beaver* knockoff, and much like various other shows about kids that were popping up at that time.

Baker was played by Roger Mobley (born 1949), who had been featured in the long-running series, *Fury* (1955–1960) and would wind down his career as a child actor with multiple appearances on *Walt Disney's Wonderful World of Color* in various roles. Danny's father was played by Robert Gerringer, who is probably best remembered as Dr. David Woodard on the ABC soap opera series *Dark Shadows*. Danny's mother was played by Joan Hotchkis (born 1927), who is probably best remembered as Oscar's girlfriend Dr. Nancy Cunningham on *The Odd Couple* (1970–1975); she also had a part in the short-lived series *My World and Welcome to It* (1969–1970), based on the work of James Thurber, which also concerned a character whose daydreams were vividly depicted in the show. Danny's friend, Eric, was played by Paul O'Keefe, who would move directly on from this to play Patty's brother Ross on *The Patty Duke Show* (1963–1965).

The pilot was produced by Richard Brill (1919–1979) and Robert Alan Aurthur (1922–1978) for United Artists TV as a Jaguar-Crossbow Production. Crossbow would be Brooks's production company until he switched to using Brooksfilms Ltd in 1979. The theme song was written by Charles Strouse with Lee Adams, but more about him in chapter 6.

United Artists had high hopes for the pilot to become a series, but of the total of five pilots produced that spring by the studio, four were picked up past the pilot stage and all four are now considered classics in one way or another: *The Fugitive*, *The Patty Duke Show*, *East Side/West Side*, and *The Outer Limits* (at the time referred to as *Please Stand By*). Brooks reflected in *Poking a Dead Frog* on the pilot not being picked up years later: "It was too personal. I was that kid. I didn't lower myself enough with, you know, sex jokes. You want things to sell; you've got to make them somehow down and dirty and attractive. It was too simple, too pure, and I was pleasing myself. I should have said, 'It's just a little too mild to get on television.'" With the demise of the show that Brooks tried to make as innocent as he could, he began to realize that sometimes you had to do more for the audience than just what worked for yourself, and it would increasingly come into play in the films that would come a few short years later. "I would think, 'The hell with this. If they don't get it, they don't get it.' . . . But I realized, how many people is this for? I've got to include some of the audience, or else."

While copies of the show would float around collectors' markets on videotape for years, it finally appeared in an official form in the Shout! Factory DVD collection *The Incredible Mel Brooks: An Irresistible Collection of Unhinged Comedy* in 2012.

While the pilot did not go anywhere, it did lead to a connection that would greatly benefit Brooks: one of the other shows piloted by United Artists, *East Side/West Side*, was produced by David Susskind's production company, Talent Associates, which would be involved with Brooks's next project, *Get Smart*.

4

And Loving It

Get Smart

nside Danny Baker may not have come off, but Brooks's next pilot would be destined for greater things.

David Susskind (1920–1987) had his own national talk show, *Open End*, which eventually became *The David Susskind Show*, both of which featured Mel Brooks on multiple occasions. What people sometimes forget, if they remember Susskind at all, is that he had been a talent agent who formed a company called Talent Associates, which developed entertainment projects for Broadway, movies studios, and television. Hired into the company was a young television executive named David Melnick (1932–2009), who saw that the company was doing fine with prestigious projects such as the series *East Side/West Side* and one-off production of serious plays, such as a 1966 production of Arthur Miller's *Death of a Salesman* that featured a young Gene Wilder in a small role. But prestige never did much for the pocketbook, and Melnick felt the company had to think ahead to more popular, mainstream programming. Which, as it turns out, wasn't really happening. *East Side/West Side*—a dramatic series with George C. Scott as a social worker—was their biggest serial success at that point, and it only lasted a season. Other attempts such as *The Baileys of Balboa*, which played like a mix of *Gilligan's Island* and *The Beverly Hillbillies*, and *Mr. Broadway*, a series starring Craig Stevens as a press agent on Broadway who eventually became a press agent who fights crime once the network got involved, had both tanked. In early 1964, Talent Associates had only one prospect that sold, and it was the game show *Supermarket Sweeps*, which featured husbands and wives competing against other couples to load up shopping carts with merchandise within a time-limit. Susskind found the game show embarrassing to even put the company name on, much less having it associated with himself. It was clear to Melnick and Susskind that they needed an idea that would prove the company could pull off making long-lasting series for television; otherwise, they would be known as an industry joke.

In 1964, Melnick examined what was selling well at the box office, which was James Bond and the character Inspector Clouseau, played by Peter Sellers in the 1963 film *The Pink Panther* and its follow-up in 1964, *A Shot in the Dark*. To Melnick, it was the perfect setup: "Inspector Clouseau meets James Bond." He presented the idea to Susskind, who agreed that it had potential and suggested to Melnick that he get someone to start working on the project.

Melnick's first choice, Mike Nichols, showed interest but could not fit it into his schedule. His second was Brooks, whom Melnick had worked with between 1963 and 1964 on the Broadway musical *Kelly* (see chapter 6 for more details). Melnick knew that Brooks had a history in television already as both a writer and producer, besides becoming increasingly known by the public at large by 1964, thanks to the *2000 Year Old Man*. Better yet, Brooks was fast with jokes and comedy ideas. With a relationship firmly established between the two of them, it seemed like a sure fit. The only problem was the same one that had plagued Brooks going back to his Caesar years—Brooks never learned to type, as he didn't want to be missing out on contributing because he was struggling to put words on paper, but rather be the guy lying on the couch or dancing around the room, playing out the material free-form. So, Brooks was a good choice, but Melnick also needed a disciplined soul who could not only type, but could keep up with Brooks in the way of humor.

To do that, he contacted an old writing acquaintance, Buck Henry (born 1930). Henry had been an actor and writer, working in both capacities through a number of shows, including one of Steve Allen's numerous talk shows and the satirical panel show *That Was the Week That Was*. Henry had also been involved with an improvisational comedy group called The Premise, as well as a series of public pranks—created by Alan Abel—between 1959 and 1962 where he fooled numerous news department by posing as G. Clifford Prout, the head of the "Society for Indecency to Naked Animals," a nonexistent group demanding pets be clothed. After *Get Smart*, Buck Henry would write the script for the Mike Nichols movie *The Graduate* (1968), which starred Brooks's second wife, Anne Bancroft; *Catch-22* (1970); and cowrite *Heaven Can Wait* (1978, which he also codirected) and *What's Up, Doc?* (1972). For those growing up in the 1970s, he is probably best remembered for numerous appearances on *Saturday Night Live* during the initial five years of the program and with its original cast, as well as creating the science-fiction parody equivalent to *Get Smart*, *Quark* (1978).

Brooks and Henry met at the offices of Talent Associates and split the next three months kibitzing about ideas for the show and alternating between hustling Melnick or being hustled by Susskind at the pool table set up in what was once the company's conference room. The main concept was clear from the beginning and never changed: "It was to make sport of a level of the government and of our relationship to it and of a style of melodrama," Henry said years later in *David Susskind: A Televised Life*. "We never considered doing it as a sitcom." Brooks himself would later state, in a 1965 interview with *Time* magazine, how much he hated the situation comedies of the time. "They were such distortions of life. If a maid took over my house like Hazel, I'd set her hair on fire!" The point was to do a funny show and avoid the clichés of then-common situation comedies: no loving family with the idiot father, no lectures about the Ten Commandments, and definitely no wiseacre housemaids like Hazel.

Brooks came up with definitive aspects of the character and the show. He offered the name "Maxwell Smart" and the name of the series—*Get Smart* (not only as an action title to suggest people were out to get Max, but also a play on the term "don't get smart with me"). It was a title that Melnick was iffy about, figuring people would think the program was a game show, but he was eventually convinced. Brooks also came up with the shoe-phone, supposedly during an office meeting where, after getting so many phone calls at once Brooks finally took off one of his shoes and answered it. Henry came up with a good chunk of things as well, including the "cone of silence," a device used in the office of Max's boss, the Chief, that was supposed to eliminate anyone other than those within the cone from hearing what they were saying . . . only for it to malfunction in one way or another throughout the series. Both agreed on Smart's agent number being 86, a code used in bars to toss a drunk from the joint, as in "86 the guy." Attempts to have his female partner be named Agent 69 were crushed quickly by the censors, however, and instead the character became Agent 99.

Henry and Brooks wrote the pilot script, dealing with Smart meeting Agent 99 for the first time and defeating the villain. Meanwhile, casting began with the production company eyeing actor Orson Bean (born 1928) for the role of Smart, before announcing in August 1964 that comic actor Tom Poston (1921–2007) would play the role. That same article mentioned that ABC had taken an interest

DVD cover for Season Four of *Get Smart*, the comedy spy series for television that Brooks created with Buck Henry.

in the script, but behind the scenes it was soon discovered that the network thought they were buying a dramatic series rather than a comic one. The network just didn't quite get it, insisting that the series become more "television friendly" by giving Maxwell Smart a mother that lives with him. "Max was to come home to his mother and explain everything. I hate mothers on shows. Max has no mother," Brooks would later tell *Time* magazine. Wanting to get away from such notions, the writers finally agreed to add Fang, a dog also known as K-13, named such because Brooks and Henry believed calling him K-9 would have been much too obvious, and even the dog only appeared occasionally up through Season Two before disappearing. Two drafts of the script were sent to ABC, who had paid $7,500 for it, with the stipulation that if they didn't like it, they could have their money back. ABC went with the second offer and sold it back to the surprised company, who unexpectedly had to scrape together the cash.

As fortune would have it, NBC had comedian Don Adams (1923–2005) under contract to do a pilot. Adams had been gaining national interest through playing a regular role in *The Bill Dana Show* (a spin-off of *The Danny Thomas Show*), which ran from 1963 through early 1965. In several episodes, Don Adams played a bumbling house detective at the apartment building where Dana's character worked. It was a character in much the spirit of what would become Maxwell Smart, and with the same staccato, nasally voice; a holdover from a William Powell impression Adams used to do in his stand-up act. It was also where the famous "Would you believe" gag from several episodes of *Get Smart* came. The script was given to Grant Tinker (1926–2016) at NBC, who liked it and suggested that Adams would be perfect in the role, but wanted some changes made. Tom Poston had always been a choice more for ABC than the producers, so making the change to Adams was no issue. The only problem was creating another draft of the script. To do that, Talent Associates turned to the man who helped with the second draft of the script, Leonard Stern.

Leonard Stern (1923–2011) had been working in movies and television for years at that point, starting off as a scripter on movies for "Ma and Pa Kettle" and Abbott and Costello in the very early 1950s. In a small piece of irony, Stern would complete the script that Mel Brooks had started for Columbia back in 1953 that finally became the film *Three for the Show* (1955). At the time of the *Get Smart* saga, Stern was a producer at Talent Associates, working on *Supermarket Sweeps* when asked to punch up the script for *Get Smart*. Stern didn't see much to change, choosing to add a couple of physical gags and leaving well enough alone. He did, however, come up with the opening credits sequence, which featured Max walking into the halls of CONTROL, the government spy agency he works for; entering through a series of steel doors that work in a variety of combinations before finally reaching a phone booth at the end of the corridor that sends him plummeting into the headquarters of the agency.

NBC finalized the deal on *Get Smart* in December 1964. The pilot was filmed soon after with Brooks's suggestion of former Caesar associate Howard Morris directing. The show at first struggled slightly from the network's standpoint—several executives did not care for Adams's vocal delivery, for one thing—but the program was gaining strong critical reviews and became a hit that would last five seasons. Buck Henry would stay on for two of those seasons as a story editor, and Leonard Stern would stay for three as producer/executive producer before moving on. Both would write episodes for the series as well.

As for Brooks, besides helping to set up the show, he cowrote three episodes in the first season before moving on: the pilot with Henry (and with input from Stern), "Our Man in Leotards" with former *Caesar's Hour* cowriter Gary Belkin, and "Survival of the Fattest" with Ronny Pearlman (1942–1977). At the time, Brooks said his reason for leaving the series soon after it started was because "I'd run dry very soon." It was clear as well that he felt his future lay not in television but elsewhere. "I'd like to write more screenplays, or a Broadway play, or a book, which—hopefully—would note people's tears and joys and say something about the human condition" (*Time* magazine). It appeared, after over fifteen years writing for television, he wanted to move away from the medium that launched his career.

At least, that's pretty much how all the biographies play up Brooks's reasons for leaving *Get Smart*. As it was, Brooks had been signed to create a pilot for another series for the network. Possibly one entitled *Triplets*, which he had sold to ABC in 1964, months before the premiere of *Get Smart* on NBC, but which never evolved to the pilot stage. Even so, he would remain a consultant on *Get Smart*, and when each episode aired, the opening credits would announce the program as being created "By Mel Brooks with Buck Henry." This demotion of Henry's input (to make it balanced, the wording would have had "with" replaced with "and"), along with entertainment industry reporting pushing Brooks's involvement over Henry's, created a wedge between the two for years afterwards. Friction also came behind the scenes in other ways, specifically as Brooks felt that Henry looked down on him in a way. "I had a reputation for being a crazy Jew animal," Brooks would say several years later to Kenneth Tynan in *The New Yorker*, "whereas Buck thought of himself as an intellectual. Well, I was an intellectual, too. . . . What Buck couldn't bear was the idea of this wacko Jew being billed over him. The truth is that he read magazines, but he's not an intellectual. He's a pedant." Once again, even after getting so far in the business, Brooks felt he was being treated without the respect he deserved.

Brooks would later state that his status in the credits had been insisted upon by his agents at the time, rather than requested by him. He and Henry would eventually reconcile and even participate in some interview segments for the Shout! Factory DVD collection of Mel Brooks material that would feature the pilot episode of the series. Both of their names would continue to be associated with the show and its various remakes and spin-offs ever since, even as the two moved on to other, bigger projects soon afterwards.

And Brooks certainly did have other options available to him. While the $200 a week he got for cocreating and being a consultant on *Get Smart* helped, there were other avenues open to him now, that showed he was becoming more than just a writer for television. And one of the biggest came through his association with a friend and fellow alumnus of Caesar, leading to Brooks's real breakthrough as a performer in front of a national audience.

5

The Difference Between Comedy and Tragedy

The Long Journey of the 2000 Year Old Man

It started as an impromptu joke in the writers' room at *Your Show of Shows*. It was 1950 and Carl Reiner had recently been hired to work on the show. His introduction to Mel Brooks earlier that year had been punctuated by Brooks leaping up and performing for everyone in the room as "a Jewish pirate who was complaining about not being able to set sail and pillage . . . because the price of sail cloth was too high," as Reiner mentioned in *Anecdotal Life*. From there, Reiner and Brooks fell into rhythm, with Reiner as the straight man asking questions of Brooks as various characters in order to break up a room full of people at parties.

Obviously, it was nothing that new to either Reiner or Brooks—the setup is the same as with Sid Caesar in the various "airport" interview sketches that would appear in many of Caesar's shows. A straight man—usually Carl Reiner once he was hired for *Your Show of Shows*—would stop an individual (typically Caesar in his Professor costume) and ask him questions about some topic. Brooks was one of the heavy lifters for these sketches when working for Caesar, and it was one of these sketches that nearly led to the altercation between Caesar and Brooks, as discussed in chapter 2. One can nearly hear Brooks's voice when Caesar spoke in such sketches, especially in the use of words like "pussycat" and a tendency to go on complex tangents being asked simple questions.

Later in 1950, Reiner had viewed a talk show on NBC called *We, the People*. The half-hour program, hosted by Dan Seymour, had various guests discussing current political or entertainment events. The show would also recreate important events from the week in order to give the news a sense of immediacy, which Reiner found "appalling and begging to be satirized." Going into the offices that following Monday, Reiner presented the idea, astonished that a news program would think they could recreate an incident where "a plumber who was in Josef Stalin's toilet repairing his plumbing, when he heard the premier say 'We're going to blow up the world Thursday.'"

It held some mild interest for the writers, but Reiner could tell he was losing everyone and pushed it further by turning to Brooks and saying, "Here with us today, ladies and gentlemen, is a man who was actually at the scene of the Crucifixion, two thousand years ago. Isn't that true, sir?" Brooks, immediately catching on, let out a low, said "Oh boy," and went into an improv about knowing Jesus, which later would be polished and become a centerpiece of the act. The two continued to play with it off and on when Reiner felt things "got into a lull," and "I would just throw something at Mel, I would make him a psychiatrist or whatever. We did it only for friends and never thought anything about it" as he told Steve Heisler.

Brooks looked back on the creation in the same interview with Heisler as largely Reiner's doing. "I think the real engine behind it is Carl, not me. I'm just collecting the fares. But he's the guy that creates the subjects, the questions, and creates a king of buoyant, effervescent, terribly naïve character."Reiner agreed to a certain extent. "It's really a writing job—the straight guy comes up with the premises. In all good writing teams, there's always someone who has a strength in one area and my strength is that I always come up with ideas." Reiner would go on to say that he relished coming up with questions for Brooks's characters for which he thinks there will be no answer. "I get the biggest kick out of . . . when I got him in a corner and there's no way out, and he finds a way out, that makes me laugh out loud." Of course, not every instance provided golden moments, and there had been times when things didn't quite gel—there was one dinner party where Brooks excused himself "for a moment" to the kitchen and then went home rather than try to come back out to the party with a good response to Reiner's question—but overall, the pair enjoyed the attempts as much as those listening would.

Out of the characters created from this came the 2000 Year Old Man: a man who probably was quite a bit older, as some stories the character would later tell have him living as a caveman. Nevertheless, the 2000 Year Old Man had seen and been everywhere, and was reporting on events that turned out to be not quite as we had come to know them: Robin Hood stole from everyone, but had a good press agent; Shakespeare's thirty-eighth play was *Queen Alexandra and Murray*; Sigmund Freud was a great basketball player, and onward. And of these characters, the one that really hooked those who got to hear them perform was the little old man who had seen everything in world history.

Soon they began to perform their act for others at dinner parties, and a short time after, Reiner began recording their little improvs on a portable Revere tape recorder to find gems that could be reused. The pair would continue in this fashion for ten years, performing interviews with a variety of characters, but always coming back to the 2000 Year Old Man. The thing was, both Brooks and Reiner agreed that it was something only for "our Jewish friends and our non-anti-Semitic Christian friends" and would never consider taking it any further. Although vaudeville has produced numerous comics who had used Yiddish accents and were accepted for that use, after World War II, it was deemed that producing comedy by parodying such an accent was making fun of the Jewish people. Entertainers quickly got away from it, but here was Brooks laying it on thick with what he deemed to be an "American Jewish" accent. To the pair, it was harmless in front of a small circle of friends, but taking it any further would probably not go over well, either with those who felt it offensive, or what they considered to be Middle America's distaste for anything spoken in such a manner. Because of that, "We were free and relaxed and we weren't worried about any kind of boundaries or hurting people's feelings, or getting letters," Brooks told Charlie Rose in 1997. "We would just entertain each other, basically."

Then in June 1960, Brooks came out to California for a business visit that climaxed with a party at Joe Fields's home. Joe Fields (1895–1966) was a Broadway producer who had several hit musicals and plays over the years, including *Gentlemen Prefer Blondes* and *Flower Drum Song*. He was well known for his lavish dinner parties, and when Reiner and Brooks could attend, he would ask them to perform for the partygoers, including some very famous names, just as at this particular function. After they performed the 2000 Year Old Man, those in attendance pounced on the pair. Comedian George Burns told them that if they didn't record it soon, he was going to steal their idea for himself. Soon after, actor Edward G. Robinson suggested they write "that thousand-year-old guy" up as a play for him to do on Broadway. Finally, Steve Allen came up to them and told them that he would pay for a studio for them to record an album's worth of material and "if you don't like what you hear, burn it" (*The Charlie Rose Show*).

The world would soon get to know the old man as well. In over fifty years, the pair have created five albums, two books, a television special, and various other appearances about the 2000 Year Old Man. Brooks would also do variations of the characters as well, over time. Below are some of the appearances the character has made over the years.

2000 Years with Carl Reiner and Mel Brooks (WP-1401, released October 1960)

Recorded in the summer of 1960 in Los Angeles at World Pacific Records, known for producing jazz albums. To help ease tension, a small audience of one hundred family members and friends were packed into the studio to watch as Reiner and Brooks performed for close to two hours. The recording was then edited down to a little over thirty-six minutes for the vinyl album. The album has Brooks doing several characters—Fabiola, a popular singer; an astronaut; beatniks in a coffeehouse; a South-American plantation owner who sounds suspiciously German; and a psychiatrist—but the majority of the time is devoted to an interview with the 2000 Year Old Man, which appears at the beginning of the album. The 2000 Year Old Man discusses how women were discovered, his longevity, "rock talk," creating a Star of David, marriage and children, Joan of Arc, Robin Hood, and the "greatest thing mankind ever devised."

Although many biographies state the album came out in January 1961, *Variety* reported its release in October 1960. *Billboard* gave it a poor review, calling it "not very funny comedy. . . . It's all ad lib, and maybe that's the trouble with the

Promotional photo of Carl Reiner and Mel Brooks for the 2000 Year Old Man, a party favorite that would end up becoming a national hit.

routines." Such an opinion didn't hurt sales, however; the album eventually sold over a million copies. Concerns about the material being too "Jewish" for others were calmed when Reiner met movie star Cary Grant on the Universal Pictures lot where Reiner was writing the screenplay for *The Thrill of It All*. Reiner had given a copy of the album to Grant, who loved it and asked for a dozen copies to give to friends. Then another dozen. Reiner feared that some may not get it, but Grant said that "Everyone at Buckingham Palace" loved the album, claiming the Queen roared. With that, Reiner and Brooks felt they were in the clear: "Who is more non-Jewish, more Gentile, more WASP-like Christian, more 100 percent shiksa than the queen of England," Reiner asked later (*My Anecdotal Life: A Memoir*).

The duo appeared on *The Ed Sullivan Show* to promote the album on February 12, 1961, which no doubt helped sales, although Sullivan's strict policy of performers doing exactly what was rehearsed found the pair having a rough time with the typically improvisational nature of the act. "It was never as good," Reiner later told the *New York* Times, "Because Mel could never remember what he said, and for him to learn when you do seven minutes, you can't ad lib for seven minutes, it may not work sometimes." Brooks agreed, adding, "I overdid everything." It should be noted that Brooks appeared without a costume, although he would develop one over the course of subsequent appearances of the character.

The album was nominated for a Grammy Award that year, but did not win. Even so, due to its popularity, it was eventually released on Capitol Records in March 1961 (catalog number SW/W 1529). The 2000 Year Old Man interview would also reappear on the 1967 "best of" album *Fly Buttons* (ST 2502). In March

1961, the pair performed at the famous club the hungry I, and then went back into the studio to do a follow-up album, this time, again, for Capitol.

2000 and One Years with Carl Reiner and Mel Brooks (SW/W 1618, released September 1961)

Recorded April 14, 1961, at Capitol's New York studios (where Brooks was busy working on the Broadway musical that would become *All American* [see chapter 6]), with over two hundred friends attending. In July that year there was talk of trying to rush-release the album after audience members began passing along some of the gags from the recording to friends, but it eventually was released in September of that year instead. The two appeared on *The New Steve Allen Show* on October 18, 1961, to help promote the album, with Brooks wearing a white long-haired wig to appear more in character.

Once again, the 2000 Year Old Man takes the first and longest cut on the thirty-seven-minute-long album. Topics discussed with the now "2000 and Six Month Man" were exercise, Shakespeare, King Arthur, Sigmund Freud, handshakes, Madame Curie and Benjamin Franklin, and Napoleon. Other interviews include a tax expert, a two-hour-old baby (a subject Reiner said was suggested to them by Cary Grant), a group of psychiatrists, and a bad poet.

Billboard was a little more up on the second album, stating, "Some of it is quite funny, even though there are many low spots." The album did well enough that the pair were asked to get another ready for the end of the year, even though both were busy with television work (Brooks working on *Inside Danny Baker* and Reiner with *The Dick Van Dyke Show*).

Carl Reiner and Mel Brooks at the Cannes Film Festival (SW/W 1815, released November 1962)

The third album by Reiner and Brooks was recorded much like the previous one in New York. It is the shortest of the original trio of albums, clocking in at just over thirty minutes. The 2000 Year Old Man actually appeared at the beginning of the second side of the album, under the title of "2,000 and Two Year Old Man." For the first time, it is not the longest cut on one of the albums. In this installment, the gentleman discusses garlic, the first comedian (in a gag revisited in the prehistoric section of *History of the World, Part I*), Antony and Cleopatra, being a doctor, knowing Rembrandt, tennis, spying in the Revolutionary War, and advice to make a peaceful, happy world. It is also the album where the 2000 Year Old-Man made the famous quote, "To me, tragedy is if I cut my finger . . . comedy is if you walk in an open sewer and die."

The first side features interviews with directors at the Cannes Film Festival, all played by Brooks, and then an interview with a doctor. The final interview is with an ad agency. The cover featured a bikini-clad young woman with the album's title painted on her torso—a cover that Reiner strongly objected to, but was told by the label that it was too late to change.

It would be eleven years before Reiner and Brooks would do another album featuring the interviewer and the old man, but there were numerous appearances that featured Brooks in character, and by 1965—when the pair appeared on a Danny Thomas special (April 23, 1965) to perform in character—Brooks finally had decided on the costume that would be his go-to outfit for the character, a black suit with a cape and a large black fedora and a cane. It was slightly askew to the image of the character from the album and later animated special from 1975—the image of one of a struggling journeyman who has seen everything but not quite benefited from it. The majesty of Brooks's costume choices worked in a mysterious way, because the voice and humor were still there.

Other appearances between the third and fourth albums included *The Hollywood Palace* on March 28, 1964; *The Andy Williams Show* on November 27, 1966; a one-off reprise of *The Colgate Comedy Hour* from November 5, 1967 that had them introduced by Dick Shawn; as well as Brooks appearing solo but in character during the 2,000th episode of the original *Jeopardy!* game show on February 21, 1972.

And speaking of solo appearances, there were a few instances where Brooks did voice work that was very much in the spirit of the 2000 Year Old Man while waiting to come back to it in 1973 on vinyl.

The Critic (Columbia Studios, 1963)

As the story goes, in 1962 Brooks had seen an abstract animated film by artist Norman McLaren (1914–1987). The animation is never named in this story, but it is easy to suspect it to be *Lines Horizontal* from 1962. As the animation played out of several lines moving back and forth on the screen, Brooks could hear an elderly man behind him muttering about how awful and dull it was.

Brooks got the idea of doing a commentary like the old man in the theater and went to Ernest Pintoff (1931–2002), a producer and director who had done a short animated film in 1959 called *The Violinist* that was narrated by Carl Reiner. They collaborated on *The Critic*, a just-over three-minute animated film that shows various objects interacting with each other, while Brooks in a voice very similar to the 2000 Year Old Man talks back to the screen ("What d'ell is this?") to the annoyance of fellow theater-goers.

The short won Brooks his first Academy Award in 1964.

My Son, The Hero Movie Trailer (1963)

It was the early 1960s, and there was a slew of what were known as "sword and sandal" movies clogging up movie theaters. Many where dubbed Italian films, featuring beefy guys who played heroes in ancient Greece, Rome, Crete, or any-place with a bit of sand lying around and a cardboard roman column nearby. And typically, these films were brought to America with the hero being redubbed as Hercules or some associate of his ("son of," "next-door-neighbor-to," etc.). The heroes would fight bad guys, save the kingdom (or destroy it if evil), and head off with the king's princess by the end.

One such film that was picked up to be redubbed for American consumption was *Arrivano I titani* (*Come Titans*), also known as *The Titans* and *Sons of Thunder*, which was released through United Artists in 1962. Although the film is a notch above some of the other such entries being endlessly made at the time—including some moments of humor—United Artists decided to redub it as a comedy, asking Carl Reiner to step in to work on it. The film was released in September 1963 and did poorly, although the *New York Times* found the "Brooklynese" redubbing "sometimes farcically fascinating."

To help promote the film, Mel Brooks stepped in and produced a series of trailers that were narrated in a voice not quite that of the 2000 Year Old Man, but in a similar style to that of *The Critic*, with Brooks as a commentator of the action seen in the clips from the film. *Variety* went as far as reviewing the ads, stating "audiences will be better entertained by the trailers and spots than by the picture itself." The film itself did not do well at the box office and was eventually redubbed with a more serious English-language dub, but a long ad created by Brooks appears on the Shout! Factory DVD boxset from 2012.

"The 2500 Year Old Brewmaster"—Ballantine Beer (1965)

In 1965, Mel Brooks was contracted to do a series of radio ads for Ballantine Beer. The ads feature up-and-coming comedian and talk-show host Dick Cavett as the interviewer, with Brooks as a 2,500-year-old brewmaster. It was obvious to all involved doing the ads and the audience listening to them that the ads were riffing off of the 2000 Year Old Man, but with Brooks adopting a German accent instead of a Yiddish one. Brooks stated that he and Cavett threw around some ideas and improvised, which were then edited down to make the commercials. "All of it was ad-libbed. Of course, since it was commercials, he had one or two stopping points where he had to mention the name of the beer. But it was great. We really enjoyed it," Brooks told Will Harris fo A.V. Club."

2000 and Thirteen (BS 2741, released November 1973)

Recorded August, 25, 1973, at L.A.'s Burbank Studios, which was set up with sofas and snacks for the guests who came to hear Reiner and Brooks perform two full shows. Brooks, having been away from the character for a few years, has reservations about whether he could voice the character as well as improv answers the way he had in the 1960s. His attempt to return to the character on an April 1970 episode of *The Dick Cavett Show* had been somewhat forced and awkward—it was clear that he was very unsure about doing the piece until talked into it by Cavett and the audience—but he had pulled through okay.

Reiner countered by writing up several cards with questions on various topics for the recording. Sitting with Brooks a couple of hours before the first recording, Reiner would pull out a card and see if Brooks began to react. If he did, Reiner would stop him and keep the topic as one to use in the show. If Brooks hesitated, kept silent, or told him to toss it, Reiner "threw those into my valise." An hour into the recording, Reiner felt that Brooks was rolling along well enough to attempt some of the tossed subjects as well. The second recording that night went even better, and the result was the longest of the 2000 Year Old Man recordings, running over thirty-four minutes of just the old man and no other characters.

Topics covered this time around included longevity, diet, the invention of fire, the mistaken anti-Semitism of Paul Revere, getting a cabinet from Jesus, Winston Churchill, and more.

"Teacher's Scotch" Print Ad—1974

In 1974, Brooks had just completed work on the next 2000 Year Old Man album and was between the successes of *Blazing Saddles* and *Young Frankenstein*. He agreed to appear in a print ad for Teacher's Scotch, featuring a photo of Brooks, dressed as a caveman, lounging on some rocks with a glass of scotch. The title on the ad states "2000 years ago, when you had a Scotch on the Rocks, you really had a Scotch on the Rocks, by the 2000 Year Old Man Mel Brooks."

The mostly text ad is full of snippets from the earlier 2000 Year Old Man pieces, such as "Rock Talk" and "Garlic," before pushing the scotch brand name. To be fair, Brooks points out that he was "monied" to advertise it, and the ad is used to promote the two movies he had just made, so "Let's be pleasant."

The Incomplete Works of Carl Reiner and Mel Brooks (3XX 2744, released December 1973)

To tie in with the release of *2000 and Thirteen* came a three-record set from Warner Bros. that contained the first three 2000 Year Old Man albums.

The 2000 Year Old Man Television Special (CBS Network, January 11, 1975)

This half-hour special aired at 8:30 p.m. on the CBS network on January 11, 1975. It aired after an episode of *All in the Family* that was the pilot for *The Jeffersons*. The animation was based on production designs by the producer, Leo Salkin (1913–1993), and directed by Dale Case, who did *The Pink Panther Show* and various Disney animated television shows in the 1990s. The program used material already recorded on the four albums and edited it down to close to twenty-four minutes with opening and closing credits.

Mel Brooks & Carl Reiner Present The 2000 Year Old Man (1981, Warner Books)

This hardback book is a transcript of all the 2000 Year Old Man material from the four albums, along with illustrations from Leo Salkin, who did the production work for the 1975 television special.

TV Guide announcement promoting the airing of *The 2000 Year Old Man* animated special in January 1975.

The Complete 2000 Year Old Man (71017, released May 17, 1994)

Rhino was originally a small record label started in 1978 that would seek out uncommon albums—in particular, novelty and older rock 'n' roll material—to reissue in various formats. As they grew, they began to release videos of older material as well. In 1992, Warner Bros. bought a 50 percent share of the company, and various older Warner Brother releases began to crop up as reissues through Rhino.

One such reissue was the 1994 collection of all four 2000 Year Old Man albums by Reiner and Brooks. They were released as a four-CD boxset and as a four-cassette version as well. Rhino also simultaneously released a videocassette of the 1975 television special. An hour-long sampler featuring material from all four albums was also released in CD form (PRCD 7056), entitled *Carl Reiner & Mel Brooks— Excerpts from The Complete 2000 Year Old Man.*

The 2000 Year Old Man in the Year 2000 (72944, released October 1997)

Variety on May 29, 1997, announced that a new recording from the pair would be released as "The Wit and Wisdom of the 2,000-Year-Old Man (for the Millennium)." As can be seen, that was soon changed to *The 2000 Year Old Man in the Year 2000.*

The album was recorded in March 1997 in L.A., in front of guests at the Complex Studios in West L.A.

Released by Rhino, it would be another album dedicated to just the 2000 Year Old Man and no other characters. Included as subjects were Moses, infomercials, wives, the "seven wonders of the world," the Inquisition, and plastic surgery. The album would end up winning a Grammy Award in 1999 for Best Spoken Comedy Album, giving Brooks his third major American award available in the entertainment business. Only the Tony Award was left (see chapter 23 for more details on that). The pair would do a promotional tour for the CD release that lasted into 1998 as well.

The 2000 Year Old Man in the Year 2000—The Book (October 1997, Cliff Street Books)

In conjunction with the release of the CD of the same name, a hardback and later a paperback book were released. The book is not just a transcript of recorded material as seen in the 1981 book previously mentioned, but rather an extension of the new material, along with some updates on some other material and some new gags as well.

The 2000 Year Old Man Goes to School (June 1999, IBOOKS, INC.)

Although at first some fans thought this was a new effort by the two men, it is a condensed collection of material from the various albums that highlights historical figures. The focus of the thirty-two-page book and accompanying CD is to not tell real stories about history, but to motivate kids to be creative and have a little fun at the same time. Included is artwork from James Bennett, who had previously illustrated Carl Reiner's children's book *Tell Me a Scary Story . . . But Not Too Scary* in 2003, along with various work in sports magazines and elsewhere.

The 2000 Year Old Man: The Complete History (8266631152, released November 24, 2009)

The latest package of material about the old man who has lived for over 2,000 years came near the fiftieth anniversary of the first album, with Shout! Factory (a company created by former Rhino founder Richard Foos) releasing a three-CD, one-DVD package that covers all the released albums, plus a handful of the "2,500-Year-Old Brewmaster" ads. The DVD contains two appearances by Reiner and Brooks (*The Ed Sullivan Show* and *The New Steve Allen Show*, both from 1961), the 1975 television special, and an interview with Reiner and Brooks from August 5, 2009, discussing the characters and albums. A booklet is included in the set that includes information about the series of albums and an interview with Reiner and Brooks.

Brooks has made no bones in stating that the ancient man helped him financially in the 1960s when he really needed it, as well as made him a public figure. Finally, he was something that people recognized. Even so, there were still areas that he had eyes on that he had yet to conquer—one was his first love, Broadway. But success on Broadway was never quite as easy to obtain as it had been in other areas, as will be seen in the next chapter.

6

All American

Early Broadway Attempts

As mentioned in chapter one, Brooks has always professed a love for Broadway, especially musical-comedy. It is what led him to working in the Catskills as a musician and jester-of-all-trades, working with B. F. Kutcher, as well as writing and directing with the Red Bank Players. Once he had established his writing career for Sid Caesar at the beginning of the 1950s, it is no wonder that he would want to branch out to the Broadway stage. It was right there, down the street, while writing for Caesar in New York. Many of the people he was working with had come from the Broadway stage, including some of his fellow writers. Why wouldn't he think he'd have as good a chance to "make it there" if he was already making it everywhere else?

But the road to the Broadway stage was not quite as simple as television. Even as Brooks's star was rising with television and as a performer himself, Broadway seemed to be one golden ring that kept eluding him, or turning out to be nothing but brass when finally caught.

Curtain Going Up (February 15, 1952–April 1, 1952)

The two-act musical revue featured sketches by Max Wilk, George Axelrod, Charles Scheuer, and Brooks. First announced in May 1951, this revue was to arrive on Broadway in the fall of that year with a budget of $100,000 and produced by the former box-office treasurer of the Ziegfeld, Daniel Melnick (not the same Daniel Melnick who later worked at Talent Associates), before Mervyn Nelson took over as the producer and director of the show in January 1952. Headlining was twenty-nine-year-old Larry Storch, a comic and actor with a heavy career in television, including starring in *F Troop* as well as the live-action Saturday morning series *The Ghost Busters* (1975).

Brooks contributed one sketch to the show, a parody of Arthur Miller's *Death of a Salesman*, with the gag being that the ailing father was a pickpocket who is devastated that his son is doing well in school and is too busy playing baseball to learn the craft of being a criminal.

Tryouts for *Curtain Going Up* began on February 15, 1952, at the Forrest Theater in Philadelphia and closed there on April 1—so quickly that Brooks once referred to *Curtain Going Up* as "the curtain never went up." The review in *Billboard* on February 23, 1952, by critic Maurie H. Orodenker laid bare that the issue was not that sketch, which was called an "even sharper definition in satire," and some of the singers and actors—especially Storch—were given good mention. What was at fault was that it ended up feeling like a mixed bag of material with nowhere to go, as if it were just another revue from one of the hotels in the Catskills. Nice, but nothing to run out to see. The show closed out of town, but some eyes were on Brooks's sketch, and it soon appeared in a bigger show that did make it to Broadway.

Leonard Sillman's New Faces of 1952 (May 16, 1952–March 28, 1953)

Leonard Sillman (1908–1982) was a Broadway producer who knew what he liked and kept producing it on a regular basis for the Broadway stage. And that was revues featuring a lot of up-and-coming talent who had fresh ideas and worked cheap. To be fair, his revues—typically named *New Faces of 1934*, *New Faces of 1952*, or *New Faces of 1968*—were solid performers at the box office and gave some later well-known performers their start. *New Faces of 1934*, for example, featured early—but not their first, as sometimes reported—roles for Henry Fonda and Imogene Coca, while much later Madeline Kahn, who will be popping up later in this book, was one of the cast members in *Leonard Sillman's New Faces of 1968*.

Nine years after his last *New Faces* revue had closed, Sillman in 1952 decided to do a new revue under the name, but did not have quite enough material. Meanwhile, Marvyn Nelson, the producer of *Curtain Going Up*, had several sketches and songs sitting around after *Curtain Going Up* stalled in Philly. So Sillman purchased the material from Nelson and incorporated it into *New Faces of 1952*. This is how Brooks's *Curtain Going Up* sketch, "Of Fathers and Sons" turned up in *New Faces of 1952* near the end of Act One, with the *Playbill* listing him as "Melvin Brooks."

Most of the other sketches for *New Faces of 1952* came from an actor and writer by the name of Ronny Graham (1919–1999). Graham worked as a comic in nightclubs and had made appearances on television variety shows before moving to Broadway, through the assistance of Imogene Coca, who had suggested Graham for the show. *New Faces of 1952* was one of his first shows, and quite an impressive debut, as he not only wrote most of the other sketches but contributed music, and was the master of ceremonies in the show.

Graham would win a Theatre World Award for *New Faces of 1952* and perform various functions besides writing on two of Sillman's later *New Faces* revues. Brooks and Graham got to know each other while working on the revue and became lifelong friends and contributors. Graham would later cowrite *To Be or Not to Be* (1983) and *Spaceballs* (1987), as well as appearing in both and *History of the World, Part I*, *Life Stinks*, *Robin Hood: Men in Tights*, and the pilot to the Brooks-produced television series *The Nutt House*.

Many soon-to-be familiar faces were in *New Faces of 1952* as well: Paul Lynde and Alice Ghostley, both of whom appeared with Graham in Brooks's sketch; Carol Lawrence, later to appear on Broadway in *South Pacific* and then as Maria in *West Side Story*; singer and actress Eartha Kitt (1927–2008), who appeared in another Brooks-related Broadway show, *Shinbone Alley*; and Robert Clary, best remembered today for playing LeBeau on *Hogan's Heroes*. Brooks noted that the popularity of the show, which lasted ten months, saw many of the cast members stopped at the

The

PLAYBILL

for the Royale Theatre

LEONARD SILLMAN'S

NEW FACES OF 1952

The *Playbill* for *New Faces of 1952*. Along with early appearances by talents like Paul Lynde, Alice Ghostley, Carol Lawrence, Eartha Kitt, and Robert Clary, it would be the first Broadway appearance of material by "Melvin Brooks," and lead to a long-lasting friendship with writer-actor Ronny Graham.   *Photo courtesy of* Playbill

stage door each night for autographs. Graham, however, usually left late, long after the autograph hounds had moved on. Brooks recalled to the A.V. Club in 2011 that even with no one outside the door, "He would burst out of the door, saying, 'Let me live! I have a life, too, you know! I can't sign autographs every night! Give me a break!'" And it would break up Brooks every single time.

The revue did well, facing some very stiff competition during its day at the Royale Theatre: *Paint Your Wagon, Pal Joey, South Pacific, The King and I,* and *Top Banana.* Like these other Broadway shows, *New Faces of 1952* was transformed into a film with most of the cast in 1954 by 20th Century-Fox, under the title *New Faces,* making it the first theatrical film credit for Brooks. This followed the earlier thrill for Brooks when the revue opened on Broadway. Not only was something he did on Broadway, but it merited a mention in the January 9th edition of *Variety*, his first mention in a national entertainment paper.

Shinbone Alley (April 13, 1957–May 25, 1957)

Brooks's next work on Broadway came in a role that he would find himself in through the next few years while on Broadway: a script doctor to help with the book. To explain in clearer terms, typically a musical has someone writing the music, the lyrics, and then the dialogue and actions that happened between all the music and lyrics. The dialogue and actions are usually referred to as the book or libretto in a musical, and it can make or break the work; a bad book can kill a musical, with critics saying that the songs were great and the dancing brilliant, but the dialogue and/or the plot didn't hold it together. Sometimes it can even be a case of someone writing great lyrics but not dialogue. When that happens, it is sometimes best to bring in a consultant to help find where the book is not working

The album that would lead to the Broadway show *Shinbone Alley* (1965), and the beginning of Brooks's early reputation as a "script doctor" to troubled Broadway shows.

and fix it. And Brooks became known for doing just that, starting with *Shinbone Alley*.

But first, a bit of backstory.

Don Marquis (1878–1937) was a humor writer best remembered today for a series of verses supposedly written by a cockroach named Archy. The poems and stories were printed in the *New York Tribune*, with illustrations by George Herriman, who created the classic comic strip *Krazy Kat*. Most were written without capitalization as Archy could not hold down a shift-key on the typewriter at the same time as pounding on the letter keys to type; thus, the characters' names are commonly written in the same manner. Archy was buddies with a female alley cat named Mehitabel, who was often discussed in the writings, besides other animals of the backstreets in Manhattan.

Eventually the series turned out to be so popular that it was later published in book form, of which editions are still available. In 1954, the idea came into play at Columbia Records to record an album about the characters, featuring actor/singers Eddie Bracken, Carol Channing, and David Wayne performing the music and lyrics by George Kleinsinger and Joe Darion. That album was popular enough to warrant a one-off concert experience on December 6, 1954, at the Town Hall in Manhattan, which went so well that in the summer of 1956 it was decided to transform the material into a full-fledged musical.

The problem was that it needed help with the book. The lyricist, Joe Darion, had created one for the musical, but many felt that the second act was confusing, with too many scenes dragging the story down. This was a major concern, as there was only limited money for the production and if it was to get to Broadway at all, it would need to do so without tryouts elsewhere, so that problems with a book can be resolved out of sight of the critics. In other words, the book had to be pretty much locked into place by the time the musical opened in April 1957.

Thus entered Mel Brooks. Brooks had built up his standing with his work with Caesar as well as having the sketch in *New Faces of 1952*, both of which are heavily mentioned in Brooks's bio in the musical's *Playbill*. He had at that point also recently worked on the Columbia lot in Hollywood; true, it was a script not used, but there was no denying he was hired to write one. Thus, Brooks was a known commodity who could write the type of material needed to spruce up the book. One element that Brooks concentrated on with Darion was developing a plot for the musical where Archy the cockroach had a crush on Mehitabel the cat, loving her free spirit, but at the same time hating her callous attitude toward others. It helped tied the music together, but some fans of the stories Marquis wrote felt it was not in character for the cockroach and the cat that they remembered reading.

In the beginning, Orson Welles was named to direct, but instead that duty went to Welles's associate Norman Lloyd, a veteran of Alfred Hitchcock's films as well. Lloyd worked on the project until just before the premiere on Broadway, when he quit over a difference of opinion between his vision for the project and that of the writers. Lloyd requested his name be taken off the billing, which was granted, and left the producer, Peter Lawrence, to direct in the last few days before opening at the Broadway Theatre.

Featured as the cat Mehitabel was Eartha Kitt, who had previously appeared in *New Faces of 1952*; and, yes, she would later appear as Catwoman in the final season of the 1960s *Batman* series. As for Archy, Eddie Bracken came back to play the role, with Tom Poston, the first choice to play Maxwell Smart for *Get Smart*, as Bracken's understudy in the show. The musical opened on April 13, 1957, to mild indifference or dissatisfaction from the critics, who seemed to wish the love felt by Archy be taken on a literal instead of spiritual level and couldn't see beyond that. Even with Brooks's help, the second act never quite came together as tightly as it needed to be either. After forty-nine performances, the show ended, with many of the dancers directly moving on to a new show called *West Side Story* that opened in June 1957. Other shows on Broadway at the time of the musical's run were *Li'l Abner* (1956–1958), *Separate Tables* (1956–1957), *Auntie Mame* (1956–1958), *A Long Day's Journey into Night* (1956–1958), and *A Visit to a Small Planet* (1957–1958).

The musical, however, was not completely dead. Over the years, it has become more appreciated, with many noting that it was an attempt to tell a musical about animals—namely cats—almost twenty-five years before the popular Andrew Lloyd Webber musical *Cats*. Most agreed that the music and lyrics were the highpoints of the musical, which was cut down to less than ninety minutes in order to be performed on television on May 16, 1960, on the David Susskind-produced series, *Play of the Week*, as "The Life and Times of Archy and Mehitabel." Once again it featured Eddie Bracken as Archy, along with Tammy Grimes as Mehitabel and Jules Munshin. In 1971, Allied Artists produced an animated movie based on the musical, naturally enough starring Eddie Bracken, along with Carol Channing returning to the role of Mehitabel.

For both the television and animated versions, Brooks's name appeared in the credits and his work was used. Further, the musical still gets an occasional airing from companies as well. Thus, while it is one of the better-known flops on Broadway, it has gone far on its nine lives, making it not quite the mistake for Brooks that one would initially believe.

All American (March 19, 1962–May 26, 1962)

Former Caesar writer Michael Stewart went on to write the book for the Broadway musical hit *Bye Bye Birdie*, which opened in April 1960. Music and lyrics were created by Charles "Buddy" Strouse (born 1928) and Lee Adams (born 1924). Both would go on to do the same for *Applause* (1970, and a Tony winner, just like *Bye Bye Birdie*); *It's a Bird, It's a Plane, It's Superman* (1966); as well as create the theme song for *All in the Family*. Strouse would also compose the music to the musical *Annie*. Probably most importantly to this book is that before all that happened, Strouse worked on the Caesar show as a musical accompanist and got to know Brooks on the show.

With the success of *Bye Bye Birdie*, its producer, Edward Padula (1916–2001), wanted to take a crack at creating a musical based on the 1957 novel *Pnin* by Vladimir Nabokov (1899–1977, who probably is most remembered today as the author of *Lolita*). The comedic novel centered on an awkward, short, and balding Russian professor who struggles as he adjusts to life in America. The novel was a success, and Padula could see in his head a version of it onstage, only to find that Nabokov had no interest in giving up his rights. Instead, Padula found another novel about a Russian professor called *Professor Fodorski* (1950), written by Robert Lewis Taylor (1912–1998), and bought the rights to it to produce. *Professor Fodorski* was most certainly dissimilar to the Nabokov's novel in every other way: while *Pnin* is a reflective study of an outsider not sure if he wants to assimilate with those around him, *Professor Fodorski* is a silly satire about how elements of sports can be used in engineering and vice versa on a campus of an American college. Nevertheless, it worked for what Padula wanted.

Asking Strouse and Adams to write the music, Padula requested from them a recommendation as to who should write the book. Strouse, hoping for lightning to

All American, the troubled 1962 Broadway show with Brooks's name proudly on the marquee. The show flopped, but would directly contribute to Brooks's vision of his homage to Broadway, *The Producers* (1967).   *Photo courtesy of Playbill*

strike twice, suggested another Caesar associate, Mel Brooks, to do the job. Brooks had by that time firmly built a reputation for writing for Broadway and had just established newfound fame with the release of the first 2000 Year Old Man album with Carl Reiner earlier that year. He was excited to take on the job, which he did in November 1960, as previous Broadway work had amounted to one sketch and being a script doctor on *Shinbone Alley*. The new musical would be his first chance to really dive in from the beginning and create his own vision instead of only building upon what others had created.

The downside was that it was Brooks writing on his own. He was working with Strouse and Adams, of course, but the dialogue and actions needed for the book were his responsibility alone. Most of his previous work had been done in committee—a style that he both enjoyed and excelled at. Taking someone's idea and molding it to make it better was one reason why Brooks was called a "comedy writer's comedy writer" in the first place. Without that competitive environment, or some would say a captive audience, Brooks tended to become unmotivated.

There was another issue as well: his marriage to Florence Baum was quickly coming to an end. In February 1961, Baum filed for a legal separation—they finally divorced in January 1962—and in March 1961 *Variety* ran an article detailing Brooks's pleads with the courts to have a weekly alimony payment of $1,000 reduced, as he was no longer making the type of money he earned while working steadily under Sid Caesar; which certainly was not the type of press he wanted. The stress of lower wages and public examination of his expenses, mixed with the growing success of his work with Reiner, left Brooks unable to concentrate as much as he should have on the book for the new musical, which by February 1961 was renamed *All American*.

Brooks turned in a book that had a healthy first act, but—as he was aware himself—stumbled a lot in the second. Like *Shinbone Alley* before it, there was simply too much story to tell in the second act, and Brooks wasn't alone in being unable to see around it. Even so, things were looking bright for the musical at the time thanks to Strouse and Adams arriving with a lot of songs for the show. Further, in September, it was announced that Columbia Pictures was looking to make a movie out of it; and, most important, Joshua Logan (famed for *South Pacific*, *Annie Get Your Gun*, *Mister Roberts*, *Picnic*, *Fanny*, *Charley's Aunt*, and many others) had agreed to direct the musical.

Besides the troublesome second act, there was still the issue of who would play the professor in *All American*. Strong support had been given for Zero Mostel, but he was rejected by the director as not fitting the image he wanted for the male romantic lead. The next suggestion was Charles Boyer, then Ron Moody. (Ironically, Mostel would eventually end up starring in Brooks's first movie, with Moody starring in Brooks's second.) Others suggested were Danny Kaye, Victor Borge, Peter Ustinov, and Jacob Pincus—all actors who could imaginatively play older, intellectual, foreign men. Finally, Logan settled on the star of his 1940 hit *Charley's Aunt*, Ray Bolger (1904–1987). Bolger, probably best remembered today for playing the Scarecrow in *The Wizard of Oz* (1939), had a long career as a comedic actor/dancer on Broadway and in the movies, but by that time had been spent years performing on television and in nightclub work when Logan suggested him as the lead. Although apprehensive, the production team agreed to take on Bolger, and it was made official in November 1961.

Yet, as *All American* came closer to its previews, the anxieties for all became greater. At one point, Strouse and Brooks had to be separated before blows were struck. In another incident, back at the hotel after one of the tryouts in Philadelphia, a financial backer had a meltdown, accusing Brooks and the others of being "untalented" and "Jews," and attacking them with a pillow—all while wearing a flimsy nightgown—before finally being hustled out of the room. As to the musical itself, it had too many songs; a book that suddenly switched from the plot of football and science to a parody of Madison Avenue advertising for too long in the second act before getting back to the main plot; and a star, Bolger, who kept changing his mind on what he wanted to do with his part.

On the plus side: many of the jokes were working, such as an early sense of the emerging un-politically correct humor of Brooks, with the first scene featuring an idiot custom officer telling the newly arriving immigrants to form lines based on the democratic method of making sure the "Krauts . . . frogs . . . Limeys . . . gooks" all stay within their own ethnic groups. Meanwhile, director Logan had also created a musical number for a song called "Physical Fitness" that featured young, well-built men stripped to the waist, which was going over like gangbusters. Finally, one song, "Once Upon a Time," was well received, and has been recorded by dozens of performers in the years since.

When *All American* opened at the Winter Garden Theatre on Mary 19, 1962, it was up against *How to Succeed in Business Without Really Trying* (1961–1965), *A Shot in the Dark* (1961–1962), and *A Funny Thing Happened on the Way to the Forum* (starring Zero Mostel and with a book cowritten by Larry Gelbart). Behind the scenes, most felt that it still needed work, and many of the reviews agreed. Several found the musical had bits that worked, although no one could agree what those pieces were. For every reviewer who found Brooks's work "heavy-handed," there would be another reviewer who felt Brooks had "held the spirit and reproduced the color of Taylor's novel." People dismissed the music, but couldn't get "Once Upon a Time" out of their heads. Bolger was considered both an obstacle and the "only thing that works," depending on who you talked to. Both Joshua Logan and Ray Bolger were nominated for Tonys that year, but Columbia Pictures quickly dropped the idea of making *All American* into a film.

Altogether, faint praise was not enough to keep the musical running, and it would fold after eighty-six performances. Strouse would muse that Brooks's work on the book was like a brawler who just "keeps swinging wildly and wildly and wildly, and when he connects, he knocks you out." As for Brooks, his own reflection was, "We had an unfortunate stroke of luck, it opened in New York when there was no newspaper strike."

Nowhere to Go But Up (November 10–November 17, 1962)

This musical comedy about prohibition bootlegging starred Tom Bosley and Martin Balsam, featured a book by James Lipton (who became famous on television decades later as the host of *Inside the Actors Studio*), and was directed by Sidney

Lumet (*12 Angry Men, Fail-Safe, Dog Day Afternoon, Network*). While the musical was in Philadelphia for tryouts, Brooks was brought in to punch up the humor in the book. It did little to help, and *Nowhere to Go But Up* folded after three previews and nine performances; but Brooks's involvement was little and not even mentioned in the *Playbill.*

Kelly (February 6, 1965)

Brooks's work amounted to little more than a week's worth of script-doctoring on *Kelly*, but he could always say he was involved with one of the biggest flops ever seen on Broadway.

Kelly had been promoted all over New York for months, only to open and close the same day, leaving its investors out in the cold and a lawsuit by the principal writers. Much has been written about the show, particularly a *Saturday Evening Post* article by Lewis H. Lapham that appeared in the April 24, 1965, issue ("Has Anybody Here Seen *Kelly*?") that showed all the clashes of a show that never came together.

The musical was set in the late nineteenth century—a popular era for musicals in the late 1950s/early 1960s (what with popular shows like *Hello, Dolly!* and *My Fair Lady* paving the way), but one that was slowly being strangled by the number of failed musicals attempting to play off those big hits by 1965. The plot dealt with a young man named Kelly who attempted to jump off the Brooklyn Bridge multiple times, but failed due to nerves, and his neighbors considered him an embarrassment for not even following through on such a stupid stunt. As the musical begins, with another attempt in the offing, several gamblers scheme to have Kelly fake a jump so that a bet can be won. Kelly must face either finally doing what he had long planned or joining the gamblers in the deceit.

It was bleak material, made even darker by the book from Eddie Lawrence (1919–2014) and music from Moose Charlap (1928–1974), which intentionally made no attempts to make Kelly sympathetic to the audience. After five years of trying to push the material to backers (including a promising one where up-and-coming actor Richard Harris was momentarily contracted to star), the material arrived at Talent Associates—the production company that made *Get Smart*. David Susskind and Daniel Melnick were enthused.

Susskind and Melnick began working to get others involved in bringing it to Broadway. Their luck would have it that that movie producer Joseph E. Levine (1905–1987) was interested. Having built a career bringing cheap foreign action films to America (including the original *Godzilla, King of the Monsters* in 1956), Levine had always prided himself on trying to bring more upscale fare to the public as well. This would increasingly become the case as the 1960s wore on, with Levine being involved with films like *The Graduate* (1967), *The Lion in Winter* (1968), and Mel Brooks's first film, *The Producers* (1968). But in 1964 when Susskind and Melnick first proposed the idea to Levine of becoming a backer, he saw it as another step up for his reputation. Levine was pretty much hands-off besides being a backer, however, and would leave the production while the show was still working through tryouts in Chicago.

In previews, the producers began to see that the bleakness of the material was working against the show, leading to songs added and dropped, plotlines abandoned, and other desperate measures in order to try to save the musical. Near the end of its tryout period, Daniel Melnick brought in screenwriter David Z. Goodman (1930–2001) to rewrite the opening act, turning Kelly from someone his neighbors booed and despised into a lovable nut. When this reinvention appeared to win the audience over at the next preview, Melnick next requested the help of two writers who were busy working on the new Talent Associates program, *Get Smart*—Leonard Stern and Mel Brooks. As Brooks knew comedy and had been involved with Broadway before, it was only natural to have him come out to look over the musical, especially as he was already on Talent Associates' dime anyway. Brooks and Stern watched the show while in Boston in late January 1965 and came back with notes for Susskind, Melnick, and director Herbert Ross. Stern remembered years later, "By then the show was a remnant of what it had been, not even a mirrored reflection. People were singing songs for which there was no motivation. . . . Mel, more experienced in theater than I was, was probably the surgeon. He had to do a lot of work that couldn't possibly be done in the week we were there."

Brooks told the group that he thought it was salvageable, but things had to change. The mother character, played by an actress that the production team had grown to dislike, wasn't working and needed to go. There were also too many songs and too many characters. Stern suggested cutting several songs, which would have made the musical a play with little music. Brooks's reaction to that was, "So what? Light the blaze under Don Francks [the actor playing Kelly]. A few happy moments for the tired businessman watching some girls jump around onstage, and everybody goes home at ten o'clock. They'll be glad to get the first cabs" (*The Saturday Evening Post*).

Susskind and Melnick liked the direction of Stern and Brooks, and told them to write two new scenes and add some gags to others. They would do just that and then go back to work on getting *Get Smart* developed. Soon enough, Lawrence and Charlap would sue, as their contract demanded that no changes be made to the musical without their permission. Word of mouth had gotten around about the show's problems, especially after the actress who played the mother was fired from the show. Brooks and Stern's jokes were considered old-fashioned and aimed for the Borsht Belt crowd rather than the "sophisticated" tastes of the Broadway audience. Essentially, by the time the show opened, every elitist on Broadway was ready to gloat at seeing the television guys and their hack movie-producer friend go down with their show. Which is exactly what occurred. The show lost $650,000 and played only one night on Broadway before closing.

Susskind felt burned by the experience, especially as it was his name front and center on the production. Soon after, when writer David Wasserman asked Susskind to produce a musical about Don Quixote, he turned it down, leading to him missing out on the chance to produce *Man of La Mancha*—which ran for nearly six years.

For Brooks, his involvement was limited, but because the *Saturday Evening Post* article had mentioned his involvement, he would be forever linked to the production. And there was still one more play before moving on.

The Best Laid Plans (March 25, 1966–March 26, 1966)

This comedy by Gwen Davis (a novelist who wrote the screenplay to the Shirley MacLaine comedy *What a Way to Go!* in 1964) starred Edward Woodward and featured Kenneth Mars as a psychoanalyst who has a female patient that is trying to romance a man by pretending to be a beatnik. The play was doing poorly, and the rumor was that Brooks was asked to come in as a script doctor to help throw in some gags.

Word had already gotten out, however, and *The Best Laid Plans* ran for a total of three performances, closing the night after it opened. Brooks would later state that he never worked on the show, but his reputation as a script doctor was so great that when he took in the show, the assumption was made. Even if he didn't work on it, going to see it did lead to Brooks seeing Kenneth Mars for the first time. It was a chance meeting that would find Mars going on to memorable performances in two of Brooks's films: *The Producers* and *Young Frankenstein*.

On reflection, his attempts at Broadway between 1952 and 1966 had produced one sketch in a popular show and several attempts to do more that got to Broadway but didn't last. By the time of *Kelly*, he was concentrating on television, with *Get Smart*—a project he entered on the ground floor—having succeeded, as had the comedy albums with Carl Reiner. Broadway had been a bit of hiccup, but perhaps someday he would go back. If nothing else, working on *All American* may have given Brooks some heartaches and frustrations, but it did lead directly to one of the most important moments of his life—meeting the woman who would become his second wife. A woman who many thought he was crazy to even bother to pursue.

7

I'm Going There, Too

Anne Bancroft

As Brooks worked on the book for *All American* between 1961 and 1962, those who were working on the musical with him got used to hearing two fantastic predictions from the writer. One was that his next production—be it a book or a play—would be a comedy called *Springtime for Hitler* (and see the next chapter for how that turned out). And once he got that out of the way "then I'm going to marry Anne Bancroft."

Those who heard him would sympathetically pat him on the back, while hoping nothing sharp was nearby. It was obviously the talk of an overworked madman. Mel Brooks? Even having a shot at Anne Bancroft? The Tony-winning, and soon Oscar-winning, dark-haired beauty with the smarts, going out with the manic little guy who thinks Hitler is funny? Oh, yeah, obviously the stress was getting to him.

But one man on *All American* knew this wasn't as far-fetched as it sounded to others. As mentioned in the previous chapter, Charles Strouse had met Mel on *Your Show of Shows*, and it was this friendship that would eventually lead to Mel being asked to take part in the development of *All American*. While working on the musical in January 1961, Mel happened to notice Strouse being visited by Anne Bancroft, who had already made much headway on Broadway by winning two major Tony Awards within two years, one for Best Performance by a Featured Actress in a Play in 1958 for *Two for the Seesaw*, and the other for Best Actress in a Play for *The Miracle Worker* in 1960. After Bancroft left the premises, Brooks begged to be introduced to Bancroft, and Strouse, who had taken a shine to Bancroft himself at one point, said okay, figuring nothing would come of such an introduction between what many saw as opposites.

Bancroft was born Anna Maria Louisa Italiano on September 17, 1931, in the Bronx, the second of three girls for Mildred and Michael Italiano. Her father was a cutter in the Manhattan garment district, and when he was temporarily laid off during the Depression, her mother became a switchboard operator and continued to work even after Michael had found full-time work again. This made them a two-income family at a time when such was a rarity, especially as Michael was doing well enough to support the family on his own, but also shows how strong-willed Anne's mother was and how it would rub off on Anne herself.

Graduating from Christopher Columbus High School in 1948, Anne was determined to get into acting and went to the American Academy of Dramatic Arts. It was there that she was spotted for a role on the live television anthology series

Studio One in April 1950, where she began using the stage name of Anne Marno. With her dark hair and photogenic, youthful face, she got a lot of work in New York television over the next year and a half, especially with evidence that she was adept at both comedy and drama. She was doing so well, Hollywood took notice, and by the winter of 1951, just as Brooks was finally getting his name established on *Your Show of Shows* and looking at a few hundred dollars an episode for writing, Anne was signing a seven-year contract with 20th Century-Fox for $20,000 a year.

Her first film, *Don't Bother to Knock*, starring Richard Widmark and Marilyn Monroe, was released in August 1952. Told to change her stage name as it would typecast her, Anne went with the suggestion of Bancroft as it was one of the few that didn't sound like "a bubble dancer." She would professionally remain Anne Bancroft for the rest of her life.

In 1953, Anne would marry Martin May, a Texan from a rich oil family. The marriage was rocky from the start, with the two separating by 1955 and finally divorcing in 1957 when they realized that they had eloped in a mad dash to get married before realizing that their worlds were very different. As the marriage was crumbling, Bancroft was discovering that Hollywood was not the dream promised her. Although she was getting more screen time with each film, the movies themselves were generally lesser "second-features"—movies that played more as an after-thought after bigger-budgeted "A-pictures"—such as in 1954's *Gorilla at Large*. Worse yet, typically as the second, third, or fourth lead in such films. By 1957, she was ready to move back to New York with the intention of getting her life in order,

Anne Bancroft—the dream-girl Brooks was determined was not going to get away.

and letting relationships stay on the sidelines. "I'm interested in only four men," she stated at the time, "my father, my agent, my press agent, and my analyst," as Bancroft reportedly said at the time, according to William Holtzman's book *Seesaw: A Dual Biography of Anne Bancroft and Mel Brooks.*

What helped in her decision to go back to New York—besides a chance to work in *Playhouse 90*—was a play written by William Gibson (1914–2008) that actor Richard Basehart had shown her called *Two for the Seesaw.* The play is a two-hander (meaning only two actors were needed to perform), dealing with an older man facing a divorce and meeting a young, lively dancer in the apartment next to his. Bancroft came back to New York determined to win the part, and did just that, only for Basehart to move on. Fortunately for all involved, powerhouse actor Henry Fonda signed on, and the play came to Broadway in January 1958, ultimately leading to Bancroft winning her first Tony. She then turned around and left *Two for the Seesaw* in 1959 to star in Gibson's next play, *The Miracle Worker,* a dramatization of how blind and deaf Helen Keller learned to communicate as a child through the help of a teacher played by Bancroft. The play opened on October 19, 1959, and costarred Patty Duke as Keller. Also in 1959, while still performing in *Two for the Seesaw,* Bancroft became friends with Charles Strouse, who was working at The Actors Studio, which Bancroft would visit from time to time.

In later years, Strouse himself admitted that he had some hopes of getting to know Anne more than just as a friend, but that was before Brooks set designs on her himself. Seeing Brooks's interest, Strouse mentioned to him that Bancroft would be rehearsing the first week in February 1961 for an episode of *The Perry Como Show* (which eventually aired February 22, 1961) over at the Ziegfeld Theater, just a few blocks from where they were working on *All American.* As usual, the kid came out in Brooks, who begged Strouse to go with him to the Ziegfeld so he could be introduced. She had just finished rehearsing the song "Married I Can Always Get" when she heard applause from the seats and a voice booming out saying, "Hey, Anne Bancroft. I'm Mel Brooks."

Hearing the voice, Bancroft imagined who was behind it, as recounted in *People* magazine. "This aggressive voice came out from the dark and I thought it must be a combination of Clark Gable and Robert Taylor, Robert Redford. It turned out to be Mel Brooks, and he never left me from that moment on." Brooks, sensing an opportunity, ran to the stage and jumped up to shake hands with her. Bancroft was taken aback. "In two years, no man had ever approached me with that kind of aggression, because I had just done *Two for the Seesaw* and *The Miracle Worker,* and people were very scared of me, especially men." Although gaining in fame, she had become known for serious dramatic roles, as well as her willingness to show that she could be neurotic and eccentric when appearing on talk shows. She was highly intelligent and, at times, a bit crazy, which did not exactly steer men in her direction.

Brooks was not only interested, he was determined, even from the start. When talking to her at the *Como* stage, Brooks asked where she would be going afterwards. When she mentioned she was going to William Morris (the talent agency), his response was a surprised "So am I!" After a visit there, she thought she may head to the delicatessen, which earned a response from Brooks of a surprised,

"Why, so am I!" Bancroft reflected later, "Wherever I said I was going, he would say he's going there. It just went on and on. The man never left me alone, thank God" (*People* magazine).

Even though she was hesitant—she was still recovering from her divorce while Brooks was separated and soon to be divorced—the two quickly began dating. Although Bancroft was financially sound, Brooks usually found cheap places for them to go to due to his financial situation and needing to treat, such as movie theaters playing foreign movies and recording sessions where Brooks knew the musicians. "All I could get into for nothing was recording sessions," Brooks told *Playboy* magazine in 1975. "Sometimes we ate in Chinatown for a buck-twenty-five." Bancroft was happily confused about the situation, "I was in love with him instantly," *People* magazine reported her saying. "Because, you see, he looked like my father and acted like my mother."

In 1963, Bancroft won the Academy Award for Best Actress in the 1962 film version of *The Miracle Worker*. At the 1964 Academy Awards, Brooks won for *The Critic*, with Anne by his side. On August 5, 1964—just as Brooks was starting to see some financial stability with *Get Smart* and Anne was doing fine with both theatrical and movie work—the two got married; asking a stranger in the court office, Andrew Boone, to be a witness, and using one of Anne's earrings as a wedding ring. To acquaintances, the union was surprising; writer Lucille Kallen reported in *Seesaw* by William Holtzman going to their house and feeling it was "sort of as though a younger brother of mine had married the queen of England." To others who were closer to the two, and knew their temperaments, and attitudes, it seemed like a good match.

The two would agree, even if, like all couples, they could sometimes disagree. One famous public argument, reported by Roger Ebert after Bancroft's death, led to Brooks wanting to take Bancroft by the arm to lead her away, only for Bancroft to yank her arms away, indignantly shouting while indicating her body, "Don't you dare touch my instrument!" Brooks nonchalantly shot back, "Oh, so this is your instrument?" "Yes, this is my instrument," she proudly replied. "Okay," Brooks replied, "Play 'Melancholy Baby.'" Bancroft would remember in interviews a time when she came home from rehearsal complaining how exhausting acting was in comparison to being a writer. Brooks set her down at a table with a piece of paper and a pencil and told her to start if it was so easy. She later admitted that she never could think of anything to put on the paper that would have proved him wrong.

Even when angry, however, they were never far away from each other. "From that day [when they met in 1961], until her death on June 5, 2005," Brooks would say in 2010 to Sean Daly, "we were glued together." As for Anne, her thoughts on Brooks were, "You know, we're like any other couple. We've had our ups and downs, but every time I hear the key in the door, I know the party's about to start."

The pair would have one son, Maximillian (Max) Michael Brooks—his first name that of Brooks's father, the second that of Anne's father—who was born on May 22, 1972, and has gone on to a solid career in show business as well. Max Brooks has worked as a writer on *Saturday Night Live*, and may be best known for his books and stories about zombies, including *The Zombie Survival Guide* (2003) and *World War Z: An Oral History of the Zombie War* (2006), which was later turned into a feature film. He has also worked as an actor and voice actor, including in *To Be or Not to Be*, which starred his parents.

Anne would pass away from uterine cancer on June 6, 2006, two months after her grandson was born. Although both Bancroft and Brooks had separate careers, they only made one film where they starred together, *To Be or Not to Be* (1983), a remake of a classic Ernst Lubitsch comedy that had starred Jack Benny and Carole Lombard (and discussed in chapter 15). When asked why they didn't do more together, Anne replied about the one film they did do, "It didn't make money." Over the years they did pop up together in a variety of projects besides in interviews or documentaries, even occasionally in films Brooks was doing at the time. Although several of these films will be discussed in more detail in later chapters, below is a list of projects that both were involved in or projects Bancroft was working on that influenced those of Brooks.

Mother Courage and Her Children

After leaving *The Miracle Worker*, Bancroft passed up on doing a musical called *Funny Girl* (which would be the breakthrough role for Barbra Streisand) to appear in the Bertolt Brecht dramatic musical *Mother Courage and Her Children*. The production takes place during the Thirty Years' War (1618–1648) and is about an old woman with three grown children who try to profit from the war by selling things to the soldiers, only for all the children to eventually die from incidents related to the war and its peace. Bancroft would have to wear padding and age makeup for the role of the mother, and the musical would last on Broadway for less than six weeks, but it would be while she was in New York with Brooks that she won the Academy Award for *The Miracle Worker* in 1963 (and thus was unable to attend the ceremony). It is also where Brooks noticed an actor playing one of the sons, Gene Wilder, for the first time. Brooks would keep the young man in mind for a role in his first film, *The Producers*, a few years down the line.

ABC Stage 67, "I'm Getting Married" (March 16, 1967)

No involvement from Brooks in this musical comedy about a young couple about to get married, but it does feature Anne Bancroft as the bride with Dick Shawn as the groom. Shawn had already worked with Brooks on material for Shawn's nightclub act earlier in the 1960s and would, of course, go on to play LSD in *The Producers*.

A Cry of Players (November 14, 1968–February 15, 1969)

This Broadway comedy-drama was another production written by William Gibson that featured Anne in a starring role. The play is about the early years of William Shakespeare and starred Bancroft as Anne Hathaway, Shakespeare's wife. Costarring as "Will" was Frank Langella. The play ran for only three months, but during that time Brooks saw it and decided that Langella would be perfect for his next film, *The Twelve Chairs* (1970), as the second lead.

Annie, the Women in the Life of a Man (CBS, February 18, 1970)

Anne starred in this hour-long, musical-comedy special for CBS in 1970. The special was a setup for numerous musical numbers and comedy bits that centered around women of various backgrounds and attitudes, from daughters to wives to starlets. Brooks had written a sketch for the special, but it "was built around the words of a Richard Rodgers song and we couldn't get permission," said producer Joe Cates to the *Chicago Tribune* at the time. One of the writers who did work on the program was William Gibson, once again writing for Bancroft. Meanwhile, two of the men acting in the program had connections to Brooks: Dick Shawn once again and producer David Susskind in a rare acting role.

This musical-comedy special typically is listed in bios as featuring Brooks in the cast, but he was busy working on *The Twelve Chairs* in Yugoslavia and could not participate in the show. Brooks being in another country also affected the film schedule for the special: While production of such a special would be done with a few days' rehearsals and then filming, Bancroft arranged the work so that the musical numbers were recorded first, and then flew to Europe to see Brooks (while studying the script for the comedy portions). She did this back and forth over a two-week period, and although it may seem excessive, she would later state to *Viva* magazine, "It was absolutely perfect. It worked out fine and it kept my marriage together. I was very happy."

Blazing Saddles (Warner Bros., February 7, 1974)

While Brooks filmed *Blazing Saddles*, Bancroft would sometimes come to the set with their toddler son, Max. Some biographies hint that Anne appears as one of the churchgoers in the town of Rock Ridge early in the film, and there is a woman who looks a smidge like her sitting by "Howard Johnson" (John Hillerman), but closer examination leads one to think otherwise. If she was one of the churchgoers, she was on the outer edges somewhere and hard to pick out.

Annie and the Hoods (ABC, November 27, 1974)

The second of two musical-comedy specials based around Bancroft, this one focused on various "hoods": parenthood, adulthood, unlikelihood, womanhood, and others. Both Gene Wilder and Carl Reiner were part of the cast, along with Brooks, who made his first professional appearance with his wife during the special, appearing in a sketch called "The Other Womanhood," where she sings the song "Guess Who I Saw Today" as a wife talking to her philandering husband, played by Brooks. The song has another link to Brooks's career in that it is from the Broadway show *New Faces of 1952*, which featured his first Broadway revue sketch.

Silent Movie (20th Century-Fox, June 16, 1976)

Besides *To Be or Not to Be*—a film that was announced in *Variety* to be done in 1975, and kept cropping up in the trade papers for years to come before finally

Ad for *Annie & The Hoods* (1974), Bancroft's second musical-comedy television special, which featured Brooks, along with friend Carl Reiner and Gene Wilder.

being made in 1983—it is Brooks's follow-up to *Young Frankenstein* (1974), *Silent Movie*, that is remembered for featuring Brooks and Bancroft on the big screen. In fact, there was heavy promotion for Anne's appearance in the film, emphasizing her willingness to be silly, what with the bonk on the head with the table, the eye-crossing with Marty Feldman, the parody of the starlet with multiple menservants.

The film has Brooks as Mel Funn, a director trying to drum up big stars for a silent movie he wants to make to save a movie studio. Among the cameo appearances of big stars of the period—Liza Minelli, James Caan, Burt Reynolds, and others—was Anne Bancroft. Playing a parody of herself, she comes into a club with a slew of men followers who are so anxious to do her bidding that they turn her cigarette into ashes with the number of lighters they all pull out in order to light it. Funn and his companions sneak into the club as flamenco dancers to try to entice her to appear in the film. The three dance with Anne, causing much destruction and personal injury along the way. At the end of the dance, Anne admits she knew it was them and asks to be in the movie.

Many had asked about Bancroft's ability to cross her eyes separately from each other. When critic Roger Ebert asked how they did the effect, Brooks replied it was not an effect. "She really can do that! That's why I married her. Twelve years ago, we're sitting in 21, I'm in love with her, I ask, 'Come on, how am I doin'?' And in reply she crosses her eyes like that. Now I know it's love. For years, I've been searching for the right role for Annie. Not *The Miracle Worker*, not *The Pumpkin Eater*, not Mrs. Robinson. The right role, where she can cross her eyes!"

Fatso (20th Century-Fox, February 1, 1980)

The first film released through Brooks's Brooksfilms production company, *Fatso* was directed and written by and costarred Bancroft. Dom DeLuise plays a heavy-set man who grew up using food as a substitute for love, but when a cousin dies from being overweight, DeLuise's character tries to go on a diet and exercise. A romance complicates his decision, and he eventually must choose between his first love of food and the woman he loves. Bancroft played the sister to DeLuise's character.

Also in the cast were Ron Carey (*Silent Movie, High Anxiety, History of the World, Part I*), Rudy De Luca (writer and actor on *Silent Movie, High Anxiety*, and most of Brooks's later movies), and Carl Reiner's wife, Estelle Reiner. The only one missing was Brooks, who—per Bancroft in an interview with *Variety* at the time of production in March 1979—was not allowed on the set. "I don't want him around. I don't want to see him during the day. Suppose he makes a suggestion and I have to say no? After all, I have to see him at night." A later *Variety* report in May that year states that Brooks "kept his word" and didn't visit the set while Bancroft was filming, but did sit through dailies, where he watched the film shot the previous day in a screening room.

However, the cinematographer on the film, Brianne Murphy (1933–2003), had a different take from the puff pieces in *Variety*. She would state in a 2002 interview for Mollie Gregory's book *Women Who Run the Show* that Brooks would arrive on the set every afternoon to pick Bancroft up to go home, and with his appearance Bancroft would appear agitated and begin to rapidly finish whatever was being done at the time. Murphy also said that, while it was true Brooks would join Bancroft in the screening room to watch dailies, no one else was permitted to see the footage. To be fair, this was not completely out of the ordinary for a director to do, and there were signs that Bancroft was feeling very vulnerable as a first-time director and wanted Brooks's support in private. Murphy agreed to a point, saying that Bancroft seemed very unsure of herself and "reluctant to tell men what to do;" yet it sent signals to the film crew that Brooks was calling the shots instead of Bancroft. "Word had gotten around that he was very controlling," said Murphy.

Things came to a head one afternoon while filming a scene when Brooks appeared on the set unannounced. Looking at the video-assist (a video system that allows everyone to see how the camera is filming a shot), Brooks yelled out "Cut, cut. That's no good, that won't work. Cut it."

Brooks, never one to stand on protocol, and always ready to speak his mind even at the worst times, had broken an unspoken rule on the set. "No one ever says 'Cut' except the director. Ever," as Murphy stated in the interview. The set went quiet, except for camera operator Bob Lavar, who glanced in annoyance at Brooks and clearly spoke for the crew to hear, "Who the fuck is that little guy?" If there was silence on the set before that, there was certainly none afterwards. After all the shouting, filming was obviously finished for the day. And the next as well, as Bancroft came to the set stating that Brooks, who was the head of the production company making the film, had demanded that Lavar be fired for being "potentially dangerous." Murphy talked Bancroft back from such an action, saying that Lavar was trying to protect Bancroft's integrity as a director. When Lavar a day later offered his resignation if it would help matters, Bancroft waved him off.

There were no further issues with the film, but *Fatso* received only so-so reviews and a lackluster performance at the box office when it was released in February 1980. It would be the only film Bancroft would direct. She would reflect later to Robert Windeler for *Family Weekly*, "I think to be a director you have to have a certain kind of personality, which I don't have. . . . Somebody has to have a very dominating hand, and I just don't have that kind of hand."

The Elephant Man (Paramount Pictures, October 1, 1980)

If Brooksfilms started with *Fatso*, it would be *The Elephant Man* that really put the company on the map, but more on that factor in chapter 20. This David Lynch–directed black-and-white film, which had Brooks as the (uncredited) executive producer, featured Bancroft in the role of "Madge Kendal," an actress of the stage in Victorian London who becomes a patron of Joseph Merrick, a man with severe deformities who is treated as a freak.

To Be or Not to Be (20th Century-Fox, December 16, 1983)

Discussed in more detail in chapter 15, this was the only film that starred both Mel Brooks and Anne Bancroft on-screen (rather than just a cameo as in *Silent Movie*).

84 Charing Cross Road (Sony, February 13, 1987)

Bancroft had read a novel by Helen Hanff that dramatizes the New York writer's correspondence with an antique bookstore manager in London over a nearly twenty-year period. The novel had earlier been made into a stage play by James Roose-Evans, and a television play by Hugh Whitemore that starred Anne Jackson. Bancroft loved the novel, leading to Brooks buying the movie rights for Bancroft as an anniversary present.

The film was made in 1986 and costarred Anthony Hopkins, who had previously appeared with Bancroft in *The Elephant Man* in 1980. While fondly remembered today, it did little business at the box office when released in 1987.

Brooks and Bancroft together in the opening musical number from *To Be or Not to Be* (1983). It would be their one costarring film.

Dracula: Dead and Loving It (Castle Rock Entertainment, 1995)

Bancroft makes a cameo appearance in Brooks's final theatrical film as Madame Ouspenskaya, a gypsy woman who is trying just a tad too hard to scare Renfield and sell merchandise. The character only appears near the beginning of the film.

Curb Your Enthusiasm, "Opening Night" (HBO, March 14, 2004)

This long-running HBO comedy series featured comedy writer-performer Larry David as the character Larry David, working in the entertainment business and the trials he goes through in everyday life, due to the poor choices he makes. The fourth season had a running story line dealing with David (the character) taking over for Nathan Lane in the Broadway musical version of *The Producers*. In the final episode of the season, Anne Bancroft appears as herself alongside Brooks, as they witness David horribly mangle his debut. It would be her last performance on-screen and—fittingly—her last appearance with Brooks.

Just as Anne's career and life affected Brooks's, so too did her passing. Brooks would admit nearly a decade after her death that he felt in "an emotional pit" and "unable to move." It came just as production was ongoing for the movie adaptation of *The Producers* Broadway musical, leaving Brooks fragmented and unable to assist as much as originally intended with the making of the film. His son, Max, would report in 2007 that his father would arrive unannounced to spend the evening—sometimes the entire night—after Bancroft's passing due to simply not knowing what to do with himself.

Over time, he found some peace for his loss through his grandchildren and through his friends, including Carl Reiner, who had recently lost his wife after decades of marriage around the same time as Brooks had. There have been documentaries, and talks, including personal appearances by Brooks to introduce his films to audiences and perform Q&As at the age of ninety that would put men half his age under the table from exhaustion. Discussions still come up occasionally about doing something (such as a sequel to *Spaceballs*, or a musical version of *Blazing Saddles*), but it is mostly fun, wishful talk.

Yet that was all in the future in 1967—just two years into their marriage. At the time, Anne was about to embark on her most famous role as Mrs. Robinson in *The Graduate* and then follow that up with a successful run on Broadway with a revival of Lillian Hellman's *The Little Foxes*. As for Brooks? *Get Smart* was earning him a small paycheck, and there were some appearances here and there thanks to the success of the 2000 Year Old Man, but things were stalling on the creative front. It certainly looked like things were going to forever stall on that *Springtime for Hitler* idea of his. But then a chance meeting would change Brooks's life forever.

8

Where Did I Go Right?

Release Date: November 15, 1967. Released through Embassy Pictures.

Hitler References

One, but it's a big extended one.

Musical Moments

Two—LSD's audition and, of course, "Springtime for Hitler."

Pre-production

The first thing beginning writers are taught is write about what you know. It's a lesson that many writers stick with or at least fall back on through the years to find material for their work.

Thus, it was no surprise after Brooks's many attempts to write for Broadway on a series of musicals that would heartbreakingly fail, Brooks would turn his attention to creating a story dealing with the backstage world of the theater. But first he needed to figure out what format his story would be told. In other words, as with many things in Mel Brooks's career, there's a bit of a jumble as to when things occurred for what would eventually become *The Producers*.

Initially, Brooks had an idea to write a novel based on a premise that had been a rather dark well to draw from for comics and gag writers for years—making fun of Adolf Hitler. Of course, such a premise goes back to the days of Charlie Chaplin in *The Great Dictator* (1940), various World War II cartoons with Daffy Duck or other characters defeating Hitler, Three Stooges shorts, and various other films of World War II, including Ernst Lubitsch's *To Be or Not to Be* (1942). Such mockery soon disappeared, though, as the war ended and the horror perpetrated by Hitler's Third Reich became clear—especially the millions of Jewish people exterminated—made Hitler no longer a laughing matter. Yet, just as the years placed the horrors of the war further away and allowed Brooks and Reiner to feel comfortable in using a "Jewish" voice for comedic purposes again (for the 2000 Year Old Man), so too came the ability to take this real-life monster and tear him apart with laughter.

No doubt that this developed out of the "sick comedy" era that began in the late 1950s. Comics were beginning to talk more about real topics—specifically, topics that were edgier and not necessarily ones that would work with a family audience or even a nonfamily audience, as some comics faced criminal and legal backlash as comic Lenny Bruce discovered. Laughs came based on dicey, taboo topics such as statements about God, Jesus, death, sex, and even Hitler.

In the mid-1950s, comedian Will Jordan had created a routine around the idea of how the entertainment industry would audition Hitler and then try to package him to a mainstream audience—a concept that Lenny Bruce would expand on in his bit "Hitler and the MCA" from his second album, *The Sick Mind of Lenny Bruce*

The initial poster for *The Producers* (1967), which emphasizes Zero Mostel and vaguely hints at the vulgar production at the center of the plot.

(1957). It was a sore topic for Jordan, who would readily point out how Bruce had "stolen his bit," as he does in Phil Berger's book, *The Last Laugh*, and mention that Brooks took it from him as well. "Incidentally, I told that bit to Mel Brooks. . . . That's the subplot of *The Producers*. . . . I'm sure he doesn't even realize he stole it from me. He sat there listening to it, screaming at it."

Yet, even if Brooks had heard the routine, the initial idea of Brooks's novel was not to sweeten the Fuhrer into something palatable, but rather the opposite: to show how, as Maurice Yacowar describes it in his book *Method in Madness*, "a nice, misunderstood Viennese boy who used to be a nifty dancer . . . grew up to be Adolf Hitler." While such a story had some amusing aspects to it, Brooks soon realized it needed something more and began investing the kernel of a story about a "gay romp" with Hitler into the center of a bigger story (if one can say there can be a story bigger than Hitler). Brooks had become an entertainer because he was enchanted by the gloss and magic of the stage, yet when he spent time there, he saw the underbelly of the business that the public at best only heard about: the once-bright stars now grasping for their past, the seedy people looking for a buck, the backers who had no business being there beyond throwing their money around, and the talents too full of themselves to realize how incompetent they are.

And at the center of all that makes up the dismal, tarnished side of the business was Brooks's Max Bialystock, a character built on the memories of producer Benjamin Kutcher, whom Brooks had worked with after World War II (see chapter 1 for more details on Kutcher); and his "caterpillar that needs to turn into a butterfly," Leo Bloom, whom Brooks built around a sweeter, innocent version of himself. It was, as Brooks pointed out in later interviews, he who noted that Kutcher was skimming a portion of investment money for himself and wondering why he didn't go bigger with the con. The idea of "Hitler as a musical" is a terrible one and central to the story, but how a mix of unethical and flat-out dumb people with no clue would even attempt to try it is the genius idea Brooks hit upon when starting to write his novel.

When Brooks showed others what he had written so far, many insisted that the material was too dialogue heavy to work as a book. Instead, a play might work better, perhaps even be the best thing for material that was about the theater. Besides, he was working in the theater industry at the moment. True, on musicals that did not last long (see chapter 6 for all the details), but at least it was an "in" that allowed him to perhaps get a shot with this play he was working on.

Then in January 1962, at a press conference for *All American*, Brooks was asked what his next project would be, and he blurted out "*Springtime for Hitler.*" It was a name he had been playing with for a while with the project, being a parody of the title for a 1934 comedy film called *Springtime for Henry*. Although many took it as a joke, *Variety* would report it in their January 24, 1962, edition as being "planned for Broadway production next season by [producer] Edward Padula," thus making it the first public announcement of Brooks's concept, not to mention probably a migraine for Padula, who had to explain that there wasn't going to be such a play to irate people who had read Brooks's announcement.

Yet, when Brooks had finished his script for *Springtime for Hitler*, he found himself in the same boat he had been in when it was being built as a novel—it was too long and with too many talking heads, as he discussed in an interview with *Written By* in 2016. When his friend and producer Kermit Bloomgarden (1904–1976)—who had produced *Nowhere to Go But Up*, which Brooks had worked on as a script doctor, was shown a rough draft—Bloomgarden's response was, "This is enchanting and funny and I love it, but you have 33 scenes and 55 actors." The producer pointed to a sign in his office that spoke "the gospel for being a Broadway producer": "One Set, Five Actors," noting that what Brooks had created was impossible for the stage. Bloomgarden then suggested that the best thing to do would be to open the story up from that of talking heads in a series of offices, into one that could take place anywhere, if it was turned into a movie script.

By the time *All American* had come and gone, Brooks was starting to see a turn in his fortunes, however. The *2000 Year-Old Man* albums of 1961 and 1962 were popular enough to get him seen on television, leading to work on television panels and additional exposure. Early 1963 would also see network interest in his sitcom pilot script for *Inside Danny Baker*, which would lead to the *Get Smart* series in 1965. There was also the marriage to Anne Bancroft. With things looking up for Brooks, he set his priorities on seeing one of his two pet projects finally getting done: be it *Springtime for Hitler* or another called *Marriage Is a Dirty Rotten Fraud* (see chapter 24 for more details), one was sure to be made.

But first there had to be a movie script. Knowing he needed to get the script in shape if he really wanted to have something to show to potential studios and financiers, Brooks turned to someone he had previously worked with, a woman by the name of Alfa-Betty Olsen. Brooks had met Olsen, a Norwegian immigrant who was looking to become a writer, back in the early 1960s at Max's Kansas City, a club in the New York City area. Brooks began working with Olsen when putting together the pilot and subsequent episodes for *Get Smart* in 1965–1965. After finishing with the script, Olsen had gone on to work as the assistant to producer Lore Noto on a musical version of the children's story (and famous movie) *The Yearling*. The musical lasted all of three performances and is considered one of the biggest bombs on Broadway, but there was a positive that came out of it: Noto agreed to let Brooks work on his script for *Springtime for Hitler* in his office as long as Olsen and Brooks kept up with his mail and other duties there. For a man struggling to get by on what little money he was getting, to have access to an office on West 46th Street was a big plus.

While much of her job as a secretary was to take Brooks's ramblings in the office and convert them into pages for an outline, Olsen was thrilled to be doing it. "I was in seventh heaven to be working with Brooks. After all, he had written for Sid Caesar." Further, she could see that the story was very important to Brooks, as she went on to tell *Vanity Fair*. "It was so evident that he wanted it very much. You could feel him reaching for the brass ring. Writing *The Producers* was Brooks creating himself; he wanted to declare himself on the world."

The days would go by with them working on a treatment, then on some of the script based on it until after four in the afternoon, when Bancroft would call to see if Brooks was ready to come home. Eventually they came up with a 150-page outline that no doubt scared some people off. A nearly 400-page script came out of that, which obviously would have given anyone looking at it a heart attack, and so sections were whacked away until finally a 122-page script came out of the sessions, along with a 30-page treatment and a 3-page synopsis.

Brooks first approached United Artists with the script; they turned it down, not because of Hitler but because, as Brooks remembered in 1997, it was "Borscht Belt humor." He next approached Universal, who liked the script, but studio head Lew Wasserman asked that Mussolini be used instead of Hitler for the musical within the story, since he would not bring as many complaints to the studio as Hitler would. Brooks saw that in trying to be sensitive, the studio was missing the whole point, "A lot of people sorta liked Mussolini—but everybody hated Hitler," Brooks reflected on the memory to *Billboard* magazine. "That's the point! We need that hatred." Further attempts were made to move the script to film producers on smaller and smaller scales, but no one wanted to touch it.

Brooks's agent at the time, Barry Levinson, thought he might know someone who could do it: a producer named Sidney Glazier (1916–2002), who had raised $90,000 on his own after finding no other backers for a documentary about Eleanor Roosevelt, whom he had worked with for a time through her cancer foundation. When *The Eleanor Roosevelt Story* (1965) won an Academy Award for best documentary, Glazier found himself suddenly being pursued by backers and studios for his next project. Glazier also happened to be a friend of Levinson, so the timing was perfect—Glazier was looking for his next project and was an outsider to the business, and Brooks had a project ready to go. Both also had been involved in Oscar-winning films (Brooks for the animated short *The Critic* in 1963), which Levinson thought made them a good match. Glazier decided to listen to Brooks's pitch, asking if he could come to his office when he "had time." Brooks rapidly agreed, telling Glazier on the phone, "I said, 'I have all the time in the world, I'm unemployed!'"

Depending on sources, Brooks either met Glazier at the Hello Coffee Shop in the building Glazier's office was located, or they met in Glazier's office. Either way, Glazier was meeting with Brooks on his lunchtime, and proceeded to pull out a cup of coffee and a tuna sandwich for his lunch, while Brooks began explaining the plot of his intended film. When Brooks finally got to the opening musical number, "Springtime for Hitler," half of Glazier's lunch came flying out of his mouth as he collapsed in hysterics. "I laughed so much during that first meeting in my office," Glazier told *Billboard* in 1997, "that I thought I had pissed in my pants until I looked down and saw I'd only spilled my coffee. Never laughed so hard in my life." Glazier was sold, telling Brooks, "By God, we'll make this movie."

Sidney Glazier, the producer who saved *The Producers* and would work with Brooks once again on its follow-up, *The Twelve Chairs* (1970).

Glazier agreed to make the movie through his production company, Universal Marion Productions (commonly referred to as U-M), in which he had partnered with "a big guy in the stock market," Louis Wolfson (1912–2007) in Florida. Wolfson would later be deemed the "father of the hostile tender offer" and would eventually go to prison for selling shares in a company he controlled that were not registered. When Wolfson was told the plot, he replied to Brooks, "Oh, good, this is getting back at Hitler. You can't bring dictators down on a soapbox with rhetoric. But if you can make people laugh at them, you've won." Wolfson also regretted not contributing to the success of Glazier's Eleanor Roosevelt documentary and wanted a chance to make a bit of money with the new project. He agreed to put up $450,000 for the film, which was a start, but not quite enough for the planned $1 million budget Brooks felt was needed to get the movie made.

Next came a visit to Chicago to talk with producer Joseph E. Levine. Levine was discussed in some detail in chapter 6, when he was involved in the financing of the Broadway flop *Kelly*, which Brooks had done some script doctoring on for a week in 1965. Although both had connections to that musical, Levine was gone from the production before Brooks arrived, so they had not met in connection to a project before discussing *Springtime for Hitler*. Levine was running Embassy Pictures (later Avco-Embassy Pictures) and was looking to expand the type of high-profile pictures he was involved with in hopes of being known more for them than for some of the exploitation films he had delivered in the past. "In the same year," Brooks remembered, "he made a deal to do *The Graduate*, *The Lion in Winter*, and *Springtime for Hitler*." Levine was hesitant, but agreed to help put up $500,000 on one condition: "'You've got to change the title. Most of the people I know in distribution will never put *Springtime for Hitler* on their marquees—they just won't do it.'" Determined to get the film made, Brooks agreed to change the title to *The Producers*.

Brooks, however, had a condition as well: he wanted to direct the movie. He brought up the fact that he had been a stage director on *Your Show of Shows*—in a summer 2012 interview with the Directors Guild of America, Brooks stated he was allowed to stage a couple of things, but as "a director of scenes, not a director of the camera." His concern when doing so was to work with the actors, and it was "only later that I would think about how to capture it." No doubt, he mentioned his work as a producer for *The Polly Bergen Show* in 1957, as well as his previous stage directing with the Red Bank Players back in the 1940s. Levine wasn't quite buying it and was hesitant to allow Brooks to direct, even if he did "know the script and know where all the actors should be." Then Brooks suggested that he show his ability to direct, and if Levine liked it, they would agree to him directing.

Now all Brooks needed to do was find something to direct. Searching around, he found that Frito-Lay was planning on filming a couple of commercials and managed to get the job of directing them. With Olsen as his casting director, Brooks did the ads, one of which featured Gene Wilder as a "daredevil aviator, complete with white silk scarf," the other featuring various townsfolks arguing over the chips at a picnic. It wasn't much, but it did show Brooks could at least put together footage in the correct order and make sense of it, and Levine relented. Then Brooks demanded that he have final cut on the picture, which riled Levine.

"He said, 'Your first movie—final cut? Who do you think you are, Attila the Hun?' But he gave in, and I've never relinquished it on a movie since."

The pieces were finally in place. Brooks would get his opportunity to make his first movie. He would have $941,000 as a budget and forty days to shoot. Now all he needed was a cast, a crew, and a script.

Cast

Still in residence at Lore Noto's office on West 46th Street, Brooks and Alfa-Betty Olsen began finding a cast for the movie. The only exceptions were the two male leads, as Brooks already had his own ideas as to who would play the roles.

Zero Mostel (1915–1977) as Max Bialystock

Mostel was born Samuel Joel Mostel to immigrant Jew parents and raised in the Lower East Side of Manhattan. His mother called him Zero because there were concerns he would end up a "zero" in life if his school grades did not improve, but his intelligence led his parents to hope he would become a rabbi. Zero, however, longed to draw and paint, at which he became so proficient that he would travel to the Metropolitan Museum of Art and copy John White Alexander's *Study in Black and Green* on a regular basis, leading to an addiction to entertaining a crowd as well as painting, as an audience was always nearby to watch him work.

Mostel would begin to lecture about artwork as an adult, leading to him obtaining work as a performer at the Café Society, a club in Manhattan. His career would blossom in the 1940s, but sputtered at times due to his leftist political leanings that

saw him being blacklisted twice in his career; the second time more severely during the "red scare" of the 1950s. Mostel eventually returned to the stage in 1958 playing Leopold Bloom in an off-Broadway play called *Ulysses in Nighttown*, which is based on the fifteenth episode in James Joyce's novel *Ulysses* (Brooks would use the name of the main character in *Ulysses*—Leo Bloom—for the second main character in *The Producers*). Mostel would return to the role on Broadway in 1974, leading to a Tony Award for Best Actor in a Play. In January 1960, Mostel was hit by a bus in Manhattan, leading to one of his legs being crushed. Although the doctors suggested the leg be amputated, Mostel refused and, although he regained use of his leg, he suffered from pain that required him to use a

Original publicity photo of Zero Mostel for *The Producers*. Mostel was hard to pin down to accept the role, and was at odds with Brooks throughout the filming.

cane for the rest of his life—one reason audiences see his character in *The Producers* using one in the film—as well as specifying in his contracts that he could only be available for a certain part of the day due to the fatigue induced by his leg. Once recovered, he began working in television and onstage again, earning his first Tony Award for Best Actor in the surreal play *Rhinoceros* in 1961, which became a film starring Mostel and Gene Wilder in 1973.

After that came two roles that would cement Mostel's fame, and ironically, both written by fellow Caesar writers from Brooks's past. The first was as the slave Pseudolus in *A Funny Thing Happened on the Way to the Forum* in 1962, with a book by Larry Gelbart, which again earned Mostel a Tony, this time for Best Actor in a Musical. It would later be turned into a movie in 1966, with Mostel in the role. The second came in 1964, when Mostel took on the role of Tevye in the original Broadway production of *Fiddler on the Roof*, with a book by Joseph Stein. Mostel's Tevye would be the prototype of most of the actors who would come to the role in later versions of the musical, and would earn him another Tony award.

Brooks had become familiar with Mostel back in the 1940s, as Mostel was friends with Sid Caesar just as Caesar was gaining fame. However, it was not until the early 1960s that they began to see each other more often as part of a group who would get together to have dinner and talk about a range of things. In the group besides Brooks and Mostel were such people as Joseph Heller, Mgoot Lee, and Mario Puzo. It would be Mostel's performances at such functions, along with what Mel had seen of Mostel onstage, that convinced Brooks that Mostel would make the perfect Max Bialystock—the down-on-his-luck producer who rages at his fortunes in *The Producers*. Glazier agreed, having come to know Mostel and given him work in the 1950s when he was suffering from the blacklist. Glazier sent half of the script to Mostel's lawyer to pass on and waited for his reply.

Still waiting for a reply from Mostel a month later, Glazier and Brooks went to see Woody Allen's Broadway show *Don't Drink the Water* and saw Mostel with his wife in the row in front of them. Glazier reached over to talk to Mostel. "I tapped Zero on the shoulder and said, 'You son of a bitch! I, your dear friend, send you a script that's perfect for you, and you don't even have the decency to reply?" (*Billboard*, 1997).

Zero had no idea what Glazier was talking about, but was told by his wife that his lawyer hated the script and refused to send it to him. "That snake in the grass," Mostel shouted in the way only Mostel could exclaim in the theater and requested that Glazier send the script to his house. Mostel's wife, Kate read it first and liked it, and Zero respected her advice on projects. "Kate read it," Brooks said later, "and told me 'He's doing it.' I said, 'What did Zero think?' She said, "I haven't talked to him yet, but I am telling you, he is going to do this.'"

Mostel would be the first person signed on to the film, forcing him to cancel appearing in the film *MacKenna's Gold* (1969, starring Gregory Peck), which was to start filming just as *The Producers* was to finish. After *The Producers*, Mostel would continue finding work in plays and movies, but his career began to drift, with lackluster secondary roles in a number of films—even his return to *Rhinoceros* on film was considered a miss. He then went back to the stage, including revivals of *Fiddler on the Roof* and *Ulysses in Nighttown*. His last major critical appearance was in

The Front (1976), which starred Woody Allen, where he played a famous comedic actor who is unjustly destroyed by the "red scare" of the 1950s, which led many to wonder how much of the plot was similar to Mostel's own experiences during that period. He would pass away a year later.

Gene Wilder (1933–2016) as Leo Bloom

Born Jerome Siberman in Milwaukee, Wisconsin, Gene became attracted to acting by way of his mother, who suffered a heart attack when he was eight. Her heart specialist pulled the young boy aside and told him to never argue with her, as she may have another heart attack as a result, and instead try to make her laugh. It would be the lynchpin to Wilder learning to perform for others, while also a reason why much of his work has featured characters with anger and tension boiling just under the surface who eventually explode, such as Bloom in *The Producers* when his blankie is taken away by Max.

Wilder would study acting upon turning thirteen and after college attended the Old Vic Theatre School in Bristol, England, for six months before returning to the United States. Drafted into the military, he worked as a paramedic for a "locked ward" at a neuropsychiatric hospital in Phoenixville, Pennsylvania, a job that helped him play the character Billy Bibbit in the original Broadway production of *One Flew over the Cuckoo's Nest* (November 1963–January 1964, with Kirk Douglas). Once out of the military, he moved on to the Actors Studio where he decided to take the stage name of Gene Wilder.

When his wife at the time, Mary Mercier, got a role in an off-Broadway production of a play called *Roots*, Wilder auditioned for the role of the husband to her character, and got the job. According to Wilder in his autobiography, this led directly to his working on television in a 1961 *Play of the Week* (a program produced by David Susskind's Talent Associates) called "Wingless Victory." That in turn led to further work on Broadway and eventually to his being cast in 1963 as one of the adult children to Anne Bancroft's mother in the Broadway musical *Mother Courage and Her Children* (discussed in chapter 7).

Mother Courage lasted less than two months—Wilder's autobiography has it lasting three months—but an important friendship came out of it. Mel Brooks would arrive every evening to pick up Bancroft and take her home after each performance, which is how Wilder met Brooks for the first time. The show was not going well for many

Original publicity photo of Gene Wilder for *The Producers*. Wilder had been Brooks's first and then third choice for the role of Leo Bloom, after an attempt to get Peter Sellers went nowhere.

in it—the musical has rarely found much success, although attempted many times afterwards—and Wilder mentioned to Brooks backstage that he was depressed that the audience was laughing at his performance. "I don't mean to be funny. I'm not trying. Why are they laughing?" Brooks was bewildered by the question. "Because you're funny," Brooks recalled to *Vanity Fair* telling Wilder at the time.. "Gene, you're funny. Get used to it. Go with what works!" Brooks obviously saw potential in Wilder, and as the play was closing, he offered to treat Gene to a weekend at the home he and Anne had on Fire Island.

When Wilder arrived a few weeks after the musical closed, Brooks pulled out thirty pages of the script—the first three scenes in the film in close to final form—for *Springtime for Hitler* and performed it for Wilder and Bancroft. After finishing, Brooks asked him if he would play the Leo Bloom part. Wilder liked what he heard and didn't see any harm in saying yes, but soon found out how passionate Brooks could be, stating in his autobiography, "Alright, now listen to me—don't take anything on Broadway or off-Broadway or anywhere else without checking with me first. Promise?" As would be typical for any actor who had been around for a bit, Wilder promised, but knew it was like most projects—if something happened, he probably wouldn't hear anything back anyway, so didn't think much of it. Later that year, when he got the part in *One Flew over the Cuckoo's Nest*, Brooks was in a fit. "Can you give them a two-week notice if you want to get out?" When Wilder said that he might be able to get a four-week notice at best, Brooks's reply was "All right, all right—we'll have to live with it."

But that was all back in 1963. By 1965 and into 1966, Brooks was shopping the script around to studios and trying various means to get interest. Thus, even with tying Wilder down to a release schedule, Brooks was not absolutely set on Wilder for the role of Leo Bloom. According to various sources, Brooks also had his eye on Peter Sellers, who was gaining international attention thanks to his work as Inspector Clouseau in *The Pink Panther* (1963) and *A Shot in the Dark* (1964)—and with many *Pink Panther* films to follow in the 1970s. Sellers had been in other roles as well, both comedic and serious, such as Stanley Kubrick's *Lolita* (1962) and *Dr. Strangelove* (1964). Sellers also seemed like the perfect fit for the role of the innocent accountant who is "set free" by the wily producer, and was a star that could help Brooks lock in a deal with a studio. It just made sense to give it a shot, so Brooks sent Sellers's agent, Dennis Selinger, a copy of what was available of the script and set up a talk to go over the project.

Brooks states in Ed Sikov's biography of Sellers, *Mr. Strangelove: A Biography of Peter Sellers*, that the meeting with Sellers did not go very well. As Brooks began describing the project, Sellers decided he needed to go to Bloomingdale's to do some shopping. Brooks tagged along, attempting to sell the project to Sellers, who grew more distant as the minutes went by. "I'd be in the middle of a very important moment—where Bialystock says to Bloom, 'Do you want to live in a gray little world? Do you want to be confined? Don't you want to fly?'—and he'd say, 'You like this buckle? What do you think of this buckle?'" Brooks wondered what he had done to turn Sellers off the project if he had been willing to meet, only for Selinger to admit that he did not think Sellers had even looked at the script and was working on so many projects at that point, he would quickly gain and then lose interest in things. As Selinger told Brooks, "This is not the right time to approach him with new material." With Sellers a long shot to cast anyway, Brooks felt it was no reflection on the script, and it was a simple matter to go back to his first choice of Wilder. "I loved Gene, because he was always an inch and a half away from hysteria. It was right there in his eyes. He was like a trapped animal, and, in *The Producers*, Max Bialystock is the thing that's trapping him."

Wilder's career was steadily building on Broadway since Brooks first approached him about the role in 1963. Established as the understudy for the two male leads in the Broadway comedy hit *LUV* (1964–1967), which starred Alan Arkin and Eli Wallach, Wilder eventually took over Arkin's part in June 1966. Wilder also appeared in the May 1966 television adaptation of *Death of a Salesman* done by David Susskind's Talent Associates. By late fall 1966, however, it was clear that *LUV* would be ending soon, and Wilder agreed to play a small part in the movie *Bonnie and Clyde* (1967). The film starring Faye Dunaway and Warren Beatty would be a tremendous smash in late 1967 and be Wilder's first appearance in film, establishing the emotional balancing act, with hysteria that bubbles over into comedy, that would be part of his film persona for years to come. Wilder filmed the small role in the winter of 1966, then went back to the concluding days of *LUV*'s run on Broadway.

After a matinee performance near the end of the play's run, Wilder heard a knock on his dressing room door and opened it to see Mel Brooks standing there with Sidney Glazier. Brooks's first words to him were, "You don't think I forgot, do you?" Brooks explained they would be filming the movie and Zero Mostel would be starring in it. The only problem was, as Brooks told Wilder, "I can't just spring you on him because he's got approval of anyone who plays Leo, so you've got to do a reading with him, just so he can see for himself how good you are."

Wilder had heard about Mostel's temperament—a man who never turned down the volume on anything he did. If he loved something, it could not be contained; the same with contempt. Wilder also felt that if he didn't get the costarring role, "I'll just be a good featured—maybe supporting—actor for the rest of my life." Arriving at Glazier's office, Brooks was the first to meet Wilder, offering him a hug. After Brooks introduced them, Wilder held out a hand to shake, only for Mostel to pull him close and give him a huge kiss on the lips. From there, Wilder felt things were going to work out, and after the reading, everyone agreed he was perfect for the role of Leo.

When filming was completed on *The Producers*, Wilder passed up the opportunity to appear in Mike Nichols's adaptation of *Catch-22*—with a script from Buck Henry—in order to film the wild, iconoclastic French Revolution comedy *Start the Revolution Without Me* (filmed in 1968, but released in 1970). That film would feature Orson Welles as the narrator and a story line about imposters and a King of France attempting to leave before the peasants can get him during the French Revolution (that may sound familiar to Brooks fans, but to be fair, this and the last portion of *History of the World, Part I* are parodies of *A Tale of Two Cities*). As with *The Producers*, *Start the Revolution Without Me* would become a cult classic after initially not doing well at the box office.

Next, in 1970, Wilder would film *Quackser Fortune Has a Cousin in the Bronx*, which he had brought to Sidney Glazier, and then played one of his most well-remembered roles in the 1971 film *Willy Wonka & the Chocolate Factory*. This would be followed in 1972 with work on the episodic Woody Allen film *Everything You Always Wanted to Know About Sex * But Were Afraid to Ask* (released 1973), while also working as a voice actor on *The Electric Company* alongside Zero Mostel and Joan Rivers in the animated shorts for "The Adventures of Letterman" (produced between 1972 and 1976) and appearing with Mostel in *Rhinoceros*. Then something occurred to bring Wilder back into Brooks's orbit, but more about that in a couple of chapters.

Kenneth Mars (1935–2011) as Franz Liebkind

Peter Sellers was not the only actor considered for the role of Leo Bloom. For a time in 1966, Dustin Hoffman (born 1937) was considered after his Obie-winning role in the off-Broadway play by Ronald Ribman, *Journey of the Fifth Horse*. Glazier was keen on Hoffman for the role, but when Hoffman was given a script, he asked if he could play Franz Liebkind, the crazy Nazi writer, instead. Brooks and Glazier were off and on about Hoffman doing the role, but when it came down to reading for it, Hoffman begged off, as Brooks told *Vanity Fair*. "I'm going to L.A. to audition for Mike Nichols to be in a movie with your wife," Hoffman told Brooks. Brooks waved away the apology, figuring, "You're a mutt. They're going to get a better-looking guy for the part. You'll be back and the part will be waiting for you."

Instead, Hoffman indeed got the starring role in *The Graduate*, written by Buck Henry, and in 1967 went off to shoot the film with Anne Bancroft playing Mrs. Robinson. Meanwhile, Brooks had eyes on Kenneth Mars, who had been building a career in commercials and in comedic roles on Broadway: *The Affair* in 1962, *Any Wednesday* in 1965, and *The Best Laid Plans*, where Brooks first saw him. Brooks would occasionally run into Mars in New York and one day excitedly told him about a part he had written for Mars in *Springtime for Hitler*: Roger De Bris, the cross-dressing director of the musical. Mars would later state that Brooks probably had him typecast into the role, as his part in *The Best Laid Plans* featured Mars as a gay psychologist.

Mars read the script and decided he didn't want to play it. He was much more fascinated by Franz, a role that Brooks hesitated on

Kenneth Mars as Franz Liebkind. Brooks initially wanted Mars to play Roger De Bris, the cross-dressing director. Mars said he'd rather play Franz and got the part when Dustin Hoffman backed out to star in *The Graduate* (1967), which costarred Anne Bancroft.

earlier with Hoffman because he was eyeing the role himself. The two argued over the role for a time until finally Olsen told Brooks, "Hire him, he's terrific," and Brooks realized she was right.

On the set, Mars would end up causing some headaches for both Brooks and Mostel. Brooks because Mars insisted that bird droppings be added to the German helmet he was wearing, which the director thought was too much (they finally compromised on the number of droppings). Also, because Mars would sometimes add a line to the script that was not there, such as noting that Hitler was such a great painter that he could "paint an entire apartment in von afternoon—two coats!"

Mostel's problem with Mars was due to the latter getting some laughs from the crew, which threatened Mostel as the head comic in the film. There was also an issue with the smell, as Mars had decided to go "method" and wore the same clothes for eight weeks of filming. He was even known to sleep in the clothes and stay in character between shots, which led Wilder to say in his autobiography, "I didn't know if the character Kenneth Mars was playing was crazy or if Kenneth Mars was crazy."

Mars would go on from *The Producers* to more television and movie work, including appearing in *Butch Cassidy and the Sundance Kid* (1969, featuring later Brooks costar Cloris Leachman) and *What's Up, Doc?* (1972, featuring another later Brooks costar, Madeline Kahn). He would make one more Brooks appearance half a dozen years later, as will be seen.

Dick Shawn (1923–1987) as LSD, the hippie playing Hitler

Original publicity photo of Dick Shawn for *The Producers*. As can be seen, Shawn is not shown in character as LSD. The original publicity photos release made it clear that Embassy Pictures was very unsure how to promote the film.

Born Richard Schulefand in Brooklyn (many bios have his year of birth being 1929), Dick Shawn had originally intended to be a professional baseball player and had landed a contract with the Chicago White Sox when he got drafted into the military. He found that the USO was looking for performers and he volunteered, soon realizing he could make people laugh. Upon returning to civilian life, Shawn performed comedy on the program *Talent Scouts*, which led to performances on *The Ed Sullivan Show* and other shows, besides working in nightclubs. In fact, in 1960 Brooks was listed in a *Variety* article as writing material for Shawn for his club act. When Zero Mostel left *A Funny Thing Happened on the Way to the Forum*, it was Dick Shawn who replaced him on Broadway. He would also later appear in an hour-long comedy play for television in 1967, leading directly to him being cast in *The Producers*, when Brooks remembered Shawn doing a bit in his nightclub act as an emptyheaded rock star, which fit perfectly with what Brooks saw as the character of LSD. He had a memorable role—some say one of the few really funny ones—in the comedian-packed film *It's a Mad, Mad, Mad, Mad World* (1963), performed as a slimy white-hat cowboy in the television movie *Evil Roy Slade* (1972), and was in the Dracula parody comedy *Love at First Bite* (1979). He was also the voice of the Snow Miser in the television animated classic *The Year Without a Santa Claus* (1974).

Shawn shared a trait in his study of comedy that was reminiscent of Brooks and Caesar before him: being funny had to be more than just doing traditional gags and premises. It had to hit closer to home, and Shawn became known for doing daring material that pushed the boundaries of good taste and the comfort zone of the audience watching. His tendency to be unpredictable in his one-man shows led to him warning crew members at such events that he may do unexpected things that should not cause concern and lead to someone spoiling the act. This contributed directly to his death on April 17, 1987, while performing at the University of California in San Diego. In a bit about the apocalypse, Shawn stumbled facedown to the stage floor. Whether it was intentional or not (some witnesses dispute this), nearly everyone behind the scenes and in the audience thought it was part of the show. When paramedics arrived minutes later, people were still unsure. It was not until the next day that it was officially announced that Shawn had suffered a fatal heart attack onstage. Ironically, he once told the *New York Post* that he would rather play colleges than nightclubs, as "At least if I die, I die in front of intelligent people who know what I'm talking about."

Christopher Hewett (1921–2001) as Roger De Bris

The role of the director was one of the few that went out to agents instead of to someone that had a connection with Brooks, as with most of the other major roles in the film. Christopher Hewett did have extensive stage experience like the others, however, having been an understudy for Rex Harrison, as well as performing in the original production of *My Fair Lady* (1956). He would also appear in *The Unsinkable Molly Brown* (1960) and for a time as Mr. Darling/Captain Hook in the Sandy Duncan version of *Peter Pan* in 1979.

Hewett, born in England, began appearing on Broadway in the mid-1950s while also doing a bit of work in television and movies. He became better known in the United States when he took over as Mr. Rourke's helper on *Fantasy Island* in its final season (1983–1984) and then starring in *Mr. Belvedere* from 1985–1990.

Andreas Voutsinas (1930–2010) as Carmen Giya, De Bris's assistant

A Greek actor, Andreas Voutsinas had joined the Actors Studio in 1957, where he became friends with Anne Bancroft, who suggested Voutsinas for the role of De Bris's assistant in *The Producers*. Voutsinas would return to do two other films for

Brooks, including his second, *The Twelve Chairs*, as well as a memorable role very much in the spirit of Carmen Giya in *History of the World, Part I*. Voutsinas acted on Broadway and even directed a comedy, *The Fun Couple*, in 1962 that costarred his then-girlfriend Jane Fonda. Into the 1970s and onward he worked in Europe, teaching acting and appearing in French and Greek movies.

Lee Meredith (born 1947) as Ulla

Just nineteen at the time of filming, Lee Meredith was cast in the small but memorable role of Ulla, the Swedish "secretary" to Max. Meredith would later appear in both the Broadway production and the movie version of Neil Simon's *The Sunshine Boys* as the nurse in the sketch being performed in the film. She would make a memorable appearance in the 2002 documentary found on the DVD release of *The Producers*, which has a brief "intermission" featuring Meredith recreating her dance from the film.

Estelle Winwood (1883–1984) as "Hold Me, Touch Me," the main play contributor

Winwood was born in England, originally working in the West End before emigrating to America in 1916. She would find plenty of work on Broadway through the years, but increasingly spent time working in television and in films, which she found a distant second to acting onstage. There are other older actresses in *The Producers*, yet Winwood is memorable as the destructive and sex-crazed "Hold Me, Touch Me" seen at the beginning of the film. She didn't quite see it that way, and is quoted in the book *Great Hollywood Wit*, "That dreadful picture. I can't bear to watch it, even on a small television. I'm rather sorry I did it. I must have needed the money—living in Hollywood weakens one's motives. [Mel Brooks] reminds me of the saying that nobody ever went broke underestimating the American public's taste."

Lobby card for *The Producers*, with Leo interrupting Max and "Hold Me, Touch Me" (Estelle Winwood) on the casting couch. Winwood would later state, "I must have needed the money," explaining her reason for participating in the film.

Ironically, she is probably best remembered for *The Producers* out of all her work. She would die at the age of 101, having worked until the age of 100. Her last film was Neil Simon's *Murder by Death* (1975), which she also panned in interviews; but then again, she felt much the same about most of her movie work, so it wasn't that out of the ordinary for her to say so.

Also Appearing

- Mel Brooks, overdubbing one of the singers in the opening song of *Springtime for Hitler*, "Don't be stupid, be a smarty, come and join the Nazi Party!" Some people will do anything to get into the act.
- Bill Macy (born 1922) as the jury head in the trial scene. Macy is still probably best known for appearing as the husband of Bea Arthur's character in the sitcom *Maude*. He plays one of the other writers in the Brooksfilms movie *My Favorite Year* (1982).
- Lore Noto, the Broadway producer that allowed Brooks and Olsen to use his office when writing the script and casting the movie, appears as one of the audience members for *Springtime for Hitler.*
- Renee Taylor (born 1933) as the actress playing Eva Braun in the musical. She had studied with Gene Wilder earlier in their careers and went on to do many roles in television sitcoms, including playing the mother to Fran Drescher's character in *The Nanny* (1993–1999). She married actor Joseph Bologna (1934–2017), who played the Sid Caesar–like King Kaiser in the Brooksfilms movie *My Favorite Year.* Brooks was listed at one point as the executive producer of *Made for Each Other*, which was written by and starring Taylor and Bologna, but the deal fell through when the production company, UMC, folded in 1971.
- Barney Martin (1923–2005) as the actor playing Göring in the musical. Martin had been in the *Kraft Music Hall* episode that Brooks cowrote in 1959, but that's probably not the reason he got hired in *The Producers.* Martin was a popular character actor on television, and a regular on the 1976–1978 sitcom *The Tony Randall Show.* He's probably best remembered today for playing the father of Liza Minnelli's character in the *Arthur* movies and Morty on *Seinfeld.*
- William Hickey (1927–1997) as the drunk at the bar. Hickey also did a lot of television and may be best remembered these days for playing the don in *Prizzi's Honor* (1985).
- Frank Campanella (1919–2006) as the bartender. Merely a cameo and mostly with his face away from the camera, but worth mentioning as he'll play a bartender once again in Brooks's *High Anxiety* nearly ten years later.
- Auditioning Hitlers: Many of the actors trying out to play Hitler were fellow singer/dancers from Broadway, and actively sought to be in it. "They were Broadway guys," Olsen remembered years later to *Vanity Fair.* "They didn't want to tell me, because they thought it would turn me off. But, no, I hired them. Agents called for people who had leads in Broadway shows." Amongst them is Rusty Blitz, who returns to a Brooks film in *Young Frankenstein* as one of the gravediggers (he also appears in Gene Wilder's 1979 film *The Frisco Kid* as a rabbi). Arthur Rubin, who had continued success on Broadway as a singer before and after *The Producers* (as well as become a producer himself), would provide the singing voice of Robin Hood in Brooks's *Robin Hood: Men in Tights.* Zale Kessler, who plays the Kaiser-dressed Jason Green in the auditions, returns as one of the disciples in the Roman Empire segment of *History of the World, Part I*, the orchestra leader in *Dracula: Dead and Loving It*, and as Bieler

in *To Be or Not to Be*. One of the dancers in the musical, Tucker Smith, would also return in *To Be or Not to Be* as one of Klotski's Klowns.

In the Crew

- John Morris (born 1926–2018) as composer of musical score and conductor. Morris had worked with Brooks on both *Shinbone Alley* and *All American* and would compose the music for all of Brooks's films up through *Life Stinks*. He also composed the music for several of Gene Wilder's films (*The Adventure of Sherlock Holmes' Smarter Brother, The World's Greatest Lover, The Woman in Red, Haunted Honeymoon, Murder in a Small Town,* and *The Lady in Question*), Marty Feldman's *The Last Remake of Beau Geste, In God We Trust,* and for his final film appearance in *Yellowbeard,* along several films for Brooksfilms (*The Elephant Man, To Be or Not to Be, The Doctor and the Devils*).

- Michael Hertzberg (born 1941) as assistant director. Hertzberg had worked as an assistant director on the film version of *Requiem for a Heavyweight* (1962). He also worked in the same role for *The World of Henry Orient* (1964), where Brooks and Sellers met up to discuss *The Producers*. Hertzberg would be brought in early into the production and would eventually end up as a producer on Brooks's next three movies. He also worked as an assistant director on Frank Perry's *The Swimmer* (1968) and would go on to produce several other films, including *Johnny Dangerously* (1984), which featured music composed by John Morris.

- Joseph Coffey (1915–2000) as director of photography. Coffey had worked as a camera operator on *Requiem for a Heavyweight*, Sidney Lumet's *The Pawnbroker* (1964), and Samuel Beckett's experimental *Film* (1965), which starred Buster Keaton. He would do the same after *The Producers* on such films as *Kramer vs. Kramer* (1979), *Fame* (1980), and *Eddie Murphy: Raw* (1987). He was the director of photography on *Up the Down Staircase* the same year he performed that function on *The Producers*.

- Charles Rosen (1930–2012) as production designer. *The Producers* would be one of Rosen's first theatrical movies for which he did production design. He would later be involved with *My Favorite Year* for Brooksfilms, as well as performing the same duty on such films as *Invasion of the Body Snatchers* (1978), *Flashdance* (1983), *Broadcast News* (1987), and *Private Parts* (1997), while also working as an art director on *Taxi Driver* (1976).

- Alan Heim (born 1936) as sound editor. Heim had worked as the sound effects editor on Glazier's *The Eleanor Roosevelt Story*. He would move up to being the editor of Brooks's second film *The Twelve Chairs* in 1970, and continue as an editor on numerous films up to the present day, including *Network* (1976), *All That Jazz* (1979), and *Hair* (1979).

- Alan Johnson (born 1937) as choreographer. Johnson, a dancer on Broadway in *West Side Story*, would go on to become a Tony-nominated choreographer (for *Legs Diamond* in 1989). One of his first chances to do such a job was for *The Producers*, and Brooks would invite him back to do more of the same in *Blazing Saddles, History of the World, Part I,* and *Dracula: Dead and Loving It*. He would direct two films for Brooksfilms—*To Be or Not to Be* and *Solarbabies* (1986). He also choreographed the dance numbers in Gene Wilder's *The Adventure of Sherlock Holmes' Smarter Brother* and *The World's Greatest Lover.*

Production

Featuring a title change pushed by Joseph Levine from *Springtime for Hitler* to *The Producers*, the upcoming film would begin appearing in *Variety* news items in early April. A full-page ad appeared in the April 19, 1967, edition of *Variety*, showcasing Zero Mostel as "The star of *Fiddler on the Roof* and *A Funny Thing Happened on the Way to the Forum*" and Mel Brooks (in just slightly smaller type) as the writer who "helped create many of TV's great hits." As for the script, a mostly completed one was done by mid-March, although Glazier reflected years later in *Billboard*, "Even when we shot the movie, I never had a real script until we were done. We just got pages every day from Brooks's secretary, a woman named Alfa-Betty Olsen, who stayed up all night, typing 'till dawn."

Besides some dialogue being dropped, there are subtle changes between the script from March 1967 and what appears on the screen:

- Surprisingly, the line about "cash" being a funny name for a play but so was *The Iceman Cometh* is not in the script at that point.
- Bialystock shows off his cardboard belt in the script but doesn't rip it up as in the film (and subsequent musical version).
- A scripted scene with Bialystock taking two dollars from a blind man so he can afford to treat Bloom to lunch is missing in the film.
- Bialystock was originally to escort Bloom to Coney Island for custard and a ride on the Parachute Jump (a parachute that would open as Bloom announces that he wants everything he had seen in the movies). However, due to disrepair on the ride and other cost factors, the film instead has the two in Central Park.
- The meeting with Liebkind to have him agree for them to produce his play is abbreviated from script to screen, relieving Liebkind of a long speech about bringing Adolph "his hot milk and opium" and how Churchill never could properly say the world "Nazi."
- Filmed, but discarded, was the "Siegfried Oath" segment, which had Bloom and Bialystock in Viking helmets to pledge an oath. (This explains Franz exclaiming they had broken the Siegfried Oath late in the film; a variation of the scene would later return to the Broadway musical version.)
- Bialystock stomps on the violinist's foot in the restaurant rather than the better visual gag of pouring champagne into his pants.
- There is more to Bialystock's pursuit of the old ladies in the script, including him being a nude model for a painting done by one of the elderly women.
- Carmen offers the pair slippers to wear when visiting De Bris. This was cut, leading to a continuity error, as Bloom and Bialystock both take off their shoes but can be seen wearing such footwear later in the scene.
- The script has Liebkind included in watching the casting call for Hitler, although this is not the case in the film.

- During the Hitler auditions, there was to have been a montage of auditioners of all shapes and sizes—including a woman—singing the very same song, "Stout-Hearted Men."
- LSD's song is much different than planned in the script, and probably influenced more heavily by Shawn than Brooks in the film.
- LSD has more to do in his first onstage appearance in the musical, allowing a better chance for the audience to want to stay than what was in the mid-March script.
- Instead of being knocked out after storming the stage as seen in the film, the script has Franz being dragged up with the curtain as it is lifted to continue the musical.
- The bombing of the theater is greatly extended in the script and was filmed, only to be edited down to what finally appears in the movie. What is shown in the film is Franz lighting the short fuse and then the theater explodes before he can stop it. In the script, he manages to stop the short fuse, then attaches the longer fuse and connects it to a detonator outside the building, only for the dynamite to not go off. After the three venture inside to fix what they believe is the problem, the drunk seen earlier in the bar with Bloom and Bialystock unintentionally sets off the explosive. (It works better in the edited form.) Also missing from the script is the business where Franz nearly shoots the dynamite.

Production was to start on May 15, but got bumped to May 22, 1967. The indoor scenes were filmed at the Production Center Studios at 221 West 26th Street in New York City, which was built in 1914 and renovated into a studio by Adolph Zukor back in the silent film days. It is now known as the Chelsea Television Studios and is currently used primarily for talk shows. The production was scheduled to be completed within forty days and for a total of $941,000, with no chance of an overrun in time or money. "There was no one to call if you needed more money, so the guys who were trained in New York had a certain way of getting things done," Michael Hertzberg recalled later to *Vanity Fair*.

The pressure was on Brooks to prove he could handle the job, which would rattle any first-time director. Brooks began the first scene shot on the first day of filming by infamously shouting "Cut!" instead of "Action!" There was no excuse for such a mistake—Brooks was experienced enough to know how directing was done—but if was meant as a joke, it backfired on some of the crew, who questioned his ability. If unintentional, it merely showed how frantic Brooks was before filming had even begun.

Those working on the set noticed the reason immediately for Brooks's anxiousness. He had come from the world of television where everything was either live or your half-hour show had to be completed within five days. In film, getting five minutes of usable footage a day was considered extraordinary, yet Brooks had trouble dialing himself down. Or when to stop obsessing on a scene. "Sometimes [Hertzberg] would take me by the collar and say, 'We're finished here.' And he'd take me to a new set that was lit. . . . He knew how much money we had to work with," Brooks told Robert Weide in an interview for the Directors Guild of America. The first day of filming was also marred by Brooks trying to treat everyone to lunch—going out to get sandwiches and coffee for the cast and crew—only to not be allowed back in the studio until Hertzberg arrived and telling the secretary refusing to let Brooks back in, "He's the director, lady!"

For some, Brooks's frantic nature helped keep the cast and crew on their toes. Dick Shawn, who admittedly was not on the set every day and did not have to deal with Brooks's anxieties, found his attitude refreshing, as he told the *New York Times*. "He keeps you on edge while you're working so you're always doing your best . . . that's the kind of people I like to work with." Some of the others felt less confident. Brooks knew what he wanted, but felt the actors could handle their roles without much assistance from him. Early on Brooks told Wilder, "You don't have to act at all, because I got all the people who are just right for the parts." When Wilder later approached Bancroft and asked, "Does he really think I'm like that?" he remembered in his autobiography. Bancroft rolled her eyes and said, "Just go along with him." His sole directorial advice to Andreas Voutsinas as Carmen was "Play it like Rasputin, but move like Marilyn Monroe."

Early in the shooting, Wilder had just rehearsed the early scene where Bloom gets hysterical and eventually wet in Bialystock's office. Wilder was drained when finished, but felt confident the scene would work when they filmed it the next day. That's when Brooks told him that they had just enough time to film the scene that afternoon. Wilder was in shock, as he had put all his energy into the rehearsal because he did not expect to have to do it again that day. Determined to prove his worth to the production, Wilder requested chocolate bars and gobbled them down for the sugar-high before performing the scene again to utter perfection. It had worked well, but only because Wilder was willing to be a trooper for Brooks.

Mostel, however, quickly soured on Brooks's attitude, nor was he thrilled with Brooks's tendency to demand that everyone play their parts exactly as he would play them in rehearsal and on the set. "Zero had a mind of his own," Brooks told *Billboard* in 1997. "I was a first-time director; he was a big Broadway star. He wasn't about to listen to a little shmeck from Brooklyn. I was firm and finally got everything I could get out of him by shaming him into it, because I could do the part almost as good as he did it, and then he would get angry and top me." Mostel and Brooks then fell into a workable relationship built on respect and anger. Brooks was known to ask "where is that fat pig?" when needing Mostel for a shot, and Mostel mocking Brooks by saying, "There's a director here? What director? Where?"

Problems came from other quarters as well. Joe Coffey continually butted heads with Brooks over the setups for the camera, which was not helped by Brooks sometimes stumbling over the technical terminology that was expected of a filmmaker. After an incident where Coffey screamed at Brooks over some of the footage shot in the first week, Hertzberg again stepped in, working as a liaison between the cameraman and the director. The dailies also were a sour pill for Joseph E. Levine—not because of what Brooks was shooting, but because he couldn't stand Wilder. "I've got $25,000 for you to get another actor," Levine told Brooks, who eventually told Wilder.

Brooks and Glazier managed to talk Levine out of it, and later, after Wilder was nominated for an Academy Award for the role, Levine would tell Wilder, "You're a great actor!" Wilder, who knew Levine wanted him fired, said in his autobiography that he thought at the time, "Thanks, Joe, for not insisting that Mel fire me." Wilder was not the only one to have issues with Levine, as he was also pressuring Glazier on what was being delivered in the dailies. "Somebody in his company would usually call and say, 'The boss doesn't like it.'" Glazier remembered years later to *Billboard*. "After a while, I got exasperated and answered, 'So he doesn't like it. What the hell does he want for half a million?'"

Brooks wasn't happy with the results either. Midway through the film, editor Ralph Rosenblum showed Glazier and Brooks his edit of the first twenty minutes of the movie. Brooks would later call Rosenblum a "great editor," but he was livid with Rosenblum at the time, according to *Vanity Fair*. After the screening, Brooks marched up to him and said, "I don't want you to touch this fucking film again! You understand? I'll do it myself. Don't touch it until I finish shooting!"

Yet Brooks was feeling the heat in trying to get the production finished on time, and it was affecting him both physically and mentally. With his insomnia kicking in strong, Brooks had trouble sleeping at night and being at his best during the day. Hertzberg, in an article about the filming, remembered Brooks's gray complexion and having to physically move him from one set to the next. The worst moment came at the worst time: Levine and Glazier snagged a photo shoot for the production, with a writer by the name of Joan Barthel arriving on the set to interview the cast and crew. Brooks, who had demanded a closed set, was boiling over in hostility toward having an outsider there "to judge him." He refused to act cordial to the writer, initiating their conversation with "I know everything and that's my problem." Upset that the article was being done months before the movie would be seen, Brooks could not see the point in having the already frantic air mixed with an outsider writing a fluff piece about it.

Although originally to have been a multipage photo layout in *Life Magazine*, the completed article appeared in the September 3, 1967, edition of the *New York Times*, with one lone photo of Brooks looking manic. The writer referred to him as cranky, but that was obviously the politest term anyone could think of for Brooks's actions, yelling at the visiting photographer with Barthel, and finishing a scene by dragging himself to a cot in despair. Glazier, Wilder, and Mostel attempted to give the writer good material for the article, but Brooks would not budge, suspiciously asking Barthel why she was there. "What did you hope for when you came here?" Brooks demanded. "What did you want?" When the author said she had no preconceived notions, Brooks called her response "too vague" and suggested she was "just a big blob of cotton," before concluding their discussion by asking her, "Do you fool around?" It was as if he was possessed by the spirit of Bialystock to doom the film in any fashion he could. While Glazier told the reporter earlier in the day, "I'm the producer. Pray for me," in a joking manner, perhaps at the time it was not so much of a joke.

From the rock bottom of that moment, however, the film continued onward without much further incident. On June 25, the company moved to the Playhouse Theatre at 137 West 48th Street to shoot both the Hitler tryouts and the musical portions of the film. "We chose the theater," Charles Rosen, the production designer stated, "because we needed the alley [for the bombing scene]" (*Vanity*

Fair). The tryout portion went smoothly, but there were issues with the musical part. Firstly, the premiere of the musical was supposed to show the hustle and bustle of audience members arriving to see the show. When it came time for filming, Brooks found himself with eleven extras. Fortunately, Glazier managed to grab people from nearby theaters to fill in, giving the theater the look needed for the movie.

As to the musical parts, Brooks had to work closely with John Morris, the composer, and Alan Johnson, the choreographer, especially as they had only two days to do all the filming needed there, and half of that was the tryouts, so the musical numbers needed to be done in a rush. The point was to make the "Springtime for Hitler" number look like the cheesiest production number in history, and that meant being so good that it looked like the characters were sloppy, not the actors and dancers playing the roles. "Alan Johnson," Brooks said in the Directors Guild interview, "was sitting next to me . . . what was wonderful about it was choreographers can bug the shit out of you. You know, 'He missed that step. . . .' But he was so cooperative." With four cameras running, the number was filmed twice, along with a bird's-eye view of the dancers forming the swastika. It was a shot that, as others have pointed out, would not have been seen by the audience, but plays into the whole broken-down Busby Berkeley feel of the number.

Shooting the scene where Bialystock convinces Bloom to join him in the scam was to occur at Coney Island; however, costs and the foreknowledge that the parachute-jump ride was in disrepair forced them to find another location. As it happened. Alfa-Betty Olsen was visiting the Lincoln Center and noticed that the Revson Fountain could possibly work for the scene's ending. It would be the very last shot filmed for the movie, which was completed on June 28, 1967. Brooks was talking to the engineer who controlled the water for the fountain, and although the fountain usually shot up to eight feet in the air, the engineer said, "I can get it up to sixteen." As the dawn was breaking, allowing the shooting to look like dusk rather than dawn, the crew managed to get in the glorious shot of Bloom demanding he get everything he had seen in the movies just as the fountain bursts up in all its power, thanks to the engineer stepping in to help.

The film was completed in exactly forty days and for $941,000, to the dollar. Brooks would then take it into the editing room for the next twenty weeks and, with Rosenbloom, put together the final version.

Backend

The film was ready for the public in early November, and Embassy Pictures decided to preview it in order to gauge how much money should be put into the marketing. Brooks had hoped to see it open in New York, but Levine vetoed the idea, saying all the theaters were booked up for season. In fact, the film wasn't so much previewed as dumped. It premiered in four cities on November 15, 1967: Detroit, Michigan (showing with *The Days of Wilfrid Owen*, and billed as "Zero Loves! Zero Lies! Zero Dances! Zero Flips!"); Philadelphia; Rochester, New York; and St. Louis. It then opened on November 22, 1967, in four more cities: Pittsburgh (where it was "Ladies Day" and women only had to pay 50 cents up until the 6:25 p.m. showing that day); Baltimore; Wilmington, Delaware; and Salt Lake City. In theaters at the time were such films as *Cool Hand Luke*, *Far from the Madding Crowd*, Neil Simon's *Barefoot in the Park*, *Camelot*, *Point Blank*, and *Clambake*, while *Bonnie and Clyde* was just about to end its run in theaters.

There were two newspaper ads designed for the release of *The Producers*: one was a variation of the first U.S. poster for the film, showing a collage of images from the film inside a box of shelves with a theater curtain and a marquee above it. The images centered on a goofy picture of Zero, and although Shawn is shown as Hitler twice in the collage, in the top photo his swastika band had been airbrushed out; and in the bottom, with his hat off and his pointer, he could be mistaken as Chaplin-ish rather than Hitler. There is a photo of the goose-stepping, saluting dancers midway up, but that is the only hint of something not in "good taste" about the film. The second ad featured a collage of Zero Mostel's face in various expressions from left to right, along with line drawings of images from the film (and even less daring than the first poster). The ad that appeared in the *Pittsburgh Post-Gazette* promoted it on Mostel's name power. Mentioning him as "The Star of *Fiddler on the Roof* . . . the irrepressible clown of *A Funny Thing Happened on the Way to the Forum*." Eventually a third poster was created and used in the nationwide release in March 1968, featuring what appears to be Ulla in a bikini wearing a little Hitler mustache, which has become probably the best known of the early posters for the film and was used on the soundtrack album.

Cover for the soundtrack album, featuring additional artwork used on one of the movie posters produced at the time.

Brooks recalled the all-important first showing of the film to the *Philadelphia Daily News*. "We opened here without special billing during an unseasonable cold spell. It was 18 degrees outside and there were 51 people in the house. You can imagine how discouraged I felt at my debut as a director, and after spending three years on the work." "Nobody laughed," Glazier recalled to *Billboard* years later. "Joe Levine turned to me and said, 'You and Brooks are full of shit. Stick this picture up your ass!'" Before walking out, Levine looked closely at a bag lady still sitting in the theater, then pointed to her and yelled back to Brooks and Glazier, "Look, even she fell asleep!"

The reviews the next day helped, however. The worst came by way of Daniel Webster at the *Philadelphia Inquirer*, who said the film "missed its calling," but still begrudgingly stated that it was "Not one for the ages, but amusing while you are watching it." Sandra Saunders over at the *Philadelphia Daily News* praised the film, finding even what she saw as the predictable backfiring of the scheme "nothing but riotous." The same with the *Detroit Free Press*, and all three reviews were used in early ads for the film.

Back in New York, Brooks went to see Levine about the marketing. Levine told him that he shouldn't expect to see much being done for it, and there were still concerns that the movie should be pulled altogether to save what money would be wasted on promoting it, as Brooks recounted to the Directors Guild. "We're not going to go crazy on this. We're going to be kind of conservative," he told Brooks. Brooks replied in a sarcastic manner, "What is that? You're going to spend about $200 on marketing?" Levine replied in all honesty, "No, no, you can double or triple that." But the reviews helped, and the film continued to run in at least Philadelphia into the Christmas season.

It was clear that Embassy had no idea how to promote the film in any kind of good taste, as can be seen by the hedging made in the posters in 1967. The publicity photos for the film played it even safer. The photo of Dick Shawn in the original press kit was not that of him as LSD, but rather in a tuxedo, most probably one of his nightclub headshots. Gene Wilder's solo photo is much the same—obviously of a slightly younger man and no suggestion of the panic-stricken Bloom from the film. It may have made it easier for Embassy, but it did little to help get across the type of madness that was in the film itself.

Then in January, Peter Sellers came back into the picture. In Los Angeles to film *I Love You, Alice B. Toklas!*, Sellers went to a party held by writer Paul Mazursky where the order of the night was to eat some pasta, get relaxed through various means on hand, and watch Fellini's *I Vitelloni*. The dinner was fine, and so were the other means, but Sellers didn't want to see *I Vitelloni*, which was just as well as they didn't have the print. They did have *The Producers*, however, and ran that instead. Sellers loved the movie so much that he called Levine to tell him, and—perhaps knowing that Levine didn't think much of it—paid for a large ad in the daily versions of *Variety* and *The Hollywood Reporter*, promoting it. While calling it "the ultimate film," Sellers praised Brooks for showing "true genius in weaving together tragedy-comedy, comedy-tragedy, pity, fear, hysteria, schizophrenia, inspired madness and a largess of lunacy with sheer magic." If Sellers recalled being asked by Brooks to be in the movie, he didn't let on in the ad at least.

Brooks was happy with the attention, as stated in his DVD commentary for the film, but in retrospect felt it may have hurt the film as well. "It was about to open in England [October 9, 1969], and he took out a double-page ad in the Sunday *Times* that said, 'This is the funniest and the best picture ever made.' The critics said, 'Hmm, we'll be the judges of that, thank you.' So I got good and bad reviews because they decided that they would judge it for themselves and not just take Peter Sellers' word for it." One thing that did come out of it was that Sellers sold Levine on the idea of renaming the movie back to *Springtime for Hitler* just as it was about to open in New York. With advertising already up, the idea was quickly nixed, except in some foreign territories where it was released much later.

The film eventually leaked out to a handful of theaters around the country, and did well in New York when released on March 18, 1968—running nearly a year there—and L.A. and Chicago on March 27, 1968. *In Cold Blood, Planet of the Apes,* and *Wait Until Dark* were playing or just about to open in theaters at the time. Yet the movie never did well in its first-run release through the middle of the country, where interest in how the entertainment industry—in particular Broadway—worked was very low. Brooks understood, as he reflected to *Vanity Fair.* "I mean, it played in the big cities, but would people in Kansas understand about raising 1,000 percent to put on a Broadway show?"

The film would slowly make its way around the world starting in the United Kingdom in October 1969, and then moving through some parts of Europe in the 1970s. When released in Sweden on May 4, 1970, it was titled *Springtime for Hitler* and did so well that most of Mel Brooks's other films would be released as *Springtime for ____* (e.g., *Springtime for the Sheriff, Springtime for Frankenstein, Springtime for the Silent Movies,* etc.). The film was finally seen in West Germany in May 1976.

Reviews of the film were mixed. Many praised parts of it; Roger Ebert called it "one of the funniest movies ever made," and Gene Shalit said, "No one will be seated in the last 88 minutes of *The Producers,* they'll all be rolling around on the floor." But several critics had issues with the homosexual jokes, finding them distasteful, and of course questioning the use of Hitler for comedy. Brooks, however, always brings up Renata Adler's review from the *New York Times* (March 19, 1968) as being the harshest he ever faced. Adler felt Mostel was "gross and unfunny as only an enormous comedian bearing down too hard on some frail tasteless routines can be." She also said that having the audience catch on in the Broadway theater and thus making the show a hit was a big mistake, feeling it let the air out of the audience watching the movie with her. But even so, overall Adler—like many critics who split hairs—was rather positive about the film. She admits that although she had issues with it, due to its bad taste, she could not leave the theater. She says at the end of her review, "On the whole, though, *The Producers* leaves one alternately picking up one's coat to leave and sitting back to laugh."

The film continued to build momentum, eventually leading to Brooks being nominated for Best Original Screenplay and Gene Wilder for Best Supporting Actor. Although Wilder would not win—losing to Jack Albertson, his later costar in *Willy Wonka and the Chocolate Factory,* for *The Subject Was Roses*—Brooks won for Best Original Screenplay, which surprised him, as he figured he had no chance against *The Battle of Algiers* and *2001: A Space Odyssey*. He would bound up onstage and thank Glazier, Levine, Mostel, and Wilder, and Wilder, and Wilder, but his cowriter Alfa-Betty Olsen got no recognition in the speech. Brooks would instead run a half-page ad in the April 21, 1969, edition of *Variety*, thanking Olsen for her work on the script and the film and thereafter commonly referred to her as the coauthor of the script.

The script won the Writers Guild of America award for Best Original Screenplay, and in 1996 the film was selected for preservation in the National Film Registry by the Library of Congress. It also led to a Broadway musical version, but more about that later. The film saw a profit by 1969, earning a little over $1.6 million by that point. Brooks, feeling that he probably could get a little bit of money out of the film, went to see Levine. Brooks said in an interview with Larry King, "You know, I'd like to see the books, Joe. I haven't seen them." Levine said that he had no problem with Brooks looking at them. "I checked very carefully where we could [see the books]. The books were in Fairbanks, Alaska. That's where he kept them. . . . The plane fare would wipe out whatever I'm going to make."

So it appears the scheme of *The Producers* was really not that far from the truth.

Reflections

There's Hitler taking it on the chin from Brooks, but let's face the fact that the film is not so much a hate letter to Hitler as an indictment of Broadway. Most of our movie memories of "putting on a show" before *The Producers* dealt with white-bread, clean-cut people trying earnestly to put on entertainment for the masses. Even in the most bitter dramas about the stage, there was always the virtuous attitude that "the show must go on" and the sun will come out tomorrow for our heroes. It was New York via Hollywood—with music leading to fantasy, goodness, bright lights, and the ability for everyone to join together in happy song and dance.

The Producers could only have come out of New York and only from a group of people who had seen the flops, the wrecks who were once famous stars, and the no-talents that seemingly get work through luck. It's in the tone of not only the characters but the costumes and scenery. It has been mentioned that Brooks wanted yellow in the film (he supposedly found it a funny color), and you do see a lot of it, but most of this world is ultimately brown and gray. Nothing looks like it should be touched for very long as it reeks of something nasty; and even De Bris's place—which is obviously showing the director as doing better than Bialystock at that point—looks cluttered and mismanaged. There are only three really "clean" moments in the film: Bloom at the fountain, the trial scene, and the musical number. Even that—the "Springtime for Hitler" number—is not of typical Hollywood gloss for a musical number: It's too bright, the seams show, the dancers are sometimes out of step, and the costumes on the women coming down the stairs are shown in shocking close-up to be obviously cheap and ill-formed, more fitting for a burlesque than the Great White Way.

Some critics complained about Brooks using medium shots and close-ups in the movie, but it works to his advantage here: we need to be too close. We need to be uncomfortable. Because in doing so, it allows us to sympathize with Bloom and Bialystock. We want out of the filth just as much as they do.

But what sometimes gets lost in the shuffle over the placement of the camera is the performances Brooks gets out of his stars—especially Zero Mostel. Mostel always worked best on the stage because he was a performer who was so powerful only the stage could hold him. In some ways, he was the equivalent for Brooks of seeing Ethel Merman blow out the back of the theaters when he was kid—the world created within the camera could hardly ever contain her, and the same with Mostel. It is only in worlds other than the here and now that he really came to life because he always seems otherworldly, and yet Brooks beats him down just enough to make him believable within this world of Max and Leo. Wilder may have been bewildered (no pun intended . . . or am I having a De Bris moment?) by Brooks saying he cast the film with people who were the parts, but it is clear that Brooks pretty much wound the players up and let them go. And they trusted him enough to let themselves go under his guidance. Anyone playing too close to the ground or too over the top would have ruined the film—Dick Shawn comes the closest to tipping the film over, but he just manages to stay in check—and that's to Brooks's credit as a director.

As to the characters, the only honest men in the film are the two crooked producers and the Nazi who wrote the play. Bloom and Bialystock know everyone else is out to get something they can't quite grasp but that they can see. De Bris talks and talks about doing something dramatic without a bunch of showgirls, but can't stop going right into the hack clichés of the musical when only slightly pushed by Bialystock. The players are in a serious musical, but immediately play up to the crowd and turn it into a comedy when they see the tide turning in the audience. The critic is delighted at being given the best seat in the house, but then insulted that such an under-the-table bribe is followed up with an obvious one.

The biggest contempt, however, is for the audience. Everyone is shocked, as they should be . . . until they are convinced that they should be laughing instead. The only honest member of the audience is the one guy applauding at the end of the musical number, and he is physically attacked for liking such a ghastly thing. Then again, who could suspect otherwise? The show is called *Springtime for Hitler*, announced as a musical, and the poster has flowers on it like some mock-hippy concert poster. This is an audience wanting to be the first to hate Bialystock's latest failure, and Brooks would play more with that concept in the Broadway musical version of the film years later. Bialystock knows they want crap, and so gives it to them.

The turnaround is when LSD starts goofing and the cast joins in. Admittedly, Renata Adler was not too far off base—the moment can feel like a letdown for viewers, but mostly because we know it most probably is what would happen. No one wants to be the fool, and they must admit either that they've been duped into seeing a Nazi musical or that they knew they were seeing a comedy making fun of a Nazi all along. Watching the film, we're not so mad at the conclusion made by Brooks, but that the audience did exactly what they probably would have done. That we probably all would have done—followed the masses and conclude we're cool for doing so. Camp is good, as long as we all believe it is camp.

As for Bloom and Bialystock, Brooks has stated that the men are the ego (Bialystock) and the id (Bloom). This isn't too far from the truth, as they are both failures in their own ways until they meet. They accomplish so much together that they form one man. One crazed man, but nevertheless one that gets things done. But there's something else here as well. Bloom is a boy—he has a blankie and is shocked by everything shown to him by Bialystock. Bialystock is a veteran of the theater who has seen it all and is sick of it, but can't escape from the dream of having one last shot at a big success and proving everyone wrong. The money isn't so much the thing for Bialystock (although he says so); it's the ability to flaunt that he is right. That his show is good and that he is loved.

Bloom is the nine-year-old Brooks, going to his first show and falling in love with theater. Bialystock is the forty-year-old Brooks, having seen one promising Broadway show after another not only flop, but be critically savaged and written off by the audiences. Who wouldn't at some point just want to blow up the theater and be done with it all?

There's more than one way to interpret Bialystock's middle finger standing up in a salute during the ending trial. *The Producers* is a love letter to Broadway, straight through the heart.

9

Tito Has the Car

The Twelve Chairs

Release Date: World premiere, October 28, 1970, through UMC Pictures

Hitler References

None. Well, it is set in 1927 Soviet Union.

Musical Moment

One—the theme song

Pre-production

Brooks left *The Producers* with mixed feelings. He had gotten his dream project done, but at a cost to his health and for little reward. "I wasn't making big bucks: I made $25,000 for *The Producers*, which wasn't a success at first," Brooks told *Tablet* magazine in 2016. The Oscar win was still in the future in the summer of 1968, but at least his film was getting some mileage in theaters, and it looked like it was at least going to cover its cost.

Still, feeling a bit like the bridges he meant to build with his first film got blown up as thoroughly as the ones he saw back in World War II, Brooks was unsure if another directing job would be down the pike. Which was a shame, as he had an idea for his next movie that would be another pet project from his past. Then, out of the blue, he heard from Sidney Glazier in early August 1968, telling him that he was planning to turn the Universal-Marion Corporation into a company that made and distributed films instead of making deals for other companies. Moreover, Glazier wanted to work with Brooks again and promised to get him at least $1.5 million to make another movie for him.

The idea came from a book Brooks had read when he was fifteen called *The Twelve Chairs*, also known as *Diamonds to Sit On*, written by Ilya Ilf and Yevgeni Petrov (commonly referred to as Ilf and Petrov) in 1928. "It's all greed, naked greed.," Brooks once reflected about the book. "But what is the treasure? Is it really diamonds or is it love?" He elaborated on this in a 1970 interview with Sheilah Graham: "All our conditioning tells us that the prize is gold and jewels, when we all know that the prize is love. In the end, when the aristocrat grabs the last chair, and hurls it away, and when the con man stays with him, you feel they have both learned something about love." The novel is comedic in many ways, but gets more serious as it goes along and ends in a rather disturbing denouement: Vorobyaninov gets paranoid and slits Bender's throat in his sleep before reaching the final chair. The novel ends with him going helplessly

Poster for a 1983 reissue of *The Twelve Chairs*, which included the animated *2000 Year Old Man* special that had been shown on CBS television in 1975.

insane when he discovers that the jewels are gone and he had killed his friend for nothing. (It should be noted that a sequel book eventually was written by the two authors, featuring Bender having survived the attack and going on to future solo adventures in search of money and a chance to escape the Soviet Union.)

The novel had been made into several movies before Brooks got to it in 1968, most famously in the United States as the Fred Allen/Jack Benny 1945 comedy, *It's in the Bag!* (featuring just five chairs); and in 1969, an Italian version featuring Sharon Tate, Terry-Thomas, Tim Brooke-Taylor, and Orson Welles was released called *12 + 1*. Brooks's film, however, goes back to the original source and characters instead of modernizing them as in the two films cited. As with nearly all of the others, Brooks also wrote a happier ending for the film than in the novel, although he does at least allow Vorobyaninov the opportunity to become violently unstable for a brief moment. By August 1968, the announcement appeared in *Variety* that U-M was to make Brooks's next movie, *The Twelve Chairs*.

Cast

Ron Moody (1924–2015) as Ippolit Matveyevich Vorobyaninov

Brooks had struck up a friendship with actor Frank Langella, who had worked with Anne Bancroft from November 1968 through February 1969 in the play *A Cry of Players* (see chapter 7), and Brooks used this opportunity to discuss with the actor who could work as Vorobyaninov in the film. Attempts were made to interest Alastair Sim, Peter Sellers—who would also be considered for the role of the priest, which Dom DeLuise eventually played—and Albert Finney, but those who were interested couldn't fit it into their schedules. Langella had an idea, however. "I took Mel to see the film of *Oliver*," he told the *Los Angeles Times* years later. As he pointed at the actor playing Fagin in the film, Ron Moody, Langella said, "There's your Vorobyaninov."

Moody was a British stage actor who had done some comedy films in the late 1950s/early 1960s, such as *Summer Holiday* (1963) with Cliff Richard and *The Mouse on the Moon* (also 1963). Then in 1960 he starred as Fagin in the original West End production of *Oliver!*, Lionel Bart's musical version of Charles Dickens's *Oliver Twist*. The show was a hit, with Moody getting some choice material to perform, and he would go on to do the role on Broadway in 1963, as well as the 1968 movie adaptation. He would also reprise the role in 1985 on Broadway, earning a Tony nomination.

It was a brilliant role for the actor, but, he felt, one that was quickly getting him typecast. When Brooks offered him the role of Vorobyaninov, Moody jumped at the chance. And signed on for the role in March 1969. Anything to get away from having to be stuck in the nineteenth century for the rest of his career. True, the jump was only to 1927, but still it was a character that was different than Fagin and a comedy—which suited his talents—to boot. Brooks

Frank Langella and Ron Moody, the stars of *The Twelve Chairs*.

was surprised, but happy, as he told the *Los Angeles Times* in 1970. "He turned down literally hundreds of $20 million pictures, all those Cromwellian things, to do this. He's one of the finest actors that the world has produced. He starts slow, like Silky Sullivan, building character, and finishes two lengths ahead of everybody else." Stories told since say that Moody was offered the part of Doctor Who that summer in 1969, but passed on it to do *The Twelve Chairs* instead. He would later tell others that he regretted passing on the role, albeit not because of anything to do with Brooks's film.

Moody would continue to work in films and television, but his career in some ways peaked with *Oliver!* He died in 2015.

Frank Langella (born 1938) as Ostap Bender

As stated above, Brooks met Langella when he was costarring in *A Cry for Players* with Anne Bancroft. Brooks looked to Langella for advice on actors for the film, but no one could be found to fill the role of Bender, the con artist. "We would sit around and throw out names." Langella remembered later. "I wasn't lusting after a film career at that point. I was doing theater work and loving it. Finally, he just said, 'Oh the hell with it. You do it,' which is not the way you get parts."

After *The Twelve Chairs*, he filmed *Diary of a Mad Housewife* for Frank Perry (although the Perry film was shot second, it was released first). He has bounced from stage to screen to television, and probably is still best remembered for his Broadway (1977) and film (1979) role as Dracula. He also won a Tony playing

Richard Nixon in the production *Frost/Nixon* in 2007 and once again reprised a role from Broadway in the subsequent film adaptation. *The Twelve Chairs* would be the only film that Langella did for Brooks.

Dom DeLuise (1933–2009) as Father Fyodor

Dom DeLuise was born to Italian immigrants and went to the High School of Performing Arts in Manhattan. In 1961, he began appear in off-Broadway musicals and comedies, finally moving up to Broadway in 1963, while starting to appear in movies (his appearance as an inept technician in *Fail-Safe* from 1964 is one of the few dramatic parts he would play over the years). A standard gig as one of the costars on the CBS series *The Entertainers* in 1964 led to him becoming a regular on *The Dean Martin Show* and finally a summer replacement series of his own in 1968. In 1969, Anne Bancroft and Mel Brooks were watching *The Dean Martin Show* when Bancroft suggested Brooks contact DeLuise about the role of the wayward priest for *The Twelve Chairs.*

Ron Moody and Dom DeLuise fight over one of *The Twelve Chairs.* The film would be DeLuise's first with Brooks, a partnership that would continue off and on up through *Robin Hood: Men in Tights* (1993).

Arriving at a bungalow at the Beverly Hills Hotel for the interview, DeLuise was surprised to find that four and a half hours would go by as they talked about their shared past of growing up in New York, Broadway, and other things. As they were wrapping up, Brooks said, "Peter Sellers is supposed to play the part of Father Fyodor, but even if he does, we'll be friends forever." Soon after, Dom got a call from Brooks telling him that Sellers wasn't going to do it, so the job was open to him. DeLuise asked about the salary and was told $15,000. "I said, 'A week?' he said, 'No, for the whole movie.' I said, "You want me to leave my home for $15,000 to go to a place called Yugoslavia?' . . . He said, 'Yeah, that's what it is.' I said, 'I'll do it.' It was the smallest salary I ever made."

It would also be the closest to the biggest role DeLuise would have in one of Brooks's movies. He acted in five other films for Brooks, but except for costarring in *Silent Movie*, all his other appearances—*Blazing Saddles*, *History of the World, Part I*, *Spaceballs*, and *Robin Hood: Men in Tights*—are extended cameos. DeLuise would also appear in Gene Wilder's *The Adventure of Sherlock Holmes' Smarter Brother* (1975), *The World's Greatest Lover* (1977), and *Haunted Honeymoon*, while also starring in Anne Bancroft's one directorial feature, *Fatso* (1980). He became quite well known for appearing in a number of Burt Reynolds films as well, including the two *Cannonball Run* films and the excellent dark comedy *The End* (1978). He also had a small cameo in the Michael Hertzberg–produced (and John Morris–orchestrated) comedy *Johnny Dangerously* (1984), which features numerous other Brooks alumni before and behind the camera.

When DeLuise passed away in 2009, Brooks stated that he "created so much joy and laughter on the set that you couldn't get your work done. So every time I made a movie with Dom, I would plan another two days on the schedule just for laughter."

Andreas Voutsinas (1930–2010) as Nikolai Sestrin

Voutsinas had appeared in *The Producers* for Brooks in 1967. He'll return one more time in *History of the World, Part I*.

Mel Brooks as Tikon

Supporting actor who slept with the director's wife.

Mel Brooks in his featured role as Tikon in *The Twelve Chairs*. Several critics mentioned that Brooks's appearance was one of the best things about the film. It would convince him to expand his roles in his later movies.

Also Appearing

The rest of the cast was divided between actors from the United Kingdom and from Yugoslavia. One of the best remembered is Diana Couplan (1928–2006), who played Madam Bruns and costarred with Sidney James in *Bless This House* (Thames Television, 1971–1976; theatrical film 1972). The other is Nicholas Smith (1934–2015), who appears as an actor in a play, within the film, and was Mr. Cuthbert Rumbold in the various *Are You Being Served?* series over the years. At one point Hermione Gingold (*The Music Man*, 1962) was asked to be in the film, but she turned it down, as reported by Leonard Lyons in 1969, "because for six weeks I'd have to lay off—or is it lie off—in Yugoslavia." The length of time she mentioned suggest she was first offered the role of Madam Bruns before Diana Couplan.

In the Crew

As mentioned in the previous chapters, Michael Hertzberg moved from assistant director to producer for this film, while Alan Heim jumped from sound editing on *The Producers* to film editing on this one. John Morris contributed the music and worked with Brooks on the opening song, "Hope for the Best (Expect the Worst)," with the lyrics and most of the melody already put together by Brooks. Jonathan Tunick (born 1938), who was the orchestrator on this film, would go on to do the same chore on *Blazing Saddles* and *Young Frankenstein*.

Production

The script was written by Mel Brooks, with Alfa-Betty Olsen once again helping to type it up and offer suggestions. Olsen also helped with the casting of the film, as Brooks himself has mentioned in many interviews.

Filming started on August 25 in Belgrade, Yugoslavia (now Serbia), where Glazier had made a deal to get equipment and technicians in an area that could pass for the Soviet Union of 1927 for much less than if they had shot in America, and with no union restrictions. "For $450,000," Brooks stated in 1997 to the *Los Angeles Times*, "we got everything—cameras, soldiers, and extras. There was no time limit. They wanted to keep as many of their film people busy, so we had a crew of about 1,000 milling around. I felt like David Lean filming *Lawrence of Arabia*." Brooks exaggerated the number of crew members involved—it was actually closer to eighty—but the film people were excited to participate in an American film.

There was one major incident during shooting, however, which involved the crew revolting, and it was another tale of Brooks's anger under stress getting the better of him. While filming a scene at the shores of the Black Sea where Dom DeLuise destroys a set of chairs (as his character is trying to find the jewels that he thinks are in one of them), Brooks got upset over a delay. "I got really mad at something, a camera broke, or I was just frustrated. My nerves were really just charred. I was burnt out." Grabbing one of the chairs, Brooks picked it up and hurled it off a dock into the water. As one, the crew walked out on Brooks, disappearing. He was confused as to what had happened until a representative for the crew came to tell him, as he recalled in his Directors Guild interview, "Comrade Brooks, we are not working until you apologize for throwing the People's chair into the Black Sea." Brooks at first was livid, telling the representative, "It's my chair. Not the People's. I can do what I want with it." Finally, realizing he was losing a day's worth of shooting over something he caused, Brooks met with the crew and humbly apologized "for being so stupid." He then showed that he had fished the chair out of the sea so everyone would know it was not lost for good.

Everyone happily accepted his apology, but they ended up not filming anymore that day for that very reason. "I heard the word 'vijnak,' which is their word for cognac. That happened at 3:00 and I lost the rest of the day because we all kissed each other and drank vijnak until we were throwing up on the floor."

The main downside to the filming was not the crew, but the location itself, as it was an area depressed and without many of the modern conveniences people in America had gotten used to, as Langella remembered. "We lived in a hotel where everything was rewired. If you picked up a phone, the lights shut off. But we were all together the whole time. We were a very tight, happy family. That's an overused phrase, but it's true." For years, Brooks himself would joke about the experience, saying, "I learned one cardinal rule of filmmaking from *The Twelve Chairs*: never shoot a film in Belgrade Yugoslavia. The whole town is illuminated by a 20-watt night light and there's nothing to do. You can't even go for a drive as Tito [Josip Bronz Tito, the president of the country] is always using the car." Brooks also had to face the wrath of people in the city who "had to miss *Bonanza* for a week when they had to remove the TV antennas from their rooftops" in order to make the scenery authentic.

DeLuise, on the other hand, loved the time there and would frequently bypass taking a taxi to see the dailies in order to pay two-cents for use of the city's trolley system. "Mel said, 'You're gonna get killed. You're gonna get killed. . . . You shouldn't be on these public trams.'" Dom felt doing the film was "the experience of a lifetime, because you just would be inventing stuff with Mel. You went to work every day. Mel said, 'We're not using you today.' You would come [anyway] . . . no matter who was in the scene, you were there." Relief from boredom also came with periodic visits from Anne Bancroft to be with Mel, while Dom's wife ventured overseas for a couple of the weeks to see Dom. Plus, although Brooks joked about being stuck there for the filming, when reminiscing about the film in 1977 to the *Chicago Tribune*, he admitted enjoying the chance to visit the homeland of his family. "I felt like I had come home. There are Russian textures of that in the film. Eating black bread. The shot of the borscht with the dollop of sour cream. I went there and said to myself, 'Ah, it's not Brooklyn: It's Kiev!'"

Principal photography continued until just before Christmas 1969; four months of hard work, especially for Mel. "In one scene," Langella reported, "I was supposed to row a boat through the moon's reflection on the water. But the arc kept moving so it appeared the moonlight was following us. Once we got so far out to sea that they couldn't find us. At 3 in the morning, Mel jumped into the water to swim out to find us." And with that enthusiasm, Brooks expected the same from his cast and crew. One day during shooting, he asked DeLuise—who had previous butted a wall of rock because Brooks told him to for a shot—to grab a chair and run up a hill. DeLuise had the choice of a chair made of mahogany or one made of balsawood and grabbed the balsawood one because it was lighter. Brooks balked, saying that the other would look better. DeLuise mentioned that he didn't think he could get up the hill with the heavy mahogany chair, and offered an alternative. "I could pick up the chair and you take a picture. I'll put the chair down." Brooks got into DeLuise's face and said, "Get the fucking chair and go up the hill!" DeLuise suggested what Brooks could do with the chair and a screaming match commenced, until DeLuise finally grabbed the mahogany chair and ran up the hill with it just as Brooks wanted. Yet, by the end of the day, the friendship and camaraderie was strong enough that, "We'd all go home, take a shower; go out to dinner, and we would scream with laughter about the day . . . even though I said, 'Fuck you, I'm not doing that!' and he'd say, 'Pick it up!'"

In January 1970, Brooks began editing the film with Alan Heim. And, as with *The Producers*, Brooks would spend months in the editing room trying to make the film perfect. "I never did what a lot of directors do," Brooks said in an interview with the Directors Guild of America in 2012. "They say, 'Well, throw it together and let me take a look and then I'll re-edit it, and we'll work together.' I would say, 'Give me everything you've got: outtakes, the works, everything you've got.' And I'd look at it all and spend a couple of days not editing, just looking. Running it through in my head."

Backend

Initial talks were to release the film in June 1970, but that was later changed to a kickoff in five cities in September. That too fell through, and it was finally sneaked into New York around October 20, and then it had its world premiere on October 28 in New York and Los Angeles. From there, the film would be released in various parts of the country over the next few months, reaching a high of sixty-eight screens by January 1971. It would continue to be shuffled around the nation through August 1971, sometimes paired with another U-M feature, Gene Wilder's *Quackser Fortune Has a Cousin in the Bronx*, or with Normal Lear's *Cold Turkey*. Oddly, the film was initially given a GP (what became PG in 1972) by the Motion Picture Association of America, due to a very mild sex scene that showed Langella on top of a woman, both fully clothed. Glazier argued the rating with the board, and *The Twelve Chairs* would be changed on December 16, 1970, from GP to G—the first film to get a reversal requested on a GP determination. Playing in theaters around the time of *The Twelve Chairs* release in the winter of 1970 were: *The Owl and the Pussycat* (with a screenplay by Buck Henry); *Tora, Tora, Tora*; *Love Story*; Carl Reiner's *Where's Poppa?*; Billy Wilder's *The Private Life of Sherlock Holmes*; and *Joe* (starring Peter Boyle).

The first poster featured whimsical artwork with Vorobyaninov holding on to a flying chair, as Bender and Fyodor hang on to him as best they can. Other chairs are seen floating up in the background, as jewels cascade around the characters. It is a striking piece of artwork, but suggests the film is about magical, flying chairs, which may explain why it was soon replaced with a poster showing DeLuise and Moody fighting over a chair, along with Bender and Vorobyaninov in the background and DeLuise again, far in the background, dressed as a peasant woman holding one of the chairs. It's uniquely chaotic and represents no particular scene in the film, but is good for a poster. The poster contains a number of review quotes, claiming *The Twelve Chairs* to be "one of the funniest films in years," "a complete joy," and "a comedy gem," amongst other quotes. When the film was reissued to theaters in 1983 by United Artists—as a Brooksfilm—the poster art was changed to one of DeLuise about to destroy a chair, while Brooks and Langella appear in front of them, and with Moody nowhere to be seen. The 1983 reissue also featured the 1975 *The 2000 Year Old Man* special from CBS as an added attraction.

The 1970 poster naturally would list positive review quotes, but not all were that way; many felt the tone of the movie was not consistent. Charles Champlin, in the *Los Angeles Times*, said that the film "does not sustain itself as slapstick and does not really define any kind of evolving relationship between the two men," even with the ending in place where the two work together in a con. Lloyd Ibert, for *Independent Film Journal*, felt "None of the actors involved give subtle or even shaded performances; they have been encouraged to bulldoze their way through. A lighter tone might have been funnier." R. J. Gardner in the *Baltimore Sun* was relentless: "*The Twelve Chairs* . . . has the advantage of uniformity. It's all bad."

But while some critics grumbled over the pacing, many were positive about the performances—some even went so far as to suggest that Brooks as an actor was the best thing in the film, leading to him saying that if he had known the outcome with audiences over his role, he would have extended it to be like a Sancho Panza-type helper to the other two characters. Many critics felt that at worst the movie had enough good moments to make the slower material worth sitting through. One of the first positive reviews came from Groucho Marx, who was quoted as coming out of a sneak preview of the film stating, "All the people who liked the Marx Brothers will like this." Roger Ebert gave the film four stars, saying "Mel Brooks has grown as a director since *The Producers*," and feeling that the comedy is used "as a tool for examining the human condition."

Tom Green of *The Sam Bernardino County Sun* said, "The performances of the trio are just beautiful. DeLuise is hilarious just being DeLuise. I think you'll enjoy the whole thing."

Glazier and Brooks went into the film hoping to promote the project as a follow-up to the Oscar-winning *The Producers* and with the well-known Ron Moody, plus with good word of mouth by critics overall. Dom DeLuise also did some solo promotions around the country, as did Brooks on various talk shows to help support the film after its release, although in some cases long before it was actually in some parts of the country. Yet, even with all that buildup, the film performed only so-so at the box office. There were a few awards, though: Brooks was nominated by the Writers Guild of America for the script (Best Comedy Adapted from Another Medium). Frank Langella won a National Board of Review award for Best Supporting Actor, but it was for *Diary of a Mad Housewife*, rather than for *The Twelve Chairs*.

Brooks came out of *The Twelve Chairs* stuck in what has traditionally been called a sophomore slump. *The Producers* may have started off rocky, but by 1971 had earned close to $5 million, thanks to the Oscar and continual interest in it; *The Twelve Chairs* had some fans, but not the momentum to keep it going. Some websites have the film making only $162,000, but that's based on a reissue back in 2002, not on the initial box office. Instead, it finally paid itself off after appearing and reappearing over the years in theaters and on video, but it was not the hit that UMC needed at the time (nor were many of their other releases). UMC would only survive into 1971 before folding, with Sidney Glazier moving on to other things. It would be his last film with Brooks.

As for Brooks, he was beginning to wonder if perhaps his luck had run out as a writer-director. Little did he know that an oddball script from a new writer dealing with a 1970s black man in an 1870s western was about to change the direction of his career forever.

Reflections

If you come into *The Twelve Chairs* after seeing Mel Brooks's films from *Blazing Saddles* onward, or even having just seen *The Producers*—as the critics did in 1968—*The Twelve Chairs* doesn't feel like it is coming from the same director. There are no gross gags, the violence is increasingly realistic (Vorobyaninov's slapping of Tikon is played for laughs early on, but when he slaps Bender, he gets a punch in the gut that sends him to the ground in agony), and the one mild sex scene may have a punch line, but it's not the outrageousness of "Little Old Lady Land" in *The Producers* or Lili von Shtupp of *Blazing Saddles*. Beyond the undercranked scenes involving Dom DeLuise being chased, the film is more realistic than most of the others in Brooks's catalogue. Of course, the jokes are there, but milder and more in connection with the characters than for the sake of slapstick. For example, Vorobyaninov may absentmindedly stamp "cancelled" on his mother-in-law's cheek, but it is obviously an accident, and—cleverly—sets up the time and place for our story without having to do it in the narrative, or with a caption. (Albeit, to have a stamp that has the date built into the rubber seems like a waste of money, but the gag would not make any sense otherwise.) Moody's Vorobyaninov is a man slowly going insane with his obsession with the chairs, and his bitterness in the palace at the end that results in howls and destruction—as close as Brooks could get to the insanity of the character in the novel—may be funny, but is genuine and understandable as well.

It doesn't all quite work. As one critic in 1970 suggested, the film is a series of red lights and green lights, with every laugh-line being followed by stretches of story with little humor. Yet, every time the film seems to stall, the action is there to lead us into another brilliant sequence. The circus scene seems disjointed and almost unnecessary, but it gets us to the funny concluding chase with Fyodor sealing his fate. Langella may appear to be too laid-back to really make one want to sympathize with his character, but ultimately, he becomes the audience's eyes and the voice of reason when Vorobyaninov becomes crazed in the final quarter of the film. Bender punching Vorobyaninov seems a bit out of left field and even a bit spiteful, but is necessary to set up the ending that is to come.

Yet such quibbles do not detract from the kinetic center of the movie. We as viewers may be thrown because it's not like other Brooks films—one goes in almost expecting a parody of Bergman's films or other heavy European dramas that filled the art houses in the 1960s and 1970s (just as Woody Allen would do with *Love and Death* in 1975), but Brooks isn't interested in giving us that. This is the story from the novel—with a few added gags, but essentially the characters and plot that he fell in love with when he first read it at the age of fifteen. Moreover, in many ways, it shows a deeper understanding of the culture than would be expected from an American writer-director. *Love and Death* may be a funny film, but it's poking fun at what Americans know of the clichés from such films it is parodying. Brooks is dealing more with the struggle, the hardships, the degradation that can find people unhappily accepting their fate because it's all they have, such as the way we can be programmed to think of a "greater good" that involves making palaces for the state instead of helping the people.

Brooks has called *The Twelve Chairs* one of his three personal favorites of his films (the other two are *The Producers* and *Life Stinks*). That may be because all three films say something personally about Brooks and where his heart is. He has also said more than once that if *The Twelve Chairs* had done better, his future projects probably would have gone in a different direction than they would have once *Blazing Saddles* came along and jump-started his career. *The Producers* was a look at his past. *Life Stinks* is a peek into his future. *The Twelve Chairs* is a glimpse into his soul. Even so, as Brooks reflected in his 2012 interview with the Directors Guild, "If I didn't have a hit with *Blazing Saddles*, I probably would have gone another way and not even been known."

10

You'd Do It for Randolph Scott

Release Date: World premiere on February 6, 1974, at the Pickwick Drive-In in Burbank, California

Hitler References

Two. The Germans raising the wrong hand when pledging to Hedley, and the actor in the commissary who is going to be out of a job after the bunker scene. Extra credit for Lili making a German spectacle of herself and her sing-along with the soldiers, but that's more to do with the character than with Nazis.

Musical Moments

Five, with snippets of others ("I Get a Kick Out of You"/"Camptown Ladies," "Randolph Scott," Lili singing to the German soldiers). Missing is a scripted appearance by Tony Martin singing "Tenement Symphony."

- Theme Song, written by Mel Brooks and sung by Frankie Lane
- "The Ballad of Rock Ridge," sung by the townspeople in church
- "April in Paris" by Count Basie and His Orchestra
- "I'm Tired," sung by Lili von Shtupp
- "The French Mistake," with Buddy Bizarre and the Boys

Pre-production

There's always television," Mel Brooks was fond of saying, when things looked bleak after *The Twelve Chairs* was released to some enthusiastic reviews but saw little revenue at the box office. Plans to follow it up by helping to produce a movie for the husband-wife team of Joseph Bologna and Renee Taylor fell through when Sidney Glazier's UMC went belly up in 1971e. The collapse of UMC also affected Brooks's adaptation of *Conquer*, Oliver Goldsmith's famous comedy from 1773, which he had been wanting to do since seeing an off-Broadway production of it. The movie was to have started filming in September 1971, and then was pushed back to 1972, with a $1.5 million budget, and Brooks had attempted to sign Albert Finney to the project. (He would try to get Finney for *My Favorite Year* in 1981 as well.) As it was, UMC had been hesitant about the film, especially after *The Twelve Chairs* had done poorly. With UMC

John Alvin's famous poster art for *Blazing Saddles*. It would be the first of many Alvin would do for Brooks, and would lead to a long career creating movie posters for Warner, Disney, and many other studios.

gone, Brooks found he had no other option than to put his pet project on the back burner and look for work.

If film work wasn't forthcoming, television at least was interested. A series of commercials for Bic pens (some featuring Richard Dimitri, who would go on to costar in Brooks's short-lived 1975 series *When Things Were Rotten*) were directed by Brooks in the spring of 1972. There was also a pilot for Dom DeLuise being discussed in the fall of 1972, along with Brooks doing voices for animation in the new PBS children series *The Electric Company*, and writing a comedy script about a gay couple in a proposed series called *The People on the Third Floor*. Plus, plenty of guest appearances on talk shows and variety programming to help pay the bills as well, but who wanted to spend the rest of their creative career guesting on talk shows?

As it turns out, such appearance did help Brooks with his main goal, albeit in an indirect way. He had been asked to appear on David Susskind's talk show in November 1970 that featured several other famous Jewish men on the topic of "How to Be a Jewish Son—Or, My Son the Success!" Seeing as *The Twelve Chairs* was about to open, Brooks agreed to do the show, which featured him, along with David Steinberg, George Segal, Larry Goldberg, and Stan Herman. The episode aired on November 29, 1970, and was essentially—and affectionately—known as "The Mel Brooks Show," as Brooks was allowed to pretty much take over the program with quips and stories (including a discussion about "making the Sign of David" that worked its way into the script for his remake of *To Be or Not to Be*). Although there were others there, most were happy to have Brooks take the weight off of them and be the focus on the program, as well as being so funny that the episode was aired once a year as long as Susskind's talk show lasted, leading to renewed interest in the careers of all involved.

"Who knew that this little roundtable interview show, certainly not a great forum for my talent, would be one of the best things I ever did in my life?" Brooks remembered later in a biography about Susskind. "It would launch me as a first-rate comic personality." It certainly helped get him more bookings on television, but better yet interest from Hollywood, which believed perhaps Brooks still had it in him for at least one more film. Being elected to the director's board for the Directors Guild in June 1971 didn't hurt either.

Make no mistake, Brooks was getting offers—he had made two films that came in on budget, with multiple nominations for awards, and with two Oscars on his mom's television set (seriously, for *The Critic* and *The Producers*). His first film was earning profits by 1971, and his second . . . well, it may have done better if by a bigger studio with more promotion behind it. There was no argument: Brooks was bankable, and the studios probably thought they could get his talent for a song now that his sophomore attempt had not done well. The problem for Brooks, however, was that after being able to do it on his own for the first two films, it was not easy to suddenly become the nameless director who did the work needed to push out a studio product. "Warner had wanted me to do a movie for them," Brooks told the *Chicago Tribune*, "and finally I said, 'All right.

Let me think of something. Stop sending me this junk.' They had been sending me about fifty scripts—a lot of marriage comedies, dopey stuff."

Agent David Begelman (1921–1995), at the time working for Creative Management Associates (CMA), saw that Brooks was attracting interest in Hollywood. One day, Begelman ran into Brooks on the streets of New York and asked him to have lunch in order to discuss his career. When Brooks mentioned that Warner was breathing down his neck to direct a movie for them, Begelman remembered a first-draft script that a story editor, Judy Feiffer—at one time married to cartoonist and writer Jules Feiffer—had recently seen. The script was from Andrew Bergman (born 1945), who was working at United Artists in 1970 when he sent his first script to Warner Bros. The script, titled *Tex X*, dealt with all the standard western clichés of the movies and television, but with the difference being a sheriff who was not only African American, but talked as if he was from modern times; Bergman said later that he based the character on voting rights activist H. Rap Brown. Warner bought it and had it on a fast track in 1971 to go before the cameras with James Earl Jones as the sheriff and Alan Arkin directing (Arkin would star in Bergman's second produced script, *The In-Laws*). But then the film never happened, and the script was being pushed around the studio with no takers. Begelman suggested Brooks take a look at it and see if he wanted to do it.

Brooks was hesitant, as appointed by Amanda Erlanson. "I wanted to do what I wanted to do. But I was fast running out of money. . . ." He also wasn't completely sold on the script, except for one aspect of it. Further, as he told the *Chicago Tribune* in 1973, there was only one aspect of the script that he thought worked. "I didn't like a lot of it [the script's plot dealt with the sheriff falling in love with the daughter of the railroad's owner], but I could just see a black sheriff riding into a white town." Brooks took it back to Begelman telling him, "I don't do things that I don't write." Begelman told him to think about how he would approach a rewrite. "This is just a skeletal outline. It's a profile of what it can be. It needs bones and flesh," Begelman told Brooks. Taking the script home with him, Brooks showed it to Bancroft, who loved the general idea and thought he should agree to work on it. If nothing else, it would bring money into the house, which would come in handy now that they had a son, as Max was born in June 1972.

Brooks agreed, but as he told the *Chicago Tribune* in 1973, on the condition "you let me have a couple of Jews and a black man and throw us in a room; we'll write it together like we did the *Show of Shows*." Brooks also wanted to hire Andrew Bergman, the original writer, which was unusual for studios to do. Typically, once a script was bought, it would go to other hands to rewrite, or else you'd end up having the possibility of a prima donna demanding his script not be touched. Brooks went straight to Bergman and asked him if he was okay with them changing his script and would he be willing to help them do exactly that. "I had the choice of saying 'You will not touch my material,' or saying,

'OK.'" Bergman said to *New York* magazine in 1981. "I was 26 at the time, and it was great experience."

Warner paid Brooks $50,000 to put together his writers, with the writers getting smaller salaries to help. Besides Bergman, Brooks brought in a writer named Norman Steinberg (born 1939). Steinberg was a lawyer in Manhattan, working in copyright law, who a few years before had wanted to be a screenwriter. One day at his legal job back in 1969, he happened to spot Brooks at a Chock Full O'Nuts shop across from his office and ran over to introduce himself and bug Brooks about a writing job. Brooks relented and got Steinberg a chance to write a script for *Get Smart* that never got produced due to the show being cancelled. However, it was enough to lead to interest in seeing his work by producers, and eventually he was hired on Flip Wilson's variety program, *Flip*, in 1970. That association led to him meeting up with Richard Pryor (1940–2006) while working on the program. It was Steinberg who suggested bringing in Pryor, as well as a fellow struggling writer working as a dentist, Alan Uger (born 1940).

Pryor, who had been steadily making a name for himself in movies and on television as a comedian and actor, was looking to expand his horizons by trying to get writing jobs. Meanwhile, Brooks and the others felt the main problem in writing the script was, as Bergman put it to Scott Saul, "if you've got three Jews in a room, you're going to be very skittish about writing jokes about a black man—what's permissible, what isn't permissible." Having someone like Pryor, who had a reputation for being outspoken, outrageous in his comedy, and talking directly about race issues, was a perfect way to find the right balance. After two months of writing with just Brooks, Bergman, Uger, and Steinberg, Pryor came in to help work on the script. Surprising to all, Pryor steadily worked on material about Mongo (Brooks credits Pryor for coming up with lines like "Mongo only pawn in game of life"), while the others would write the "black material" and then run it past Pryor to see if it worked or not. "I said, 'I can't say the N-word,' Brooks remembered to Dick Cavett. "I need him—he has to bless it. I need a black guy to bless that word.'" From reports, Pryor was rather laid-back about the material, only showing displeasure with any gag that crossed the line by saying, "You can do that, but it's not funny." The writers enjoyed having his help and writing with him, but it was soon apparent that Pryor was itching to move on to other things. Further, his drinking and drug use on the job—Pryor's initial meeting with the other writers saw him snorting cocaine and then offering some to Brooks, who begged off saying, "Never before lunch"—was a tad too obvious to even people outside of the writers' room and was making some of the studio people nervous.

Pryor stayed for about a month, waiting until a first draft had been put into place, before moving on and on good terms. After all, the consensus in the writers' room was that Pryor had done a lot of heavy lifting on the script for the group, and besides, everyone was sure that Pryor himself would end up playing Bart in the film that was now being called *Black Bart* instead of *Tex X*.

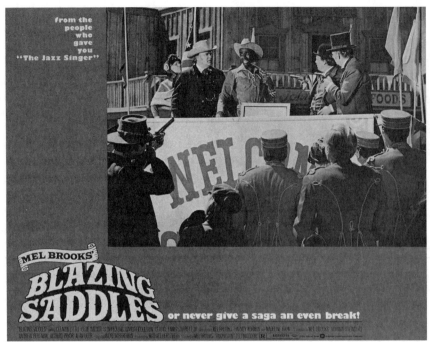

from the
people
who
gave
you
"The Jazz Singer"

MEL BROOKS'
BLAZING SADDLES or never give a saga an even break!

Cleavon Little as Bart, a character created for co-scriptwriter Richard Pryor. Warner refused to hire Pryor, having heard about his drug use and volatile nature. Pryor was involved with the hiring of Little, who was then known for his starring role in the television comedy series *Temperature Rising.*

The first draft was a hefty 412 pages, when a normal script would run about 100–120 pages. The second draft was still too long at 275 pages. Even so, when the second draft was given to the studio, Warner felt it had enough merit to allow for another draft, and the sixth draft would end up the final script.

With a script that was so large being reduced, obviously, some gags caused concern that the writers might be going too far. The campfire scene where all the cowboys pass various sound levels of gas was a first for American films, but it worked because it pricked at the western cliché of men sitting around a campfire after riding horses all day managing to shovel beans and black coffee into their stomach and yet not have any gastric issues. Although some animal-rights viewers protested the punching of the horse by Mongo, Brooks could back that up from having heard of Sid Caesar once doing so in a fit of anger after a horse on the streets of New York nipped at his wife; not to mention that the horse was trained to take such a fall and the punch was faked, so there were no injuries to the horse or to Alex Karras's hand from doing the gag. Still, Brooks was worried about some of the other material in the movie, such as the comical beating of the old woman, as he mentioned in his interview with the Directors Guild of America. When he asked Warner studio chief John Calley, "Can I beat the shit

A running gag filmed and then cut from *Blazing Saddles* had the major characters completely ignore stage-coach robberies happening in the background of various scenes.

out of this little old lady? I mean, really, with sound effects of breaking ribs and punching?" Calley's reply was, "Mel, if you're going to go up to the bell . . . ring it." This, Brooks felt, gave him the freedom to try anything, and he passed that feeling on to the writers as well.

Besides changing some lines for better comedic tone (for example, when told of killing off the first-born male child in each household, Hedley Lamarr's response is "No, that's been done to death," rather than the film's "Too Jewish"), the major changes over the multiple scripts were:

- Brooks himself singing the opening "Blazing Saddles" theme, in the style of "Tony Bennett and Frankie Lane."
- Many of the scripts have a running gag of a stagecoach being held up in the background of scenes, with no one ever going to help the people being robbed. (These scenes were shot but later cut from the film.)
- Lyle was to do some fancy rope tricks before throwing it around the handcar in the quicksand. Bart then argues with Taggart about rescuing them before Bart and Charlie finally drag themselves out on their own.
- Lamarr molesting the statue and his looking up the word "snatch" are added very late in the script process.
- The script shows us the shooting of the sheriff of Rock Ridge—in a comical fashion—and some other business that was obviously changed on location (tying a boy's pet snake in a bow, dumping paint over a Jewish painter, etc.).
- As per Norman Steinberg to columnist George Anderson "The part of the villain was written for John Carradine, and we even used his real name. All through the script whenever someone would mention the name John Carradine, everyone would freeze in terror." As it turns out, Carradine wasn't interested in being in the film, but it is easy to see how this concept drifted to one of Hedley Lamarr—whose name keeps being confused with famous actress Hedy Lamarr.
- The discussion for finding a new sheriff goes on for a time in the script, with the townsfolk considering letting a little boy be the new sheriff before finally deciding to wire the governor.
- Pryor had written a scene for Bart as he waits to be hung where he recites "The Pimp's Lament," about being a pimp for a prostitute who has done him

wrong. On the official Mel Brooks website, www.melbrooks.com, it states that Brooks cut the song because "it slowed the film down and would make it less likely for audiences to sympathize with his plight."

- "The Pimp's Lament" scene was rewritten and shot with Bart stopping his hanging by leading everyone in prayer. As everyone bows their heads, Bart continues the prayer as he slowly works his way out of the gallows, only to be stopped by Lamarr, who shoves a gun in Bart's face and asks him for a moment of his time. (A photo from this scene of Lamarr and Bart with the gun appears in the paperback novelization.) Instead, the final cut of the film shows Bart being led to the hangman's noose and Lamarr laughing at the possibilities before cutting to Lamarr taking Bart to see the governor, thus losing the prayer. This scene most probably was cut as deemed too similar to Bart's later escape from the townspeople when arriving at Rock Ridge (which plays better than the prayer escape anyway).

- Governor William J. Le Petomane meeting Bart has a lot of dialogue changes, giving Bart some dialogue in the scene and cutting every utterance of the word "nigger" that the governor says in earlier drafts of the script (the closest he comes is calling Bart a "Ni," which is funnier than the planned running gag of the governor saying "Nigger, uh, no offence," over and over again). It should be noted that the governor's name is based on a famous late-nineteenth-century performer of the Moulin Rouge who could not only pass gas at will, but with enough force to blow out a candle from a distance; his name meant "the fartomaniac."

- Pryor had written two pieces for Bart to do when in the sheriff's office: one was to crumple up a wanted poster for a black man ("He's got enough trouble without a bunch of honkies chasing his ass all over Mexico," Bart says), and the other was to have him painting over a jockey ashtray in white-face. Both pieces were cut, and instead, we only see Bart putting up two posters. The shot cuts away from him just as he pauses to look at the third poster, suggesting that the dialogue was shot but then discarded, and probably for the same reason "The Pimp's Lament" was cut—it makes Bart lawless and less lovable to a middle-American white audience.

- More of the chess game is played between Bart and Jim than is seen in the film.

- The governor is interrupted while playing a ukulele and singing to his secretary, after which he reads the letter from Rock Ridge. The governor is shocked they call him an "asshole," and loudly blurts out the word. This causes his secretary to reply "Anything you want, sir" as she begins to get into position for him. There are stills of this scene in the press kit, but it is missing from the movie. Brooks would tell Gene Siskel that he cut the scene after filming it, deciding that the joke passed beyond what could be deemed as good "bad taste."

- Bart's attempt to get to know the townspeople goes far beyond the little old lady in the script. The results are the same, however.
- The capture of Mongo takes more than just the Candygram seen in the film. Multiple other methods occur to help beat down on Mongo, including an automated showdown game that shoots a cannon in Mongo's face and diving in a well without oxygen in his diving suit. This footage was reinstated in the film when it aired on CBS a few years later.
- Many people come to apologize to Bart after saving them from Mongo besides the little old lady, who is the only one seen doing so in the film. All have conditions to their apologies and offers of assistance to Bart, however.
- Lili von Shtupp (shtupp is Yiddish for—in the nicest way possible—"to have sex") was originally to be called Lili von Dyke; an obvious play on the unsubtle manliness of Marlene Dietrich in several of her films, in particular *The Blue Angel*, which is parodied briefly in *Blazing Saddles*. The February 22, 1973, draft of the script says to change "all references to Lili von Dyke to Lili von Shtupp."
- Lili's assistant, Leopold, who looks like Erich von Stroheim, is missing in the film.
- Lili's intro to "I'm Tired" is trimmed in the film. The main gag missed is one repeated later with Bart in her dressing room—wanting to get into something more comfortable—so no loss. Her song has slightly different lyrics in earlier versions of the script, along with her using a whip onstage, and without soldier-dancers as in the film.
- As repeated in every history of the film, Bart's comment in the dark to Lili that she is sucking on his arm was cut for "good taste."
- Lili's "What a nice guy!" line is missing.
- Jim calling Bart "one crazy nigger" in the script is missing from the film.
- The aforementioned Tony Martin (1913–2012), singing "Tenement Symphony." This song, speaking of people of all races joining together in happiness, was in the Marx Brothers film *The Big Store* (1941) and is just a touch smarmy and hacky in its lecturing tone. In the script, Bart and Jim check in with Charlie about where the train is going, and Tony Martin—dressed in a tux and cowboy hat—interrupts the scene to begin singing "Tenement Symphony." When Taggart and his men arrive, Taggart shouts, "Get back to work, Martin," and Martin goes back to working on the railroad in his tux. The bit was cut when Warner could not get the performance rights to the song.
- After beating up and switching clothes with the Klan members, Jim was to ask Bart, "Did you have to stick the cactus up his ass?" Bart was to have replied that he had to do it. This may have been filmed and then edited out before the movie's release.
- Filmed but then cut was Bart and Jim arriving at a baptism. This scene appears in the "edited for television" version shown on CBS, but it tapers off unexpectedly with no real punch line. This is because . . .

- . . . The script has Taggart and his men catch up with Bart and Jim at the baptism, where Jim tried to hold Bart down in the water so he won't be seen. When they are discovered, they take off on a horse, only to find Taggart and his men close behind. Bart and Jim then jump off the horse and run at "lightning speed," getting away.
- A tad more to the townspeople meeting out in the prairie with the railroad workers appears in the script, but it's all setup for the meeting and easily dropped.
- A shot of lumber being lifted by white arms would appear at this point. The camera would show the arms struggling with the lumber until black arms appear, joining to help lift the wood higher. Then yellow arms join in as well. Then giant green arms join in, causing all the other arms to let go as screams are heard and someone shouts, "What the hell was that?"
- The governor comes into the fake town with the press. He doesn't even notice that the people are not real as he gets his picture taken with them. They are all there when Taggart and his horde arrives. The governor's arrival was filmed and featured in the television cut of the movie.
- When the dynamite doesn't go off, Lili makes a suggestion in German that Gabby Johnson interprets in his own special way. He gets beaten with hats by everyone around him. This is replaced in the film with the preacher starting a prayer and getting beaten down in the same manner.
- No "French Mistake" in earlier scripts, nor Buddy dressing down the men for their dancing errors.
- Norman Steinberg in March 1974 stated that the original ending was to feature "an elaborate railroad race in which an entire train popped out of the ground at the finish line." This probably goes back to Bergman's *Tex X* script and the proposed romance between Bart and the railroad owner's daughter. Steinberg said it was quickly taken out of the script when Warner said that the effects needed would cost $500,000.

Norman Steinberg would move on to produce all thirteen episodes of *When Things Were Rotten* for Brooks in 1975, as well as write the script for the Brooksfilms *My Favorite Year* (1982) and *Johnny Dangerously* (1984). Alan Uger would write for the series *Family Ties* and eventually become first a producer and then co-executive producer on that show. Andrew Bergman would write the screenplays for *The In-Laws* (1979), the clever but little-seen *So Fine* (1981), *Fletch* (1985), *Honeymoon in Vegas* (1992), and *The Freshman* (1990, with Marlon Brando and Matthew Broderick). Richard Pryor, of course, went on to an explosive career as a stand-up, a writer, and actor, eventually working with Gene Wilder in a number of movies, starting with *Silver Streak* in 1976. He'll return to the world of Brooks's films briefly for *History of the World, Part I*, which will be discussed in more detail in that chapter.

With a script in place, Warner announced in November 1972 that *Black Bart* would commence filming in January 1973 at their Burbank Studios. That would be pushed back to March, with casting being set as late as April for some parts in the film.

Cast

Cleavon Little (1939–1992) as Bart

Born in Oklahoma, Little was raised in San Diego, moving to New York when he got a scholarship to Juilliard. A run in several off-Broadway shows led to him being cast in *Jimmy Shine* on Broadway in 1969, which starred Dustin Hoffman. Little would follow that up as the lead in the musical *Purlie* in 1971, which earned him a Drama Desk Award and a Tony for Best Actor in a Musical. Both he and costar Sherman Hemsley would be spotted by Norman Lear and cast in episodes of his new series *All in the Family* (Hemsley would become a semi-regular as George Jefferson; a character spun off in his own series, *The Jeffersons* later on). That *All in the Family* appearance led to starring as the conman-like lead in the hospital sitcom *Temperature Rising* (1972–1974, with Little being the only constant in the various casts brought into the show over the years it aired.

As mentioned earlier in the chapter, Richard Pryor was the first choice for the role of Bart. Brooks had watched Pryor play out the part with the writers, and he could not see how anyone else could play it. Although it would be easy to suggest that Brooks may have retroactively remembered things in a way to make him out as a good guy for Pryor in historical pieces about the making of the film, all witnesses to the events support that Brooks tried hard to get Warner to consider Pryor for the job, even meeting face to face with Warner to try to talk them into going with Pryor. On his official website, Brooks said he nearly quit over the incident, but was talked out of it by Pryor, who wanted to see the film made because, as Pryor told him, "Don't quit, I haven't got my last payment for writing!"

But Pryor had two strikes against him. First, he may have been rapidly getting work in movies and was better known through his comedy albums, but the superstardom he would achieve came later in the 1970s; if it had come sooner, Warner would have probably ignored the warning signs and signed him. Secondly, Pryor was already earning a poor reputation in Hollywood that preceded his growing public acceptance. "Warner Brothers wouldn't touch him with a ten-foot pole because his reputation was so dubious in terms of reliability," Andrew Bergman recalled. "He was a known sniffer," Brooks years later in the PBS documentary *Make a Noise* admitted this was the main reason for Warner to be uninterested as they felt he was uninsurable. "I couldn't get him because Warner Bros. said, 'Richard takes drugs, we can't take it.'"

Cleavon Little, on the other hand, was a Tony-winning actor who had been in several films by that point and at the time was seen regularly on television in *Temperature Rising*. Brooks couldn't fault their logic. Further, he had seen Little in both *Purlie* and *Jimmy Shine* and knew he was an accomplished performer.

His conman character on *Temperature Rising* naturally led to him being signed to play the trickster character of Bart in *Blazing Saddles* as well. There was also another reason that Little was perfect for the role. Per Brooks in an article for *Entertainment Weekly*, Pryor recommended Little when they cast the role, saying, "If I was the black sheriff, I could pass for Cuban because I'm coffee-colored. Now, this guy Cleavon Little: he's classy, he has poise, and he's really charming. But he's black as coal. He will scare the shit out of them."

It should be mentioned that Pryor would state many times afterwards that he was not happy with the loss of the role, and sometimes suggested that Little had wormed his way into the film in order to push Pryor out. He would suggest the same about the other writers as well, with them taking credit for things he added to the script. Yet Pryor's name was associated with the project in every article or review that talked about the writers before and after its release, usually with special mention. When asked about this, the other writers disagreed with Pryor, always saying that they never tried to claim ownership over certain aspects of the script. Only Brooks would designate some material as being from particular writers, and it would always be either what he or Pryor brought to the script.

As for Little, "*Blazing Saddles* never started anything else," he reflected in 1986 to the *Pittsburgh Press*. "After that my career did not move in any appreciable

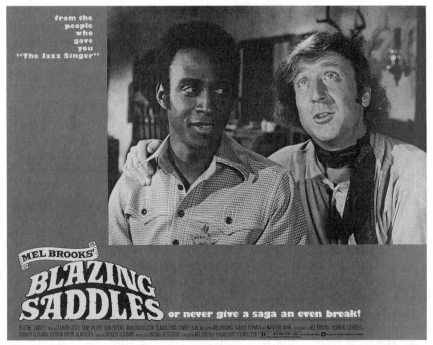

The pairing of Cleavon Little with Gene Wilder was a happy accident, as Wilder came in with only a weekend's notice after the original actor to play Jim, Gig Young, had to be released due to health issues.

way. Things stopped working for me creatively and financially." Little began appearing in smaller roles, including, he said, being replaced as the lead in the film *Greased Lightning* (1977) by Richard Pryor. "The reason they told me was that [the main character] was much lighter than me, and that Richard would be better. . . . I think they were just giving me a lot of bunk because Richard was about to be hot. I'd rather they'd just have been straight with me."

Little would continue appearing in films and television, receiving some notices for his role in the horror comedy *Once Bitten* (1985, with Jim Carrey). Eventually he returned to the stage, finding renewed success with Judd Hirsch in the play *I'm Not Rappaport* by Herb Gardner. He also returned to television in 1991 with the series *True Colors*, which only lasted for a short time, and later won an Emmy for a guest-starring role on the Judd Hirsch series *Dear John*. He died in 1992 from colorectal cancer.

Gene Wilder as Jim, the Waco Kid

After finishing *Everything You Wanted to Know about Sex * But Were Afraid to Ask* for Woody Allen in 1972, Wilder began thinking of writing a script. It was not his first attempt—two earlier scripts had been completed but never produced—yet this time he thought he had something. As will be explained in the next chapter, this led to him meeting up with Brooks, who showed him the script to *Blazing Saddles*. Brooks then asked Wilder if he would like to play Hedley Lamarr. Wilder liked the script but felt he was wrong for the part of Lamarr. Instead he asked if he could play Jim. Brooks was set on the character being played by an older actor, as Jim is supposed to be a legendary, but washed-up, cowboy. Brooks couldn't see beyond that description to even think of using someone as young as Wilder.

Initially, the writers envisioned the part being played by one man: Johnny Carson. Carson had done some cameos in the past (including on *Get Smart*) for brief gags, but shied away from anything bigger. When Brooks and Norman Steinberg went to discuss the role with Carson on the set of *The Tonight Show*, Carson flatly told them, "I'm not an actor. I can't do this."

Respecting Carson's wishes, the production began looking elsewhere. In February 1973, musician and sometimes-actor Roy Clark flew into Los Angeles to discuss playing the role, but things did not work out. Attempts to get Sterling Hayden fell through almost immediately as "He won't leave his boat for less than $15,000 a day," Norman Steinberg said in 1974. In March, actor Dan Dailey (1915–1978)—best known for his work in musicals, and recommended to Brooks as one of the best horsemen around who could act—was hired to play the role, and for weeks *Variety* and other daily papers reported his involvement in the film. Then, just before filming, Dailey reluctantly called Brooks and backed out due to his eyesight. "I'm blind," Brooks remembered Dailey saying. "I'm wearing coke bottles for glasses. It would be dangerous."

With Dailey out, Brooks happened upon John Wayne (1907–1979) in the studio commissary (Wayne was on the lot to film *Cahill U.S. Marshal* at the time). Taking a chance, Brooks gave him the script and asked him if he would like the role of the Waco Kid. The next day, Wayne came back saying, "I can't do this. This is too dirty. I'm John Wayne. But man, I was up all night screaming, laughing. I'm gonna be the first one on line to see this movie." (As an aside, when Gene Wilder was about to make his film *The Frisco Kid* in 1979, Wayne was set to be in it, but then backed out when the studio tried to renegotiate his salary. It would have been his last film instead of the 1977 *The Shootist*.)

The production next turned to Robert Mitchum, but he wasn't interested in the role. Finally, the production signed actor Gig Young (1913–1978), once a leading man who had bounced back as a strong character actor thanks to his work as the emcee in *They Shoot Horses, Don't They?* (1969). Young was hung upside-down for his first scene as Jim in the jail cell. As he began to speak his lines, Young began to shake, which Brooks mistook as him simply being in character. "He's giving me the alky shakes," Brooks remembered in an interview with AMC thinking as he watched Young. "I said, 'Keep doing what you're doing.'" When the actor began to scream and started foaming at the mouth and nose, Brooks realized that Young wasn't faking it. Per Brooks, he was told later that Young had stopped drinking for the role and had developed a case of delirium tremens (the DT's). After an ambulance took the actor away, Brooks shot what he could of Little for the scene and then cancelled the rest of the day's filming, as it was clear that Young would not be ready to play the part.

Remembering Wilder's request to play the role, and knowing that he had seen the latest version of the script (Brooks had been sending Wilder each new draft as they were completed), Brooks ran to a payphone by the set and called Wilder in New York. Wilder was about to head to Europe in two weeks to film his role as the Fox in Stanley Donen's *The Little Prince* (1974), but asked Donen if his filming could be pushed back in order to help his old friend out. Donen agreed and Wilder flew out over the weekend to Los Angeles to get fitted for a costume and familiarize himself with the horse he was to ride in the film. The next day, he was on the set, handing upside-down and asking Little, "Are we black?"

While all that was going on, Wilder's idea for a spoof of horror movies was gaining traction, but more about that in the next chapter.

Harvey Korman (1927–2008) as Hedley Lamarr

With John Carradine out and Wilder out, other actors were looked at for Hedley Lamarr. Many, many actors. Korman would even joke in the documentary on the DVD special edition of the film that he saw his name was way down on the list of actors for the role. It was okay, though—by that time in his career, he was used to being the "second" person people thought of for acting jobs.

Born in Chicago, Korman studied acting at the Goodman School of Drama for four years, eventually obtaining lead roles in productions at various summer

Slim Pickens, Madeline Kahn, and Harvey Korman. Korman came into the film knowing he got the role of Hedley Lamarr after both John Carradine and Gene Wilder turned it down.

theaters in the Chicago, Green Bay, Wisconsin, and the Arizona area. In 1950, he attempted Broadway, but ended up in the ensembles of two short-lived musicals before being cast adrift. "Then all the doors shut and I ended up selling candy at Radio City Music Hall," Korman remembered in an interview in 1964 in the *Chicago Tribune*. He moved to Hollywood and played Hamlet with a small stock company in L.A. before returning to Chicago. He made his first movie upon arriving back home, a film by Herschell Gordon Lewis called *Living Venus* (1961), and then started getting jobs in television and is most remembered in this period for his numerous appearances on *The Munsters* (1964–1966) and doing the voice of the Great Gazoo in the last season of *The Flintstones* (1965–1966). He also appeared in the "Gallagher" series on *Walt Disney's Wonderful World of Color* in 1965, which starred Roger Mobley, who played Danny Baker in Brooks's *Inside Danny Baker* pilot (see chapter 3 for more details).

Performing as the second banana on *The Danny Kaye Show* in 1966 led directly to him being cast for his most famous acting job on television, the variety series *The Carol Burnett Show*, which he was on for ten years and which landed him four Emmy Awards over those years. And that work found Korman being cast as Lamarr in *Blazing Saddles*. Brooks discovered that he enjoyed working with Korman and would use him in *High Anxiety*, *History of the World, Part I*, and *Dracula: Dead and Loving It*, as well as costarring with Cloris Leachman in the short-lived Brooks-related series *The Nutt House*.

Korman over time would occasionally try to expand his work so that he was the star of the series (including a pilot based on *Fawlty Towers* in 1978 called *Chateau Snavely*), but eventually resigned himself to being considered "the best second banana in the business." He would continue to work in television and movies, as well as perform live with fellow *Burnett* cast member Tim Conway, for many years. He passed away in 2008.

Madeline Kahn (1942–1999) as Lili von Shtupp

Born Madeline Wolfson in Boston, Madeline graduated from Hofstra University with a degree in speech therapy, while also studying music and drama. Although she would turn her career toward working with children in public schools, she found herself being drawn to public performances, especially after finding that she had a strong voice as a singer while working in college at a hofbrauhaus, where she was a singing waitress. Taking her stepfather's last name for her stage name, Kahn began struggling to work on Broadway, eventually landing a part in *Leonard Sillman's New Faces of 1968*, the newest edition of the musical revue that back in 1952 had featured Brooks's first Broadway work.

Her first film work was in the short *De Duva: The Dove* in 1968, which was a spoof of Ingmar Bergman's films. She would continue working on Broadway and off-Broadway before being selected by Peter Bogdanovich to play the part of the shrewish fiancée in the comedy *What's Up, Doc?* (1972, and cowritten by Buck Henry). Bogdanovich would use several of the same actors from that film in his follow-up in 1973, *Paper Moon*, which earned Kahn an Academy Award nomination for Best Supporting Actress. In November 1972, she was signed to appear in *Mame* (1974) with Lucille Ball in the character of the nanny, Gooch, but was unexpectedly fired when Ball decided during rehearsals that she wanted the actress who played the part on Broadway, Jane Connell, for the role instead.

Undeterred, Kahn had read about Brooks's upcoming film in the *New York Times* and decided to audition for the role of "Lili von Dyke." "I had a hunch," she told Charlie Rose in 1996. "I read that there was going to be this take-off on a German kind of world; a western parody, and Mel Brooks." Knowing her background singing German songs at the hofbrauhaus, Kahn thought she had

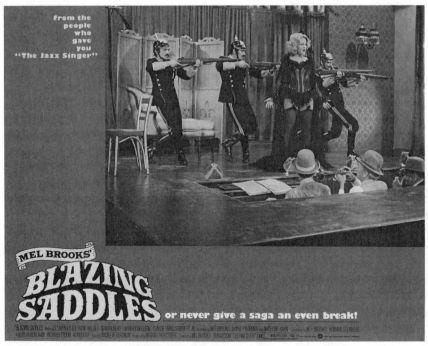

Madeline Kahn in her most famous role as Lily Von Shtupp. She would go on to appear in three more films for Brooks.

a chance. "[I thought] I must try and see if I can inquire about this, even though I'm not a Marlene Dietrich type at all. But I understand this sort of thing . . . potentially."

Kahn came in to audition for the part privately with Brooks, who had seen her in the Bogdanovich films and was happy with the audition, but asked to see her legs. "And she said, 'Oh, it's one of those auditions,'" Brooks remembered later to Virginia Rohan. "I said, 'No, no. You got me all wrong." Explaining that the parody of Marlene Dietrich would involve straddling a chair and showing off the character's legs, Kahn did exactly that. Brooks was happy but then quickly said, "Okay, okay, lower your skirt in case someone walks by the office right now." Kahn would be signed for the role in February 1973.

Although they have no scenes together, Wilder watched Kahn while filming and suggested to Brooks that perhaps she would be good in the film they were talking about as their next project together.

Slim Pickens (1919–1983) as Taggart

Pickens was born Louis Lindley Jr. in Kingsburg, California, where he began working at rodeos as a rider when still in his teens. "My father was against rodeoing and told me he didn't want to see my name on the entry lists ever again," Pickens said to UPI in 1979 about his stage name. "While I was fretting about what to call myself, some old boy sitting on a wagon said, 'Why don't you call yourself Slim Pickens, 'cause that's sure what your prize money'll be."

Pickens would work in the rodeo into his thirties when he found out that stuntmen in Hollywood were getting good pay for falling off horses and jumping off crashing wagons—the type of things he was doing as a career "when I was paying rodeo fees to get my neck broke." What attracted Hollywood to Pickens was that he could not only act, but could ride horses and stagecoaches without needing a double, thus saving money. He would soon start appearing in westerns, with occasional roles outside of that genre, including a pivotal part in the Stanley Kubrick dark comedy *Dr. Strangelove* (1964) in a role that originally was to go to Peter Sellers and that found him riding an atomic bomb to its destination like a bronco rider—one of the top images in movie history.

Brooks noted to *The New Yorker* that Pickens gave him the best advice he ever received about working on a movie set. "I said to him, 'Look, you've done a thousand movies.

Mel Brooks as the governor in a scene cut from the film by Brooks, as he deemed it going beyond good "bad taste."

I have done three or four. Is there any piece of advice you could offer me?' He said, 'Sit down . . . Sit down any time you see a chair. Otherwise as you're working you don't realize you're on your feet for twenty hours. You're more tired than you know. Get off your feet and sit down.'" For Brooks, who had been known to drive himself frantic on his previous films, it was perfect advice.

Candygram for Mongo! Bart's take-down of Mongo goes far beyond the Candygram in scenes shot but then cut from the film before release. Those cuts would eventually appear in the CBS airing of the film and later as extras on the DVD/Blu-ray releases of the film.

Pickens would continue working in movies and television until 1982. He passed away in 1983.

Alex Karras (1935–2012) as Mongo

Karras, born in Gary, Indiana, was a professional football player with the Detroit Lions. In 1968, he played himself in the film version of George Plimpton's nonfiction book about his brief time playing with the team, *Paper Lion* (the film starred Alan Alda, who would go on to play Hawkeye in the television series *MASH*, which would feature Karras in an episode). That would eventually lead to roles in television and finally to *Blazing Saddles* as Mongo.

After co-announcing *Monday Night Football* for three years in the mid-1970s, Karras went back to acting in television and films, appearing in the 1982 Blake Edwards comedy *Victor/Victoria*, and then in the long-running ABC family comedy *Webster*, with his wife Susan Clark (1983–1989). He died in 2012 due to kidney failure.

Mel Brooks as Governor William J. Le Petomane, Indian Chief, and Hooligan

Actor with blackmail material on writer-director.

Also Appearing

Beyond Madeline Kahn, it was obvious that Brooks had seen Peter Bogdanovich's *Paper Moon* and *What's Up, Doc?*, as represented by the first three actors listed below:

- Liam Dunn (1916–1976) as Reverend Johnson. He had earlier appeared in *What's Up, Doc?* as Judge Maxwell. He would later appear early in *Young*

Frankenstein as Mr. Hilltop, the patient in the lecture and as the unfortunate news vendor in *Silent Movie*.

- Burton Gilliam (born 1938) as Taggart's underling, Lyle. He had earlier appeared in a small but pivotal role in *Paper Moon* as Floyd, the desk clerk.
- John Hillerman (1932–2017) as Howard Johnson. He had appeared in Bogdanovich's *The Last Picture Show* (featuring Cloris Leachman), *What's Up, Doc?* as the hotel manager, and *Paper Moon* as Deputy Hardin and Jess Hardin. He would pop up in one other Brooks film, as a rich man in the French Revolution scene of *The History of the World, Part I*. Hillerman has appeared in many television shows and other films, like *Chinatown* (1974), but is probably best remembered for playing Higgins on the long-running *Magnum, P.I.* television series.
- David Huddleston (1930–2016) as Olson Johnson ("Blow it out your ass, Howard."). Huddleston was a popular figure on television and would reappear as the judge in the 2005 version of *The Producers*. He is probably best remembered as the Big Lebowski in *The Big Lebowski* (1998).
- Dom DeLuise as Buddy Bizarre. Making his second appearance in a Brooks film after *The Twelve Chairs*. He'll be back again in Brooks's 1976 film *Silent Movie*.
- Carol Arthur (born 1935) as Harriett Johnson ("I'm not used to public speaking. . . ."). The wife of Dom DeLuise, she will return in three more Brooks films: the pregnant woman near the beginning of *Silent Movie*, and as a villager in both *Robin Hood: Men in Tights* and *Dracula: Dead and Loving It*. She also appears briefly in Gene Wilder's *The World's Greatest Lover*.
- George Furth (1932–2008) as Van Johnson ("Howard Johnson is right!"). This was his only appearance in a Brooks film, but it was hard to watch any television from the 1960s onward without seeing Furth in something. He also worked many times on Broadway as a writer, such as creating the book for Stephen Sondheim's *Company*, which earned Furth a Tony for Best Book for a Musical and a Drama Desk Award for Outstanding Book. He also wrote the book for Sondheim's *Merrily We Roll Along* and the dramatic play *Precious Sons*, which starred Ed Harris in 1986.
- Jack Starrett (1936–1989) as Gabby Johnson ("The sheriff is a n--!"). A director and actor, who usually made low-budget action films (*Cleopatra Jones*, *Slaughter*, *Race with the Devil*). He had been spotted by Brooks at a party doing his dead-on impression of Gabby Hayes, a popular actor in John Wayne westerns, and Brooks asked him to play the role in *Blazing Saddles*.
- Jimmy Martinez as Scared Mexican Man ("Mongo! Santa Maria!"). It's just one line—a pun really—playing off the name of a famous jazz musician, but Martinez will pop up again in Brooks's work, first in various roles on the television series *When Things Were Rotten*, and then as a waiter in *High Anxiety*.
- Paul Mazursky (1930–2014) as Second Indian. Mazursky was a well-known writer and director, made such films as *Bob & Carol & Ted & Alice* (1969), *Harry and Tonto* (1974), *An Unmarried Woman* (1978), and *Moscow on the*

Hudson (1984). He plays the Indian next to Brooks as the Indian chief in the flashback scene. He would later appear in *History of the World, Part I* and in several episodes of the series *Curb Your Enthusiasm*, which also featured Mel Brooks.

In the Crew

- Michael Hertzberg took on the role of producer after Sidney Glazier bowed out for personal reasons dealing with a divorce and wanting to raise his daughter in New York rather than Los Angeles.
- John Morris also returned to write the score and work with Brooks on the songs performed.
- Danforth Greene edited the film with Brooks, and later performed that duty on *Spaceballs*.
- John C. Howard also worked on editing the film and would do so on *Young Frankenstein, Silent Movie, High Anxiety*, and *History of the World, Part I*.
- Production design was by Peter Woolery, who came back for *High Anxiety* to do the same.
- Terry Miles was the makeup artist on this film and *High Anxiety*.
- Also working on this and other films in the same roles for Brooks were Gene S. Cantamessa, Les Fresholtz, Arthur Pantadosi, and Raul A. Bruce for sound; Gene Marks as the music editor; Jonathan Tunick as the conductor for the orchestra; Dan Wallin as score mixer; Alan Johnson as choreographer; Julie Pitkanen as script supervisor; Anthony Goldschmidt as the title designer, and too many stunt people to list here.

Production

November 1972 saw the first announcements in the daily papers about Brooks's new film, *Black Bart*—a title Warner was never completely sold on. In the early 1970s, several films appeared showing African American characters as the protagonists, be they heroes or villains. Most were low-budget exploitation films, typically crime drams, and usually with our hero fighting both evil and racism from various white characters (usually rich, powerful men who are a billion times eviler than anyone else in the film). The genre was called blaxploitation and petered out after 1975, but in 1972 it was really kicking into gear. Which is why Brooks felt he had to explain the name even before filming began. As he told the *Baltimore Sun* that November, "It won't be a 'black' movie but more of a juxtaposition of hypocrisy, greed, flat-out fun and clichés that I've been watching since I was three years old. The white characters will keep saying 'I'll be hornswoggled' and 'they went thataway,' and the sheriff will answer 'right on, man!'"

Filming had been announced back in November 1972 as starting in either January or February of the following year, but most of the casting was not completed until March 1973. Filming instead started March 6, 1973, at the Warner Bros. studio lot in Burbank for both interiors and scenes taking place in Rock Ridge, which were shot on the studio's then-permanent western set at the studio. The entire western town is now gone from the lot, torn down in the 1980s when it was realized that they were underutilizing precious studio space by keeping the western set but only filming on it less than 10 percent of the time each year. The only thing remaining is the barn door that Jim is sitting by at the end of the picture, which can still be seen on the Warner Bros. studio tour.

In April, the scenic western location footage was shot in the Mojave Desert for the opening railroad scene, the moment where Bart comes across Count Basie, Taggart telling his gang that they need "a shitload of dimes" at the thruway, and the final shot of Jim and Bart riding off the movie in the limo. Brooks remembered to the *Minneapolis Star Tribune* Count Basie arriving for the shooting: "Count Basie was amazed to find himself sitting in the desert. He said, 'When are we goin' to town to shoot it, man?' I said, 'This is it.' He said, 'You're kiddin.' That was the greatest day we had. They just wailed on the desert."

Shooting continued at the Vasquez Rocks State Park (Captain Kirk fought a Gorn in this area in an episode of *Star Trek*, to give you some perspective) for scenes featuring Bart going back to see Charlie at the railroad camp and Lamarr's sign-up for desperadoes. The breakout from Warner Bros. near the end of the film was, naturally enough, shot on location in Burbank, and the final confrontation between Bart and Lamarr at Grauman's Chinese Theatre just a few miles away on Hollywood Boulevard.

Any concerns by Brooks or others that they were going too far with the racial gags was tossed Little's way for his input. Brooks recalled to Lisa Rosen: "I said, 'Could you really do that scene, "I'll blow this nigger's head all over this town?"' He said, 'No problem. We're on the right side. We can do anything because we're on the right side.'"

Bart with Count Basie. Basie did not know until he arrived in the desert that they were shooting the orchestra outdoors for the gag in the film.

Filming outside the studio must have made for some interesting negotiations as it started just as the Writers Guild of America West staged a strike against the studios. This strike lasted from March through June 24, 1973, and featured picket lines at the gates of the studios in Los Angeles, including Warner Bros. Complaints were filed against writers who crossed the picket lines to direct (and only direct, not write) features, including Brooks and Michael Crichton, who was directing *Westworld* (1973) over at the MGM studio lot at the time. The complaints led to a Supreme Court ruling (*American Broadcasting Companies, Inc, et al v. Writers Guild of America West*) that what were called "hyphenates" (aka writer/directors), as long as they were not asked to perform writing duties, were protected under the National Labor Relations Act.

Additional issues were still to come: Gig Young sued over his departure from the film (little is known of the outcome to the suit), while an item was placed in a Jack O'Brian column, "Voice of Broadway" from May 9, 1973, that "both Dan Dailey and Gig Young refused star roles in Mel Brooks's *Black Bart* so-called satire. Because the script's too filthy." In June 1974, actress Hedy Lamarr "didn't get the joke," as Brooks stated, and sued in Manhattan Supreme Court for $10 million over the use and misuse of her name in the film. She would settle out of court for $10,000 and a public apology from Brooks.

With filming completed, Brooks went into the editing room and came back with a cut for the executives to watch in the fall of 1973. It was an unpleasant experience, he recalled in the Directors Guild of America interview. "We screened [the film] for the Warner Bros. COO and CEO and all the executives. There were no laughs. I had flop sweat. And this guy got up [Leo Greenfield, the domestic distributor for the studio] and said, 'I've worked here a long time, and I've never told the studio that a picture was so bad we should eat it. But this picture is very embarrassing and I don't think I can sell it.'"

Brooks was worried, and began to suggest to his production team that they needed to go back to the drawing board and re-edit the film. His producer, Michael Hertzberg, convinced him to try another screening, this time for the secretaries and other employees on the lot. The second screening was a great success, and word of mouth began to spread within the studio. Late the next day, studio head John Calley—who had been the only executive who laughed at the initial screening and had told Brooks to "ring the bell" if attempting anything outrageous—called Brooks to let him know, "Everybody's talking—I even got a call from our distributor who said, 'Well, let's take a chance on these three cities.'"

Studio chairman Ted Ashley wasn't satisfied, however. Seemingly not aware that Brooks had rights to the final cut of the film, Ashley pulled him into Calley's office and gave him a list of two dozen things that needed to be cut from the film. "No farting, you can't punch a horse," Brooks told a crowd at a TCM Classic Film Festival in 2014. "If I took all his notes, we'd have a 12-minute movie. Calley was with me, and after Ted Ashley was finished, I took all the notes and threw them in a waste paper basket, and Calley said, 'Good filing.'"

There was still an issue with the title of the film, however. Warner felt *Black Bart* sounded too much like a low-budget blaxploitation picture title. "The Warners people said, 'Why not make it a funny title?' I said, 'I think it is a funny title, and it's only funny for those who get it, which is good'" (*Chicago Tribune*). Eventually, the writers suggested the title *Purple Sage*, invoking an old Zane Grey novel and various film adaptations, *Riders of the Purple Sage*. Warner wasn't thrilled with that title either, thinking it was trying to be vaguely dirty.

Finally, Brooks came up with the nonsensical title *Blazing Saddles*, which Warner agreed to use in the middle of November 1973, a year after the film was first announced. This did create a slight problem in the film, as we see Lamarr and Bart reach the Chinese Theatre with the marquee displaying the name of the film as *Black Bart*. As some viewers may have noticed, effects are used to cover up the marquee and replace the names there with that of *Blazing Saddles*, although it still shows as *Black Bart* in a still from the film seen in the paperback novelization.

With a title settled upon, the theme song was still needed. Brooks had assumed he would either end up singing it himself (as listed in earlier script drafts) or hire someone to do it in a style similar to Frankie Laine. Laine (1913–2007) had started his career as a jazz singer, later becoming quite famous for singing songs for westerns in the late 1950s, especially with the theme from the television series *Rawhide* and the movie *3:10 to Yuma*. Such songs were heavily orchestrated but talked of the Old West in a rugged way along with Laine's bold and sure vocals that seemed perfect to parody for *Blazing Saddles*. Then they found out they could get the real Frankie Laine to record the song, which was impossible to pass up. Even so, it was said that Brooks was nervous as the recording took place, fearing that Laine may find out that the song was not so much a "tribute to the West" but more of a send-up of it, and reportedly kept telling people to keep the laughing down while Laine recorded the song.

Laine later did see the film in 1974, but admitted that he couldn't really tell much from what he saw. "I saw it with the censorship board [in the Union of South Africa]," Laine recalled in 1975 to the *Cincinnati Enquirer*. "The original film runs about 94 minutes. After cutting by the South African censors, it was reduced to 22 minutes." Laine didn't seem to mind the cutting of the film, however. "By the time the picture starts, I'm finished anyway."

Promotional material for the film centered around a poster painted by artist John Alvin (1948–2008). Alvin was working at an animation studio when someone suggested him for the poster, which looks serious from a distance, but on closer inspection shows that appearances are deceiving. What looks to be Bart on his steed, with an Indian nickel behind him, actually shows the following details:

- The Indian is, of course, Mel Brooks.
- His headband reads "Kosher for Passover" in Hebrew.
- The front white feathers on the headdress are on fire.
- The coin says "Hi, I'm Mel. Trust Me."
- Bart has a microphone overhead and is giving the peace sign.
- Bart's horse has a wind-up key in its rump.
- A jet can be seen flying near the bottom of the poster.

The poster would bring about an avalanche of poster work for Alvin, as he remembered in 2007 to the *Santa Fe New Mexican*. "I didn't look for work for fifteen years after that; it came to me. I just kept getting calls from strangers who asked, 'Are you the guy who did so-and-so film?" Alvin would create poster art for such films as *Young Frankenstein, E.T. the Extra-Terrestrial, Blade Runner, The Princess Bride, The Goonies, Batman Returns, Jurassic Park*, and many posters for Disney.

The posters and newspaper art came with two taglines: "Mel Brooks's Blazing Saddles or never give a saga an even break!" and "From Warner Bros. the people who gave you 'The Jazz Singer.'" Both would be used on some lobby cards for the film. Speaking of lobby cards, plenty were created, including some showing scenes not in the film.

Other promotional tools were a standard series of TV and radio spots for the film as well as four "TV Excerpts" from it, each running about three minutes long, that could be aired on news and interview programs. The four clips were "Welcome" with Bart arriving in town; "Robyn Hilton" showing the secretary (played by Robyn Hilton) with Lamarr and the governor; "Fast Draw," showing Jim displaying his fast hands; and, "The Vamp," with Lili trying to seduce the sheriff. There was also a 45 RPM record available from the Warner Bros. Record label (WB 7774) that plays Frankie Laine singing "Blazing Saddles" on one side and Madeline Kahn with "I'm Tired" on the flip side.

In an interview in 1974, Brooks mentions that there were additional television ads created that featured Carl Reiner as a "doddering British film critic, who falls asleep just before mentioning the title of the film" while Brooks can be heard yelling at the critic, "Wake up! Hey England, wake up!" "It's hysterical," Brooks said about the ads. "If you're from Brooklyn to call him England is hysterical." Sadly, these ads have yet to appear on any official video releases for the film.

Backend

The film premiered at the Pickwick Drive-In Theatre in Burbank, California, on February 6, 1974. The event was a special one, where anyone who came to the show riding a horse got free admission to the advance showing, which included many of the cast members attending along with the two regular features for the drive-in afterwards: *Cinderella Liberty* and *Hannie Caulder* (a western featuring Raquel Welch). At least 100 riders came in to see the film in this manner, with the rest of the lot filled with paying customers who drove in to see the premiere.

Newspaper ad announcing the special sneak preview event at the Pickwick Drive-in, Burbank, California, on February 6, 1974. Anyone who came in with their horse got in free.

The next day saw the film released to two theaters in the country: in Los Angeles, at the Avco Center Cinema, and New York, the Sutton Theater. Playing in theaters at the time were such films as *Zardoz, American Graffiti,* and *Walking Tall.* A month later, the film began to spread out to other areas of the country, mostly in March 1974. Playing in theaters at that time and into April and May were such films as *The Sting, Serpico, Papillon, Magnum Force, Sleeper,* and *The Exorcist.* Unlike Brooks's previous two films, Warner Bros. was a major studio with vast promotional and distribution departments, and for the first time Brooks was seeing one of his films handled as a major Hollywood movie, instead of a personal effort that somehow escaped through a hole in the asylum wall.

A novelization was released for the movie, written by Tad Richards, who had written comedic work as well as a western historical novel, *Cherokee Bill* (1974). Brooks did not care for Richards's first draft and requested various changes be made to get the novelization more in sync with the film. The published novel includes text and photos of scenes not in the film itself.

Reviews came quickly, although not always positive. Vincent Canby in the *New York Times* (and syndicated to other papers throughout the country) was one of the first, and he had very mixed things to say. Comparing the film to Chinese food, Canby felt that "a couple of hours later . . . you wonder why you laughed as consistently as you did." Calling many of the gags as "desperate bone-crushing efforts to be funny," Canby still ends up implying that people laughed throughout the film, making one wonder if he secretly liked it but wanted to hate it walking in and couldn't let go of that hope. Charles Champlin in the *Los Angeles Times* was more positive, calling it a "mock-down, knock-down, bawdy, gaudy, hyper-hip burlesque western [that] is irreverent, outrageous, improbable, often as blithely tasteless as a stag night at the Friars Club and almost continuously funny." Roger Ebert gave the film four stars out of four, while *Variety* seemed to like it as a "raunchy, protracted version of a television comedy skit."

Although Brooks hoped to have the film nominated for an Academy Award for the screenplay, the movie received only three nominations, of which it won none: Madeline Kahn for Best Actress in a Supporting Role, John C. Howard and Danford B. Greene for Film Editing, and John Morris and Mel Brooks for Best Original Song ("Blazing Saddles"). The writers did win for Best Comedy Written Directly for the Screen by the Writers Guild of America, USA, and in 2006 the film was selected by the Library of Congress as being culturally significant and was chosen for preservation by the National Film Registry.

The film, made for $2.6 million, has earned over $119 million domestically over the years and was popular enough to see a pilot being made in 1975 based on Andrew Bergman's original story called *Black Bart.* The pilot episode, which aired April 4, 1975, on CBS, was written by Michael Elias and Rich Eustis and starred Louis Gossett Jr. as Bart and Steve Landesberg as a sleepy-eyed, wavy-haired, drunk-on-the-mend quick-shooter, who was nothing at all like the Waco Kid (sarcasm intended). While the cast is not bad and the idea of at least one new character—the female saloon owner who looked like Kitty from *Gunsmoke* if she had been a pirate, and thus possibly having some good back stories to tell there—was clever, but it lacked the needed racial tension that would be impossible for the family-hour world of television, and the outrageous silliness of the film. With none of the creative minds that worked on the film available, that's understandable.

Reflections

Blazing Saddles started out as iconoclastic; it became an icon.

The film began as a seedling of an idea based on Andrew Bergman's original script for *Tex X*—that of a hip, young black man of 1974 dealing with a redneck society in the West of 1874. That's it. There's nothing else to hang the story on but the one premise. And yet, with the help of his gang of writers, Brooks created a movie that would open doors for comedies to come in the 1970s.

To be fair, however, all those elements had been there already—many from years in comedy film past—but in *Blazing Saddles* reawakened and with a harder edge. Most notably is the "breaking of the fourth wall." When one or more of the characters in a movie or play acknowledges our existence—and thus acknowledges their own status as being within a movie—that's "breaking the fourth wall." Brooks had done it before in *The Producers* with Max's asides to the camera, but it had been there since the days of silent movies. Oliver Hardy silently voicing his frustrations with Stan Laurel by looking directly at us; Groucho telling us to go out to the lobby "until this blows over" as Chico begins a piano piece in *Horsefeathers*; Hope and Crosby acknowledging that they can't die in *Road to Morocco* as "Paramount will protect us, 'cause we're signed for five more years." All these were earlier signs of this practice, so *Blazing Saddles* was nothing new in that respect.

What it did do new was demonstrate that comedic device with anger. When Lamarr asks us how to get the people out of Rock Ridge, he says in disgust, "Why am I asking you?" Lamarr shoves aside people in line at the movie theater—the audience going to see *Blazing Saddles*—because he's got important things to do and wants to know how the movie ends (an idea that would be borrowed and expanded upon in *Spaceballs*). The cast doesn't merely stumble upon another movie set (again, see the Hope-Crosby *Road To* pictures for earlier examples of this gag), they smash through the wall and tell the one person trying to stop them that they "work for Mel Brooks," before flowing through the studio lot and finally out into the streets and our reality. There's no barrier any longer—our world is not safe on the screen.

And anger from the world events of the 1960s and 1970s became part of the comedies of the 1970s and onward. Reality began to settle into the fantasy of the movies just as easily as pointing out to people that eating nothing but beans and black coffee probably did have the cowboys farting around the campfire at night. Some would eventually call it "shock comedy," but usually it was there, as with *Blazing Saddles*, not to parody the western but to parody ourselves. The reason the use of the word "nigger" works in *Blazing Saddles* is because we know in our core that racism is too easily a thing to trigger. And look at the use of the word within the film; as noted by Brooks himself, the only people using the term are stupid people. It's obviously why Brooks decided not to have Jim call Bart "a crazy nigger" midway through the film, and why Bart's scripted "Keep the peace, niggers!" at the end was replaced with "Keep the peace, brothers!" To let the heroes use it offhandedly soils the message about how racist comments are really the work of idiots. Even Lamarr doesn't use it, because he may be a bad guy, but he's smart enough to not think in those terms.

Better yet, take a look at the film once Bart saves the town from Mongo. Everyone rises up a notch; the old lady apologies for the "Up yours, nigger" line from earlier that morning and bakes Bart an apple pie. Of course, she asks him to not say anything about it, but I didn't say they all suddenly became enlightened. Still, a notch up is a notch up. After that sequence, the word is only heard twice more in the film and both times by way of the people still being morons. If one must find a moral in *Blazing Saddles*, it is that through friendship and cooperation people get things done. Lamarr is counting on the town falling apart because of the color of Bart's skin, but once they were able to get beyond their prejudices about it—even accept that he's a smarter man than they are—then things start working out for them. When Olson Johnson in an obvious immigrant accent tells everyone that he doesn't want the Irish there, he knows it is "prairie shit" because they've all gone too far to be prejudiced any longer if they want to survive.

In terms of relationships, Bart and Jim are another male couple in Brooks's films that complete each other. Not in the way of *The Producers*, where it was the wise and the innocent/the id and the ego; not as in *The Twelve Chairs*, with class differences coming together between the two main characters; but this time as two smart men who recognize in each other that they can achieve more together than alone in a world that judges them by appearances. Jim is a drunk, an "alky" who can't handle a gun, but Bart treats him as a fellow human being and supports Jim crawling out of the bottle and becoming better than he was when he was "the Waco Kid." Jim, on the other hand, warns Bart that the world is going to judge him by his skin, not the badge, because they're "morons." They know there is prejudice against them both, and are smart enough not to ignore it or hide from it. When it comes to Jim shouting to the KKK members, "Oh, boys! Lookee what I got here!" and Bart asks where the white women are at, we know they didn't even have to plan the ruse out—they knew even the slightest provocation would send those racist men over to the rock to be beaten and stripped, because they understood their world better than anyone else around them.

Some over the years have suggested that the film would have even more bite to it if Brooks had been able to convince Warner to cast Richard Pryor. Yet, while Pryor created the Bart we see in the film, his ability on the screen was not quite there yet. In subsequent films, he may have had a touch of anger in his voice, but he tended to fall back on the standard for all comedic heroes up to that point—the coward who does the right thing when pushed. Pryor worked best when given a character who is struggling, unsure, worried about getting hurt, and only in moments really becoming brave—and that just isn't Bart of *Blazing Saddles*. Bart is a trickster. He knows he is in a movie, and better yet, he knows that he is untouchable (like Hope and Crosby knowing Paramount will protect them). Having "Merrily We Roll Along" play as Bart leaves Mongo with the Candygram fits because this world he inhabits is a cartoon, and he's Bugs Bunny. To fit that role, an actor was needed who could stay rooted in that world while inviting us into it as our guide. Pryor would have been too real, too hurt over being told "Up yours, nigger," too angry when hitting Taggart with that shovel.

Admittedly, that may be part of a weakness in the film as well. There's anger about racism, but Bart is perhaps too perfect. Brooks took out Bart's "Pimp's Lament," his crumpling up the wanted poster for the black man, and his shoving a cactus up one of the KKK members' ass because they all could have easily turned the audience—a predominantly white audience—against our hero. Thus, just as with the erasing of the word "nigger" from the story as it progresses, Bart is (okay, pun intended) whitewashed as well to appease the audience. *Blazing Saddles* may in some ways have been a poke at our own racial boundaries, but only so much. The real story is still the clash of the times, and our reality leaking into a fictional western one. In doing that, the sharp jabs at racism evaporate in favor of the surrealism of Hollywood filmmaking that takes up the last third of the film. At the time, perhaps it is just as well. *Blazing Saddles* was pushing boundaries, but one can only push so far with each attempt, and this was about as far as you could go in 1974 America and still be a hit.

In connection with its parody of Hollywood, the film is not only iconoclastic about reality and race, but also—naturally—about western clichés. However, if *Blazing Saddles* killed off anything, it was not the movie westerns but television westerns. By the early 1970s, spaghetti westerns had changed the scope of the genre, which had already been trying to snap into a twentieth-century mindset since the days of "adult westerns" like *High Noon* back in the 1950s. The concept of friendly, dusty towns with evil railroad owners and politicians, and "head 'em off at the pass!" had by 1974 already been buried by films like *The Good, the Bad, and the Ugly*, and other modern westerns. But these concepts were still the norm for television westerns. In fact, many of the cast members in *Blazing Saddles* had been regular guest stars on the television westerns from the late 1960s and early 1970s, the actors no doubt feeling right at home and/or worried they were biting the hand that feeds them when making *Blazing Saddles*. To be fair, television westerns of the time were trying to modernize and deal with more contemporary issues like racism, bigotry, and violence, but *Blazing Saddles* came by and said, "You'll never be able to point out how silly all this 'Cowboy and Indian' stuff is to people of today." Even though such westerns were mainly off television by the mid-1970s, *Blazing Saddles* helped bury that concept for good on television.

The print ad included in the *Blazing Saddles* press-book that—not surprisingly—never appeared in your local paper.

Over the years, Brooks and others associated with the film have been asked if the same movie could be made today. The typical response is no, that we've become too politically correct and the word "nigger" could not have made it into the film, leading to a good chunk of the film not really working. I disagree in some respects—perhaps the major studios would have rejected the film for that reason, but a smaller studio probably would have been okay with it. The word certainly does get used these days in films; usually with an R rating, but that's what *Blazing Saddles* has anyway. Where the film would be in trouble is that far too often comedy films have gone beyond the now-charming fart scenes and beating up of old women seen in the movie from 1974. People too often today expect something stronger, like urination or defecation instead of just guys passing gas. It would have to be more shocking than ever, and in doing so would not be anywhere near as effective as what we got in 1974.

Blazing Saddles has stayed with us, and showed that crude comedy can sometimes produce not only great laughs, but deep thoughts as well. In an interview with Brooks from 2014, a writer by the name of Drew McWeeny mentioned going to a screening of the film right after the second trial over Rodney King (a black man badly beaten by police on camera). The audience was "pretty much split, black and white. And by ten minutes into the film, everyone was on the floor. It was such an amazing room to be in on that night and to feel everyone laughing at the same things."

Brooks told McWeeny that he had been there and witnessed it as well. "It was like this movie audience saw the 'new world' of cinema for the first time, and they really celebrated the shit out of it. They went nuts. It was probably, as far as watching one of my movies, you know, on screen, it was probably the greatest night of my life."

Now who can argue with that?

Quiet Dignity and Grace

Young Frankenstein

Release Date: World premiere at the Avco Theater in Westwood, California, on December 17, 1974. General release between December 18 and December 22, 1974, throughout the country.

Hitler References

Surprisingly, none for a movie that takes place in some mythical version of Transylvania at an indefinite time period. You half-expect the monster to save a little boy only for his mother to call out for "Little Adolph" to come in for dinner, but no.

Musical Moments

Two and a half. "Puttin' on the Ritz" by Frankenstein and his Monster. The theme song played at various times to attract the Monster (and Frankenstein). Brief snippets of "Sweet Mystery of Life" by Elizabeth and Inga, while Elizabeth sings a snippet of "Battle Hymn of the Republic." Blücher (neigh!) gets a chance to play a bit on the violin, and Igor on the . . . ram's horn thingie.

Pre-production

Sometimes fate lends a hand. In trying to help out a friend, Brooks ended up earning him the title of "King of Comedy" in Hollywood in 1974.

In April 1972, as he said in his autobiography, Gene Wilder was piecing together a new script idea he had about "What might happen if I were the great grandson of Beaufort von Frankenstein and was called to Transylvania because I had just inherited the Frankenstein estate." It was his third attempt at writing a script, and he wrote at the top of the page where he was fleshing out his idea, "Young Frankenstein." Later he would realize he was subconsciously thinking about an old Mickey Rooney movie called *Young Edison*, as well one Anne Bancroft had made called *Young Winston*, when he came up with the title. Happy with what he had, he called Brooks to tell him about the concept. Brooks's response was, "Cute. That's cute."

The story would have ended there, but later that summer Wilder received a call from his agent Mike Medavoy, who suggested that Wilder make a movie with Marty Feldman and Peter Boyle. Wilder knew of Boyle from his growing success in movies after *Joe* (1970), in which he starred, and had seen Marty

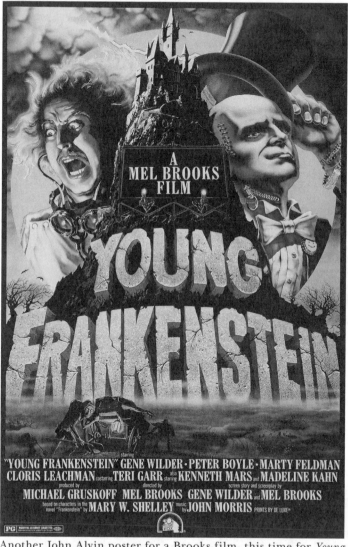

Another John Alvin poster for a Brooks film, this time for *Young Frankenstein*. With this and *Blazing Saddles* both becoming major hits in the same year, Mel Brooks had a lock on the title of being a comedy genius.

Feldman in the summertime television series *The Marty Feldman Comedy Machine* (1971–1972). Still, Wilder was curious as to why Medavoy thought of the pairing and was told "Because I now represent you and Peter and Marty." Gene's often-quoted response was, "Well, with that kind of wonderful artistic reason, how can it go wrong?"

As mentioned in the DVD documentary for the film, Medavoy asked if Wilder had anything, and Wilder thought back on his "Young Frankenstein" concept. Working away through the night, Wilder then sent Medavoy four typewritten pages of a scene for the proposed script that plays out almost exactly like in the film of Frederick first meeting Igor at the train station. Medavoy called back two days later and thought he could sell it to a studio, and then asked if Mel Brooks would be willing to direct it. Wilder was reluctant and told Medavoy that he knew Brooks probably would not direct anything that he himself hadn't written.

The following day Wilder received a call from Brooks. "What are you getting me into?" Brooks demanded. Wilder replied, "Nothing you don't want to get into." Brooks kept hesitating on the phone, but by the next day Medavoy called Wilder to say that Brooks had agreed to direct the film. At that point in time, Brooks was still working on the project that would become *Blazing Saddles*, and Wilder stated later that if Brooks had already found renewed success with that movie or had seen a bigger success with either *The Producers* or *The Twelve Chairs*, Brooks probably would have passed. It was only because he needed to take a chance and help a friend that he agreed to do the film. Columbia was offered the package of Brooks, Wilder, Feldman, and Boyle and agreed to the picture. Now only the script needed to be done.

It should be noted that Brooks tells a slightly different story—or two—as to how *Young Frankenstein* began. In the most common version, Brooks was working on the set of *Blazing Saddles* when he spotted Wilder writing something on a pad of paper. Asked what he was doing, Wilder mentioned it was an idea about the young Dr. Frankenstein, and then they went from there. Brooks, however, corroborated Wilder's version in a 1974 interview with Bob Thomas of the Associated Press, stating the *Blazing Saddles* script had just been completed when he heard from Wilder about the *Young Frankenstein* concept.

In June 1973, Columbia Pictures announced that they had gathered up the project with Brooks, Wilder, Feldman, and Boyle. Everything looked great as the contracts were about to be signed, except there were two problems that stood in the way: the budget and the filming. That may sound like a joke, but it was what it all boiled down to. The first had to do with the budget. After looking through the script, Brooks determined that they would need a budget of $2.25 million; Columbia felt it should be $1.75 million. Brooks and Wilder were hesitant on what to do until Brooks said, as recounted in the DVD documentary, "We're nuts! We should just go in there and say, 'You guys are crackerjacks. Your budget is right on the nose. So I'll tell you what, you come up, and we'll come down and we'll meet in the middle. $2 million."

With the first issue resolved, the second issue appeared. Just as they were about to leave, Brooks mentioned the film was to be in black and white. Wilder had been the first to recognize this idea when beginning on the script, and Brooks saw it as a must for the look of the film as well—if they were to parody that style, being in color was not going to do it. "I've watched all the great James Whale horror films over and over again," Brooks stated. "I love them because of his incredible portraiture, all the backlighting. They'd always have this sort of little halo and white light around the head." There was also a more down-to-earth reason: "The other issue was the monster makeup for Peter Boyle. We did some tests in color; and it was a shade of green that was way too much. Terrible. Shoot the same makeup in black and white, looks gorgeous."

Besides, it was not like the black-and-white format was completely dead— Peter Bogdanovich had created an Oscar-winning movie in 1971 that was in black and white, *The Last Picture Show*, and that was from Columbia as well. Ticket buyers were smart enough to understand using the film format there, and it could easily be reasoned that they would feel the same with *Young Frankenstein*. Columbia, on the other hand, didn't buy it. "Peru just got color," Brooks remembered in various interviews over the years. The company did not want to do a comedy in black and white, especially for $2 million, and then be unable to sell it overseas because it wasn't in color. Columbia came back with an offer, however, as Brooks told Yahoo in 2014. "If you [film] it on color stock, in some important places like New York, Chicago, and L.A., we'll [screen it in] black and white. But everywhere else, it's got to be in color." Brooks nearly agreed, but finally declined, thinking, "Nah, they'll screw it up. I don't trust them." Columbia said if they could find another studio in a short amount of time to take on the script, they would release them to go elsewhere, and Brooks agreed.

With Brooks and Wilder at the meeting was producer Michael Gruskoff, who had coproduced the well-received and now-considered-classic science-fiction film *Silent Running* for Universal the year before. Gruskoff had worked with Brooks at the William Morris Agency and with Wilder's agent, Mike Medavoy, at CMA. He had also become friends with Alan Ladd Jr. (born 1937 and the son of actor Alan Ladd) back in 1969 when they both worked in London. Ladd had become the Vice-President for Creative Affairs at 20th Century-Fox in January 1973, and was a natural for the trio to meet to discuss the film. Ladd signed them on, and the film was announced in the trade papers in June 1973, with a budget of $2.7 million (it eventually was completed for $2.78 million).

And with all the negotiations out of the way, the only thing left to do was to get the script in order, which they continued to do through the production of *Blazing Saddles*. While writing it, there were only two arguments that disrupted their work. In his autobiography, Wilder couldn't remember what the first argument was about, but it was enough for Brooks to scream at Wilder and stomp out the door of where Wilder was staying. This was followed up ten minutes later by Brooks calling Wilder and saying "Who was that madman who you had in your house? I could hear the yelling all the way over here. You should never let crazy people into your house—don't you know that? They could be dangerous!"

The other, and more important, argument came when Wilder presented Brooks with the "Puttin' on the Ritz" sequence. Brooks read through the scene and then confronted Wilder, "You have the audacity to put in this musical number in here? After all the hard work we've put into this you do this?" Wilder, furious over Brooks's comments, argued his reasons behind the sequence for about twenty-five minutes when Brooks jumped in and said, "It's in!" When asked why he would suddenly change his mind, Brooks said, "I wanted to see how hard you'd fight for it. If you gave up right away, I'd know it was wrong. But when you turned blue—I knew it must be right." In 2014, speaking to Yahoo, Brooks had another take on the story, however: "So I made a deal with him. I said, 'Okay, we'll shoot it. We'll shoot it properly, but when we see it in the dailies, stitched together with the other scenes, you're going to want to cut it. But I'll spend the extra money and let's shoot it.' So we did, and it turned out to be the best scene in the whole movie, that's all. I apologized profusely to Gene after the opening night."

To go back further, however, perhaps Brooks was also remembering a few years back to when he argued with Sid Caesar over a joke to use on his program until he poked at Caesar, demanding he do it. Although Caesar did not like the finger in his chest, he felt that Brooks must have felt strongly enough to risk it; and the same when Wilder argued for nearly a half-hour over the "Puttin' on the Ritz" number in *Young Frankenstein*.

The script would still be tightened as the production came closer to being filmed. Much of what appears in the movie goes back to Wilder's original solo draft before Brooks came in, only with certain elements dropped, including a long musical sequence and some of the scenes being moved around for a better pace. A good number of lines came by way of Brooks, as well as pitching Igor—with his various showbiz references ("Nice working with you" and making a rim-shot sound after saying "Call it a hunch" and pointing at his hunch, for examples)—to be more in tune with the modern world than the other characters. Brooks was very proud of one element in particular, as he told Robert Ross: "The whole thing is dripping with Jewish humor, of course, and the scene that I consider closes the second act is when the monster breaks out of the castle and goes off on his own. Gene shouts out the line: 'What have I done?' Which is the line that would close every second act in every Jewish play in New York."

A comparison of the script drafts with what audiences finally saw shows the following cuts:

- A complete opening sequence that came through all the drafts from Wilder's first was filmed and then cut. The scene features the surviving members of the family hearing the will of Beaufort von Frankenstein (voiced by John Carradine) on the twentieth anniversary of the man's death. A record—on 78 rpm—is played with the Baron explaining that each surviving member would get a piece of his estate . . . unless his great-grandson Frederick had become a doctor. This premise does explain why the coffin is displayed and the box retrieved from the mummified remains in the first place (it had been there for twenty years), but it sets up a lot of characters that are never seen again and comes too close to having audiences expecting a *Ten Little Indians/The Old Dark House* plot, with relatives trying to bump off Frederick. Besides, Herr Falkstein explains the plot quickly and efficiently in the lecture hall, so it's all unnecessary exposition. The scene is included in the special edition DVD and the Blu-ray of the film (and features actor Leon Askin—General Burkhalter of *Hogan's Heroes* fame).

- Wilder's original version of Frederick is much more of a stuffed shirt than in later drafts; yelling at his assistant in the lecture hall over a mishap with an incorrect cauliflower that ruins part of his lecture (but foreshadows Igor getting the wrong brain for the creature later). He also demands that the medical student who called him Frankenstein be removed from his lectures the next semester.

- Another sequence filmed but discarded had Frederick and Herr Falkstein walking down a street, discussing Frederick going to the see the estate. (Later drafts make mention of Frederick's impeding wedding.) They walk past a man playing a violin for change, with the man playing the "eerie Transylvanian Lullaby that was heard at the opening" of the film. Frederick appears stricken with a headache and returns to the man to discuss his violin. He then breaks it in two and hands it back to the man. Herr Falkstein asks why he destroyed the man's violin, but Frederick has no memory of doing so. Frederick agrees to go and Herr Falkstein gives some change to the man who is now playing half a violin. This scene establishes that the music played, which we see later affects the creature, affects Frederick as well. Herr Falkstein in the filmed scene also hints that it's a family trait to be affected by the music. It was probably cut as we never really see it affecting Frederick again until the end of the film, and there it is assumed it is because of the mind-swap.

- Elizabeth comes off better in the goodbye scene in the initial draft, without the concerns about her appearances that made the scene really hysterical in the final draft and film. In other words, she's rather dull in the first draft and more of a warm body rather than a flesh-and-blood character as in the film. Oddly, some of their dialogue is switched in the first draft.

- The older couple on the train, loudly complaining first in English and then in German about "someone" doing "something" every night, do not appear in the earlier drafts of the script.

- It is clearer in the drafts that the pronunciation of Igor's name is Igor putting Frederick on. Feldman's response in the film is quicker than intended, and thus the uncertainty as to if he really is called "Eye-gor" doesn't play out.

- In the first draft, Frederick, Igor, and Inga walk past Dracula and a wolfman on their way to the wagon.
- "Walk this way," according to Feldman, was his ad lib while they were rehearsing the scene on set. Brooks liked it enough that he told them to do it for the camera, which both Wilder and Feldman balk at; Wilder, as he stated in his autobiography, because he didn't know the meaning of the joke, and Feldman because he did and thought it was a corny "old music hall joke." "We both said, 'Mel, please take that out,' and he left it in," Feldman said later. "He said, 'I think it's funny.' Audiences laugh at it. Gene and I were both wrong. Mel was right."
- The portrait of Victor von Frankenstein does not appear in the earlier drafts of the script.
- The business with the revolving bookcase came later in the drafts.
- The drafts of the script have Frederick flicking the switch on to his grandfather's private library to a shower of sparks. It was Feldman, however, who suggested changing the scene so that Igor would be the one to spot the switches, with Frederick shouting "Damn your eyes," after the sparks fly, and Igor pointing out his eyes saying, "Too late." "No one got it during the preview screening or press releases" Brooks said in Robert Ross's biography of Feldman. "It was a bit of Victoriana from England and the cliché wasn't known [in America]. I loved it and trust the English audiences got it."
- Upon finding Victor von Frankenstein's book, Frederick suggests that he take it along to read, as "we could all use a good laugh." Inga and Igor laugh with Frederick, only for lightning to frighten them into holding each other. This was filmed, and a snippet appears in some television ads for the movie, but is not included in the "deleted scenes" of the DVD/Blu-ray.
- Frederick is shown reading Victor von Frankenstein's book over a longer period of time; at first in a condescending manner and then finally—as seen in the film—in intense conviction.
- As Frederick announces that "It could work!", lighting would have then repeatedly struck, showing the faces of everyone in the flash of light, including Frau Blücher (neigh!) somewhere else, smoking a cigar. The shot of Frau Blücher (neigh!) with the cigar appears in some ads ("and Cloris Leachman as the lady with a cigar . . . "), but not in the film.
- Also missing is Beaufort von Frankenstein's coffin opening with his skeleton saying "Oh, shit!" after Frederick agrees that it could work.
- The policeman meeting Frederick with the dead man's hand sticking out is from a later draft of the script.
- The drafts establish that Hans Delbruck died from VD, so maybe he wasn't that smart after all.
- The in-jokes about Igor's hump changing sides was developed by Feldman on the set and not in any of the drafts.

- There's a tad more dialogue with the villagers before Inspector Kemp is introduced. They also seem to understand him perfectly in the earlier drafts and not listening in confusion when Kemp's German accent really goes full-tilt gonzo as in the film.
- The first draft has Frederick and Igor visiting what they think is the lifeless creature on the slab, not realizing he is slowly coming back to life. They then go to eat.
- It has been presented in several histories of the film that Feldman came up with the line about "I'll never forget what my father said to me" on the set, but these lines appear in the third draft of the script and onwards, before filming commenced.
- In Wilder's first draft, when Frederick asks the creature to "give me your hands," the two would go into a production number with a song called "Alive." From here, the first draft deals with Frederick teaching the creature dancing and music, leading directly to the "Puttin' on the Ritz" number and bypassing Inspector Kemp's visit and the creature getting loose the first time.
- The film cuts directly from the trio giving the creature a sedative to Frederick playing darts with the Inspector. The later drafts have Kemp being met at the door by Inga before Frederick arrives and takes the inspector into the study. This scene was shot, but then cut, although it appears on the Blu-Ray.
- When the little girl asks what they can throw in now, the creature was to pick her up high over his head . . . and then place her on the teeter-totter. The look on the creature's face instead of all that business actually drew more laughs, so the creature picking up the girl was cut from the film.
- Again, histories of the film suggest that Gene Hackman came up with the espresso line on the set, but the line appears in the third draft of the script from December 1973.
- A sequence was filmed with Jack Sprat, the highwayman trying to rob the creature only to get beaten up instead. It isn't very funny and obviously was cut for this reason.
- Upon finding the creature, Frederick suggests they kill him. Frau Blücher (neigh!) pulls out a gun and tells Frederick "to be a Frankenstein." Going back to his grandfather's notes, Frederick realizes that the creature feels unloved. This leads directly to the scene in the film where Frederick goes into the cell to talk to the creature and, finally, admitting he is a Frankenstein. Stills exist of Blücher (neigh!) holding the gun on the others, so the scene was shot. It does not appear in the deleted scenes on the DVD, but is included in the special edition Blu-ray.
- The exhibition of the creature is longer in the drafts and was filmed but edited down. In addition to the creature walking forward and then backwards, Frederick puts a blindfold on the creature and has him balance two

Frau Blücher (neigh!) pulls out a gun to halt the execution of the monster in a scene cut from the final version of the film.

milk bottles—one empty, one full. Igor brings out the milk bottles. When Frederick asks Igor where his hump has gone to, Igor replies indignantly, "Never in a tux!" This does explain why Frederick is holding a blindfold in his hand in the film, as the portion of the scene dealing with the blindfold is missing. This part of the scene was cut but is included in the special edition Blu-ray.

- Frederick's and Inga's full "intellectual discussion" was filmed, but then edited down to just the beginning of the scene. The full scene, along with a brief reprise after Frederick is kicked out of Elizabeth's room, appears on the DVD/Blu-ray.
- Igor's Groucho Marx–like reading of the line "Certainly, you take the blonde and I'll take the one in the turban," along with his attacking of the fur around Elizabeth's neck, was added by Feldman (with the encouragement of Brooks) while filming—which explains why everyone has trouble controlling their laughter in the scene, especially Wilder.
- The drafts have the villagers arriving to speak to Frederick just as the creature kidnaps Elizabeth. They then leave to hunt the creature down, while Frederick and Igor work on a way to bring the creature back to the castle.
- In the first draft, Elizabeth sees the creature's "schwanzstucker" and is enthusiastic for a romp with him. In the third draft, the creature takes

The monster rips out the arm of the Inspector (Kenneth Mars)—
an action that does appear in the movie, but not with the monster's reaction as seen in this lobby card for the film.

Elizabeth to a cave, where she resists more than the somewhat conflicted
participant seen in the film. The song she sings is "Cheek to Cheek" instead
of "Sweet Mystery of Life."

- The villagers stop to regroup and decide to go back to the castle, thinking
  they had been tricked. By eliminating the initial visit at the time Elizabeth
  is kidnapped, there's no need for this scene, and it was cut.
- It should be mentioned that some additional filming was done showing
  the villagers doing silly things while searching for the creature. However,
  it gets too far away from the main plot and slows down the pace of the film,
  so wisely it was edited out. Some of this footage does appear on the Blu-ray
  edition of the film, however.
- The creature's speech begins by him stating he is a relative of the doctor's
  and is a much longer speech than the one in the film that starts with him
  directly saying he is "the monster!"
- Frederick and Inga are seen in domestic bliss, with Frederick arriving
  home from work, rather than on their wedding night. The results are the
  same, however.
- A final cast bow, with the full cast coming down the staircase of the castle,
  singing "Sweet Mystery of Life" and walking past the camera. Wilder can
  be seen dragging Brooks out to take a bow as well. Brooks had been trying
  to place such a nod to the players in every one of his films. He would finally
  achieve it somewhat in his next film, *Silent Movie*, and only properly in the
  film he starred in but didn't direct, *To Be or Not to Be*.

With the script in completed form, the time came for casting and gathering
the crew.

Cast

Gene Wilder as Frederick von Frankenstein

Besides his promised filming as The Fox in *The Little Prince*—which hit theaters about the same time as *Young Frankenstein*—Wilder worked on getting *Young Frankenstein* ready. While working on the film, he had an idea for another script, this one being about another brother to the famous literary detective Sherlock Holmes. He would ask Marty Feldman and Madeline Kahn to appear in the film if it was green-lit. After 20th Century-Fox saw footage from the film in early April, they asked Wilder if he had anything else he'd like to work on, whereupon he signed a five-year contract with the studio, and began writing *The Adventure of Sherlock Holmes' Smarter Brother*, which he also directed.

His next film after that was *Silver Streak* (1976), which saw him share the screen for the first time with Richard Pryor. They would go on to make three additional movies together over the years: *Stir Crazy* (1980), *See No Evil, Hear No Evil* (1989), and *Another You* (1991). Wilder would continue to make movies in the very early 1990s, some doing better than others, including three with Gilda Radner—*Hanky Panky* (1982), *The Woman in Red* (1984), and *Haunted Honeymoon* (1986, which also featured Dom DeLuise in his third appearance in a Wilder–directed film)—who he was married to until her death in 1989.

In 1994, Wilder would star in the short-lived sitcom *Something Wilder*, lasting only fifteen episodes, and then appeared in two murder-mystery films for the A&E cable network in 1999, *Murder in a Small Town* and *The Lady in Question*, which he cowrote with his brother-in-law, Gilbert Pearlman (who wrote the novelizations for *Young Frankenstein* and *The Adventure of Sherlock Holmes' Smarter Brother*). A couple of appearances on the sitcom *Will & Grace* led to Wilder winning an Emmy for Outstanding Guest Actor on a Comedy Series, but it would be his last professional work on-screen. From 2003 onward, he would concentrate on writing short stories and novels, with an occasional appearance to do an interview. In 2013, he was diagnosed with Alzheimer's disease, which he kept private so as not to upset any of his fans. He died in 2016.

Over the years there was a lot of talk about Wilder working with Brooks again, sometimes from Brooks himself. Wilder did appear to witness the Broadway version of *The Producers* and

Teri Garr and Gene Wilder about to head to the bookcase and Von Frankenstein's secret library. Wilder had originally wanted Madeline Kahn for the role Garr played in the film.

came onstage when *Young Frankenstein* was made into a musical for Broadway, but original projects with Brooks were never to be. The tabloids, especially in the later 1970s, tried to build up a feud between the two, but there never seemed to be much spark to the idea, with Wilder always presenting Brooks as someone who had guided him as a writer and director, as well as giving him early work that helped to create his film career. They continued to talk often as friends in the last few years, although never as partners on a new project.

Although it may be a cliché to say so, Brooks and Wilder together were another case of two men finding friendship and complementing each other, just as in so many of Brooks's early films. It was something Wilder himself noticed in 1975, looking back on their collaborations: "My job was to make him subtler. His job was to make me more broad. I would say, 'I don't want this to be *Blazing Frankenstein*,' and he'd answer, 'I don't want an art film that only fourteen people see.'" As their work diverged from each other, so too did their styles, with Brooks more willing to go for the cartoon-type gags, while Wilder would incorporate such a light touch in his later films that they seemed more quaint than laugh-out-loud funny. Separately, they were always worth a look, but together they made classics.

Marty Feldman (1934–1982) as Igor

Born in London, England, the son of Jewish immigrant parents, Martin Alan Feldman had grown up as an odd man out: Jewish with a slightly lazy eye—Feldman's protruding eyes came late in his teens after an attempt to treat a thyroid problem badly backfired—bad grades, a weak build, and a heavy amount of antisocial behavior. At the age of eleven, he was punished for writing a poem at school that the teachers assumed he had to have plagiarized. The punishment backfired, however, as Feldman was convinced that if his teachers had problems with what he did, then he would become a writer as a form of rebellion against them.

In 1954, Feldman met a fellow writer, Barry Took, and the two would unite to write several episodes for various series on British television and radio, including *The Army Game* (1960) and *Round the Horne* (1964–1967). Took later at the BBC helped band together the writers that became *Monty Python's Flying Circus*.

Marty Feldman as I-gor ain't got no body . . . but although Feldman was already gaining some success in America, *Young Frankenstein* would help catapult him to Hollywood stardom.

A time as script editor and head writer on *The Frost Report* led to Feldman joining fellow writers John Cleese, Graham Chapman, and Tim Brooke-Taylor as an actor and writer on their own series *At Last the 1948 Show* in 1967. That series would spearhead Feldman into starring in his own series, *Marty* (later titled *It's Marty* in its second series), from 1968-1969, as well as branching out into movies with a small role in the apocalyptic comedy *The Bed Sitting Room* (1969) and his first starring role in the self-penned *Every Home Should Have One* (1970).

In 1971, an attempt was made to produce a series for Marty that could be shown in the United States as well. The series, *The Marty Feldman Comedy Machine*, which was produced by Brooks's old cowriter on the Caesar shows, Larry Gelbart, would air for only fifteen episodes in the summer of 1972, but Gene Wilder happened to see a few episodes. He immediately pictured Marty in the role of Igor, the hunchback, and began thinking of him in the role as he sketched out more of the script. When the offer of working with Wilder and Boyle came up, Feldman jumped at the chance, not only because soon enough Mel Brooks was on board, but also because it meant a chance to work in a Hollywood picture.

Marty would go on to appear in Wilder's *The Adventure of Sherlock Holmes' Smarter Brother* (1975) and an Italian comedy released in the United States as *Sex with a Smile* (1976) before returning to Brooks's next film, *Silent Movie*.

Peter Boyle (1935–2006) as the Monster

Boyle was looking around for anything to get him away from the character he had become known for in the early 1970s, the homicidal bigot in the film *Joe* (1970), and a chance to play in a comedy by Wilder and Brooks seemed like a perfect opportunity. Boyle was born in Norristown, Pennsylvania, and grew up in Philadelphia, where his father was a local television personality known as "Chuck Wagon Pete." Growing up around the entertainment business, Peter found that his studies to join a Catholic order were not going anywhere and eventually drifted into acting, bouncing around between New York and Chicago before joining Second City, the improvisation group. He would move on to a small part in the film *Medium Cool* (1969) and then to *Joe* in 1970. While *Joe* had an antiviolence message, it was praised by many who enjoyed watching Boyle's character in the film killing hippies, which is why Boyle began looking for more parts to break away from that image even though the film made him famous. "I was concerned," he mentioned in 1974 to the *Philadelphia Inquirer*, "I'd be doing Joe forever." Although other dramatic roles had come along, Brooks's film was the first to really allow him to play comedy on the screen. The film would also be important to Boyle as he would meet his wife, Loraine Alterman, a writer for *Rolling Stone* magazine, on the set of the film and the two would marry in 1977, eventually having two daughters.

Young Frankenstein was the only film Boyle would do with Brooks, but he would team up with Marty Feldman twice more—in the Feldman-directed film *In God We Tru$t* (1980) and writer-star Graham Chapman's *Yellowbeard* (1983), which also featured other Brooks alumni Kenneth Mars and Madeline Kahn. Boyle would continue with a large career of television and movie credits over the years, even after suffering a stroke in 1990, from which he eventually recovered. Besides playing the Monster in *Young Frankenstein*, and perhaps his role in *Taxi Driver* (1976), Boyle is probably best remembered today for the character Frank Barone, which he played for nine years on the popular series *Everybody Loves Raymond* (1996–2005)—which certainly is a nicer legacy than *Joe*. He passed away in 2006.

Cloris Leachman (born 1926) as Frau Blücher (neigh!)

Leachman was born in Des Moines, Iowa, becoming involved with acting as a teenager and eventually studying acting in college. Contrary to popular belief, Leachman was not once Miss America, although she did rank into the top 16 in 1946. That publicity along with a $1,000 she won from the contest was enough to help her get work in New York—mainly on television. She would join the Actors Studio soon after that. She would also understudy for the lead role of Nellie in the original production of *South Pacific* on Broadway.

Although she would work off and on during the next ten years on Broadway, most of her work in the 1950s and 1960s came from television, including on the series *Lassie*, although she would occasionally get a role films as well, such as the briefly seen girl that gets Mike Hammer involved with a deadly search for a box containing "the great whatsit" in the cult classic *Kiss Me Deadly* (1955). By the 1970s, Leachman was starting to drift into more movie roles, just as she began as a regular on the popular sitcom *The Mary Tyler Moore Show* in 1970—a series that found her character of Mary's friend Phyllis spun off into her own show, *Phyllis* (1975–1977). Her performance in the 1971 film *The Last Picture Show* gained Leachman an Oscar for Best Supporting Actress, but she went back to television just as quickly, filming a comedy called *Thursday's Game* for the ABC Network that was written by James L. Brooks (*Lou Grant*, *Taxi*, *The Simpsons*) and starring Bob Newhart and Gene Wilder. A couple of years later, as work was beginning on *Young Frankenstein*, Mel Brooks remembered her from *The Last Picture Show*, while Gene had worked with her in the television movie *Thursday's Game*, a rather good dramatic comedy, that was initially shelved by the network until April 1974 when the popularity of the actors involved naturally found the film being aired.

Leachman had never tried to use a German accent before, according to her autobiography, and arrived on the set having to "cram" for the role by listening to Brooks's mother, who was visiting the set. "In the film," she would go on to say in her book, "I pronounce my first line . . . very carefully because I was still a little unsure about the accent." The drawn-out method of her speech there

Gene Wilder looking ready to crack up again as Cloris Leachman makes her debut in a Mel Brooks film as Frau Blücher (neigh!). Leachman would go on to play roles in two later Brooks films, as well as have a costarring role in *Nut House*, Brooks's 1990s television series.

and elsewhere in the film works well; heightening the tension as one feels there is a lot of mystery hidden behind Blücher's (neigh!) words, even if it is just Leachman making sure of her accent.

As an aside, for years the rumor went around that the word "Blücher (neigh!)" means "glue" in German. It doesn't. Nor is it "glue" in Yiddish. For some reason people assumed that the horses fearing the name comes from a hidden meaning, and the idea that it meant "glue" came to pass. It is nothing that simple, and actually somewhat nastier—that the horses fear Frau Blücher (neigh!), not her name. Which begs the question, what on Earth is she doing to those poor horses when no one is around?

Teri Garr (born 1947) as Inga

Born in Lakewood, Ohio, Garr was the daughter of a vaudevillian named Eddie Garr, who would appear in some films and television before passing away in 1956. Her mother, Phyllis Garr, was a former Rockette who eventually became a wardrobe mistress in Hollywood, working on such films as *The Graduate*, *Silver Streak*, *The In-Laws*, and *Young Frankenstein*. Having studied acting and dancing, Teri landing one of her first big roles in the L.A. road company of *West Side Story* just after finishing high school. The role only lasted six weeks, but she would join the dancing class of David Winters, who had played the part of A-Rab in the movie version of *West Side Story* and appeared in the road company version Teri had done. Later, Winters was signed to choreograph the classic Elvis movie *Viva Las Vegas* (1964) and asked his students to audition. Garr would end up dancing in nine Elvis movies, as well as taking roles in other movies and films, including a rather large part in an episode of *Star Trek* ("Assignment: Earth,"

1968) and a small but memorable role in the Monkees' film *Head*, which she got due to being in the same acting class with the film's scriptwriter, Jack Nicholson.

Garr's big break on television came in 1971 when she became the female second banana on *The Sonny and Cher Comedy Hour*, where Brooks first saw her. She also got a small role in Francis Ford Coppola's 1974 film *The Conversation*. As mentioned above, Garr's mother had been working in movies by that time, dealing with costumes and wardrobe, and Teri had made a habit out of asking her mother if there were any roles still open on the films she was hired to work on. When *Young Frankenstein* came up, Teri was surprised to find that they were still casting. The part was for Elizabeth, Frederick's fiancée, and Garr auditioned three times for the part, with the understanding that they were trying to get Madeline Kahn to play the role. When Kahn finally agreed, Brooks had been impressed enough with Garr that he told her if she could come back the next day with a German accent, there may be another role for her, the part of the laboratory assistant, Inga.

Just as Leachman had studied Brooks's mom on the set, Garr studied the accent of a German woman who was Cher's wig stylist behind the scenes on *The Sonny and Cher Comedy Hour* to try to perfect the accent needed. The other thing she needed was mentioned as part of the character's description in the script: "A large-breasted laboratory assistant lying in the hay." It's what leads into the whole "What knockers" line, after all. "When I read the part," Garr remembered in her autobiography, "I realized it was really all about boobs, and I was not about to let my lack of them hinder my performance. The next day I went in to do my imitation of [Cher's wig stylist] for Mel Brooks wearing a fuzzy pink sweater and a huge padded bra stuffed with socks." The next day she got a call telling her she got the job, which convinced her she needed to stuff her bra with socks more often when auditioning.

Although her mother was working on the same film with her, her mother wanted Teri to not mention anything to Brooks about their relationship, figuring there had to be a divide between the cast and the crew. Yet Teri told Brooks anyway, who gushed about her in front of her mother. Garr was proud of getting the role against many other actresses (Farrah Fawcett being one): "For one thing, it was the first major role in which I actually got to talk—not just dance, as I'd done in the Elvis movies, or get buried in sand, as in *Pajama Party*. And Mel Brooks had chosen me over so many other actresses, including every good-looking starlet who ever got off the bus in Hollywood."

Garr, surprisingly, never returned to the world of Mel Brooks's films. Then again, that may not be too surprising, as she began to get bigger roles as time went on. One of the first big ones was *Oh, God!* (1977), written by Larry Gelbart and directed by Carl Reiner. That was followed close behind by Steven Spielberg's *Close Encounters of the Third Kind* (1977), *Tootsie* (1982, with Larry Gelbart contributing), *Mr. Mom* (1983), and a handful of films connected with Francis Ford Coppola, including *The Escape Artist* (1982), *The Black Stallion* (1979), and the fascinating but little-seen *One from the Heart* (1981). Her film and television career—including multiple appearances on *Friends* as Phoebe's mother—continued into the 2000s. In 2002, she announced that she had multiple sclerosis. After 2007, and building back her strength from a brain aneurysm she suffered in 2006, she had to concentrate on maintaining her health, although she has made rare appearances in the years since to promote medical causes.

Madeline Kahn (1942–1999) as Elizabeth

While filming *Blazing Saddles*, Wilder went to Brooks and suggested that Madeline Kahn would be perfect as the laboratory assistant in the *Young Frankenstein* film they were going to do next. Brooks thought she would be good too, but in the role of Elizabeth instead. The only issue was that Kahn was looking to play more dramatic parts and was getting a bit tired of doing comedy after comedy. It was only when they neared filming and were close to signing someone—most probably Teri Garr—for the role that Kahn finally relented and agreed to do the part.

After *Young Frankenstein*, Kahn would return to the stage in the drama *In the Boom Boom Room*, for which Kahn was nominated for Best Actress in a Play Tony, and won a Drama Desk Award for Outstanding Performance in 1974. In 1975, she would return to Bogdanovich for the quirky musical, *At Long Last Love* and then star with Wilder in *The Adventure of Sherlock Holmes' Smarter Brother*. She

Garr, Wilder, Kahn, and Feldman in the notorious baggage scene in *Young Frankenstein*, which had to be redone many times due to Feldman making Wilder laugh while filming.

would skip over the next Brooks film after *Young Frankenstein*, but would be back in 1977 for *High Anxiety*.

Kenneth Mars as Inspector Kemp

After *The Producers*, Mars moved on to a costarring role on the short-lived, but well-remembered, television series *He & She* (1967–1968). He appeared in *Butch Cassidy and the Sundance Kid* in 1969, which featured Cloris Leachman and was edited by John C. Howard, who worked on many of Brooks's films, and *What's Up, Doc?* (with Madeline Kahn) in 1972. Although he is memorable in *Young Frankenstein*, it would be the last film he worked on with Brooks. He would restrict most of his time after this to television, including doing voice work for animated series. He would pass away from pancreatic cancer at the age of seventy-five.

Gene Hackman (born 1930) as the Blind Hermit

Hackman was already an established name by the time of *Young Frankenstein*, having starred in *The French Connection* (1971), *The Poseidon Adventure* (1972), and *The Conversation* (1974, with Teri Garr). He had also costarred in *Bonnie and Clyde* (1967), Gene Wilder's first film, and was a friend of Wilder. "He was playing tennis with Wilder every weekend," Brooks remembered later to Yahoo, "and he said, 'Is there anything in that crazy movie I could do?'" Wilder would say in the DVD documentary on the making of the film that Hackman expected to play "third officer on the left" or some such, but instead Wilder and Brooks decided that the only role for him was that of the Blind Hermit. "I told him," Brooks continued, "'There's no money in it.' But he said, 'I don't want that. I just want to do it.'"

Gene Hackman as the blind man, about to innocently do bodily harm to the monster (Peter Boyle). Hackman performed in the role on the agreement that his appearance would be a surprise for audiences.

Although the casting was supposed to be a surprise, newspapers announced his appearance in the film back in November 1974 (a month before it was released). The announcement listed him as appearing as a monster in the film, however, rather than the role he did play. As it turns out, most people didn't see the spoiler, and it was not unusual for audience members to find something strangely familiar about the actor playing the part under the wig and long beard, and they were genuinely surprised to see it was Hackman in the role when the ending credits appeared. This would be the only film appearance for Hackman in a Brooks film, although he would later reteam with Garr in the comedy *Full Moon in Blue Water* in 1988.

Richard Haydn (1905–1985) as Herr Falkstein

The man who comes to tell Frederick about his inheritance is played by an actor who many remember from *The Sound of Music*, where he played Max Detweiler. He also did the voice of the Caterpillar in Disney's *Alice in Wonderland* (1951). *Young Frankenstein* would be his last role on camera in his career.

Danny Goldman (born 1939) as the annoying Medical Student

Goldman had appeared as Capt. Murrhardt in Robert Altman's *MASH* (1970). He would go on to concentrate on television work. He has done an extensive amount of voice acting, including the voice of Brainy Smurf, throughout the 1980s.

Mel Brooks as Cat Screech and Werewolf Howl

Reduced to making animal noises to get work. So sad.

Also Appearing

- Liam Dunn as Mr. Hilltop at the beginning of the film. Popping up from *Blazing Saddles*, along with Wilder and Kahn, where he was Reverend Johnson. He'll make one more Brooks appearance as the news vendor in *Silent Movie*.
- John Dennis (1925–2004) as an orderly. Appeared in a lot of television, typically as a cop or a bartender. He'll play an orderly again in *High Anxiety*.
- Jeff Maxwell (born 1947) as one of the medical students listening to the opening lecture. He would go on to play Igor (yes, Igor) on *MASH*, the television series.

In the Crew

There were many members of the crew who would work on this film and Brooks's follow-up, *Silent Movie*, in the same capacity:

- Mary Keats as hair stylist.
- William Tuttle, a longtime makeup artist who had worked on Hitchcock's *North by Northwest* (1959) and *Singin' in the Rain*, amongst many others, did the makeup in *Young Frankenstein*. He would have to design the makeup for Boyle in the film, being told that they could not use the same type of

makeup as in the Universal *Frankenstein* films. He would later work on Wilder's films *Silver Streak* and *The World's Greatest Lover.*

- Frank Baur as production manager. He would also work on Wilder's *The World's Greatest Lover.*
- Anthony Goldschmidt was brought back after *Blazing Saddles* as title designer for this film, *Silent Movie,* and *Spaceballs.*
- Don Hall as sound editor.
- Gary L. King and Jay King both worked as special effects technicians on this film and *Silent Movie.*
- Jesse Wayne did stunts for this film and *Silent Movie.*
- Stanford C. Allen was an assistant editor on *Young Frankenstein* and returned as the editor on *Silent Movie.*
- Ray Quiroz as script supervisor.
- Gerald Hirschfeld was cinematographer for the film. Hirschfeld had done the brilliant black-and-white photography in *Fail-Safe* (1964), amongst other films before this one. He would work with Brooks's production company as the director of photography on *My Favorite Year* (1982) and *To Be or Not to Be* (1983). He also was cinematographer on *The World's Greatest Lover* for Gene Wilder. He would never directly work under Brooks as director again—check out the Production section below for a reason why that may have been.
- John Morris created the musical score once again for Brooks, with Jonathan Tunick as orchestrator. This would be Tunick's last film for Brooks. John R. Harris was the music editor on this film, *High Anxiety,* and *History of the World, Part I.*
- Jack M. Marino was property master on this film, *History of the World, Part I, Life Stinks, Robin Hood: Men in Tights,* and *Dracula: Dead and Loving It.* Hendrik Wynands had been construction coordinator on Wilder's film *Willy Wonka and the Chocolate Factory* (1971), and would perform the same duties on *Young Frankenstein, Silent Movie,* Bancroft's *The Turning Point* (1977), *High Anxiety,* and Wilder's *The Frisco Kid.* Gene S. Cantamessa, who had done sound on *Blazing Saddles,* returned for this film as production mixer and did the same on *High Anxiety.* He would also be the production sound mixer on *History of the World, Part I* and *To Be or Not to Be.* Richard Portman did sound re-recording on *Willy Wonka and the Chocolate Factory* before *Young Frankenstein.* He would go on to be the re-recording mixer on *Silent Movie* and *High Anxiety.*

Production

One thing Wilder was adamant about was that Brooks should not appear in the movie. "One of the deals Gene Wilder made with me is 'You're not in the movie. If you're in the movie, I won't do it.'" Brooks recalled forty years later in an interview with Yahoo. "He thought I'd be in a suit of armor, and the camera would whip by him and I'd open the visor and say, 'Hello folks'—that I'd break the fourth wall every chance I had. He said, 'You can pay more attention to saluting James Whale's early *Frankenstein* [films].' And I said, 'You're right.'" (Oddly enough, he would make such a cameo appearance in a suit of armor in the first episode of his 1975 television series *When Things Were Rotten*.)

Wilder was referring to James Whale, the director who did *Frankenstein* (1931) and *Bride of Frankenstein* (1935), two classic monster movies that many generations had grown up seeing in theaters and on television. There were more movies in the series after Whale left, however; in particular *Son of Frankenstein* (1939) and *The Ghost of Frankenstein* (1942). Brooks and Wilder even tracked down Ken Strickfaden (1896–1984), who had created the original electronic gizmos found on the set of the 1931 *Frankenstein*. "He had all that in his garage," Brooks remembered in another Yahoo interview, this one in 2014. "We gave him like $2,000 and he was thrilled. He said, 'I don't care about the money; my stuff is going to be in the movie!' I said, 'Yep.' Because I wanted the original, rinky-dink, crazy turn-of-the-century imaginative electrical, bubbling, and static-y stuff. And we got it!"

Naturally, the look of the creature is a satirical version of the original Boris Karloff design—with the clothing, the five-inch-high boots, and the protruding forehead . . . along with a zipper in the neck. The castle created—for $360,000— and the village all look as if lifted from the earlier films, along with the standard "angry villagers with burning torches" and antiquated vehicles and clothing for everyone. Other elements that made it into the film that reflected the previous *Frankenstein* series of movies:

- Wilder's mustache, although not exactly the same, is similar to the style worn by Basil Rathbone in *Son of Frankenstein*. He really does look as if he could be related to Rathbone.
- Kemp is based on Inspector Krogh from *Son of Frankenstein*, including the wooden arm. In that film—and in the introduction scene between Frederick and Kemp that was cut from *Young Frankenstein*—each inspector lost their arm after having it ripped out of its socket by the monster.
- The later arrival of fiancée Elizabeth and the creature arriving in her room comes from *Frankenstein* (although she is only frightened by the monster in the original film).
- Frankenstein and Igor at the cemetery, with Frederick telling his assistant to get down when it's pretty clear that they're in the eye-sight of the gravedig-gers, is a direct parody of a scene in *Frankenstein*.
- Igor's mishap with the brains is also a parody of the same in *Frankenstein*.
- The little girl playing with the creature comes from *Frankenstein*, and it is our fore-knowledge of what happens to the little girl in the original film— drowning at the hands of the creature, who thinks she is a pretty flower that will float—is what makes the scene funny in *Young Frankenstein*.
- Brain swaps to "fix" the creature were a centerpiece of a couple of the sequels, and a prime one in the comedy sequel *Abbott and Costello Meet*

Frankenstein (1948). *Young Frankenstein* is the only case of it being a true success, however, and didn't involve physically swapping brains either.

The main objection for Brooks and Wilder was—unlike *Blazing Saddles*, which ripped at the clichés of the genre—that *Young Frankenstein* was a tribute to the *Frankenstein* films. As James Robert Parish reported Brooks saying in his biography *It's Good to Be King*, "What I wanted was the truth behind the horror conventions, the way real people—crazy but real—would behave in that castle. And I wanted to do it with the greatest affection for those great old films." As mentioned by many working on the film and who would see it later, the plot of the film could just as easily be the latest in the sequels from those 1930s originals, it is only the characters and what they do that make it a comedy. Thus, once again, making black and white the way to go.

Filming began February 19, 1974 (after initially being set to start February 11) at the University of Southern California, where the opening lecture scene was shot. Before that, Brooks had all the actors meet to rehearse for three weeks, which was more usual for him on a film, as he told the Directors Guild of America in an interview. "On *Young Frankenstein* I needed three weeks. I thought it was a play more than a movie. And I really needed time, but I got the three weeks. And they all gave their time—Teri Garr, all of them. It was so lovely."

Brooks and Wilder asked Gerald Hirschfeld, the cinematographer, to watch the original *Frankenstein* (1931) and *Bride of Frankenstein* (1935) to get the look of those films for the new one. As footage came back, Hirschfeld felt things were going well, until about a week and a half into filming, Brooks and Wilder had a meeting with Hirschfeld after watching the dailies. Brooks was unhappy with what Hirschfeld was giving them, stating that they wanted to satirize the look, not copy it exactly. Hirschfeld fought back, saying he was never told to do it that way. As he remembered later, "Gene Wilder piped up and said, 'Mel, he's right. We never told him that.'" Hirschfeld experimented with the filming the next day, and Brooks and Wilder agreed that Hirschfeld knew what he was doing, which he described in the DVD documentary. "Halfway through the picture," Hirschfeld stated, "Mel said to me in the lunch line, 'Jerry, I'm glad I didn't fire you four weeks ago.' I thought to myself, 'Mel, you're lucky I didn't quit.'"

Besides the University of Southern California, the only other location filming outside of the studios was that of the "Puttin' on the Ritz" number. This was filmed at the Mayfair Music Hall in Santa Monica, California. It would later be used in the film *Someone to Love* (1987). The theater was demolished in 2010 after being damaged in an earthquake in 1994. The rest of the film was shot on the Fox lot, with some exteriors—such as a train station where Elizabeth says goodbye—done over at MGM.

Beyond the original *Frankenstein* movie electronics that Ken Strickfaden brought, and the makeup on Boyle's face, the only other big effects in the film were the little girl flying through the air—a simple wire rigging did the trick there—and the moment where Boyle's head appears to glow from within during the reanimation scene. This was done fairly simply thanks to a cast having already been made of Boyle's head to help with creating his daily makeup while filming. Using that cast, the makeup artists were able to build a hollow plastic version of Boyle's head that was then painted on the inside to show teeth and the eye sockets when a light on a dimmer switch was turned on inside of it.

The rest of the film took place on the Fox lot, with sets built to look like the European villages of the Frankenstein films. While Strickfaden's electronic equipment—such as Tesla coils—was old and dangerous, there appeared to be no issues with the working conditions on the set. As it turns out, the only problem on the set was the cast and crew getting on so well that their laughter was spoiling takes. Brooks got around this with the crew by having them chew on handkerchiefs if they felt the urge to laugh—a technique he picked up while filming *The Twelve Chairs*. But Wilder had enormous trouble keeping his composure, especially in light of Feldman's need to improvise bits of business during the shooting. Feldman had become known for this tactic when filming his earlier television shows—wishing to hear the laughs of the crew who would eventually stop laughing once they got used to a joke in the script, and thus putting in new bits of dialogue or actions in order to try to goose them into laughing. But Wilder's laughter only drove Feldman on. Brooks—a man commonly very strict about his script being done to the letter—also enjoyed Feldman and would allow him to play around with the text if something occurred to him, leading to the various theatrical, and sometimes fourth-wall-breaking, asides Igor has in the film that are not in the script. Brooks and the others also knew that stopping Feldman wasn't going to do much good anyway. "If I or Madeline, or Cloris were not doing what Mel wanted, he would pull on the reins and if he wanted more he would start tugging," Wilder remembered to Robert Ross. "Marty didn't respond well to the tugging. I'm not saying there was anger, but as soon as the reins were loosened, Marty would respond like anyone with freedom. That means that maybe he would go off half-cocked in the wrong direction, but the next take he'd go off full-cocked in the right direction."

Yet Leachman found that Wilder was an easy laugh, stating in her autobiography that some of her best lines ended up not making the film because they could not get Wilder to stop laughing when she spoke. "Every time I'd say a line, he'd break up, so we'd have to shoot the scene again. And again. I had a little better control than he did but the same thing would happen to me. Gene would say a line and I'd look at him with that hat he had on, at his surprised eyes, his consuming naivete, and I couldn't help but laugh."

Eventually it got to the point where some scenes had to be shot through the laughter. This can be seen even in the outtakes found on the DVD and Blu-ray, where Wilder muffs a line but the others continue onward anyway, in hopes that something can be salvaged from the take. The scene where Igor attacks Elizabeth's fur had to be shot multiple times and then stitched together to get one fluid version (and in the end, none contain Igor with fur in his mouth as seen in the multiple outtakes). Sometimes such a method caused problems as well. When the creature attacks Frederick in the sedative scene, Wilder breaks up mid-scene and Brooks requested that a reaction shot of Inga be inserted to cover it. Brooks was then told that there was no close-up of Inga to put in the shot because Brooks didn't shoot such footage. Fortunately, John Howard remembered there was a tight close-up of Garr's face from another scene in the film and used it, covering for the error (and if you look, you can tell from the background that it is not from the same set, but only if one really looks for it).

All reports point to the set being a congenial one, which worried Brooks, as reported by James Robert Parish. "All the time we were shooting, I was sure the picture was going to be a failure. We were having too wonderful a time. Work should be painful, I thought. How can this be good if we're enjoying it so much?" Wilder, who had a brief affair with Garr during the making of the film, had his own melancholia about the film. Enjoying himself filming with the others, Wilder realized that it would soon be over. On the last day of shooting, Brooks found Wilder sitting alone on the castle set in deep thought and asked him why he was looking so sad. Wilder replied, "I don't want to leave Transylvania."

One sidenote to the film: As the production was ongoing, a fourteen-year-old kid by the name of Alan Spencer was sneaking into the studio to see the filming, as Spencer reflected on with Robert Ross. "You could do that kind of thing back then. The first time I did it, the guard on the gate didn't ask me anything. The second time he did stop me and I told him I was Mel Brooks's son. He said he could see the resemblance!" Spencer got past the guards but not Feldman, who—no doubt through his own misspent youth—picked up that Spencer wasn't supposed to be there. Spencer had researched Feldman's career and knew about his television and radio work, making the kid one of the few who had an idea of Feldman's history in comedy. Feldman would take Spencer under his wing, and they would spend time together when Feldman was in L.A., with Feldman helping him work at becoming a writer. Spencer eventually would create the series *Sledge Hammer!* (1986–1987) as well as *The Nutt House* with Mel Brooks in 1989.

Filming was completed the first week of May, with the cast bow shot being the last before the wrap party. Brooks and Wilder then moved on to the editing room to piece together the film until the beginning of September. At that time, Brooks began inviting people on the Fox lot to come see reels of the film, but none of the executives, and specifically told those who were invited "not to bring their bosses." Brooks had learned from *Blazing Saddles* that the money men were the last ones that should see the movie as all their fears about a film could cause massive mistakes to occur. Eventually a 142-minute version was put together and shown to a select group, which was then trimmed to the 90-minute version that would be released. By October the film was ready, and Fox decided to go with a Christmas release, banking on how well *Blazing Saddles* had done for Fox earlier that year.

Backend

Fox pushed heavily for the film, with Boyle being sent out on a nine-city tour in early December 1974 to help promote it, while little notices about the film were placed in the newspaper over the fall, leading to its release that Christmas. John Alvin returned after doing the poster for *Blazing Saddles* to do the one for *Young Frankenstein*, and the little in-jokes return as well, although all are situated on the person of the creature. The monster tips his top hat with a label inside that gives the size as "Incredibly Large." His zipper on his neck is larger and more fashionable, and he wears a bracelet that lists his name as "Monster." Instead of a carnation in his lapel, he is wearing a smiley button. The emphasis is on Wilder and Boyle at the top of the poster, with Feldman appearing at the bottom pushing the cart with the dead body to be used for the experiment. In some later versions of the poster, Feldman's caricature from the bottom of the poster was enlarged and placed at the top to attract audiences that either loved the character or knew of Feldman.

Fox had the usual advertising for television and radio, with Brooks as the announcer, talking quickly about the film—sometimes to the point of barely talking at all in a series of ten-second spots. A soundtrack album from ABC Records was released in December 1974, while there was also a paperback novelization to tie in with the movie. Promotional ideas mentioned in the pressbook suggested tying in with the soundtrack album—"The monster theme will also serve as ideal intermission music in your theater, and you may even want to pipe it out to the street. It's that catchy!"—and the novelization—"Place a pair of passes in one of every fifty or one hundred copies of *Young Frankenstein* offered for sale at selected stores!" Another idea was to have a costume contest, with a local radio or television personality hosting.

The world premiere of the film occurred on December 17, 1974, at the Avco Theater in Westwood, California. It then opened on December 18,1974, in Los Angeles and New York, with the rest of the country getting the film between December 19 and 23. In theaters at the time were such films as *The Godfather, Part II*, *The Man with the Golden Gun*, *Earthquake*, *Towering Inferno*, *Airport '75*, and Billy Wilder's version of *The Front Page*. *The Little Prince*—the film Wilder had to delay his filming on in order to do *Blazing Saddles*—also had a limited run in parts of the country while *Young Frankenstein* was opening.

Reviews were notably praising and better than for *Blazing Saddles*, although there were still some pans. John Dorr at *The Hollywood Reporter* felt it "works more for movie buff nostalgia than flash or spectacle," and showed "no cumulative effect beyond its succession of hard-worked jokes." Charles Champlin in the *Los Angeles Times*, however, called the film "a detailed tribute to the original *Frankenstein* and all the monster films which Wilder, Brooks and the rest of us grew up on. . . . And the tribute is respectful, loaded with updating jokes, but stopping well short of the tear-apart parody which leaves the object of the tribute in a crumpled heap." Roger Ebert, a champion of Brooks's earlier films, called *Young Frankenstein* "his most disciplined and inventive film . . . it shows artistic growth and a more sure-handed control of the material." Pauline Kael, who could be very hit or miss about Brooks's films, praised the director for carrying the story through and keeping the film "remarkably consistent in tone."

The film was nominated for two Academy Awards, but lost in both categories, Best Sound and Best Adapted Screenplay. It did win some other awards, namely for science fiction and horror, including a Hugo for Best Dramatic Presentation, a Nebula Award for Best Dramatic Writing, and several Saturn Awards for Best Horror Film, Best Direction, Best Supporting Actor (for Feldman), Best Make-up and Best Set Decoration. In 2003, it was listed as worthy of preservation by the National Film Preservation Board. At the box office, *Young Frankenstein* has domestically made over $86 million, putting it second to *Blazing Saddles* out of Brooks's films. It also means that within one year, 1974, Brooks made two films that have grossed over $200 million over time. There was a good reason for Hollywood to suddenly see Brooks as the new king of comedy.

Young Frankenstein even had its own rip-off, done in Turkey in 1975, *Sevimli Frankenstayn (My Friend Frankenstein)*. There's no really good way to describe the genre other than that Turkey had an industry based on making their own versions of popular American films (*Jaws, The Exorcist, E.T.*) for domestic consumption. Most were poorly shot with bad effects and obvious copyright infringement, the most famous being *Dunyayl Kurtaran Adam*, which uses special effect shots from *Star Wars: A New Hope* in the wrong framing. Some such borrowed material for an original story; others, like *Sevimli Frankenstayn*, are nearly scene-for-scene copies of the original film. In this case, it is clear that someone was told the film was successful, but didn't really understand what the jokes meant or what the homage was about—it's just the film remade as if remembered by someone who saw *Young Frankenstein* while sick with the flu.

Beyond such questionable plagiarism for the lawyers to sort out, two other issues did arise from the film's release. Some viewers did object to the film's use of rape imagery for jokes—especially in Elizabeth's scenes with the creature. The film was picketed for this reason, although *Variety* took the unfortunately common view of brushing it off as nothing serious ("Gal Pickets Hit Mel Brooks's Rape for Laffs Scene" is how the headline read). The other, more serious issue had to do with how the film began being promoted. When advertising first appeared for the film, including one on the Playboy building on the Sunset Strip in L.A., the poster stated it was a "Mel Brooks Film." Which in a way it was, but it made no mention that Gene Wilder had cowritten the script, which was seen by the Writers Guild of America West as a violation of "basic agreement in connection with writing credits." The WGA would sue Fox over the advertising, and eventually received $10,000 in damages for "selling Mel Brooks, not Wilder." Wilder received $3,000, while the guild received the remainder. There were no indications that this caused any rifts between Brooks and Wilder, however, even though it's hard not to notice that they never worked together again on another film after this one.

Reflections

Sometimes the best creative projects are the ones that get steamrolled over the participants. *Young Frankenstein* came to be due to negotiations for an agent's clients, and a page or two of notes that one of the actors had for a story. Within days, the project had a studio and nearly $3 million ready to film it, so the ball was in motion. It was written while another film was being created by the two men writing it, and completed in less time than normal for a Brooks film. Yet it has become a classic of both the horror and comedy genres.

Wilder's performance is the most personable of his career. Although usually laying bare emotional discomfort in many of his roles, it is almost always hidden behind a wall, leaving a number of his characters somewhat cold until they go off the rails, and then into a hyper-drive of emotions. In some cases, that works wonders—his Wonka in *Willy Wonka and the Chocolate Factory* is excellent because we can never be sure if he's playing at being crazy or really is crazy; and when his temper finally erupts near the end, we don't feel his pain as much as our own—because we sympathize with Charlie—and feel bad that Wonka appears to not like Charlie/us anymore. In other cases, however, we end up with an amusing caricature, such as in *Stir Crazy* or *The Woman in Red*; fun to watch, but we can't really tell what is inside the character's head beyond what we see on the screen.

Frederick is different. We know he lives in a logical world, where you can't reanimate the central nervous system and you don't want to spoil your fiancée's hair right before a party. He's too polite to flat-out mention to Igor that his hump is probably faked, and while curious about his grandfather's private library, laughs it all off at first. Later, after being influenced by the world he has entered, he accepts the unknowable, allows himself to be with Inga, regenerate a human, and even suggest forthright to Elizabeth that they should spend the night together (only to slip momentarily back into her logical world). And we want him to succeed because he feels he deserves the chance after all he must go through. He's not the man typically seen played by Wilder who is swept away thanks to the events around him; Frederick is a man of action. Crazy action, but still determined and in control. (It would have been interesting to have seen how audiences would have accepted the character from the first draft, who is more arrogant, obnoxious, and self-aware than the somewhat innocent Frederick of the film.)

Many, including Wilder, have suggested that the real heart of the film is Igor, thanks to Marty Feldman's performance. More importantly, Igor is our eyes (I would nearly say, no pun intended, but his eyes suggest the fractured nature of this world anyway). He's the only one (besides a couple of glances from Frederick and the creature) that suggests he knows he is in a movie. He even talks directly to us at one point—something done in both *The Producers* and *Blazing Saddles* before it—and what he says is not confrontational as in those two films, but rather acknowledges our own thoughts at that point ("Quiet dignity and grace," he sarcastically says, after Frederick has a tantrum). He gets away with being able to climb down from the castle roof to the floor of the lab within two seconds because we know he knows he is in a movie reality. It is clear—at least in the script—that he is messing with Frederick about his name being pronounced a certain way because he knows Frederick is being uptight about his own pronunciation; his hump changes because it's just for show and he figures that no one is impolite enough to call him out on it (in the cut scene where Frederick notices the hump is gone, Igor is insulted he would even ask where it is). In many ways, he is an extension of Bart from *Blazing Saddles*—he's a trickster who moves the film along—and it is only fitting that he ends the film on his own terms by blowing the horn and setting up the final piece of music over the ending title.

It is worth noting that *Young Frankenstein* has the most number of relevant parts for actresses of all of Brooks's films. Typically it is just one, and not even always important to the story. *History of the World, Part I* may have more, but it is an anthology of stories, with only one main female character in each. Better yet, the ones in *Young Frankenstein* are all fleshed out characters, independent of each other. Blücher (neigh!) may at first be simply the "creepy housekeeper" of gothic lore, but we learn quickly enough that she was the grandfather's lover and is determined to see Frederick sent down the same path to prove Victor was right (besides, early on, attempting to hit on him with the suggestion of some Ovaltine). Her actions direct the narrative and give Frederick the incentive to do what he does; without her influence, nothing would happen in the film. We may still worry about the horses, but she was right about everything else.

Inga is a bit harder to place. It is easy to see that she started out as a dream girl—the beautiful blonde who not only sees you as a god (the first few drafts even have her calling Frederick one), but wants to hang out with you. The joke of elevating Frederick may be groan-worthy, but it plays into that fantasy, as well as giving us a chance to see that Inga can be both sexy and funny at the same time. If Kahn had played the part, as Wilder originally wanted, she would have laid on the smolder a bit too thick and then dismiss the advance in anger. Garr is more puppylike in her longing and then embarrassed in her realization, thereby making the gag work better. Saying all that, Inga is brainy enough to understand what Frederick is talking about—such as at the breakfast table as he reads from his grandfather's notes—as well as being able to carry on his experiments when he himself becomes part of it. Inga represents Frederick's freedom from the tight reality he was used to before, and it is fitting that they end up together.

Elizabeth is an even more tightly wound version of the Elizabeth character found in the James Whale movies. And unlike Frederick, who finds himself when allowed to live beyond what he knew before, Elizabeth explodes. Her hair goes nuts, as well as her prim attitude. By the end of the film, she's embarrassing the creature alone in their bedroom with her shenanigans, demonstrating how some people can go from one extreme to the other when faced with a life-changing event. Kahn manages to pull that off.

And, in mentioning Elizabeth, it should be noted that we have a film considered a comedy classic—a film classic, even—that hinges on what many now see (and some even then saw) as a rape joke. We can dance around it as much as we want and try to pretty it up, but let's look at the setup: woman is uptight prude who is kidnapped by well-endowed man and taken to a secluded spot where he forces himself on her, whereupon she suddenly blossoms into an enthusiastic sexual creature. That can be dressed up in many ways, but it is the core of the gag, and it is part of the final punch line as well—Frederick gains in size and jumps on Inga, with her even shouting "NO!" before finally belting out "Sweet Mystery of Life."

In *Blazing Saddles*, Brooks barely squeaked by with the first rape joke he does because we discover soon enough that Taggart's men are so stupid they raped the cattle instead of the women. The second time he used rape imagery in that film it isn't funny ("You said rape twice." "I like rape."), but it's just dialogue from the bad guys, and the film quickly moves on from there with no further reference, so we let it go. Here, they soften the visuals by making Elizabeth a bit conflicted about the idea of possibly being with the creature when she sees the size of him. In the original draft, Elizabeth is even more of a willing participant.

We have to remember, this material where the creature, and later Frederick, force themselves on the female characters for cheap laughs really is a reflection of a mentality that still existed in the 1970s—where people still looked at rape and sexual molestation as punch lines to jokes, even on television. It's a product of its time, just as the jokes about gay men were much harsher in Brooks's earlier films than his later ones (even up through *To Be or Not to Be* in 1982 Brooks was using the term "fag" in many of his films). Today, it makes us wince, almost more because we know we used to find rape something to laugh about, more than the jokes themselves. Hand it to Wilder and Brooks to try to at least swing the setup so that Elizabeth is enticed by her situation, but it is still something that you look at today and have to hang an asterisk on in order to explain why it was acceptable at the time. Oddly enough, when the 1974 film *Rocky Horror Picture Show* had a similar scene between a woman and a man-made creature, it is the woman who takes the initiative (and, to be fair, the audiences of the 1970s would call her a slut to the screen for doing so, so perhaps it wasn't that much more progressive).

Getting back to things that are good about the film, it was a perfect choice by Brooks and Wilder to film in black and white. Not only because of the homage they wanted to bring to the film, and that of the makeup for Boyle, but also because it deals with one final aspect of the old monster movies that needed to be sent up: that these films never seem to be of any time-period. The original script hints at modern conveniences (there's an apology about the record being on 78 rpm when played, hence the people there know it's old-fashioned), but these were cut, and in the film the most modern thing besides the electronics in Frederick's lab is the train. Otherwise, it's horses and carts, and the villagers all dress as if they're about to go to Octoberfest at the beginning of the twentieth century. It was never quite clear if these films were supposed to be happening in 1931 or 1935 or 1895, and the black-and-white photography hides the time period because it settles us into a foreign world of black and white. In color, the contrast of these people living in another world would have us disbelieving in all that is shown. Brooks and Wilder were correct in choosing the look of this fantasy world—one that we don't even notice when looking at the film today—proving that a greater vision beyond making sure it played Peru can gain us a film classic.

12

Which One of You Is Funn?

Silent Movie

Release Date: Sneak preview at Avco Center Cinema, Westwood, California on June 18, 1976; Opened nationally on June 30, 1976, by 20th Century-Fox.

Hitler References

Once again, no Hitler references. Give it a couple more movies and we'll see them again.

Musical Moments

We may not get Hitler from Brooks, but we do get musical numbers, even in a silent movie. Mel, Marty, and Dom all dance with Anne Bancroft at the club; Mel and Vilma (Bernadette Peters) dance on the wedding cake; and Vilma has two production numbers of her own in the club: the Calypso number, where she is peeled out of the giant banana, and later dressed as a bunny to sing "Here Comes Peter Cottontail."

Pre-production

Brooks had witnessed *Young Frankenstein* debuting to great reviews and ticket sales. This gave him some breathing room. Sure, he was already signed to the three-film deal with 20th Century-Fox, but to have both *Young Frankenstein* and *Blazing Saddles*—his last two movies—be blockbusters gave him leverage over the studio. Yet he was already contemplating his next film as his homage to horror films was being released. And once again, as with *Blazing Saddles* and *Young Frankenstein*, the new movie would be a case of someone approaching Brooks with the initial concept.

In December 1974, Brooks went to a party at former Caesar writer Larry Gelbart's place. Attending the party was writer Ron Clark (born 1934). Clark had written material for several comics before moving on to writing for variety shows in the late 1960s and early 1970s, including *The Smothers Brothers Comedy*

Hour. For a time, he partnered with Sam Bobrick, writing a number of plays, including the 1970 comedy *Norman, Is That You?* The play, about a couple discovering their son is gay, ran for a little over a week on Broadway. However,

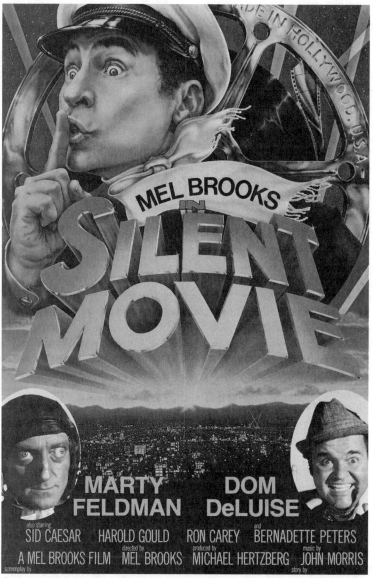

Once again, John Alvin does the movie poster for Brooks. Variations of the poster would later add photos of the many guest stars in the film, but it was at first decided not to feature the other actors in order to make their appearances a surprise for the audience.

it would continue to be produced around the country in community theater for years and was eventually turned into a movie starring Redd Foxx in 1976.

Brooks had seen *Norman, Is That You?* and approached Clark to let him know that he enjoyed it. As they talked, Clark suggested they meet for lunch to discuss an idea he had for a movie, filling Brooks with dread. "Lunch is for people who don't make me nervous," Brooks said to AP in 1976 about this offer. However, he found Clark to be very personable and good-natured. "Ron was the 10,000th person to tell me 'Let's have lunch—I got a great idea.' This time I accepted."

The idea was a silent movie, which Brooks found completely underwhelming. He too had thought about the idea a few years back, but didn't see how a movie in "black and white and no sound" could be sustained for the length of an entire picture for a modern audience. Clark countered that he envisioned something different: a movie in color, set in the current time, with all the modern camera techniques available, and with big movie stars . . . but without sound. "I had this crazy notion about a silent comedy with a modern setting," Clark said to AP in 1977. "I knew if I took it to a studio, I'd get thrown out on my ear. I decided there were only two men who could pull it off: Woody Allen and Mel Brooks. Mel seemed the better choice, so I asked to have lunch with him." Brooks warmed to the idea, as did the studio when he presented it. There was the obvious joke, of course, "First you make a movie with no color and now a movie without sound, what's next? You go door to door and show paintings to people?" Still, this was Brooks—the "king of comedy"—and he seemed to know what he was doing to create box-office comedy hits, so the studio came on board quickly, and by January 14, 1975, *Variety* was reporting that Brooks had signed a deal to make his next movie, *The Hollywood Silents*.

Beyond Brooks's reputation, it wasn't that hard to convince Fox. Silent movies may have been a page from the past, but the late 1960s had seen a resurgence of interest in the 1920s and early 1930s through fashion, design, and film, with the success of *Bonnie and Clyde* helping to resurrect the gangster films for a brief period in the early 1970s. Further, kids of the 1950s and 1960s had grown up watching silent movies and early talkies—especially slapstick comedies of the silent era—on television and were now reaching adulthood and nostalgic for their childhood days. Art theaters began running such films to wide attendance, as well as films like *That's Entertainment* showing that audiences were a bit savvier about the movies and the industry. Even the downside of the 1970s, which saw the demise of several actors and comedians of those long-ago days starting to die off due to old age—Charlie Chaplin would pass away in 1977, for example—only reinforced the public's interest, because soon those people would no longer be with us to recapture that past. The public knew silent movies, and so there was no need to have to explain over and over to ticket buyers that a movie called *Silent Movie* was probably going to be . . . well . . . a silent movie.

The studio did have one request, as Brooks told Roger Ebert: "The studio was, 'Go ahead,' they told me, 'make your silent movie. But, Mel, do us a favor.

Just as a safeguard, record dialog. Please.' What? Just as a safeguard? I banned the microphone! We didn't even rent one for the picture!" It was a repeat of Columbia suggesting to Brooks to shoot *Young Frankenstein* in color "just in case." Brooks quickly shut down the suggestion. After additional consultation by the studio, "They just told me, 'If anyone can pull it off, you can,'" Brooks related. Even so, Brooks was worried about how successful it would be and what effect it would have on his career. "What do you think?" Brooks asked a *Newsweek* writer in February 1975. "Do you think a silent can work? They'll let me make it. They'll let me do anything now—once."

With the wheels in motion, Clark quit his job producing the then-new Normal Lear television series *Hot L Baltimore*, based on an off-Broadway play by Lanford Wilson and starring James Cromwell, in early February 1975 to concentrate on the Brooks film. Just as well; the controversial Lear series, with lead characters that were prostitutes and the first appearance of a gay couple as regular characters in the stories, was cancelled after thirteen episodes.

Clark had a proven track record, but Brooks wanted to return to the days of *Blazing Saddles* and suggested they get a couple more writers in on the project to beef up the quota of gags; especially in a film that would need to rely on visual gags, which were not always the easiest to conceive. Clark recommended two fellow writers he had met while working on *The Tim Conway Comedy Hour* in 1970 and had recently completed scripts for *Hot L Baltimore* alongside him: Rudy De Luca (born 1933) and Barry Levinson (born 1942). Both had also written and acted with Marty Feldman for the series *The Marty Feldman Comedy Machine*, which meant they knew how to write for Feldman, who Brooks was already envisioning costarring in the film. Brooks quickly agreed.

However, both writers were working full-time on *The Carol Burnett Show*. "Because I couldn't pay them enough to quit *Burnett*," Brooks related in July 1976 to Bob Thomas for AP, "we had to meet at lunchtime at a delicatessen. We took along a tape recorder so we wouldn't lose a single thought. When the tape was transcribed, the gags were interspersed with sentences like, 'I'll have the pastrami, hold the mustard,' and 'Who ordered the cole slaw?'" Brooks also only had limited time to invest in the script in the first part of 1975, as he was working to help produce the Robin Hood parody television series *When Things Were Rotten*.

As work went along on the script, Clark suggested that Brooks himself should play the lead role. "You'd be perfect," Clark said. "Our hero is manic, arrogant, strong, silly, wacky." Brooks's response was a disappointed "Am I really like that?" He was hesitant to do the role, however. "I always felt I'd rather have somebody really talented carry my message," Brooks responded when asked about starring in his movies. Brooks instead hoped that he could get Gene Wilder to do it, but Wilder was already prepping *The Adventure of Sherlock Holmes' Smarter Brother* at Fox and couldn't get involved. Yet it didn't take long to convince Brooks to play the part. "I said, 'Well, what the hell? They don't even talk. Me, Marty Feldman, and Dom DeLuise—how bad can that be?'" By mid-February 1975, Brooks was already telling *Newsweek* that he would be starring in the film, alongside Dom DeLuise, Marty Feldman, and Madeline Kahn.

Brooks had a good lock on most of the actors that would star with him in the early days of the script. Dom DeLuise was an easy early choice who signed on as soon as possible. Feldman had based a chunk of his comedy career in Britain writing homages to the silent movie comedians, performing skits involving his own variations of the type of physical stunts Buster Keaton and Harold Lloyd used to do in their films. To have his next Hollywood film directed by someone he had already worked with and performing material he felt was his calling? It took little effort to get Feldman to sign on. Even the role of the studio chief was easy to find, as all the script drafts note the studio chief's name as "Sid Caesar" long before they finally hired Caesar to do the role in November 1975.

Although Madeline Kahn was listed as being in it as late as December 3, 1975, in *Variety*, she passed on making the picture. Brooks even delayed the start of filming in hopes of getting Kahn, along with DeLuise and Feldman, who were all busy making Gene Wilder's *The Adventure of Sherlock Holmes' Smarter Brother* earlier in the year. Yet Kahn passed on *Silent Movie*, and in mid-December 1975 Bernadette Peters was signed on.

As for the "superstars" who would be in the film—that was left open when writing the script. Brooks mentioned to the *Baltimore Sun* in May 1975 that he hoped they could get Robert Redford, but then jokingly added "if Redford doesn't want to do it, we'll get Paul Newman." Beyond the joke, however, Brooks and the writers had no idea who would be in the film. "When we wrote the script for the picture," he told Gene Siskel in August 1976, "we numbered the cameo bits, 'Star 1, Star 2, Star 3, Star 4, Star 5.' . . . So, I'm sitting with Ron Clark, Rudy De Luca and Barry Levinson. We wrote the script together, now it's finished, and we're asking each other, 'How are we gonna get the stars?'"

The first star came to Brooks around Christmas 1975. James Caan had been slowly building a career for himself with lead roles in films back during the late 1960s that led to strong roles in two popular films, the television movie *Brian's Song* (1971) and then *The Godfather* (1972). His picks could be sometimes hit or miss in popularity, but he continued with a strong run of offbeat roles in films like *Cinderella Liberty* (1973), *Funny Lady* (1975), and *Rollerball* (1975). Caan called Brooks to say, "I know from the secretaries at Fox that there are stars in your picture . . . I want to be dealt in." When Brooks told him that there was "no money in it," Caan brushed it off, saying that he wanted to work with Brooks and money wasn't important.

Next was Burt Reynolds, who was just about to reach the pinnacle of movie stardom in 1975 after a string of hit action films like *White Lightning* (1973), *The Longest Yard* (1974), and *W.W. and the Dixie Dancekings* (1975). Brooks contacted Burt Reynolds's manager about a role, once again saying that there was no money to be had, and "that I wasn't going to offer Burt anything in return. I would not direct a picture for him. I would not offer him advice on a script. I would just work with him on this movie, and he might have to work as long as five days." Reynolds immediately said yes, taking time off from Peter Bogdanovich's *Nickelodeon* (another film about the silent movies) to do his cameo. Brooks said that Reynolds did the film for two reasons: out of mutual respect and because Reynolds was eager to be in a hit after starring in *Lucky Lady* (1975)—a film that was already being designated a bomb before its release. *Silent Movie* would be the first film to feature Dom DeLuise with Reynolds together, with the duo acting together in several movies in the years to come, such as the *Cannonball* films, *The End*, and *Smokey and the Bandit, Part II*.

Reynolds's costar in *Lucky Lady*, Liza Minnelli, would soon join the cast as well. Burt Reynolds hosted an episode of *The Tonight Show* on December 15, 1975, to promote the film, with his *Lucky Lady* costars, Gene Hackman and Liza Minnelli, with Mel Brooks as an additional guest on the program. During the interview with Brooks, he discussed *Silent Movie*, and Minnelli herself asked if she could be in it, whereupon he instantly agreed.

As the stars started piling up for the film, Brooks asked his wife, Anne, if there was anyone else who may be good for the film. She asked him if he was going to ever get around to asking her. Brooks was surprised that she felt she even had to be asked, assuming she would be in the film one way or another. When he asked why she was concerned, she said, "Well, I haven't been in a big, big, runaway hit since *The Graduate*, so I may not be box office. And I don't want to hurt you; I only want to help you." To that Brooks said, "Well, I think we'll take a chance with you, kid." After filming, Brooks could not stop bragging about his wife's dedication to the movie. "She did the most work. Two weeks. The risks she took! You know, in that dance number that really is her head slamming into that wall. She didn't wear any pads in the scene," as Brooks told Gene Siskel. According to Carl Reiner in his book *My Anecdotal Life*, he taught Anne Bancroft how to cross and then shift her eyes to the left and right for the film, although this conflicts slightly with Brooks's story about her doing it when they were first dating.

After attracting world-famous mime Marcel Marceau to the film for his one-word performance, Brooks set his sights on Paul Newman, who was one of the top Hollywood stars from the 1960s until his death in 2008, with films like *Cool Hand Luke* (1967) and *Butch Cassidy and the Sundance Kid* (1969) already behind him at that point. To be truthful, Brooks first hoped for Steve McQueen, who was the highest-paid actor at the time with hits like *The Great Escape* (1963), *The Cincinnati Kid* (1965), and *Bullitt* (1968). Brooks and the writers even parodied his multiple motorcycle jump in *The Great Escape* in their script, with the wheelchair jump to try to entice McQueen to do the film.

With no word from McQueen, Brooks turned to Newman, who could easily accommodate the script with a minor change here and there. Newman called Brooks soon after getting the script, saying he would like the role, which involved a chase around the hospital on souped-up motorized wheelchairs, but he did have a question. "How fast can the wheelchairs go?" Brooks, knowing that they could go as fast as forty miles per hour, assumed that Newman was worried about hurting himself, and lowballed the speed at a maximum of ten mph. This disappointed Newman, as he was hoping they went faster. Newman then offered suggestions on how to get the wheelchairs up to seventy mph, and volunteered to test-drive the wheelchair out on the tracks when Brooks's production crew proceeded to build one to Newman's liking. "It was scary," Brooks said of the test. "There was no insurance on him. He could have killed himself. When it came to the filming, we literally couldn't catch him. He had to slow up. He can't help but win. He's a winner." And a look at the film shows exactly that, with Newman constantly pulling away from the others, even when the pursuit should be closer. Feldman later stated in an interview that Newman liked the wheelchair—which cost thousands of dollars to customize—so much he took it home with him after filming was completed.

Dom DeLuise achingly riding up the steps in his wheelchair—a moment from the Paul Newman chase scene that was cut from the final version of the film.

Almost immediately after Newman agreed to do the film, Brooks heard from McQueen, asking if the "wheelchair guy part" was still open. When told that Newman had already agreed to the part, McQueen, who had a long-term friendly/not-so-friendly rivalry with Newman, said, "Ol' Blue Eyes, that SOB, he gets all my parts." Brooks asked him why he never called back about the role if he was interested, and McQueen stated that he was just being shy. Besides, "I'm wearing this beard for the Ibsen film I'm doing [*An Enemy of the People*, based on the Henrik Ibsen play, which was filmed in 1976 but released in 1978]. You would've had to take me with the beard . . . it wouldn't have been McQueen, you know, the McQueen they know, the *Great Escape* McQueen."

With the cast pretty much in place, the film was ready to start production on January 5, 1976. Now only the title needed to be settled upon. By May 1975, *The Hollywood Silents*—as the film was first reported, had changed to *Silent Movies Madness*, with Brooks telling the *Baltimore Sun* at the time, "Maybe it will be called *Mel Brooks's Silent Movies* or *The Silent Movie of Mel Brooks*." Instead, by December 1975 it would bounce around a bit as either *The Silent Movie* or simply *Silent Movie*, before finally being named *Silent Movie* in early 1976.

Cast

Mel Brooks as Mel Funn

Actor known for small roles; given his big break through the generosity of the director.

Marty Feldman as Marty Eggs

Feldman would jump straight from *Young Frankenstein* to *The Adventure of Sherlock Holmes' Smarter Brother*, as well as a small role in the Italian comedy *Sex with a Smile*, before climbing on board to do *Silent Movie*. It would be his last film with Brooks, as he moved on to direct two comedies of his own, *The Last Remake of Beau Geste* (1977) and *In God We Tru$t* (1980). In later films, Brooks commonly would state that he was looking for actors who could be his next "Marty Feldman," which shows how much of an impression Feldman's work made on him.

Feldman clashed with Brooks over the stunt work, which Feldman felt he could do—and had done in his own television work—but that Brooks thought should be left to the stuntmen. Feldman usually got his way in this case and in others throughout his career, before and after *Silent Movie*. It has even been suggested by composer John Morris, who worked on Feldman's last screen appearance, *Yellowbeard* (1983), that Feldman's insistence on doing his own stunts, as well as his other health problems led to him having the heart attack that killed him one day before his filming was to be completed.

Dom DeLuise, Marty Feldman, and Mel Brooks motoring through the city in *Silent Movie*.

Dom DeLuise as Dom Bell

DeLuise appeared in his own sitcom, *Lotsa Luck* (1973–1974), and then played a substantial role in Wilder's *The Adventure of Sherlock Holmes' Smarter Brother*. He would immediately follow up *Silent Movie* by appearing in Gene Wilder's next movie, *The World's Greatest Lover* (1977), before appearing in his first film with Burt Reynolds, *The End* (1978), kicking off their multiple films together. DeLuise would direct and star in the 1979 film *Hot Stuff* and star in Anne Bancroft's *Fatso* (1980) before returning to Brooks in *History of the World, Part I*.

Bernadette Peters (born 1948) as Velma Kaplan

A child actor who gained notice in 1968 when appearing in the off-Broadway musical *Dames at Sea*, which won her a Drama Desk Award for her performance. She went on to appear in several Broadway productions after this, probably

Bernadette Peters with Brooks near the end of the film. Madeline Kahn was initially to be in the film, but backed out and Peters joined the cast soon before shooting began.

remembered as the best thing in otherwise complete misfires: playing the lead in the musical *La Strada* (1969) and in *Mack and Mabel* (1974).

Feeling that she may have better luck in Los Angeles, Peters moved there in late 1974. Soon after, she appeared as a guest star on an episode of *The Carol Burnett Show*. The *Burnett Show* at the time had two of the writers working with Brooks on *Silent Movie*, and their recommendation led Brooks to checking out her performance on the program and then offering her the role of Velma when it was clear that Madeline Kahn would not be able to do the film.

Silent Movie is the only film Peters would make with Brooks. She would move on to a sitcom called *All's Fair* that lasted a season (1976–1977) before appearing in two films with her then-boyfriend Steve Martin: *The Jerk* (1979, and directed by Carl Reiner) and *Pennies from Heaven* (1982). She continues to bounce between television and theater since, appearing in such series as *Ugly Betty*, *Smash*, and *Mozart in the Jungle*.

Sid Caesar as Sid Caesar, Studio Chief

Caesar had been busy since the days of his own television series, commonly appearing in stage shows and in guest roles on television. He also began appearing in more films as the 1960s moved on, but his only starring roles were in two mild comedies for producer William Castle in 1967, *The Busy Body* and *The Spirit Is Willing*. By 1976, Caesar was falling deep into an alcohol and medication addiction that he would later relate in his autobiographies as being a period where he had only vague recollections of what he was doing when performing, going into a type of autopilot. His performances would still be solid at the time, which only helped perpetuate the problem. In the 1980s, Caesar kicked his habit and bounced back, with a long, solid career making guest appearances in films and television. Caesar would make one more appearance in a Brooks film, in *History of the World, Part I*.

Harold Gould (1923–2010) as Engulf

Gould was a character actor who seemed to be in just about every possible thing you could think of on television. He studied acting after fighting in World War II, and was a professor at the University of California for a time before beginning to get work in films. As he was already in his forties when he started, he tended to play businessmen, fathers, and conmen, including originally playing Ritchie's father in the pilot of what would become *Happy Days*. Gould's career got a boost with his recurring role as Rhoda's father in *The Mary Tyler Moore Show* spin-off, *Rhoda* (1974-1978), as well as appearing in *The Sting* (1973) and Woody Allen's *Love and Death* (1975). *Silent Movie* is the only film Gould would make with Brooks, but his career would continue strongly up to the year he passed away.

Ron Carey (1935–1997) as Devour

Starting out as a stand-up comic in the 1960s, Carey began his acting career with a small role in the Neil Simon comedy *The Out of Towners* (1970) and in *Made for Each Other* (1975), a film that Mel Brooks was originally supposed to produce in its early stage of development. Most of his acting work centered on television, and he is probably best known today for his role as Officer Levitt in seasons three through eight of the series *Barney Miller* (1976–1982). Carey's participation in *Silent Movie* would lead to a large supporting role in Anne Bancroft's *Fatso*. He also appears in *High Anxiety* as Brophy and in the Roman Empire segment of *History of the World, Part I*.

Sid Caesar returns to work with Mel Brooks in *Silent Movie*. The studio chief is specifically named "Sid Caesar" in the final version of the script, so sure was Brooks of getting Caesar for the role.

Also Appearing

- Charlie Callas (1927–2001) as the blind man with the dog. Originally a drummer for such performers as Tommy Corsey and Buddy Rich, Callas became a comedian doing a variety of weird noises and physical movements and asides in his act. He'll return in *High Anxiety, History of the World, Part I,* and *Dracula: Dead and Loving It*
- Harry Ritz (1907–1986) as the man leaving the tailor shop. Harry was a member of the Ritz Brothers, a team of dancer-comedians who became headliners in vaudeville and then moved into the movies. For a brief period in the mid-1930s, the Ritz Brothers were one of the most popular teams in comedy, and many comedians coming of age in the 1940s, such as Brooks, Danny Kaye, Sid Caesar, Jerry Lewis, and others, all would readily admit that they were born out of what the Ritz Brothers had done before them. When brother Al passed away in the mid-1960s, Harry continued with his other brother Jimmy, including appearing in the 1975 Madeline Kahn movie *Won Ton Ton, the Dog Who Saved Hollywood.* Harry appeared solo in *Silent Movie* for his cameo.
- Henny Youngman (1906–1998) as man at outside restaurant. Youngman was known for always carrying a violin in his act and for telling terribly creaky one-liners ("Take my wife . . . please!") that worked because he kept slinging them out so fast that you eventually gave up and joined in. This is

why his one line in *Silent Movie* is simply a throwback to an old gag about yelling at the waiter about a fly in his soup (one of the variable responses would be "Not so loud or everyone will want one!"). Youngman was signed to appear in *High Anxiety*, as a patient in the asylum who keeps throwing out one-liners while a nurse patiently pats him on his head. His character would be cut, and instead he would make his next and final appearance briefly in *History of the World, Part I*.

- Fritz Feld (1900–1993) as the maître d'. When did he not play the maître d'? When did he not play a maître d' named Fritz? It's like there was a tear in the space-time continuum and this man decided that instead of conquering countless worlds, he'd just show people to tables throughout history. He was also famous for doing a popping sound with his mouth, which he does in *Silent Movie* as well. He played other things, of course, but was quite content in having found stable income playing a particular type of role.
- Chuck McCann (born 1934) as studio guard. McCann played in a lot of comedies, and is remembered by a certain generation still for a CBS Saturday morning comedy called *Far Out Space Nuts*. He would later have bit roles in *Robin Hood: Men in Tights* and *Dracula: Dead and Loving It*.
- Jack Riley (1935–2016) as an executive for Engulf and Devour. Riley is probably best remembered as Mr. Carlin on *The Bob Newhart Show* (1972–1978). Riley later appeared in four additional Brooks-related films: *High Anxiety*, *History of the World, Part I*, *Spaceballs*, and *To Be or Not to Be*.
- Phil Leeds (1916–1998) as waiter loudly forgetting Funn ruined his career with drink. Leeds appeared in a lot of television, including several times on *Barney Miller*. He'll pop up again as the chief monk in *History of the World, Part I*.
- Appearing as executives around the Engulf and Devour table were two of the three writers, Barry Levinson and Rudy De Luca. They were joined at the table by Howard Hesseman (born 1940), a few years before he found greater success as Dr. Johnny Fever on the television sitcom *WKRP in Cincinnati* (off to the right and thus rarely on camera); Al Hopson (1920–1998), who will return to be shot by Dr. Thorndyke in *High Anxiety*; and Lee DeLano (born 1931), who returns as Norton in *High Anxiety* and the wagon driver in the Roman Empire segment of *History of the World, Part I*.
- Returning to a Brooks film after *Blazing Saddles* were Carol Arthur (Dom DeLuise's wife) as the pregnant lady and Patrick Campbell (who played emcee for Lili in *Blazing Saddles*) as the bellhop.
- Liam Dunn, who appeared as the reverend in *Blazing Saddles* and the patient in the lecture hall in *Young Frankenstein*, appears in *Silent Movie* as the unfortunate news vendor. It was his last appearance in a Brooks film.
- Eddie Ryder (1923–1997), who plays the British officer in the dailies being shown to the studio chief returns in *High Anxiety* as one of the doctors at the convention.

- Robert Lussier (born 1934), who is the projectionist near the end of the film, returns briefly in *High Anxiety* as Dr. Thorndyke's father in the flashback near the end of the film.
- Valerie Curtin (born 1945), who was the wife of Barry Levinson at the time (they would divorce in 1982), played the nurse in the Intensive Care Ward. She would later play the woman hitting on Gene Wilder's character in *Silver Streak*.

In the Crew

Mary Keats, William Tuttle, Frank Baur, Don Hall, Gary L. King, Jay King, Anthony Goldschmidt, and Ray Quiroz all returned in the same jobs they performed on *Young Frankenstein*. John Morris returned to compose the score, with Ralph Burns and Billy Byers orchestrating the music. John C. Howard also returned as editor, and with the help of Stanford C. Allen, worked with Brooks to edit the film. Howard will return with *High Anxiety*.

Production

Filming began in Los Angeles on January 5, with additional shooting on the Fox lot. Shooting in the commissary with Liza Minelli occurred in mid-March, causing some complaints from people on the lot who had to find lunch elsewhere while Brooks was shooting inside. Filming took place over twelve weeks, wrapping up at the end of March 1976. The script was filmed pretty much as conceived by the team of writers, including 375 pieces of stunt work done for the film. The main problem Brooks ran into was that the crew refused to laugh. "We're shooting silent, people," Brooks told them. "You can laugh if you want to."

One element that did change quickly was Brooks's initial idea that there would be no sound at all in the film, not even a musical score. Once he saw the dailies, however, he realized that something needed to be there, at least to audibly keep hold of the audience. He then pressed John Morris into service to write a score, which Morris was enthusiastic about . . . until he realized just how much work was involved.

"The first thing was," Morris told *Film Score Monthly* in 2001, "I decided not to use a note of piano in the whole score to get away from that cliché. What was hard about scoring *Silent Movie* was that it was an interminable amount of music. I think we had something like forty recording sessions. We had stacks of scores. It became a joke." Morris realized at the first recording session that he would never be able to finish it in the six weeks he was told he had to compose, orchestrate, and compose the score. He quickly brought in Ralph Burns and Billy Byers to orchestrate while they listened to the recordings. "There were 120 cues and I had thirty days [left]. That means I have to do four pieces of music a day. If I get behind it's going to be horrible."

During the months of April and May, Brooks worked with John C. Howard and Stanford C. Allen to edit the film down to size, and with that came some more changes to the film. What changed or went missing:

- Big Picture Studios was scripted to be Sunshine Studio. This was changed before filming began.
- The film was to zero in on each character to give us a little history of each as the film opens. This was not done, and instead the audience just assumes that Bell and Eggs are simply friends of Funn.
- After Caesar goes sailing across the room in his chair, a hidden projector screen was to drop down and repeatedly knock him in the head while a musical scene from *Mother Wore Tights* plays on Caesar's face.
- The business with James Caan punching a bag and knocking everyone around in the process was added before filming began. In earlier drafts of the script, Caan merely invites everyone into his trailer. (It was probably changed as the wobbling trailer would have been given away before they entered it unless Caan was on the outside.)
- The lunch in the trailer was filmed but edited to only the eating of the melon balls and then DeLuise peppering a piece of bread, forcing him to sneeze. Filmed but cut was everyone getting an ear of corn, only for Feldman to salt his corn heavily, forcing the others to do the same to balance out the trailer. (The flip pictures in the paperback of the movie shows DeLuise trying to eat the corn, only to spit it out.) To shake off the salty taste, everyone gets a glass of lemonade from a pitcher, and when DeLuise spills some on himself, everyone reluctantly does the same to balance out the trailer. (If one watches the movie, a pitcher magically appears on the table between the four putting down their toothpicks from the melon balls and DeLuise peppering the bread.) In the script, a belch from DeLuise was to send everyone sailing, but instead in the movie it is his sneezing that does it.
- DeLuise's trip to the men's room involved him looking to be urinating against a tree, but it turns out to be him watering some plants with a hose.
- When DeLuise asks to stop to get a blueberry pie, Feldman spots a blonde with a bag of groceries and propositions her. She slaps him and he returns to the car. When he describes to Brooks what he had said to the woman, Brooks slaps him as well.
- Added to the projection room scene was Caesar being told that Engulf and Devour are on their way out.
- Filmed, but cut, was Brooks, Feldman, and DeLuise entering the commissary in their suits of armor and trying to pay for their order before reaching Minnelli's table. Minnelli was supposed to know it was them all along, but

this was changed to her being surprised in the film itself, probably because it plays too close to the later scene with Bancroft knowing it is them.

- Brooks was to first snap the cigarette out of Feldman's mouth before being blindfolded when using the whip. This slight edit merely saves some time.

- The ending to Bancroft's dance is different in the script, stopping just as DeLuise finishes dancing on the table and the crowd going wild, rather than the leap off the table into the arms of Brooks and the boys as seen in the film. Added too was ramming Bancroft's head into the wall, and then her reemergence later to show the audience (both in the restaurant and watching the movie) that she was okay.

- The script has Feldman taking the stairs to Caesar's room, rather than getting into an elevator with a woman who slaps him as he gets out next to Brooks and DeLuise.

- Cut from the wheelchair chase was Newman taking a ramp near some stairs. Brooks follows smoothly on his wheelchair, but Feldman and DeLuise nearly kill themselves trying to drive their chairs up the stairs next to the ramp.

- When Brooks begins to leave with Peters, Feldman, and DeLuise trying to remind him of the movie they're making, Brooks was to reply (via card), "Who gives a shit?" You can see them asking the question, but not Brooks's response in the film.

- Filmed, but not in most drafts of the script, is a scene where Brooks tries to use a phone booth, drops his change, and then a woman enters as he is bent over. When he stands up, she is on his shoulders and sticking out of the top of the booth. This was an old gag of Buster Keaton's that Brooks added to the filming, but the movie worked better going straight from the hotel to the bums in the alley.

- At one point in the film, there was to be a scene showing a restaurant where human-sized lobsters are the customers and wait staff. The customers get to pick out their own small human to eat, and a claw should be shown grabbing a terrified human out of a tank and taking it away to be cooked. Although filmed, with equipment built to create the giant claw hand that grabs a person from a pool of water, the scene was cut when it did not go over well in test showings.

- The final bum picked up was to be Dean Martin instead of Brooks. This then goes straight into Brooks sobering up in the restaurant, so was probably cut because the gag didn't lead into the next sequence at all.

- Peters was to prove her love by tearing up the check, whereupon Brooks tells her he loves her, but his breath is so bad that she asks him not to speak any longer. (This is rather like an ending gag in *The Jerk*, which also starred Peters and was directed by Carl Reiner.)

- The biggest sequence cut from the film shows Brooks shooting his silent movie within the film. This included him on a camera crane shouting,

"Lights! Camera! Action! No sound!" DeLuise was to be shown looking over costumes, with a woman dressed as a gaudy Christmas tree, and DeLuise deciding the small earrings needed to come off in order to make the costume perfect. A scene from the silent movie being made was to have "all the superstars" in swimsuits, doing an Esther Williams–like production number as they line up by the side of a pool and then dive in, one by one. Brooks was then to look down and say, "Good. It's going to work. Now let's try it with water." The camera was then to cut to show the "superstars" all groaning in pain at the bottom of the empty pool.

- All that was discarded—it appears the swimming portion was never filmed, but the rest was—and instead a gag appears showing first a *Variety* front page stating that the film "starts shooting today!" followed by another immediately afterwards saying that it is "completed in record time!" This makes for a punchy gag and speeds up the film to its ending chase scene (not to mention that maybe some of the actors didn't feel like getting into swimsuits for the Esther Williams joke anyway).

- Engulf and Devour were to get into a crash-test car thinking it is a cab after the coke machine attack. They were to end up crashing, with the two men moving in slow motion inside the car like how the crash-test dummies move in testing footage. They then were to emerge with their clothes all torn up, but unharmed.

- The ending was to be another attempt at the "cast walking by the camera" salute that Brooks tried in *Young Frankenstein*. Instead, the ending credits show the superstars saying goodbye as the film comes to a close.

By late May, the film was ready to be released, with *Variety* announcing that it would be released on June 30, 1976, in 350 theaters. Brooks was concerned, however. He felt there were so many gags in the movie that it might be overloaded, leading to a perfect response from his wife, which Brooks later described to Harry Tessel in an interview. "When will people have time to breathe?" Brooks asked Bancroft. "Don't worry about it," she consoled him. "They'll have time to breathe during the jokes that fail."

Backend

Once again, John Alvin did the poster art for the film, although it featured no hidden jokes beyond Mel Funn's name being written into his captain's hat. Funn appeared in front of a reel of film, which is marked "Made in Hollywood, U.S.A." He is holding a finger up to his lips in a "shh" position with the logo reading "Mel Brooks in Silent Movie." All this above a sunset over Hollywood, with premiere studio lights shooting out into the sky. At the time of release, it was decided to not show the "superstars" that make guest appearances in the film, which is why their names do not appear on the poster. There is a rather odd insert placement of both Feldman and DeLuise into the original U.S.

movie poster, as if they were an afterthought. Later versions of this poster used overseas and in re-release would insert pictures of the "superstars" as well as Feldman and DeLuise. Television commercials were created for the film, and they too seem a bit rushed and a bit "on the cheap." Instead of a logo superimposed over the various clips of the film, as is typical for most movie trailers, the movie poster is awkwardly inserted, while an announcer quickly states, "Silent Movie."

A paperback was published connected with the film, but instead of a typical novelization, the book is the movie in script form, with many photos. It also included photos in the outside corners of each page, which when quickly flipped through gave the images motion.

The film was sneak-previewed on June 18, 1976, at the Avco Center Cinema in Westwood, California. It was then released across the country on the same date, June 30, 1976—a first for one of Brooks's films, which usually were opened region by region. In the theaters at the time were such films as *The Omen*, Neil Simon's *Murder by Death*, *The Outlaw Josey Wales*, *Food of the Gods*, and *Logan's Run*.

Critical reviews were positive, although mixed. Variety leaned toward saying the film would do well, but the reviewer seemed to have an intense dislike for Marcel Marceau before even seeing it and concluded that the movie was simply the cast mugging at the camera. Yet, while some critics felt *Silent Movie* only verified their hatred for Brooks's work, some were converted, such as Joe Baltake of the Philadelphia Daily News, who started his review saying, "When I'm wrong, I'm wrong. I used to be Mel Brooks's least supportive follower—but, then I saw the light, namely his latest flick, *Silent Movie*. It's everything a film comedy should be—short, irresistibly inventive and, best of all, falling-down funny." Roger Ebert once again gave one of Brooks's films four-stars out of four, claiming the movie made him laugh a lot. Charles Champlin at the Los Angeles Times called it "a joy for summer" and wrote that "*Silent Movie* is certain to have the year's noisiest audiences."

Budgeted at $4.4 million, the film has grossed over $36 million domestically, which was sure to have been a help to Brooks, who told Gene Siskel that he made the film for no money upfront, and instead would take a piece of the gross "after it breaks even." The film would be nominated for a number of Golden Globes (Best Actor for Brooks, Best Supporting Actor for Feldman, and Best Supporting Actress for Peters), as well as for Best Comedy Written Directly for the Screen by the Writers Guild of America. It would only win one award, designated one of the Top Ten Films for 1976 by the National Board of Review.

In July 1978, the studio announced that they planned to rerelease the film in theaters that August as *Silent Movie—Plus*, with all the additional scenes that were cut from the film, including the lobster restaurant, edited back into the film. This did not occur, however, and the film was reissued that August without such additions.

The film was another success for Brooks, but as it turns out, he had writers already talking to him about doing another film. And while *Silent Movie* was still in theaters, he was gearing up for this next film, already titled *High Anxiety.*

Reflections

Up to this point, Brooks's films had never followed a standard formula when it came to plots. *The Producers* was a satire of show business with a dash of Hitler and bad taste in the mix. *The Twelve Chairs* was a sweet adventure film showing two characters bonding. *Blazing Saddles* touched upon bigotry, as well as the inanity of western clichés. *Young Frankenstein* was a homage to horror films of our youth, while at the same time telling a rather serious new *Frankenstein* story. Everyone by this time and today seems to put Brooks into the corner of being a master of parodies, but none of his films are simply that.

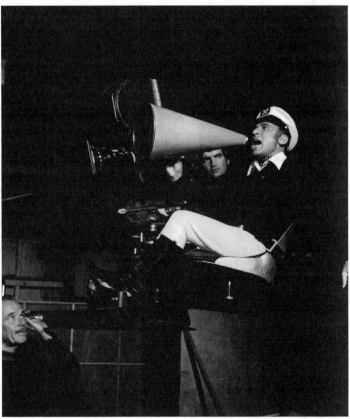

A very popular shot of Brooks that came from the press kit of *Silent Movie.*
This is from a montage of the silent movie within *Silent Movie* being
filmed, which was cut before the movie was released.

The same holds true with *Silent Movie*. While there are jokes about the concept of silent films, the movie really isn't about that. Nor is it the symbolism of male friendship as seen in his earlier film, although Brooks himself noted that Funn is more physical with his two male friends than he ever gets to be with Vilma. Further, Brooks said to Gene Siskel, "my gripe in *Silent Movie* is the capitalist corporations which engulf smaller organizations. I suppose one day we may have to succumb to the fact that Renault will own the Louvre." Yet even this is quickly tossed off with Gulf and Western (the company who had bought Paramount Pictures in the 1970s) becoming Engulf and Devour and their slogan of "Our Fingers are in Everything." It simply creates a villain for the film, rather than a statement like Brooks wished.

Instead, the real purpose of this movie is to give us ninety minutes of sight gags. When Funn, Bell, and Eggs are stalled in traffic, or simply driving around, the point is not to tell us anything about silent movies, but to allow Brooks and his writers to throw in another unrelated gag. Because of this, *Silent Movie* is really the first film to draw our attention to an avalanche of jokes that do not have anything to do with the plot, but are there just to get us to laugh. When we see the restaurant serving food so hot that people literally have steam pouring out of their mouths, or the tailor shop where the clothes in the window are actually the style worn by the man leaving the shop, we're seeing a level of background visual humor that would be put to good use in films like *Airplane*, *Johnny Dangerously*, and the *Police Squad* films. It was a style that was becoming increasingly popular as the 1970s wore on, but Brooks really perfected it in *Silent Movie*.

The downside of *Silent Movie* is that it pigeonholed Brooks. *Silent Movie* is a gag-fest, but audiences and critics only saw a film that parodied silent movies, which really wasn't the point. At the time of its release, Brooks told Gene Siskel in the *Chicago Tribune*, "Now maybe I can take a chance again, because I'm not worried about obscurity like I was after *The Twelve Chairs*. Obscurity? Shit, I was worried about making a living."

And yet, just a few paragraphs away he is already talking about his Hitchcock parody. Brooks had found himself . . . not so much in a rut, but willingly being considered exactly what people wanted him to be—a parodist. It allowed him to be with a group of writers again, being silly, acting in films, using the undercranked camera style that he enjoyed using in both *The Twelve Chairs* and *Blazing Saddles*. The man who wanted to see if he could possibly revive his *She Stoops to Conquer* script in 1976 was conflicted in feeling he may be better off giving the audience what they wanted. The box office certainly agreed with his second thoughts there.

The man who wanted to say something more than simply gags would return, but it would take a few more films before Brooks decided to take that chance again.

13

I Got It

High Anxiety

Release Date: Premiered in Los Angeles and New York City on December 26, 1977. Regional release throughout the United States starting February 1, 1978.

Hitler References

A treatment center for the insane and no Hitlers? Oh, Doc, why did you do it?! Why did you do it?!

Musical Moments

Dick Van Patten's character is killed while being forced to listen to the Mel Brooks–penned song, "If You Love Me, Tell Me Loud." Dr. Thorndyke sings "High Anxiety."

Pre-production

The idea of creating a parody of Alfred Hitchcock's many suspense films came about as Brooks was writing with Ron Clark, Barry Levinson, and Rudy De Luca on *Silent Movie*. "We got to talking about Hitchcock and his films," Brooks told Art Sarno in 1977. "I can't recall who first broached the subject. [We] wondered about the possibility of doing a spoof. The more we talked about it, the better we liked it." By the time *Silent Movie* premiered in June 1976, Brooks was already negotiating the deal for *High Anxiety* with Fox.

It seemed like a solid idea to the Fox studio, and not simply because it was their moneymaker, Brooks, at the helm. Hitchcock and his films had been going through a renaissance in the 1970s, notably the films he made after he came to Hollywood, starting with the release of *Rebecca* in 1940. The general audience of the time was really the first to become aware of the styles of individual directors, and the popularity of Francois Truffaut's book *Hitchcock/Truffaut*, which transcribes an interview Truffaut did with Hitchcock, became a classic text for anyone wanting to learn about filmmaking. People were acquainted with his films, such as *North by Northwest*, *Notorious*, *Vertigo*, and *Psycho*, and they received multiple airings on television and in rerelease in theaters. This way Fox had an upcoming film that would bring the Mel Brooks fans as well as the Hitchcock fans together, so it was an easy decision to make.

One of the movie posters for *High Anxiety*.

Brooks, however, didn't want to simply make a parody of Hitchcock's films but to do like he did in *Young Frankenstein*—transcend the material to take it to a high realism that would make it funny. Plus, Alfred Hitchcock was alive and still trying to work, with his last movie, *Family Plot*, having been released in April 1976, just a couple of months before Fox would announce Brooks's *High Anxiety* parody. Brooks wanted to make sure that Hitchcock understood his wish to make a film that was respectful of his original work, while at the same time poking some gentle fun.

As it turned out, Hitchcock was a fan of Brooks's work, especially *Blazing Saddles*. Hitchcock quickly granted a visit at his bungalow/office on the Universal Studio lot with Brooks in order to discuss the project. When they met, however, the kid in Brooks couldn't help being less than serious. "So I was talking to Hitchcock," Brooks remembered in 2012 to Salon, "and he said, 'Mel, I think what you should do. . . .' And I said, 'Al, call me Mr. Brooks.' He looked at me like I was a shithead. But then he took a moment, and he burst into laughter." It was a joke that could have terminated their talk right there, but because so many fans and even people in the industry that Hitchcock met were in awe of his talent, Hitchcock seemed to enjoy talking with someone who wasn't going to play the "respect" game.

Brooks has said in various interviews that his initial discussion with Hitchcock concentrated on wine. Yet, per Brooks in various interviews over the year, this initial visit with Hitchcock grew into a weekly session where Brooks would bring new script material for the film to Hitchcock's office every Friday afternoon and they would go over it while having lunch. Such sessions would occur up to just three days before filming began.

Brooks recalled in the same Salon interview: "He was my rough editor on the script. He'd cross something out and say no good. And he'd add something and say, 'You forgot this.' He was such a good amanuensis, such a good help in making the script. I should have given him screenwriting credit." Brooks admitted in a 2013 interview with NPR that it was Hitchcock who came up with the idea of the birds attacking in the film. "He said, 'What are you going to do about *The Birds*?' I said, 'Well, gee, at the moment I haven't included it.' And he said, 'Well, why don't you have them attach you with . . . their doody? If they all shit all over you, I mean, it's going to be funny.' I said, 'Thank you. Thank you, Mr. Hitchcock.'"

Although not widely discussed, many in Hollywood knew that Hitchcock was not in the best of health and had problems with his knees, which Brooks saw when they met; sometimes he would have to assist Hitchcock to get from his office to a dining room in his bungalow for their lunch sessions. On one occasion, Hitchcock found himself stuck in the doorway between the two rooms, with Brooks behind him. Later admitting that it was "a little obstreperous," Brooks told Hitchcock, "Come on, Al! I'm hungry here!" and pushed Hitchcock in the behind with his knee, forcing Hitchcock through the doorframe. "He just turned red and screamed for about ten minutes in laughter," Brooks said. "'Your nerve! Your nerve!' He loved being treated like a buddy." Brooks noted in 1973 to *Rolling Stone* that Hitchcock understandably wanted some friendship in his last years. "When I visited him, he very matter-of-factly explained that no one in the company hierarchy came to visit him anymore. In the old days, the executives used to attack him. I didn't know if the new ones didn't care or if they'd just forgotten him, so I called them up and said, 'Will you please go bother this man?' He'd have a glass of wine with anyone, there's a billion thoughts in that head. He's a marvelous storyteller!"

High Anxiety was announced in July 1976, with the goal of releasing it by January or February 1977. Brooks also hoped he could entice Gene Wilder and Dom DeLuise back to do the film, but neither appeared. For DeLuise, it was simply a case of not being able to fit the filming into his schedule. It was a bit more complicated for Wilder, however. He was busy working on his film *The World's Greatest Lover*, which would be released in December 1977, but he also didn't see the point. As he told Jean-Claude Bouls in an article about his relationship with Brooks: "So long as he wants to act the leading role and can fulfill it, there's no need for him to call on Gene Wilder." Brooks countered with an offer for a cameo appearance—most probably as the patient Ron Clark plays in the film—but Wilder turned this down as well.

Instead, Brooks took on the lead again, after having done so in his previous film, *Silent Movie*. In the case of Dr. Thorndyke, Brooks saw the character as a dream role for himself. Not only was he to play a leader in the field of psychology after having studied it briefly in college after the war, but he was to be the true hero of the film, which he relished as he told Gene Siskel in 1977. "I've always wanted to be the character I'm playing: Professor Richard H. Thorndyke. I mean, I like a hat that comes down on both sides. I like a Phi Beta Kappa key. I like a gray suit. I mean, there it is, a dream come true: I'm a Nobel Prize-winning psychiatrist in an Alfred Hitchcock picture. That's a kid's fantasy, especially a kid who loved *The 39 Steps* and *The Lady Vanishes*."

The rest of the cast fell into place pretty quickly. Both Madeline Kahn and Cloris Leachman were signed in October 1976, with Ron Carey, Harvey Korman, and Howard Morris soon added as well. By January 1977, Fox was already running ads in *Variety* for the upcoming production that was to begin filming on April 25, which simply showed the title along with a photo of Brooks leaning away in fear.

Cast

Mel Brooks as Dr. Richard Thorndyke

Since he did okay in *Silent Movie*, the producer/director must have decided to give the kid another chance at starring.

A behind-the-scenes shot of Brooks filming the first appearance of Brophy at the airport.

Madeline Kahn as Victoria Brisbane

Kahn returns to the raucous land of Brooks for this film after declining to appear in *Silent Movie* the previous year. Right before filming began, she spent two months performing in the off-Broadway comedy *Marco Polo Sings a Solo*. As Hitchcock usually preferred his heroines to be blonde, Kahn appears as a blonde for *High Anxiety*. She'll return in Brooks's next film, *History of the World, Part I* in 1981.

Cloris Leachman as Nurse Charlotte Diesel

Another Brooks veteran, Leachman arrived at this production after playing Frau Blücher (neigh!) in *Young Frankenstein*. Leachman had concentrated her time on her series *Phyllis* (1975–1977), as well as reprising the same role in the last season of *The Mary Tyler Moore Show*.

Leachman was looking forward to the role when discussing it in late October with UPI: "[Mel] wants me to play the head nurse in an asylum for the very, very nervous. She's a sex maniac, even more so than Frau Blücher. I was a little kinky in *Young Frankenstein*, and I'm letting it out another notch in this one." Brooks also noticed the link with Frau Blücher and suggested Leachman play Diesel the same way, but she wanted to try something different. Noticing that the costume created to build up the impossible pyramid-like breasts of the character forced her to scrunch up her body, she decided to play the character as if ready to explode and trying so hard to hide the fact that she only accentuates it through her makeup of grey, glistening skin, the faint mustache, and the over-application of lipstick to try to look "cheery." The look extended to the voice as well, which has Diesel talking through clenched teeth and mumbling out of the side of her mouth, as if she were hiding fangs in her mouth.

Like Kahn, Leachman will be back in *History of the World, Part I*.

Harvey Korman as Dr. Charles Montague

Like Leachman, Korman had previously worked in a Brooks film, and like Leachman, had returned to television afterwards; in Korman's case, working on *The Carol Burnett Show*. He described to the *New York Times* his role of Montague as "loosely molded after Leo G. Carroll in *Spellbound*. On the outside, I'm a very elegant man, nattily dressed in satins and such. But inside, I'm corrupt."

And like Leachman, he will return in *History of the World, Part I*, and the pair would team up one more time for the short-lived Brooks-produced series *The Nutt House* in 1989. And as one last tie-in, he, Leachman, and fellow *High Anxiety* costar Dick Van Patten all appeared in the first pilot for the series *The Love Boat*, which was shot in 1976.

Ron Carey as Brophy

Carey had by this time started appearing semiregularly on the television series *Barney Miller* as Officer Carl Levitt. He will be back for *History of the World, Part I*, like Korman and Leachman. The running gag of Brophy saying "I got it! I got it! I got it! I ain't got it!" is based on a routine that Carey used to do in his stand-up comedy days before becoming a full-time actor. Incidentally, Brophy is named after actor Edward Brophy, a character actor who usually played the sidekick (hence the joke of Brophy in the film announcing he is the sidekick) and probably is best remembered for voicing Timothy Q. Mouse, the mouse sidekick in *Dumbo* (1941).

Howard Morris as Professor Lillolman

After leaving Sid Caesar behind, Morris began doing voice work as well as directing, including the pilot episode of *Get Smart* in 1965, and the ensemble comedy film *Who's Minding the Mint* (1967). He also appeared in two Jerry Lewis films, *Way . . . Way Out* (1966, with Dick Shawn) and *The Big Mouth* (1967 with Charlie Callas). *High Anxiety* would be his first time acting with Brooks in a film. As you may have guessed by this point, he too will be back in *History of the World, Part I*.

Dick Van Patten (1928–2015) as Dr. Wentworth

Van Patten had been an actor that popped up on television ever since the days of *Mama* back in 1950. Van Patten first appeared on Broadway back in 1935 at the age of seven in the play *Tapestry in Gray*. He would continue on Broadway in various roles until he started working on television and then spent many years as a guest star on television programs, typically playing variations of ineffectual middle-management weasels. He landed in Brooks's orbit when he was hired to play Friar Tuck in the series *When Things Were Rotten* (1975), leading directly to his being hired for *High Anxiety*. He would come off of *High Anxiety* to star in the popular series *Eight Is Enough* (1977–1981). While miraculously not appearing in *History of the World, Part I*, he returns to appear in Brooks's *Spaceballs* and *Robin Hood: Men in Tights*.

Also Appearing

- Jack Riley (1935–2016) as the desk clerk. He had previously appeared in *Silent Movie* as one of the executives, and will return in other Brooks films.
- Charlie Callas as the cocker spaniel. He will pop up in *History of the World, Part I* and was to have appeared in *Dracula: Dead and Loving It*. He stated at the time that he came up with most of his mannerism as the dog himself during rehearsals.
- Brooks's fellow screenwriters on *High Anxiety* all appear in the film in small roles: Ron Clark as Zachary Cartwright, the recovering patient; Barry Levinson as the bellboy; Rudy De Luca as Braces, the killer. Each writer had acted out the material with his respective character in writing sessions so well that Brooks convinced them that they should perform in the film. De Luca's character, Braces, is a parody on the villain Jaws from the James Bond series (*The Spy Who Loved Me* and *Moonraker*), who had teeth made of steel.
- Lee Delano as Norton, the orderly with half a mustache. Delano was the executive slapping around Ron Carey in the boardroom scene in *Silent Movie*. He'll next appear in—yes, you guessed it—*History of the World, Part I*. In that film, he appears as a wagon driver in the section taking place in Ancient Rome.
- Murphy Dunne (born 1942) as the piano player. Dunne is probably best known as Murph from Murph and the MagicTones in *The Blues Brothers* (1980). He tended to portray piano players in movies, such as the one on the out-of-control luxury bus in *The Big Bus* (176).
- Al Hopson as the unfortunate man who is shot by Braces pretending to be Dr. Thorndyke. Hopson was another of the executives in the boardroom in *Silent Movie*.

- Robert Ridgely (1931–1997) as the man propositioning Thorndyke in the airport bathroom. Ridgely had played the hangman in *Blazing Saddles* and would turn up again in *Life Stinks* and the hangman again in *Robin Hood: Men in Tights*. He's probably best remembered today for his role as Colonel James in *Boogie Nights* (1997).
- Albert J. Whitlock (1915–1999) as Arthur Brisbane. Whitlock was an illustrator who became known for his matte design work with Alfred Hitchcock going back to the 1934 version of *The Man Who Knew Too Much*. Whitlock did the visual effects in *High Anxiety*, as he had done on several Hitchcock films, when Brooks decided that he would be perfect as the industrialist in the movie. He also appears as a used chariot salesman in *History of the World, Part I*, as well as doing the matte paintings in that film and in *Spaceballs*.
- Arnold Soboloff (1930–1979) as Dr. Colbun. Soboloff appears as the man leaving the acupuncturist in *Silent Movie*.
- Deborah Dawes as the stewardess. She'll reappear as a "game show girl" in the Roman section of *History of the World, Part I*.
- Ira Miller (1940–2012) as the psychiatrist with his daughters. Miller had appeared as a villager in *When Things Were Rotten* and will continue to have small roles in all of Brooks's remaining directed films.
- Beatrice Colen (1948–1999) as the hotel maid who interrupts Victoria with Thorndyke. Colen was a common sight on television in the 1970s and played Marsha the waitress in the first season of *Happy Days* (1974–1975) as well as Etta Candy in the first season of *Wonder Woman* (1976–1977).
- Hunter Von Leer (born 1944) as policeman at airport. He later appears as Lt. Bob in the Ancient Rome segment of *History of the World, Part I*.
- George "Bullets" Durgom (1915–1992) as the bald man trapped in the phone booth. A manager for various Hollywood talents, he occasionally popped up in films.
- Mitchell Bock as bar patron. He'll pop up as one of Jesus's disciples in *History of the World, Part I*, and operating the video in *Spaceballs*.
- Alan U. Schwartz as a psychiatrist . . . somewhere there . . . in the audience. He was Brooks's attorney in real life and turns up again in *History of the World, Part I*, as one of the Roman Senators.

In the Crew

- John Morris returned to compose the score, with Ralph Burns orchestrating again after *Silent Movie*.
- Jack Hayes (1919–2011) contributed as an orchestrator on this film and for each Brooks-directed film up through *Robin Hood: Men in Tights*.
- John C. Howard also returned as editor. Patricia Norris, who had designed the costumes for *Silent Movie*, did this film and *History of the World, Part I*.
- Ed Koons, who had been the camera operator on *Silent Movie*, did the same on *High Anxiety*, as did Paul Lohmann as the director of photography.

- Peter Woolery, who was the production designer on *Blazing Saddles*, came back to do the same on *High Anxiety*. He also worked as a set designer on Hitchcock's 1966 film *Torn Curtain*. Ray Berwick, who had trained the birds used in Hitchcock's *The Birds* (1963), was the trainer of the birds seen in *High Anxiety*.
- Harold Michelson, who had worked as a storyboard artist on *The Birds* and *Marnie* for Hitchcock, would do the same on *High Anxiety*, as well as work as a production designer on *History of the World, Part I*, and as the art director on *Spaceballs*.

Production

As production came closer, Brooks and the director of photography, Paul Lohmann, reviewed many of Hitchcock's movies for additional pointers to use in *High Anxiety*. "I watch the kind of film we're making with the DP, so he knows not to be frivolous." Brooks said in an interview with the Directors Guild of America. "For *High Anxiety*, it was, 'What is a Hitchcock film? What does it look like? What does it feel like? How does he light them?'"

Brooks was also working with other people in the industry who had previously worked with Hitchcock, in hopes of bringing the look they gave to Hitchcock's films to his. This included Albert Whitlock for the matte paintings (such as the bell tower at the institution on the cliff) and even the bird trainer who had done the same work on *The Birds*. At the same time, Brooks was determined to make sure that the film did not overindulge in references to the point that he would lose the part of the audience that had no knowledge of Hitchcock's films. For this reason, the references tend to be there for audience members to pick up, without Brooks emphasizing them. Some of the Hitchcock references included:

- Nurse Diesel—although commonly thought of as a parody of Nurse Ratched in *One Flew over the Cuckoo's Nest*, Diesel is more in line with the uptight smothering mother figure seen in several Hitchcock films, such as Mrs. Danvers (Judith Anderson) in the 1940 film *Rebecca* and Leopoldine Konstantin as one of the main conspirators in *Notorious* (1946).
- The man who asks Thorndyke to come to the men's room at the airport is an example of an authority figure who suddenly thrusts the main character into an adventure out of the blue, such as happens to Cary Grant's character in *North by Northwest* being taken away thanks to a mistaken identity. In *High Anxiety*, however, it's just a setup for a joke where the authority figure turns out to be a nut wanting to expose himself to Thorndyke.
- The birds attacking Thorndyke is, of course, a parody of the bird attack in *The Birds*.
- The man who calls and changes Thorndyke's hotel room to a higher floor is named "Mr. MacGuffin." A MacGuffin is a phase Hitchcock commonly

used to refer to anything in one of his movies that served no purpose other than to advance the plot.

- The shower scene is shot in a very similar style to the one done in *Psycho* (1960), only with a newspaper instead of a knife. Brooks stated after the film came out that Hitchcock enjoyed the idea that the ink from the newsprint is going down the drain, as he used chocolate syrup to substitute for the blood in the *Psycho* murder scene.
- Thorndyke's fear of heights comes directly from *Vertigo* (1958), with James Stewart's character in that film suffering from the effects of vertigo.
- *Vertigo* also is where the high tower comes into play as well as the location under the Golden Gate Bridge seen in *High Anxiety* where Thorndyke is being strangled. The same location, Fort Point at the base of the Golden Gate Bridge, was used for when Kim Novak's character in *Vertigo* jumps into the bay.
- Professor Lillolman, a former mentor to Thorndyke who helps him trace his "high anxiety" to a childhood event is likened to Dr. Brulov in *Spellbound*, including the "not dead, only sleeping" gag used in both *Spellbound* and *High Anxiety.*
- Lillolman's chair spinning is similar to that used in *Psycho* to reveal mother.

Dr. Thorndyke is on the run and heading to a phone booth at the location famous from the Hitchcock film *Vertigo* (1958). The area is Fort Point, at the foot of the Golden Gate Bridge, and it is still a tourist attraction, although going through renovations in 2016, as seen in the top photo.

- The heroine being blonde, as mentioned earlier in the chapter.
- Dick Van Patten's character appearing to be "caught in a web" is a visual reference to a similar visual look in *Suspicion* (1941). Another example is his squinting while driving in the rain, which is similar to Marion Crane doing the same in *Psycho* (1960).
- Victoria kissing Thorndyke and vice versa, in order to avoid suspicion by others, is a common device used in several of Hitchcock's films.
- The scene were Diesel and Montague discuss their plans while placing dishes on a glass table and thereby obstructing the view of the camera comes from Hitchcock's *The Lodger* (1926), which featured a scene of a character looking up to imagine people walking on a glass floor above.

Brooks had more ideas to link to Hitchcock, such as having Thorndyke at one point hiding in the nose of George Washington at Mount Rushmore, only to drop out in a green jumpsuit, but such ideas never got past the laughing stages of early thoughts on the script. Indeed, much of the script went straight to film with very little being cut, which is unusual for Brooks up to this time; even whole sequences would normally hit the editor's floor before the film was finished. There were at least two, however, that were shot but not included in the release. A planned scene with Henny Youngman being at the institute as a man who can't stop telling one-liners was ultimately cut, even though Youngman was signed to the role. The other main one filmed but then cut by Brooks as being too odd for audiences at the time was one that Leachman claimed was her best scene in the movie: celebrating after seeing the newspaper headline about Thorndyke killing a man at the convention, Montague and Diesel discuss their next move. What got the scene cut was that Diesel is dressed in a Cleopatra outfit, and Korman is hanging from the ceiling in a BDSM contraption and dressed as a Roman slave. Diesel is so excited that she finally lets her hair down and lowers Montague, alias Spartacus, on to her. While the scene itself was perhaps one kink too far, it conflicts somewhat with the pair's later concerns about the photo in the newspaper, and its deletion makes more sense for the plot.

Filming began on April 25 in San Francisco at the Hyatt Regency, where the scenes centering around the "American Psychiatric Convention" were filmed. To get the shots from the glass elevator looking down on the concourse and of Brooks looking out for the newspaper photo, three panels of glass in the elevator were replaced with clear glass at a cost of $7,000. Other locations in San Francisco where filming took place were Fisherman's Wharf (where Braces gets the call to kill Thorndyke) and Fort Point (where Braces tries to kill Thorndyke in the phone booth). The filming then moved to Los Angeles for interiors at the Fox studio and some additional exteriors at Mount St. Mary's University, which was used for exteriors of the institute. The bird attack on Thorndyke was shot at Brookside Park. Some additional hotel filming was done at the Bonaventure Hotel in Los Angeles. Only Brooks Carey, De Luca, and Levinson were needed for the San Francisco filming when it came to the main cast, while Leachman's

Dr. Thorndyke shoots a man in the lobby of the hotel . . . or does he? This scene was shot in the lobby of the Hyatt Regency in San Francisco. The scenery had not changed much in nearly forty years when this second photo was taken in 2016.

first scene shot was of her at the dining table slurping down fruit in front of Korman.

Filming was completed on July 18, 1977, and according to *Variety*, "four days ahead of schedule." The film was budgeted at $3.5 million and was completed at close to $4 million. During the filming and editing, Brooks kept the writers around to discuss needed changes. "Mel was very receptive to having us on the set during shooting," De Luca stated in an AP interview in 1977, "and he asked us to keep the time open. He wants to have us continue right in to the editing process and even the scoring. Music can be very important in a comedy."

Brooks did believe that the music composed would lend direction to how the comedy played and would participate in the studio when the soundtrack was being recorded, making suggestions. John Morris and Brooks decided that for the shower scene they would avoid the shrieking violins used in *Psycho*, as it would be too obvious a homage. Instead, Morris said that the idea was to hint at the style of score written by Bernard Herrmann—Hitchcock's composer on many of his movies—without merely copying the sound. "The Theremin was the device I used in the main title," Morris described to *Film Score Monthly*. "I used it as a joke, like for *Spellbound* and such."

By September 1977, a rough cut of the film was ready to be shown at the studio. Running fourteen minutes, this cut was assembled and shown at the 21st Annual San Francisco Film Festival on October 9, 1977, and then again at the Granada Theater in Chicago on November 9, 1977. In both cases, Brooks was on hand to discuss his work and the upcoming film. A final version of the film was then screened at the Academy of Motion Picture Arts and Sciences on December 14, 1977, in order to possibly obtain some nominations from the Academy for the picture, though it would receive none. Instead, it would eventually pop up in Los Angeles and New York City on Christmas Day, 1977.

Brooks also had one audience that he wanted to make sure enjoyed it—Hitchcock himself. When a special showing of the film for him was over, the great director left the screening room without a word, suggesting to Brooks that he hated the film. "I was so worried," Brooks reflected years later to *Cinema Retro* magazine. "I thought this is no good. I guess he didn't like the picture. The next day on my desk in my office at 20th Century-Fox there was a beautiful wooden case of 1961 Chateau Haut-Brion. Six magnums. Priceless. Unbelievable to this day. There was also a little note: 'Dear Mel—I have no anxiety about *High Anxiety*, it's a wonderful film. Love Hitch.'"

Backend

High Anxiety would continue to play exclusively in Los Angeles and New York City until it was rolled out to other parts of the country during the first two weeks of February 1978. In theaters at the time were such films as Neil Simon's *The Goodbye Girl*, *Close Encounters of the Third Kind*, Anne Bancroft in *The Turning Point*, Richard Pryor in *Which Way Is Up?*, Gene Wilder in *The World's Greatest*

Lover, and even Fox competing against itself by reissuing *Young Frankenstein*. Initial markets show the film ran an ad campaign in the newspapers offering a "Free *High Anxiety* paperback to first 100 patrons." The novel was written by Robert H. Pilpel and is unique in that it is written in the first person as told by Dr. Thorndyke, and Pilpel is allowed to expand on the histories of the characters, which makes the novelization the most fully realized of the ones done for Brooks's films.

There was also a vinyl soundtrack album released, featuring music from *High Anxiety* and songs from all of Brooks's other films. The album was announced in November 1977 as a double album, with the score of *High Anxiety* on one record and a "best of" collection on the second record. This was reduced by the beginning of 1978 to just one record, with *High Anxiety* material on one side and the "greatest hits" from the other films on the flip side. This does probably explain why the packaging it came in has a gatefold cover, however, which is not typical for a single-disc release. The back cover shows the movie posters for the other films directed by Brooks before *High Anxiety*, along with the text "Mel Brooks's Greatest Hits Featuring the Fabulous Film Scores of John Morris." The inner gatefold cover gives biographical information about John Morris and details about the compositions created for the films. Brooks would go on a five-day tour to promote the soundtrack album in March 1978, which helped to promote *High Anxiety* as well.

The initial cover art for the album as well as the movie displayed Brooks with his arms and legs outstretched in the hypnotic swirl that is seen in the movie whenever he experiences "high anxiety." Soon after there was another poster that still showed Brooks in the center, but with artwork depicting various characters and scenes from the movie illustrated by Robert Tanenbaum. It was this poster artwork that would be commonly seen when the film was released in foreign markets.

Critical response to the film was more mixed than it had been since the days of *Blazing Saddles*. Roger Ebert, who commonly had given Brooks's work four stars up to this point, gave *High Anxiety* only two-and-a-half stars. In doing so, he pinpointed a criticism that several other reviewers noted as well: Hitchcock commonly would make light of his own work within his films. "Hitchcock's films are often funny themselves," Ebert would write. "And satire works best when its target is self-important." Charles Champlin was more positive, although he too felt the film was not as riotously funny as many of Brooks's earlier films, calling it "a high good time, if a calmer Brooks than most." Joe Baltake of the *Philadelphia Daily News*, who could be very hit or miss about Brooks, loved *High Anxiety*, calling it "refreshingly restrained." For the most part, critics seemed to find the film filled with good moments, but not quite paying off as one would expect it would be based on Brooks's earlier films.

The film would eventually earn $31 million domestic, which was lower than *Silent Movie* and less than half of what *Young Frankenstein* had made, but still a strong success for a film that only cost $4 million to make. There were hopes that it would get some nominations by the Academy, and Brooks was disappointed that it seemed the further along his career went, the less likely it was that the industry would recognize him. "The only two people who ever said I was a good director were Hitchcock and Billy Wilder. I never heard from anyone else in the business." Although disappointed with the results, Brooks was still looking ahead to another project to film at 20th Century-Fox, and the word was that he would be working with the same writers he had before on a war movie—specifically one dealing with a group of fighter pilots. That would change, as seen in the next chapter.

Reflections

High Anxiety accomplishes what it sets out to do—give audiences a fun roller-coaster ride while poking fun at some of the well-known conventions of Hitchcock's films. Better yet, it has weathered well over the years, still paying off with a story that could have been used in a Hitchcock film itself. For example, people always talk about the *Psycho* parody, but Braces smashing his way through the phone booth in an attempt to kill Thorndyke only to set up his own death is genuinely clever and rivals some similar threats to the hero in Hitchcock's own films.

Speaking of which, many people, including Brooks himself, have pointed out that *High Anxiety* features Brooks doing his Frank Sinatra impression, which he used to do on various talk shows in the years previous. Yet to be fair, that's not quite the case: Brooks's impression dealt with Sinatra's tendency to scat his way through songs—adding additional sounds and inserting words into a song with pausing that would impress William Shatner. Besides some of the pausing, Brooks's rendition of his song "High Anxiety" within the movie is more of a new invention. In the film, he is playing with the way lounge singers take over a room full of strangers, making inane

Brooks singing "High Anxiety," allowing him to dust off some of his old Frank Sinatra impression that he used to do on the talk show circuit years before.

small talk and trying to be dramatic with the microphone cord, but only looking silly in the process.

That comparison to something Brooks used to do in his career does pinpoint an interesting subtext in the film; it is a homage not only to Hitchcock, but to Brooks as well. If nothing else, *High Anxiety* is the first instance in Brooks's films where we can see him falling back on material from previous sources—much like the Sinatra bit. The orchestra playing from out of nowhere, but turning out to be located nearby in the reality of the characters—as seen when Thorndyke spots the orchestra on their bus going by—is directly from Count Basie playing in the desert in *Blazing Saddles*. Lillolman turning the word "necessary" into a word called "nece" is essentially the same gag as when the governor in *Blazing Saddles* calls Bart a "Ni." As much as we like the cast, Diesel is obviously a descendant of Frau Blücher (but without the neigh!), and Montague is a beaten-down variation of Hedley Lamarr. Even Brophy can be easily seen as the grandson of Brooks's servant character in *The Twelve Chairs*.

Everything was starting to look a bit familiar, and this may have been one of the reasons some critics found themselves not as enthusiastic as for previous films by Brooks. It is also quite possible that he could see the writing on the wall as well. *High Anxiety* may have been fun, but the seams were starting to show, as well as getting pigeonholed as a man who just made spoofs. It was time for a recharge.

14

They Stink on Ice!

History of the World: Part I

Release Date: Released nationally on June 12, 1981, by 20th Century-Fox.

Hitler References

One, and it's the biggest laugh heard in the theater—"Hitler on Ice!"

Musical Moments

Eight in all, some longer than others. Chief Caveman conducting abuse of other cave people for "Hallelujah"; Josephus dancing at the slave auction; Empress Nympho singing her approval to Ponchielli's opera *La Giaconda*; Caladonia and her "high erotic temple dance"; a guy with a boombox listening to "Funkytown" by Lipps Inc. in Ancient Rome; Comicus and his friends singing "Off on the Road to Judea;" "The Inquisition" number; incidental music for Hitler; and "Jews in Space."

Extra Credit to "It's Good to Be the King," a rap song that does not appear in the movie but was used as a promotional tool that ended up becoming popular on its own. The single was produced by Pete Wingfield, who cowrote the song with Mel Brooks. Wingfield was a keyboardist who has played for and produced a variety of rock and soul performers, such as Alan Parsons, Olivia Newton-John, B. B. King, Paul McCartney, and the Everly Brothers. The song, which has Brooks rapping a brief history about being King Louis XVI, was released in multiple countries in 1981–1982, through RCA. Created as a promotional item only, the single managed to get airplay on radio stations throughout the world and reached #67 on *Billboard* magazine's Dance chart and #69 on their R&B chart. Thus, Brooks is credited as the first white artist to enter the R&B charts with a song done completely in a rap style. The song would do so well in France that it reached #2 on the R&B charts there, selling 375,000 copies. The single featured Brooks rapping on the A-side, with an instrumental version of the song on the B-side. With its success, Brooks would return to the rap style for his next movie, *To Be or Not to Be*, but more on that in the next chapter.

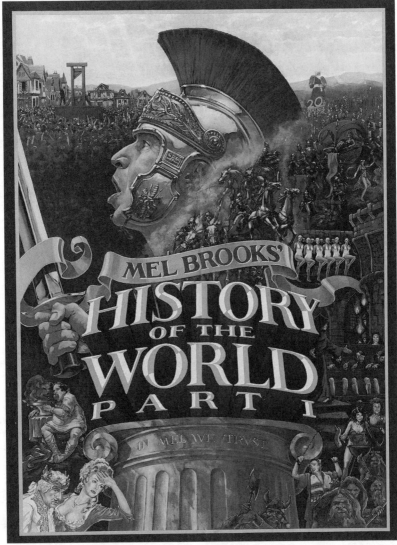

John Alvin once again with a movie poster for Brooks. In this and nearly all of the others, the image is always of Brooks in profile, with some type of tapestry incorporated into the poster as well.

Pre-production

High Anxiety was Brooks's fourth comedy in four years, and it was only natural for people to see him as a high-producing movie machine. Thus, as he began promoting *High Anxiety* to the press in 1977, it was understandable that reporters would ask what was next. The first concept discussed by Brooks in such interviews was a parody of war movies, sometimes referred to as *Bombs Away*, and described by Brooks to the *Washington Post* in 1978 as "a World War II bomber movie with Marty Feldman as the tailgunner, Dom DeLuise at the controls." Brooks was also still hinting at parodying Hollywood musicals, as he told Roger Ebert in 1977: "And I still haven't done my underwater movie tribute to Esther Williams, which will open with six dozen piano players in formal wear, all seated at their grand pianos, playing underwater, their tails steaming out in the water and all these bubbles coming up behind them. God knows what they're doing. . . ."

There was also a newer concept percolating in his head, as he told Gene Siskel in November 1977. "I feel our real enemy is the economy and the people who construct it. I really want to nail some of these bastards. I mean their profit margins never go down. And without going too deeply into politics, I'd love to be able to say something about how absolutely corrupt I think all politicians are. So what I'm looking for now is a story that says all that and still is very funny." This idea would have to wait a few years to come to fruition in his movie *Life Stinks*, but for the time being in 1977 and into 1978, the emphasis was on *Bombs Away*, which he planned to write with his collaborators on *Silent Movie* and *High Anxiety*: Ron Clark, Rudy De Luca, and Barry Levinson.

The problem was Brooks had too many ideas he wanted to do that could not sustain a full feature. Thus, he wondered if perhaps a collection of skits would be better. By February 1978, Brooks began to toss around possible movie titles such as *The Follies of 1979* or *Brooksomania* in interviews and hinting at possible story lines or gags. "I might have fun with *Star Wars*, but I'm not going to do a whole movie about it. It ain't worth it," Brooks told Susan Stanley in 1978, which suggests the spark of "Jews in Space" and possibly the beginning of what would become *Spaceballs*. There was also talk of directing a "restoration comedy where they are very rich and very poor, and when they speak, they are so smart and so English that we need subtitles!" For the most part, however, "it'll be a series of short pieces, with some crazy hunks. I think it'll be more fun and relaxing for me."

One day, as Brooks was walking to his bungalow at Fox, a grip asked him what the name of his next movie would be. On the spur of the moment, he shouted back, "History of the World," and like *Springtime for Hitler* before it, the new title stuck in Brooks's head. Over time he added "Part I" as a knowledgeable and pointed take on Sir Walter Raleigh's five-volume study called *The Histories of the World, Volume 1*, which only got as far as 130 BC before his death by execution (not because of writing such a text, but for political reasons). Thus, Brooks planned a "Part 1" that, like Raleigh's study, would never reach a "Part 2." Although he hinted in 1981 to AP, "If it's a hit, I might want to do others."

Brooks brought his new idea to his fellow writers, who felt that there was not enough of a hook to the idea to flesh it out into a feature-length film; that it would be too episodic. Brooks told them, "I'll hold it together. I'll be in everything." As he later explained to *Newsday* just as the film was coming out: "Playing all those parts was more than immodesty. It was mortar and glue. It was a Mel Brooks concept, therefore wouldn't it be proper if Mel Brooks were in every episode to give it a unity that the different chapters need?" No doubt, Brooks too was looking at his previous work with the 2000 Year Old Man character, who had seen everything and been everywhere. There was talk about how Brooks would play a chamberpot salesman, and his ancestors in the same business throughout history, but in the end, he decided to go with himself playing fresh characters throughout the script. Meanwhile, the other writers were getting offers to do other work, and their time was becoming limited. It was looking like success was going to finally break up that old gang of Brooks's, and he began to wonder if maybe he could do the next movie on his own and forsake the group strategy he had successfully used since the days of *Blazing Saddles*.

"I spent a lot of time walking around the park and thinking," Brooks told Bob Thomas in 1981. "I almost got arrested twice for talking to myself. Finally, I said, 'Yes, Melvin, you can do it!'" He knew that in doing so, he was putting himself in the position of looking like an egomaniac—a producer, director, writer, and star of his own movie—but thought it ultimately would be for the best. "I am a brand name, like Chateau Lafitte, and I don't mind comparing myself to the best of wines. The audience knows that if it's a Mel Brooks movie they can expect a certain quality." Thus, he began writing, with the only thing set in stone for the film the new title—which was made public in September 1978—and that his wife, Anne Bancroft, would star in the film.

"Then began two years of writing," Brooks said to the *Los Angeles Times* just as the film was coming out in 1981. "First of all, I had to choose what parts of history to do. For instance, the Spanish Inquisition beat out the Black Plague—it was like baby birds fighting in the nest." Brooks had other projects he was working on at the time as well: acting as Hitler in the De Luca-Levinson project *Peeping Times* (1978), appearing briefly in *The Muppet Movie* (1979), and—most importantly—endeavoring to get his new production company, Brooksfilms (covered in more detail in chapter 20) off the ground, with the production of *The Elephant Man*, starring Anthony Hopkins, John Hurt, and Anne Bancroft. He was also setting up production for a movie based on Brooks's career with Sid Caesar, *My Favorite Year*, and another focusing on the life of actress Frances Farmer, *Frances*. With all this production work, and the filming of *The Elephant Man* delayed until October 1979, Brooks decided to push back the start on *History of the World* from November 1979 in hopes of getting started in February 1980. It would actually be May 1980 before filming would finally commence.

Such delays did lead to changes in casting already being reported in the trade papers. Early on, coverage on the production claimed that Brooks was looking to cast the film with a variety of comedy stars. John Cleese, of Monty Python fame, had signed on in June 1979, but had to back out due to other commitments as the start of production kept getting pushed back. The same issue arose with Carl Reiner, who had been signed to play the role of the aristocrat that eventually went to Harvey Korman (once again playing into the joke

Korman tells that he was never the first on anyone's list for a movie role). More widely known is that Richard Pryor was signed to star in the film back in 1979, only to nearly kill himself by setting himself on fire just days before he was to appear on the set, causing his role to be recast with talented dancer/actor Gregory Hines. At long last, *History of the World, Part I* was set to start filming on May 5, 1980.

Cast

Mel Brooks as Moses, Comicus, Torquemada, Jacques, and King Louis XVI

Mel Brooks. You've probably heard of him. He played five roles in the film, nearly fulfilling his suggestion that he would link all the material together, but he doesn't appear at all in the caveman segment or in the previews for *Part II*.

Sid Caesar as Chief Caveman, guiding the other cavemen in the first segment of the film

Returning to work with Brooks after *Silent Movie*, Caesar was finally clearing his head and putting more into his work again after his physical and mental slump of the 1970s (as described in chapter 2). Comparing the performances between *Silent Movie* and *History of the World, Part I*, it is easy to see the more energized man of the early *Your Show of Shows* years in the latter film. It would be the last film he would make with Brooks, although Caesar would remain active in the theater and on television for many more years. He would pass away in 2014.

Ron Carey as Swiftus Lazarus, the agent for the stand-up philosopher Comicus

Swiftus—named after famous Hollywood agent Swifty Lazar—would be the last role Carey would do for Brooks. He would continue working in television, including several episodes of an Italian comedy-western series based on the comics series *Lucky Luke*, starring Terrance Hill, in 1992. He died in 2007.

It's good to be . . . you know. Brooks as the King, in the French Revolution segment of the film.

Mary-Margaret Humes (born 1954) as Miriam, the vestal virgin

Humes had moved to Hollywood in the late 1970s and decided to promote herself with a billboard near the Fox Studio lot. "I was driving down Sunset Boulevard," Brooks said in 1982, "and there on a billboard I saw one of the most beautiful girls I had ever seen in my life. She was almost wearing a little pink toga, and it looked to me she might be perfect as Miriam, a vestal virgin." After meeting with Humes, Brooks hired her for the role. Humes would go on to appear in a variety of television programs, typically crime-action shows, and have a regular role on the cult series *Eerie, Indiana* (1991–1992) and *Dawson's Creek* (1998–2003).

Gregory Hines (1946–2003) as Josephus

Hines first worked on Broadway back in 1954 in the musical-comedy *The Girl in Pink Tights*. He and his brother Maurice became a double act as tap dancers when still kids and would eventually perform together on film in Francis Ford Coppola's, *The Cotton Club* (1984).

As mentioned earlier, Richard Pryor was to report the following week to the *History of the World* set to film his role as Josephus when he set himself on fire, leading to a long hospital stay. In a crunch for time due to a possible upcoming actors' strike (and with a writers' strike looming right behind it), Brooks needed to move ahead quickly with the filming and hired Gregory Hines, remembering him from the Broadway revue *Eubie!* from the previous year. Hines's first day on the set was actually his audition as well, and within hours Brooks told him to relax as he had the part.

Hines received good notices from the critics for his performance in *History of the World, Part I*, and it quickly led to roles in other films, including *Wolfen* (1981), *White Nights* (1985), and *Running Scared* (1986). He also had a series on CBS, *The Gregory Hines Show* (1997–1999). He died in 2003 from liver cancer.

Madeline Kahn as Empress Nympho

After *High Anxiety*, Kahn seemed to accept her fate as being thrown into broad comedies, appearing in Neil Simon's *The Cheap Detective*, the *Life of Brian* knockoff *Wholly Moses!* (1980), Buck Henry's *First Family* (1980), and Graham Chapman's *Yellowbeard* (1983). She would have her own sitcom, *Oh Madeline* (1983–1984), and appear as a regular on *Mr. President* (1987–1988). *History of the World, Part I* would feature Kahn's fourth and final appearance in a Brooks film. Brooks would later attempt to interest her in playing Molly in *Life Stinks* and Latrine in *Robin Hood: Men in Tights*, but she passed on both—some claim—due to the salaries offered being too small. Her final role came as a regular on the series *Cosby* for CBS (1996–1999), and when she passed away from cancer in 1999, a special episode of the series would focus on her.

Dom DeLuise as Emperor Nero

DeLuise also appeared in *Wholly Moses!* and continued to have a vigorous career, appearing in two *Cannonball Run* films, a pivotal part in *The Best Little Whorehouse in Texas*, and in drag for a role in Gene Wilder's *Haunted Honeymoon* (1986). He'll be back—in voice only—for *Spaceballs*.

Rudy De Luca as Primate, Cave Dweller who gets speared, and Captain Mucus of the Roman Legion

Former cowriter De Luca may have left the script to *History of the World* to Brooks, but he was still happy to appear as an actor in *History of the World, Part I*. Interestingly, he would cowrite the script to *Caveman* (1981), starring Ringo Starr, which was playing in theaters at the same time he acted as a caveman in Brooks's film. De Luca next appears in *Spaceballs*, and would cowrite and act in both *Life Stinks* and *Dracula: Dead and Loving It*.

Shecky Greene (born 1926) as Marcus Vindictus

A popular stand-up comic, Greene also acted, including in several episodes in the first season of the World War II drama series *Combat!* and later in the Ron Howard comedy *Splash* (1984). Marcus Vindictus in *History of the World, Part I* is probably his best-remembered role out of all of his film appearances.

Harvey Korman as Count de Monet

As mentioned earlier in the chapter, Korman was the second choice for the role of the villainous Count de Monet in the French Revolution segment, after Carl Reiner had to pass on it. Possibly the third choice, as it appears this was initially to be John Cleese's role. Korman will be back in Brooks's final film, *Dracula: Dead and Loving It*, as well as the television series *The Nutt House*, which is covered in chapter 21.

Cloris Leachman as Madame Defarge

The role of the French Revolutionary Defarge would be Leachman's last role in a Brooks film, but not her last association with Brooks overall, as she will later appear alongside Korman in *The Nutt House* television series.

Howard Morris

After the rather large role of Dr. Lillolman in *High Anxiety*, Morris returns for a small role as the Court Spokesman in the Roman Empire segment. He'll have a bigger role again as Sailor in *Life Stinks*.

Pamela Stephenson (born 1949) as Mademoiselle Rimbaud

Born in New Zealand, Stephenson became widely known for starring in the British comedy series *Not the Nine O'Clock News*. Her work on that program led directly to her appearance in *History of the World, Part I*. She later appeared in *Superman II* (1983) and was grossly misused on her one season as a regular on *Saturday Night Live* (1984--1985). In 1989, she married actor/comic Billy Connolly, and trained to become a clinical psychologist, focusing on children's issues and human sexuality. She has written several autobiographies.

Andreas Voutsinas as Bearnaise

Korman's assistant in the French Revolution segment. He had appeared in both *The Producers* and *The Twelve Chairs*. This would be his last appearance in a Brooks film.

Spike Milligan (1918–2002) as Monsieur Rimbaud

Writer and actor, who had cocreated *The Goon Show* with Harry Secombe, Michael Bentine, and Peter Sellers for BBC Radio. Considered by many to be the father of "alternative comedy," Milligan was known for his stream of consciousness and often on-the-edge humor. He had worked with Marty Feldman in *The Marty Feldman Comedy Machine* series, and would work with Feldman in *The Last Remake of Beau Geste*. He also appeared in *Yellowbeard* and *Life of Brian*. This would be his only appearance in a Brooks film, and his contribution to comedy is more than can be noted in just one paragraph of this book.

Orson Welles (1915–1985) as the narrator

Famous writer, actor, director, and magician, who created the legendary film *Citizen Kane* (1941). Thanks to studio interference and his own struggles to live up to that early success, by the 1970s Welles had become known more for appearing on talk shows and narrating various films, including the comedy *Start the Revolution Without Me* (1968) starring Gene Wilder, which also dealt with mistaken identity in the court of King Louis XVI during the French Revolution. Brooks hired Welles for $5,000 for five days guaranteed work. Welles completed all his narrative on the first day, picking up a check for all five days after being needed for only one. His last voice work was as Unicron in the animated *The Transformers: The Movie* (1986).

Also Appearing

Brooks really did want to try to give as many comics and old names a shot in his film as possible. Among the many faces seen are:

The main cast from the Roman segment of the film. Gregory Hines was brought into the film after Richard Pryor had to drop out due to his injuries from setting himself on fire. Hines's audition was essentially the takes of the slave auction scene used in the film.

- J. J. Barry (1932–1990) as primate and cave dweller. Appeared in several episodes of *Barney Miller*.
- Sammy Shore (born 1927) as primate and cave dweller. A stand-up comic, Shore would create the well-known Comedy Store in Hollywood. He'll later appear as the Preacher in *Life Stinks*.
- Earl Finn (born 1937) as prehistoric man and one of Jesus's disciples. He'll pop up again as a guard in *Spaceballs*.
- Bea Arthur (1922–2009) as the unemployment clerk. Best known as Maude and as a regular on *The Golden Girls*, Arthur was also a regular on the last season of *Caesar's Hour*, which Brooks contributed to as a writer.
- Charlie Callas as the soothsayer. This was the third Brooks film in a row for Callas, and the first time he got any real dialogue (he appeared as the blind man in *Silent Movie* and made dog sounds as the cocker in *High Anxiety*).
- Paul Mazursky as the Roman officer asking everyone what the punishment is for striking an officer. Mazursky had previously appeared as one of the Indians on horseback with Brooks for Bart's flashback scene in *Blazing Saddles*.

- Dena Dietrich (born 1928) as Competence, the servant of Empress Nympho. Dietrich appeared in a lot of television comedies over the years, but she probably became best known in a series of commercials for Chiffon margarine. Dietrich, as Mother Nature in the ad, would say "It's not nice to fool Mother Nature," when a character mistakes the margarine for real butter, which because a catchphrase for many years, even after the ad was long gone.
- Ron Clark as stoned soldier #1. He was one of Brooks's cowriters for *High Anxiety* and *Silent Movie*. He'll be writing again for Brooks for *Life Stinks*.
- Jack Riley as stoned soldier #2. Appeared in *Silent Movie*, *High Anxiety*, and will appear next in *To Be or Not to Be* with Brooks as one of the actors at Bronski's theater.
- Henny Youngman as the chemist. He had popped up in *Silent Movie* and was signed to appear in *High Anxiety*. This was his last film appearance for Brooks.
- Pat McCormick (1927–2005) as the plumbing salesman in the Roman Empire segment. McCormick was a famous comedy writer; he's probably best known for appearing in the *Smokey and the Bandit* movies as Big Enos.
- Sid Gould (1912–1996) as the barber/bloodletter in the Roman Empire segment. He was a comic actor who appeared frequently on Lucille Ball's later series.
- Barry Levinson as the column salesman. Brooks's cowriter on *Silent Movie* and *High Anxiety* returned briefly after stabbing Brooks with a newspaper in *High Anxiety*'s shower scene.
- Hugh Hefner (born 1926) as the man who discovered the centerfold. Hefner was the mastermind behind the magazine *Playboy*, and many of the vestal virgins were either Playboy models or "Playmates" (i.e., women who had posed for said centerfolds).
- Albert Whitlock as the used chariot salesman. Whitlock would also do the special visual effects for the film, as he had previously done for *High Anxiety*.
- Ronny Graham as Oedipus in the Roman Empire segment and Jew #2 in the Inquisition. Graham was Brooks's friend from the days they worked together on *New Face of 1952*. This was the first time he appeared in one of Brooks's films, while also cowriting the lyrics with Brooks for "The Inquisition." Graham will be back as cowriter and acting as Sondheim in *To Be or Not to Be*, and as the priest in *Spaceballs*.
- John Hurt (1940–2017) as Jesus. He agreed to appear in the film after starring as John Merrick in *The Elephant Man*. He would tell *Variety*, "It's my first out-and-out comedy, but I don't have anything funny to do!" He'll pop up again in a memorable cameo for *Spaceballs*.
- Jackie Mason (born 1931) as Jew #1. Mason is another famous stand-up comic who was signed early for his role in the film. He became famous for being censored from *The Ed Sullivan Show* for supposedly using a rude gesture (possibly a middle finger, although no one seems to be quite sure, as

Mason himself said it didn't happen) just out of camera range when being told to quickly finish up his spot on the show. He would gain widespread popularity after his 1987 one-man show, *The World According to Me!* This would be his only appearance in a Brooks film.

- Phil Leeds as the chief monk. He had previously appeared in *Silent Movie* as the waiter who nearly gives Mel Funn an alcoholic drink at the club.
- John Hillerman as the rich man stopped by the vendors in the streets of Paris. Hillerman played Howard Johnson in *Blazing Saddles*.
- Jack Carter (1922–2015) as the rat vendor. The comedian who hosted the program before *Your Show of Shows* during its first season. This was his only appearance in a Brooks film.
- Jan Murray (1926–2006) as the vendor selling nothing. Another comedian and actor. This was his only appearance in a Brooks film.
- Andrew Sachs (1930–2016) as Gerard in the French Revolution. Although Sachs had a vast television career in England, he'll probably be forever remembered as Manuel on the British series *Fawlty Towers*.

In the Crew

- Stuart Cornfeld (born 1952) as associate producer. Cornfeld had been the producer on Anne Bancroft's *Fatso* and executive producer on *The Elephant Man*. He was an assistant to the producer on *High Anxiety*. He'd later produce *Zoolander*, *Dodgeball*, and *Tropic Thunder*, amongst others.
- Alan Johnson as associate producer. Johnson also worked as a choreographer on this and many previous Brooks films. He'll be back as the director of *To Be or Not to Be*.
- John Morris composed the music, with Ralph Burns as the orchestrator on "The Inquisition" and Jack Hayes again on other orchestrations.
- John C. Howard as editor.

Production

Shooting began May 5, 1980, on the Paramount Studio lot in Los Angeles starting with the Primates opening of the film and then the Cavemen segments with Sid Caesar. Upon seeing the set, with all the rocks and primitive vegetation, Brooks got the idea to film the "Old Testament" sequence. "I was going to skip the Bible and go to Rome," he reflected in 2012 to the Directors Guild. "I said, 'No, I've got the set, just turn that thing round and it will be the mountaintop, and I did the Moses bit."

Speaking of the Fifteen Commandments, the website Jewishhumorcentral. com on May 22, 2013, posted a translation of what the tablet that Moses breaks in the film says, reducing the number to the Ten Commandments. The translations are:

Mel Brooks as Moses—a short segment in the film that was created when Brooks saw the set built for the cavemen scene and decided it would be cost-effective to use it again for a gag about the Ten Commandments.

- Thou Shalt Not Pass.
- Thou Shalt Not Laugh.
- Thou Shalt Not Buy.
- Thou Shalt Not Tolerate Us
- Thou Shalt Not Break.

After the filming for the Cavemen and Moses scenes, rehearsals began for the dance number on the huge Spanish Inquisition set on Stage 32 of the Paramount lot. The pool used for the water dance sequence looked great in rehearsal, but by the time the team was ready to film the next day, algae had turned the water green, leading to a time-consuming cleanup to get it to look acceptable for the cameras and the swimmers.

The "Square of Warriors" backlot at Universal Studios was used to film the outdoor marketplace scenes that appear in the Roman Empire story line, with June 16 being the first day Gregory Hines was needed on the set for his Josephus character. A few days later, the shot of Moses parting the waters for Comicus and the others in their chariot was filmed at Park Lake, located in the Universal lot as well (the lake was being used as part of the tour ride Universal had at the studio for tourists at the time). Meanwhile, the footage of the chariots and wagons racing through the countryside was shot at Cheeseboro Canyon in Old Agoura, California. As the filming went into July, the production moved to Francis Ford Coppola's Zoetrope Studio to film the interior scenes at Caesar's Palace.

Nearly a full hour of the finished film was completed within roughly ten weeks, which was a bit of a rush for Brooks for one of his films, especially one with so many different sets and characters, but there was a good reason for this. As mentioned earlier, there had been talks of a strike by the Screen Actors Guild, and Brooks wanted to make sure they could get as much done as possible before that occurred. As it turns out, just as the production was to move to England to film the French Revolution segment, the SGA strike began on July 20, 1980. This caused some delays as Brooks and the production had to get permission from the SGA to continue filming, as although the strike was only for actors in the Screen Actors Guild, it affected productions with those actors in other parts of the world. Although the strike would go on for three months, Brooks was granted permission to continue filming after signing a pact that said the studio would agree to whatever terms were set with any new industry contracts that resulted from the conclusion of the strike. Production started up again on July 28, 1980, at Blenheim Palace, once belonging to Winston Churchill's ancestors, for the outdoor segments of the French Revolution sequence. Interiors for this segment were then shot at Shepperton Studios in London.

At the start of filming, Brooks had estimated that it would take four months to shoot *History of the World, Part I*, with a budget of $8–9 million. Filming was completed by September at a cost closer to $12 million, with the Inquisition set alone supposedly costing $1 million. One unintentional bonus was a $200,000 payout by the insurance company for the production over Richard Pryor being unable to film. Editing then took place over a period of several months, with Fox screening the film in sneak previews across the country, starting with a showing on April 24, 1981, at the Avco Center Cinema in Westwood, California. At the time, such sneak previews allowed audiences to stay for the regular feature that was then currently playing in the theater after seeing the "sneaked" film. Oftentimes, the film playing with *History of the World, Part I* was John Boorman's *Excalibur* (a fantasy film about King Arthur), although other films in certain locations ranged from Jerry Lewis's *Hardly Working* to Michael Cimino's *Heaven's Gate*.

Although the film title was never mentioned in any of the sneak-preview ads, the showings were sold out; the Westwood screening was oversold, with viewers who weren't turned away having to sit in the aisles. Such previews gave Brooks a good understanding of what needed to be trimmed, and there was at least one whole comedy skit excised thanks to this process; one that had been shot for the "previews of *Part II*" portion at the end of the movie. The scene dealt with a look at the modern "nuclear family." "I had a father and a mother," Brooks told Gene Siskel, "made up to look like half a dog and half a cat as a result of a nuclear meltdown. But the audience was seriously chilled and didn't laugh, so I left it out."

On May 12, 1981, it was announced by *Variety* that *History of the World, Part I* was "in the can." Everything was looking good for the film to be released in June 1981, as the studio had predicted back in late December 1980. After three years, the world was about to get a new Mel Brooks comedy.

Backend

Fox released *History of the World, Part I* nationally on June 12, 1981. The movie poster was once again by John Alvin, who kept to a similar style used in his previous posters for *Blazing Saddles* and *Silent Movie*: a head shot of Brooks, posing to the side, this time as a Roman Centurion; Brooks's name on a ribbon (or scarf, as in the case of *Silent Movie*); and the title in a 3-D font. The artwork around Brooks's head consists of drawings from incidents in the film, as well as one not featured—cave dwellers cooking meat on a grill.

As mentioned at the start of this chapter, a promotional music single was released for the film. A book from Warner was released in spring 1981, a few months before the film was released, in order to generate interest in the film; the book featured photos from the film along with some brief narrative to set up some of the gags. Brooks also promoted the film in interviews and on talk shows during the summer of 1981 as well.

In theaters at the time the film was released were Alan Alda's *The Four Seasons*, Richard Pryor in *Busting Loose*, Cheech and Chong's *Nice Dreams*, *Raiders of the Lost Ark* (which came out the same day as *History of the World, Part I*), and *Clash of the Titans*. There were some concerns as the film was being released, due to the news in May 1981—about six weeks before the film was to be in theaters—that RCA would be releasing it on videodisc in the fall of 1981. To some theater owners, this suggested a short lifespan for the film and the first signs that the age of video could soon be driving the theaters out of business. This was also one of the concerns that drove the SGA strike the previous year and the one that occurred soon after that by the Writers Guild, as writers and actors were seeing this new medium of video and cable giving studios a new way to make profits that were not being shared with the people who worked on the film. For the moment, the studios pacified theater owners by claiming that the new outlet of video was too expensive for the younger people who like to go to movies anyway. That would of course change over time, and in 1981, *History of the World, Part I* was making history in that battle.

Reviews were mixed when the film was released. Gene Siskel gave it three out of four stars, but called it "scattershot" and felt the Roman and French sequences ran too long. Sheila Benson at the *Los Angeles Times* asked where Brooks's sense of humor had gone, and called the film a "big, overblown, crashing bore." On the flip side, Desmond Ryan of *The Philadelphia Inquirer* wrote that "the groans run into the laughs," but he also felt the film had some "genuine inspirations," such as "The Inquisition" number, which nearly all of the critics complemented and found to be the best part of the film along with the "previews" for *Part II*. Such reviews didn't matter to the audiences, who poured in over $31.6 million to see the film domestically over the years. It was a slightly bigger hit than *High Anxiety* even, proving that Brooks still had staying power with the public, even if the critics were starting to slip away.

No matter whether one likes the film or not, there can be no argument that it did create a catchphrase that many—including Brooks—has used since. Every time we see King Louis XVI do something rude that cannot be questioned, he turns to the camera and says, "It's good to be the king." At the time, Brooks himself probably felt that way about his position in Hollywood. Life was good, no doubt about it.

Reflections

One thing to be said for *History of the World, Part I* is that Brooks achieved what he wanted to do—the film is in his voice and with his level of humor. "The height of my vulgarity," as he once called it. Saying that, the Roman Empire segment also spins its wheels a lot, rushing through introductions of characters and then spending much too long with bad sex jokes before sputtering out into a small joke about the Last Supper before closing out completely. On the other hand, the gladiator fight between Brooks and Hines is perfect, as well as Bea Arthur's "bullshit" jokes near the beginning of the segment. And Hines is in good form for his first movie. Humes, unfortunately, has nothing to do but look pretty, but she seems game enough to try to remain perky in order to give some character to her role.

The Inquisition number usually goes over well with audiences and does get across the point that it was an atrocity that inflicted a lot of bizarre torture in

One of Brooks's biggest musical numbers naturally centers on a taboo subject—the Spanish Inquisition.

order to convert many innocent people, which Brooks aimed for and achieved while getting some laughs along the way. The French Revolution sequence works much better than the Roman Empire one, even with its occasional lapse of taste. At least Stephenson as the woman wanting to get her father out of prison has a character to play that even gets a couple of laughs ("Hump! Hump! Hump!"), and Spike Milligan is always a guarantee for a few funny bits as well. Korman doesn't have much to do other than play an ancestor of Hedley from *Blazing Saddles*, but Andres Voutsinas as Bearnaise has a lot of good throw-away material in the background that never takes away what is happening in the foreground, but is fun to see if you're looking for it.

And, of course, there's "Hitler on Ice"—the bit that probably got the biggest laugh in the theater when I saw it on opening night back in June 1981. Hard to beat that.

Longtime fans may spot some repetition from *Blazing Saddles* beyond Count de Monet having to correct people on the pronunciation of his name like Hedley before him in *Blazing Saddles*: the "repeat after me" gag in the French Revolution segment with Leachman's character; the shouting of "bullshit" in unison by a group; and the "hung" joke in the Roman Empire. But they are quickly over and, let's face it, were good gags that hadn't been seen in close to ten years by that point, so forgivable. And in fairness, the blackouts leading to titles for each segment look very much like a prototype for the Monty Python gag with their subsequent hit film *The Meaning of Life* (1980), as well as the gag with the Chief Caveman directing the pain of others to create music coming very, very close to a gag in Terry Gilliam's *The Adventures of Baron Munchhausen* (1988). So what goes around, comes around.

Brooks also borrow a gag from the *2000 Year Old Man* album, with the caveman who gets eaten by a dinosaur being the first comedian. And in a way, it is too bad that the film didn't try to bridge the segments together by having it be a 2000 Year Old Man film, with Brooks in character, and perhaps saying a bit more about how often things stay the same no matter what progress we make as a species.

Yet in the end, any criticisms of the film mean little. *The History of the World, Part I* was a hit. Brooks was proven right. Even so, it would be the last film he would write on his own, and it would be six more years before he'd direct again.

Not that the next film featuring Brooks hasn't always been mistakenly considered one he directed as well, as will be discussed in the next chapter.

15

And Nobody Saw It

To Be or Not to Be

Release Date: December 16, 1983 by 20th Century-Fox

Hitler References

It's Nazi-palooza! Featuring Brooks playing a fake Hitler, the real Hitler—albeit, shown only from behind—multiple references to Hitler, and more Nazis than one usually sees even in a war movie.

Musical Moments

Three full songs: "Sweet Georgia Brown" by Ben Bernie, Maceo Pinkard, and Kenneth Casey is sung in Polish by Frederick and Anna Bronski at the start of the film; "A Little Piece" by Mel Brooks and Ronny Graham is sung in the sketch *Naughty Nazis*; and "Ladies," also by Brooks and Graham, which is sung by Bronski as Sasha tries to escape the Nazis.

Bits of four other songs also appear: a good bit of the patriotic "Leci Liscie Z. Drzewa" ("Leaves Are Falling from the Tree") by Chopin, sung in the Officers Club with Siletski; brief parts of "You and the Night and the Music" by Arthur Schwartz; "Will you Remember?" (also known as "Sweetheart, Sweetheart, Sweetheart") by Sigmund Romberg and Rida Johnson Young; and "Heart and Soul" by Hoagy Carmichael, which are all sung by Anna while trying to delay Siletski at his suite.

As with *History of the World, Part I*, special mention should be made to a rap single created to help promote the film, this one called "To Be or Not to Be (The Hitler Rap)," written by Mel Brooks with Pete Wingfield (born 1962). Wingfield also produced the song. The song is in much the same spirit as "It's Good to Be the King" from *History of the World, Part I*, with the rap sung by Brooks having historical content about the character being sung about. The song appears on the soundtrack album and was released as a single by Island Records in several parts of the world, reaching #12 on the UK Singles Charts and #3 on the Australian charts. It was released through Island Records in Great Britain as a 7" vinyl single, a 12" vinyl single, and a 7" picture disc. The A-side has the rap version with Brooks singing, while the flip side has an instrumental version of the song. The artwork for the single was done by Graham Humphreys and features Brooks as Hitler posing at a podium onstage, with stormtroopers on the floor below him serving as guards. The front of the podium says, "We have ways of making you dance."

Pre-production

First off, Brooks didn't direct this movie.

Secondly, he didn't write the script to this movie.

Yet it's still considered a Mel Brooks movie by many fans, and is included on many DVD and Blu-ray box sets of his films. Most of all, however, this was a dream project of both Brooks and Bancroft for several years before it was finally filmed in 1983.

To Be or Not to Be is a remake of an Ernst Lubitsch (1892–1947) production from 1942 that starred Jack Benny and Carole Lombard. Lombard, who was Clark Gable's wife, would die in a plane crash while on a war-bonds tour two months before the film played in theaters, and *To Be or Not to Be* is considered her best role by many. Lubitsch, a German film director and writer who moved to America in the 1920s, became known for his sophisticated comedies, including *Ninotchka* (1939) with Greta Garbo and *The Shop Around the Corner* (1940) with James Stewart and Margaret Sullavan. Lubitsch cowrote the script with Edwin

To Be or Not to Be was a remake of the 1942 Ernst Lubitsch film, with the plot following the earlier film in many places, like this scene where Bronski (Brooks) and the other actors hunt down the spy in the theater.

Justus Mayer, based on a story by Melchior Lengyet, and the plot remains very much the same for the 1983 remake.

It is understandable why Brooks would fall in love with the original film. Not only is Lubitsch's *To Be or Not to Be* considered a comedy classic today, it also ridicules the Nazis and Hitler. Furthermore, it is a perfect type of film for married actors, such as Brooks and Bancroft, who wanted to perform together. On July 5, 1975, a UPI report stated that "Producer-director-actor Mel Brooks bought remake rights to the 1940s hit *To Be or Not to Be* to star his wife, Anne Bancroft." Not much more was heard about the project until December 18, 1975, when Fox announced the film would be released in 1976, with Brooks writing, directing, and acting with Bancroft.

In May 1976, there was news that William Allyn and David Lunney were to produce the film for Brooks, with James Kirkwood writing the script. Kirkwood (1924–1989) had written the novels *There Must Be a Pony!*, *P.S. Your Cat Is Dead*, and *Some Kind of Hero*. He also had coauthored the book for the musical *A Chorus Line*, which earned him a Tony Award in 1976. Interest eventually died down on the project as both Bancroft and Brooks went to work on other projects, but there was a brief mention of it again in December 1977 when Gene Wilder said in an interview that he had been contacted by Brooks about playing a role in the remake and was considering it. This suggests that Wilder was to play the pilot in the film in a variation of the plot that would have put the love triangle on a more level playing field, with a more mature Sobinski and Frederick fighting over Anna, rather than the quickly dismissed, one-sided, lovesick pilot of both the original and the remake. If so, it would have made for an intriguing diversion from the original plot, and given audiences a chance to see Brooks and Wilder working together in the same film as actors, but it was just a brief moment of interest as everyone went back to their other projects instead.

Brooks again approached Fox about the film in September 1980, now that the Brooksfilms production company was becoming functional. Fox was still interested in the idea, but Brooks had one condition: he didn't want to direct if he was going to star, as he told the *Philadelphia Inquirer*. "It's a brilliant plot with some sensational comic sequences. I kept looking for a way [to do both] and then I thought to myself that if I do the leading role, I won't have time to direct it." Instead, Brooks suggested to Fox executives that they hire Alan Johnson, who had been Brooks's choreographer for his films since *The Producers* in 1967. Brooks joked at the time, "I knew that in an emotional tug-of-war [over the film], I could smash him," but on the serious side, Brooks had decided that the film would be more than just a comedy; it would be a musical. With Johnson on board, there would be someone behind the camera that knew what Brooks, who was the producer, wanted, while also being able to do any choreography that was needed for the film.

Variety began reporting Johnson as the director by May 1981 as news spread about the upcoming production, while in July 1981 UPI ran a story stating that a new writer had been selected to work on the script, Thomas Meehan

Artwork used for the press kit for *To Be or Not to Be*, the only Mel Brooks film that is not a Mel Brooks film. It is also the only film where Brooks and Anne Bancroft would costar as the two leads, although they did briefly appear together in *Silent Movie*.

(1929–2017). Meehan had worked with Bancroft on her two television specials in 1970 and 1974, as well as written an episode of Brooks's Robin Hood parody series from 1975, *When Things Were Rotten*. Meehan was also responsible for writing the book (dialogue and action) for *Annie*, the vastly successful musical based on Little Orphan Annie, which originally ran from 1977 through 1983. If Brooks were to reinvent *To Be or Not to Be* into a musical, Meehan was a good man to have on board.

Writing began in the summer of 1981, with Meehan, Johnson, and Brooks working with Ronny Graham on the script. The first thing suggested was to change the type of theatrical group the main characters worked in. "In the 1942 film," Meehan stated in an article he wrote for the *New York Times*, "the actors were members of a Shakespearean repertory company. But to liven up the picture, we've decided to make them a vaudeville troupe that does song-and-dance numbers and satiric sketches that are only occasionally interspersed with interludes of high-brow theatre. 'Highlights from *Hamlet*,' rather than the entire play." This change would allow the production to insert musical numbers into the script as a natural part of the plot without characters suddenly bursting into song out of the blue, and by late 1981 it was decided that the film would open with Brooks and Bancroft singing "Sweet Georgia Brown" in Polish.

As the weeks dragged on, Brooks left Graham and Meehan to work on the script without his everyday involvement. The pair would suggest to Brooks that they had to do some major rewriting of the dialogue in order to suit the different personality of the manic Brooks from the original star, Jack Benny, as well as to pick up the pace of the action and dialogue for a modern audience. Brooks was okay with that suggestion, as long as the majority of the scenes and the plot did not change. He did warn the two, though. "Believe me, you two are going to get it in the neck from the critics for what you're about to do. [They'll say] 'How dare they tamper with Lubitsch's masterpiece, how dare they rewrite an already perfect screenplay?' But if you don't, we're not going to make the picture."

In October 1981, Fox announced that Brooks would be making the remake to be released "next summer." That would end up being delayed, with Brooks being occupied with production on two Brooksfilms, *My Favorite Year* and *Frances*. He was also flirting with the idea of his next movie being based on the legend of Robin Hood, going so far as to suggest that it would star Marty Feldman and Spike Milligan, but then decided to concentrate solely on acting in *To Be or Not to Be*. In early 1982, Graham and Meehan finished a fifty-page outline for the movie, which was accepted, and the pair began working on the script. Brooks then increasingly began to buzz the two, contributing his own ideas to the script and working with Graham on songs to be used in the film. Songs written were "A Little Piece" and "Ladies," while a "nutsy gypsy number like Harry Ritz used to do," called "Gypsy Love, Gypsy Hate," was eventually dropped after the first draft of the script was completed.

Filming was to begin in the fall of 1982, but a lawsuit filed in November 1982 by the original producers, William Allyn and David Lunney, delayed things for several weeks. The complaint by the two men was that they had been pushed out of the way and not allowed to do their jobs as producers on the upcoming film as had been promised in an agreement back in April 1976. At one point, the studio offered the pair their salaries for the production, but instead they sued for $10 million. The matter was eventually settled out of court with the two men receiving a "production suggested by" credit in the film.

In December 1982, casting was completed and filming was to begin on January 24, 1983.

Cast

Mel Brooks as Frederick Bronski

Husband of the star. Possible nepotism at work.

Anne Bancroft as (Anna Bronski)

Bancroft was happy to make the film, not only because it gave her a chance to work with her husband, but also it allowed her to step briefly away from the serious dramatic roles she usually had and got to play for comedy, as well as dance and sing. Many noted that neither Brooks nor Bancroft were hoofers, but most critics seemed to appreciate them being game enough to try. This would be the only film where they are teamed up on-screen for the entire length of the film. Bancroft will make one more appearance in a Brooks film—a cameo as a gypsy woman in *Dracula: Dead and Loving It*.

Tim Matheson (born 1947) as Lieutenant Andre Sobinski, the dashing young pilot

Matheson started his career in television, in the 1960s, including doing voice work as Jonny Quest in the popular animated series of the same name. One of his first well-known movie roles was as Mike, the son of Henry Fonda's character in the comedy *Yours, Mine and Ours* (1968). He moved into the 1970s getting season-long roles in *The Virginian* and *Bonanza*, but usually appeared as a guest star on various series before landing the plum role as Eric Stratton in the hugely successful film *Animal House*. At the time of *To Be or Not to Be*'s release in 1983, Matheson reflected on *Animal House*, saying to Nancy Mills, "It was nice to have been in a really successful film. Unfortunately, I haven't been in one since then."

Matheson always appeared to look younger than his years, playing college students well into his thirties, which allowed him to play the young, naïve Sobinski at the age of thirty-five. Matheson would appear in *Fletch* (1985), which was cowritten by *Blazing Saddles* writer Andrew Bergman. He has continued to work mostly in television, including four seasons on the CBS series *Hart of Dixie* (2011–2015).

Charles Durning (1923–2012) as Colonel Erhardt

Durning started his career as a professional ballroom dancer before working as an actor in the New York area in a number of theatrical productions. As the 1960s wore on, he began to appear on television and eventually movies. Even so, he did not neglect the stage, such as appearing in the 1973 production of *In the Boom Boom Room*, starring Madeline Kahn. Movie success came thanks to appearing as a police officer in first *The Sting* (1973), followed by *Dog Day Afternoon* (1975). The year before *To Be or Not to Be*, Durning had received critical raves for his part as the governor in *The Best Little Whorehouse in Texas* (1982) and would repeat those accolades with his role as Erhardt, including an Academy Award nomination for Best Supporting Actor.

Durning would appear in the only other film directed by Alan Johnson, *Solarbabies*, in 1986. He would continue working in movies and on television, including several episodes of the series *Rescue Me* (2004–2011) and as Peter Griffin's stepfather Francis on *Family Guy*, until his death in 2012.

Jose Ferrer (1912–1992) as Professor Siletski

Another actor from the Broadway stage to star in a Brooks film, Ferrer became known for his portrayal of Cyrano de Bergerac in a Broadway production of the play by the same name. Ferrer would win a Tony Award in 1947 for the role and then an Academy Award as Best Actor in 1950 when a film adaptation was made with him playing the character, the first Hispanic actor to win the award. As the 1970s wore on, he made many disaster and exploitation movies (*The Swarm, The*

Anne Bancroft, Mel Brooks, and Tim Matheson in *To Be or Not to Be.*

Charles Durning as Colonel Erhardt with Brooks. Although Brooks at one point would rip into Durning for his performance while they were filming, Durning would end up earning an Academy Award nomination for Best Supporting Actor for his role.

Concord . . . Airport '79, Dracula's Dog, Bloody Birthday) that somewhat diminished his reputation. Nevertheless, he continued to get some solid roles on television, including several episodes of *Newhart* (1985–1987). He would pass away in 1992.

James Haake (born 1932) as Sasha, Anna's Dresser

Haake was working at a Los Angeles nightclub called La Cage aux Folles, which featured female impersonators, when Brooks and Bancroft saw him in 1981. Haake had been the emcee of the nightly show, performing as a character called Gypsy. Impressed by his performance, Brooks worked Haake into the plot of *To Be or Not to Be*, for a subplot showcasing that, in addition to Jews, homosexuals and other persecuted groups were also rounded up and forced into concentration camps.

Christopher Lloyd (born 1938) as Captain Schultz

Lloyd is best known and probably will be forever remembered as Doc Emmett Brown in the *Back to the Future* films, but he had already established a recognized character as Reverend Jim Ignatowski on the sitcom *Taxi*—a role that won him two Emmy Awards for Outstanding Supporting Actor in a Comedy Series. His first film role was as one of the patients in the film version of *One Flew over the Cuckoo's Nest* (1975), and he spent most of his early film career playing criminals

A scene not in the 1942 version has the theater being closed after Anna Bronski's dresser is captured for being a homosexual. While other films before the 1982 remake hinted at the Nazis sending homosexuals to the concentration camps, this was one of the first Hollywood films to deal with it directly.

or crazy people. He would follow up *To Be or Not to Be* with roles in *Star Trek III: The Search for Spock* and *The Adventures of Buckaroo Banzai Across the 8th Dimension* in 1984. All this before acting in the iconic *Back to the Future* film in 1985.

Also Appearing

- Ronny Graham as Sondheim, the stage manager. As mentioned, Graham cowrote the script as well as two songs for the film. He'll be back in *Spaceballs* as a cowriter and actor. And, as many probably noticed, the character is named Sondheim so that Bronski can tell him to "send in the clowns" in reference to composer Stephen Sondheim, who wrote "Send in the Clowns" for his musical *A Little Night Music* (1973).
- George Gaynes (1917–2016) as Ravitch, the overacting ham of the actors. After a long career in television, including acting as the father figure in *Punky Brewster* (1985), Gaynes began appearing more frequently in films, typically as a somewhat clueless, self-important man. He appeared as Commandant Lassard in the *Police Academy* film series and was in *Tootsie* (1982) as a pompous, hammy actor right before appearing in *To Be or Not to Be*.
- George Wyner (born 1945) as Ratkowski, one of the Bronski Theater performers. Wyner had previously appeared in the Brooksfilms *My Favorite Year* (1982) and would go on to have a much larger role as Colonel Sanderz in *Spaceballs*.
- Jack Riley as Dobish, Bronski's driver and Frederick's understudy. Riley will return one more time in *Spaceballs*.
- Lewis J. Stadlen (born 1947) as Lupinsky, the actor who finally gets to play Shylock. Stadlen began his Broadway career playing Groucho in the musical about the Marx Brothers, *Minnie's Boys* (1970). He eventually would play Max Bialystock in the Broadway production of *The Producers* from April 2003 to October 2003.
- Estelle Reiner (1914–2008) as Gruba, the woman hiding the refugees in the theater. Estelle was the wife of Carl Reiner. She is probably best remembered for *When Harry Met Sally* (1989), directed by her son, Rob Reiner, as the woman telling the waitress "I'll have what she's having."
- Max Brooks as Rifka's son, the refugee boy that Gruba invites into the theater. Max is the son of Mel Brooks and Anne Bancroft. He'll later go on to write for *Saturday Night Live* (2001–2003) and then go on to write the zombie novel *World War Z* (2006) and *The Zombie Survival Guide* (2003).
- In more incidental roles were Henry Kaiser as a Gestapo officer, who will return in *Spaceballs* as the magnetic beam operator; Zale Kessler as Bieler, who will return as the orchestra leader in *Dracula: Dead and Loving It*; and Terence Marsh as the startled British officer, who returns as the Spaceball Drum Beater in *Spaceballs* and was the production designer on *To Be or Not to Be*, as well as *Spaceballs*.

In the Crew

Besides Terence Marsh mentioned above, other members of the production team included John Morris, once again composing music for the film, with Ralph Burns and Jack Hayes as orchestrators. Irene Walzer, who was a publicist on *History of the World, Part I*, became an associate producer on *To Be or Not to Be*. Gerald Hirschfield, who was the director of photography on *Young Frankenstein*, returned to do the same on *To Be or Not to Be*; and John Franco Jr., who did set designs on *History of the World, Part I*, would also do the designs for this film.

Production

Filming began on January 24, 1983, with the New York Street standing set on the Warner Bros. lot in Burbank, California, used for the exteriors of the Bronski Theatre. Most interiors were done at the American Zoetrope Studios and the Mayfield Senior School in Pasadena, California. The high school was used for filming of scenes that take place at Hotel Europa (the film's location of Siletski's room) and the Officers Club in England, where the Polish officers are shown singing together.

Although initially planned since the late 1970s to be a musical, it became clearer as filming came closer that the songs were overwhelming the script, causing the plot to be sidelined too much by the various musical numbers. Thus, all musical numbers not essential to the plot were cut from the script, and the "Sweet Georgia Brown" number moved to the beginning, where it would make an immediate impact on the audience. This was a disappointment to all involved who were looking forward to creating a musical, but the deletion helped the pace of the film overall.

One scene actually filmed and then cut due to lackluster response from test audiences was to have appeared near the end of the movie, as Brooks mentioned to the *Philadelphia Inquirer* right before the film was released. "We had a scene that shows Hitler and a Nazi audience staring at the empty stage. Suddenly he starts stamping his feet and clapping his hands like a kid and yelling, 'We want a show! We want a show!' I thought it was hysterical, but [the preview audience] were too caught up in the escape and they didn't want an outside joke. You can't futz with an audience."

While most of the plot is the same, there are several changes made between the 1941 original film and the 1983 movie. Besides the change of a female dresser to Sasha for Anna and the actors changing from a Shakespearian troupe to a vaudevillian one, some of the other changes are:

• Character names changed: The main characters are changed from Joseph and Maria Tura in the 1941 version to Frederick and Anna Bronski in the 1983 version. The pilot's first name changed from Stanislav to Andre. The double agent's name changed from Siletsky to Siletski. Colonel Ehrhardt in the original became Colonel Erhardt in the remake.

- The 1941 film starts with Joseph Tura playing a Gestapo agent in a serious drama called *Gestapo*. The 1983 film has Frederick Bronski playing Hitler in a musical sendup called *Naughty Nazis*.
- In fact, Joseph Tura never plays Hitler in the original film. It is played by a character called Bronski—whose name is used for the last name of Brooks's and Bancroft's characters in the 1983 film.
- "Heil me!" appears in both films—once in the original and twice in the remake. Yet in the remake it is an intentional gag-line in *Naughty Nazis*; in the original it is a suggested line that is quickly shot down in a rehearsal.
- The theater is the Polski Theatre in the original; it is the Bronski Theatre in the remake.
- Speaking of which, with the theater being Bronski's, it is natural that Frederick would essentially be running the show as the producer. In the original, a character by the name of Joseph Dobosh is the producer of the plays and also the mastermind of many of the plans done by the group to outwit the Nazis in the film.
- It's insinuated that Joseph has had to deal with Maria's flirtations before. In the 1983 film, Anna's visits with the Polish flyer appears to be a first for her and innocent on her part.
- Joseph's Hamlet has a book as he comes onstage; Frederick's Hamlet has a knife.
- Anna is only seeing Sobinski for a second night in her dressing room when war breaks out in the 1983 movie. In the original, Maria has been up in Sobinski's plane, and they meet again the following week when war breaks out.
- In the remake, Anna has a dog . . . for some reason that hopefully wasn't just for the silly leap by the dog into the plane at the end of the film.
- In the original, there is more about the Polish underground and citizens turning against the Nazis, including a successful bombing of the train station near the end. In the remake, there doesn't seem to be much of an underground anywhere except in passing. (This may have been done to avoid the audience asking why Sobinski didn't simply go to the underground upon arrival rather than Anna. Out of sight, out of mind, as it were.)
- The Polish officers in the Officers Club sing a rousing anti-Nazi song in the original film. In the remake, they sing a sad song about those who have died.
- Maria gets the information to the Underground in the original film, thus showing her being pro-active to fight the Nazis. There is no such scene in the remake.
- Siletsky is very clear that he wants Maria to be an agent for the Nazis. Siletski merely hints at this with Anna in the remake.
- It is Joseph's idea to kill Siletsky by inviting him to the made-up Gestapo headquarters. In the remake, Frederick is forced into the plan by the others.
- Maria goes through an elaborate plan to make it appear Siletsky has committed suicide. It turns out not to be needed and probably was jettisoned from the script in the remake as it's a plot point with no payoff.

- Hitler is a piece of cheese in the original. He's a pickle in the remake. Fans of the original film for years have discussed what the joke actually meant, and this probably is why the joke was changed and given an explanation in the remake ("because he's a sour puss!")
- Ehrhardt tells Maria that Siletsky's body was found in the Polski Theatre when the Nazis began preparing the theater for an event planned there that night for Hitler. In the 1983 film, Anna is invited to talk to Erhardt when there is a phone call telling Erhardt and Anna that Siletski was found dead in a trunk in the middle of a street. (The remake clarifies a couple of things—for example, if Siletsky's body was found hidden away in the theater, even if they knew he was killed by the British agent running around, why would the Gestapo not suspect someone in the theatrical group of helping him? Why allow Hitler into a possible trap later that night? With his body being found in the streets, there is no concern about the theater. Also, Joseph returns as Siletsky to Erhardt because he is concerned about Maria, but it is not exactly clear. And if it isn't, then why would he risk going? The remake makes it clear that there is a concern Anna is in trouble, making Frederick's risk understandable.)
- In the 1941 film, there is only the theatrical group that escapes, dressed as Nazis. In the remake, there are also additional refugees that were hiding at the theater who escape dressed as clowns.
- There is no comical attempted suicide attempt by the Colonel in the remake.
- Joseph does not go in to retrieve his wife from the Colonel in the original, but it is still someone dressed as Hitler who does so.

Production went smoothly on the film, although it was clear that Brooks could still throw his weight around, even if he was not directing the film himself. At one point in the filming, he had a scene with Charles Durning as Erhardt. Brooks took him to task over a take that didn't go well. "[It] happened on a movie I made this year for Mel Brooks," During recalled to the *Los Angeles Times* soon after filming was completed. "He's a brutally honest man, Mel. After I'd done one scene, he said, right in front of everyone, 'Garbage you give me.' That absolutely rocked me." Brooks would also later admit that he had a hard time stopping himself from telling Johnson how to direct. "[I wanted to say] 'Are you crazy? You can't put the camera there!'"

To be fair, Brooks also made sure his performance could be stacked up against that of the other actors, although he found his methods conflicted with Bancroft's, as he told Bob Thomas. "Her approach to a scene is always totally honest; she wants to know what the character is feeling at that point in time. My approach is: The audience must be entertained, no matter what. She says they will be entertained if everything is honest. We managed to reach a compromise." The pair also took lessons from a teacher at UCLA in speaking "very rude Polish" in order to sound somewhat authentic in the opening of the film.

Filming was completed in April 1983. Editing was next, but the studio was pushing Brooks to have the film ready in quick order so that it could be released that Christmas, something that did not set well with Brooks, who liked to take his time with screenings to get the right feel for his films. The film was in a completed form by late September, with some special showings in October through early December, including one at the Gotham Cinema in Manhattan on December 5, 1983, that was for 500 related family members—most with the last names of Kaminsky or Italiano, the real last names of Brooks and Bancroft. The film was then released nationally on December 16, 1983.

Backend

There were initially two movie posters created for the film by Drew Stuzan. The first is much in the style of one of the posters done for *High Anxiety*, with images of characters surrounding a central image; in this case, images of Brooks as his various characters in the film along with Bancroft surrounding an image of Frederick and the dog running to the plane with Nazis in pursuit. The better-known poster is a continuation of those that had come before it for Brooks's films, with a profile shot of Brooks, only this time joined by a profile of Bancroft, above a scenic view of a town, with planes and parachutists in the sky, and the movie title in a 3-D font. Brooks's name appears first, with Bancroft's name in parentheses, which is a continuation of a running gag in the film dealing with Anna's billing on posters being in parentheses. The poster adds the tagline, "That is the movie!"

In theaters at the time of the film's release were Brian DePalma's *Scarface*, Clint Eastwood in *Sudden Impact*, *Terms of Endearment*, *The Right Stuff*, Barbra Streisand in *Yentl*, and *A Christmas Story*. To help promote the film, Brooks filmed an hour-long program for London Weekend Television on August 17, 1983. The program, titled *An Audience with . . .*, was one in a series done by the show, and featured an artist doing what was essentially a solo performance in front of a live audience, filled with celebrities. In the program with Brooks were Ronny Graham and Anne Bancroft to help with some musical numbers related to the film, including the Polish version of "Sweet Georgia Brown." The program would later be exported to the United States and shown on the cable pay-channel Showtime. Beyond that, in November 1983, news filtered through the entertainment papers that Brooks told Fox he would not be helping to promote the film when it went into theaters, instead taking his family on a three-week vacation in Hawaii that Christmas.

Critical reviews leaned toward the positive for the film, mainly from critics who were happy to see Brooks dialing down a bit from the gross-out gags of *History of the World, Part I*. Some, however, took offense with the film treating Nazis with laughter; and yet, ironically, many such reviews praised Charles Durning for playing a funny Nazi in the film. Roger Ebert gave the film three stars, saying, "*To Be or Not to Be* works as well as a story as any Brooks film since

Young Frankenstein." Vincent Canby for the *New York Times* called it "smashingly funny," although he found the addition of the gay Sasha "not one of the film's great inspirations." Elsewhere, Marshall Fine called the film, "[Brooks's] most disciplined and consistently funny film to date." Kevin Thomas of the *Los Angeles Times*, however, dismissed it, saying, "It would have been better not to have been attempted in the first place." One thing that didn't happen, as Meehan mentioned after the reviews came in: "We were not, as we'd anticipated, taken to task for having too heavily rewritten the 1942 screenplay. Instead, we were chided for having scarcely rewritten it at all."

That observation appeared to be shared by a number of theatergoers as well. The film, which cost $9 million to make, earned only $13 million when released in the United States and would be seen as a flop. Attempts were made in trade ads in *Variety* to drum up some nominations for the film and actors, but only Charles Durning would be nominated for an Oscar. The script would be nominated for Best Comedy Adapted from Another Medium by the Writers Guild of America, while Bancroft and Durning would be nominated for Golden Globes, but there would be no win for the film in any of the award ceremonies.

In his interview with the *Philadelphia Inquirer*, Brooks was still looking ahead to his next parody film, even before *To Be or Not to Be* was released: "I want to do a flat-out take-off on science fiction. You know what I mean. We'll open up with somebody saying, 'Don't use your lasers, men, they may be friendly.' All that terrible dialogue. They've gone too far. Those guys are waiting to be shot down." As it turns out, Brooks would be on the right track for his next project. But after the slow returns on *History of the World, Part I* and the fate of *To Be or Not to Be*, and Brooks's disappointment over what he saw as Fox rushing the film to release before it was ready, he would soon find himself leaving Fox after nearly ten years and five films together

Reflections

Lubitsch's *To Be or Not to Be* is a classic in writing and performance. It also faced a certain amount of criticism at the time for suggesting that in war, by laughing at the Nazis, we were in a sense making them harmless. To Lubitsch, the laughter came not from seeing such men as silly, but because the audience has contempt for them. In the 1983 version, the same holds true. Brooks and all involved do not find death camps, the bombing of Warsaw, and the invasion of Poland as something to make light of, but rather as no matter how aloof and horrible people try to make themselves, such men commonly are the first to cower—such as Erhardt and Schultz in the film—when threatened. We need to have contempt for them, and laughter is the great equalizer. Surprisingly, even forty years on, Brooks would run into the same wish of critics to categorize his film as "fluff" just as they had with Lubitsch's.

Saying that, it is hard not to compare the films and find the earlier version had more of a dramatic impact and that it said more than the remake. Some of this may be due to additional comedic moments, but some of Johnson's directorial decisions also contribute. The killing of Siletsky in the theater is a masterful piece of editing in the 1941 film, making his death real and our watching—just like the actors in the seats below the stage—transforms us into accomplices. The remake takes that scene and pulls the camera back much too far, keeping us at a distance and thus doesn't involve us as deeply as it did in the first film. On the other hand—and I know this is treason to fans of Lubitsch's original—the writers of the remake eliminate some of the plot holes of the original while creating new moments of interest as well.

One interesting comparison when watching the two films side by side is noting how much the original is an ensemble piece—all the actors have things to do and contribute to the plot. Jack Benny's Joseph does provide action, but he isn't the mastermind of the final gambit, nor the main instigator in any way. He doesn't even get to play Hitler. In the 1983 film, however, it really is about Frederick and Anna. All the action centers on them, as they make every move that propels the plot, while the other characters help out in small ways. This doesn't necessarily make such a change a wrong move; rather it helps to focus the audience's attention upon the two main characters and their actions, rather than those of a number of other characters as in the original film.

One final observation: although this film was not written or directed by Brooks, he had a great deal of input on it. He chastised actors about their performances—as seen with Durning earlier in this chapter—pushed to veto camera moves, and was hovering over Meehan and Graham during the writing process. There is no indication that this was unwanted, but it was obviously there. Yet, even with his heavy involvement, the film feels different from others in his career thanks to new voices being heard. The camera work and lighting, for example, are more striking than in *High Anxiety* and *History of the World, Part I*, and this was no doubt due to Alan Johnson working with the director of photography, Gerald Hirschfield. There are new players, with only Ronny Graham returning from a previous film; and he had only been involved with one scene in the previous movie. (One can imagine the film being made with Harvey Korman as Erhardt and Dom DeLuise as the gay dresser if Brooks had directed.) There are new writers that would come back to work with Brooks again in the future.

In many ways, the movie works as a chrysalis to what was to come in the remaining years of Brooks's film career. There will be four more movies made by Brooks, but none of them look like his 1970s output, and with the exceptions of cameo appearances by some of his old repertory of actors in later films, many of the actors will be new to Brooks. True, with one exception, they will all be parody films, but there will be something new added as well.

To Be or Not to Be may not have been Mel Brooks's film, but to survive into the 1980s and beyond, it was probably the film that he needed.

16

Just Plain Yogurt

Spaceballs

Release Date: June 24, 1987, distributed through MGM

Hitler References

None, really. The princess's stuntman does have a little Hitler mustache, however. And when one of the Spaceballs shouts out a "jawohl," Dark Helmet gives him a look.

Musical Moments

Three quick snippets: The *Ghostbuster*-ish theme song for *Spaceballs* being played as everyone evacuates Spaceball One. Princess Vespa sings a little of "Nobody Knows the Trouble I've Seen" while in prison. The alien makes his getaway from the diner by singing a bit of "Hello! Ma Baby" like Michigan J. Frog in the Warner Bros. cartoon *One Froggy Evening* (1955).

Preproduction

It took time for Brooks to come around to the idea of doing a science-fiction parody. In fact, although he adored Flash Gordon as a kid, the love for such movies didn't stay with him, which he acknowledged when it was pointed out that all his parody films up to that point had been from genres of his youth. "[Science-fiction movies are] not my favorites, but I had done westerns. I had done horror films. I had done Hitchcock. And to make a successful parody, you need a really big target . . . I may not be a fan of the genre, but I do think the first two *Star Wars* films are classics that will live for a very long time." Brooks also admitted he was doing it for one person in particular. "My son," Brooks told Gene Siskel. "My 14-year-old son, Max. He loves space movies. He loved the *Star Wars* pictures. He loved the *Alien* pictures."

As *To Be or Not to Be* neared completion in 1983, Brooks turned to the two writers of that film, Thomas Meehan and Ronny Graham, to come up with ideas for his next. By January 1984, Brooks was already talking up a science-fiction parody as his next film; it was just the title that needed some work. "I have in mind a picture called *The Planet Moron*," Brooks told *Parade Magazine*. "It'll be the first really rich satire of all the science fiction movies' 'Don't fire your lasers, they may be friendly.' That sort of dialog. When they invade, I want to be able to say, 'We're surrounded by Morons.'"

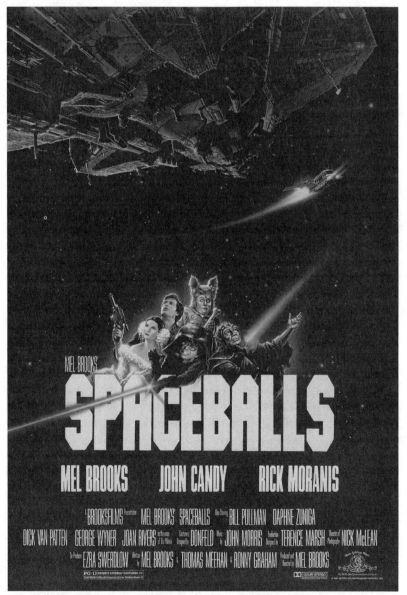

Spaceballs: the movie poster. Although the film would do only so-so at the theaters, on video it has become a cult hit, leading to years of speculation of a sequel.

The title would change from *The Planet Moron* to *Return to the Planet Moron* in February 1984, then just *Planet Moron* in May 1984. However, another title change was needed when it became clear that a comedy film from the United Kingdom called *Morons from Outer Space*, which had been covered in *Variety* since February of that year, was going to be released in 1985. Brooks, Meehan, and Graham decided the word "space" had to be in the new title, and they began going through the alphabet, looking for a second word to go with it. In the special-edition DVD and Blu-ray release of *Spaceballs*, an interview between Meehan and Brooks has Brooks saying that he remembers spilling his cup of coffee and saying "Balls!" in reaction. (Admittedly, Meehan looks rather unconvinced with the accuracy of Brooks's version of this story in the interview footage, but goes along with it anyway.) Thus, the film's title was announced as *Spaceballs* in October 1984. Oddly enough, *Morons from Outer Space* features a character playing "Space-ball" early in the film, and the film features a spaceship version of a 1950s Caravan camper, but this appeared to be mere coincidence between the two films.

A title was in place, but the script was long in coming, and this was due to Brooks's responsibilities for his Brooksfilms production company. There were also delays as Brooks had decided to move from 20th Century-Fox to MGM after former Fox executive Alan Ladd Jr. became president of MGM/United Artists in early 1985. Ladd had been the studio leader at Fox who saved *Young Frankenstein* when Brooks was hunting for a studio, and it had led to a long-time deal between Brooks and 20th Century-Fox up through the release of *To Be or Not to Be*. One of the first acquisitions by the Ladd-run studio in January 1985 was distribution of Brooksfilms's upcoming productions, including the troubled *Solarbabies* (see chapter 20 for more details on that film's production), with *Spaceballs* being announced to be made through MGM in July 1986.

As he stepped back into the public eye on a new film, Brooks knew he had been essentially missing for many years. "I know it's been a long time between directing movies for me," Brooks noted to the *Los Angeles Times* while filming *Spaceballs*. "But I only direct things I write. I'd rather write the Ninth Symphony than conduct it. And these days, it takes three years to do the script and set up the deal and—well—I just won't direct a picture I haven't written."

Brooks would state in many interviews as *Spaceballs* began filming that the script took two years to write, but later would amend that to be roughly six months of actual writing, broken up over two years due to various delays. Like many scripts Brooks wrote, the first draft was immense, running close to 400 pages, and then reduced over time. Initially, Brooks and his fellow writers intended the script to satirize multiple science-fiction films and center around an "invasion from outer space" involving very stupid people; an idea that Tim Burton's *Mars Attacks!* would later attempt. That changed in May 1984 to one "set 1 trillion years from now when there's no place left to hide and make love," according to Brooks to columnist Liz Smith. Even so, the emphasis was still on making fun of multiple films in the genre, as he told Desmond Ryan:

"I'm turning my anger against space. We are going to send up everything out there—*Star Wars*, *E.T.*, *Star Trek*, everything. It's going to be *Blazing Space*." Yet, as the script was finally trimmed to a manageable state, it was clear that the script's main target was the *Star Wars* franchise, which worried Brooks. He knew the creator of *Star Wars*, George Lucas, kept a tight rein on the franchise. "I was afraid to get sued by Lucas," Brooks told *Entertainment Weekly* in 2003. "I sent him the script and he said, 'It's fine.' He had one caveat: 'You can't do merchandising. You can't actually have a Dark Helmet action figure, because they'll look too much like ours.'" Brooks understood how important the merchandising was, as he said in an interview with a laugh, "Fox and Lucas were making a fortune, and [*Spaceballs*] really, you know, was stealing."

Brooks also noted one additional reason Lucas may have greenlighted the script was that the *Spaceballs* production used Lucas's Industrial Light and Magic special effects company. "I called Lucas and I said, 'I want you guys up in San Francisco—at the ranch or whatever—to do all the post-production of the movie.' And he said, 'Oh, great, great.' . . . So it was wise, you know? I was playing ball with the people who could have said no."

Originally production was announced to begin in March 1986. It was then delayed until the deal with MGM was finalized in July 1986 with filming to begin on October 28, 1986, making it the first film to be greenlighted by the merged MGM/UA studio. United Artists had just been involved with the spiraling budget for the film *Heaven's Gate*, which nearly killed the studio a few brief years before and led to MGM buying out the company. Because of this, MGM/UA promoted to the press that *Spaceballs* would be firmly held down at a $13 million budget, but that swelled to $22 million by the time cameras began rolling.

Casting was the next hurdle, and came very close to the beginning of filming, with many of the leads hired in August and September 1986. Easily filled were some of the smaller roles, with actors Brooks had used before happily signing on just to work with Brooks again, such as Dick Van Patten, Ronny Graham, Rudy De Luca, and Dom DeLuise. Van Patten even says that he got offered his role as the king from Brooks at a social event and agreed without seeing a script. As for the main leads, however, "We'll also be doing a national search for a lot of new faces," Brooks told Marilyn Beck in October 1985. And for the first time since *Young Frankenstein*, Brooks would not be playing the lead, although he certainly found ways to incorporate himself into the movie.

Cast

Mel Brooks as President Skroob and Yogurt

A man so desperate for work, he is willing to hide his face behind gold makeup and walk on his aching knees for hours during filming. How could the director do that to the man?

And, yes, as mentioned in various sources, the name Skroob is not Brooks spelled backwards, but an anagram of the name.

Daphne Zuniga (born 1962) as Princess Vespa

Zuniga was one of the first of the "new faces" to be hired, after Brooks had seen her in the starring role as Alison in Rob Reiner's film *The Sure Thing* (1985). Before that film, Zuniga had been working in film and television—including a short-lived recurring role as Alex Keaton's girlfriend on the sitcom *Family Ties* in 1984. When auditioning for *Spaceballs*, Zuniga told Brooks that she didn't feel she was suited to playing the type of broad comedy he usually made, but Brooks told her that "half the battle" was playing the comedy straight and she would be fine.

Zuniga starred in *The Fly II* from Brooksfilms after *Spaceballs*, and she was a regular on the television soap drama *Melrose Place* (1992–1996). Besides other film and television appearances, she also has done voice work in animated series, including twelve episodes of *Spaceballs: The Animated Series*.

Rick Moranis (born 1954) as Lord Dark Helmet

Moranis had worked in radio and as a stand-up comic for years before being hired for the Canadian comedy series *SCTV* in 1980, the year before the series moved to the NBC network as a ninety-minute late-night series on Friday nights. The series would introduce Moranis's and Dave Thomas's beloved characters of Bob and Doug McKenzie. Written and performed by Moranis with Dave Thomas, this pair of Canadian goof-offs were given a few minutes most weeks to showcase Canadian culture as they understood it (such as by drinking beers and eating back-bacon). The pairing would develop into a record album and tour through America and finally a feature film for MGM, *Strange Brew* (1983), featuring the characters.

By the time of *Spaceballs*, Moranis had gone through a prolific period of filmwork, usually playing slightly dweebish men who have secrets, as in *Streets of Fire* (1984), *Ghostbusters* (1985), and *Little Shop of Horrors* (1986). Although increasingly wary of being promised he could incorporate some of his improvisational skills, he was curious to work for Brooks and signed on in August 1986.

Moranis continued to have leading roles in films like the *Honey I Shrunk the Kids* films for Disney; two more films with Steve Martin, *Parenthood* (1989) and *My Blue Heaven* (1990); as well as Barney Rubble in the live-action version of *The Flintstones* (1994). He has recorded two musical albums, *The Agoraphobic Cowboy* (2005) and *My Mother's Brisket & Other Love Songs* (2013).

John Candy (1950–1994) as Barf the Mawg

When Moranis signed on, he suggested Candy would be a good choice for the role of Barf the Mawg. Like Moranis, Candy was also going through a rather hot streak in movies in the 1980s, although he had started appearing in films in the 1970s, as well as Canadian television while working in the Canadian

Brooks as Yogurt. The makeup gave Brooks an allergic reaction, causing him to work as quickly as possible through his scenes in-character.

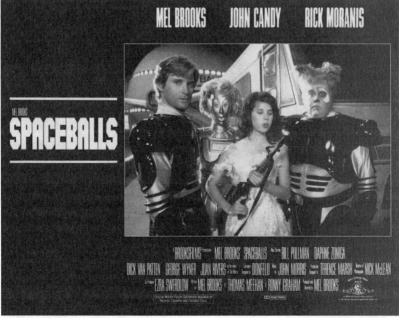

Daphne Zuniga as Princess Vespa, showing the boys how to shoot. Vespa ends up being the most proactive character in the film and one of the very few times a female character in a Brooks film is the lead.

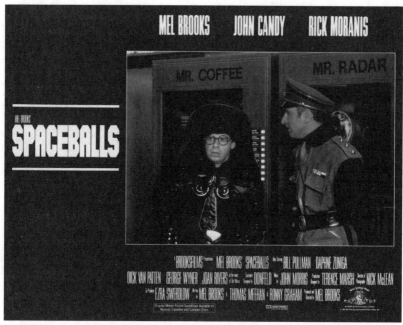

Rick Moranis as Dark Helmet, with George Wyner. Moranis was allowed to improvise some of the material on the film, as was John Candy; something that Brooks was usually very much against.

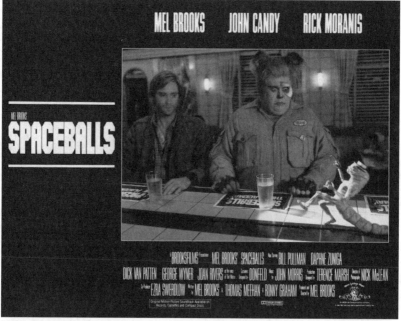

Hello, My Darling! John Hurt makes his second guest appearance in a Mel Brooks movie in a parody of his earlier role in the film *Alien*.

version of the Second City improvisational theatrical troupe. It was with that group that he would help create with several of the other actors and writers *Second City Television*, a half-hour program parodying television programs that eventually was transformed into *SCTV* for NBC. Candy was one of the few members of the group to headline major Hollywood films after leaving *SCTV* and had already appeared in such films as *The Blues Brothers* (1980), *Stripes* (1981), *National Lampoon's Vacation* (1983), and two films with Tom Hanks, *Splash* (1984) and *Volunteers* (1985) before being offered *Spaceballs*. Candy had also worked with Moranis on two films by that point, *Little Shop of Horrors* and *Brewster's Millions* (1985, and starring Richard Pryor). After *Spaceballs*, Candy appeared in *The Great Outdoors* (1988), *Uncle Buck* (1989), *Home Alone* (1990), and *JFK* (1991). He died while filming his last movie, *Wagons East* (1994).

Bill Pullman (born 1953) as Lone Starr

With Brooks having hired such recognizable names as Candy and Moranis for *Spaceballs*, MGM was happy with Brooks's choices, but there were still concerns about finding a big movie star to play the role of Lone Starr. Suggestions made by the studio included Tom Berenger, Tom Cruise, and Tom Hanks. None of those candidates worked out, but depending on who is speaking, it was either Brooks's decision or was completely taken out of his hands. "The studio fought me," he told Gene Siskel in 1987. "They wanted Tom Cruise or Tom Hanks—anybody named Tom who costs $2 million. That's what's wrong with this business. If you make it a 'Tom' movie it's no longer a parody, it's a 'Tom' movie, and you have to build scenes around him." However, Bill Pullman, who eventually got the role, had a different take, as he told an audience at the ArcLight Cinemas in Hollywood in 2011: "[Mel] said, 'I tried to get a Tom and I couldn't get him. I tried to get Tom Cruise, Tom Hanks, and I couldn't get them, so I got a Bill!' And I said, 'Is that a joke, Mel?' But it's true. He really crafted the part and he imagined he was going to get a big box office draw at the time and I think he was hurt that they didn't take him up on it, you know?"

Bill Pullman had worked for years by that point as a theater teacher and had just gotten his first movie role as the mistress's boyfriend in *Ruthless People* (1986). Pullman had impressed Brooks with the film, and after seeing the actor as the lead in a Los Angeles production of the Michael de Ghelderoe play *Barabbas*, Brooks offered him the role. Pullman asked why the studio didn't make a fuss after the concern about getting a well-known name for the role, and Brooks said that once they had "two of the big comics at the time: John Candy and Rick Moranis," Brooks figured "'Heck, I'll get somebody nobody knows!'" Pullman certainly didn't argue that point and signed on for his first major starring role in a film.

After *Spaceballs*, Pullman was typically cast as the lead or costar in films such as *The Serpent and the Rainbow* (1988), *A League of Their Own* (1992), *Sleepless in Seattle* (1993), and *Lost Highway* (1997). He is probably still best remembered as playing the president in *Independence Day* (1996).

George Wyner (born 1945) as Colonel Sanderz

Rumors were circulating that Brooks had offered the role of Colonel Sanderz to Steve Martin, but if such an offer was made, Martin declined; thus denying the audience a second film that starred him, Moranis, and Candy (all three had appeared in *Little Shop of Horrors*). Instead, Brooks went with someone he had worked with before on *To Be or Not to Be*, George Wyner. Wyner at the time was a regular cast member on *Hill Street Blues* and was eager to sign on when he found out he would be working with Moranis. Sanderz would be Wyner's last role for Brooks.

Dick Van Patten as King Roland

Van Patten returned to the world of Brooks's films after last appearing in *High Anxiety*. He'll be back for one more Brooks film, *Robin Hood: Men in Tights*.

Lorene Yarnell (1944–2010)

Yarnell appeared as a dancer in films and on television, going back to the movie *Bye Bye Birdie* in 1963. She is remembered for her years working with her then-husband Robert Shields as a pair of mimes on *The Sonny and Cher Show* (1976–1977) and in a summer replacement series called *Shields and Yarnell* (1977). She typically was hidden behind either greasepaint or other appliances, much like in that of *Spaceballs*. Yarnell moved to Norway in the late 1990s with her third husband. A ruptured intracranial aneurysm caused her death in 2010.

Joan Rivers (1933–2014)

A popular comedienne who would eventually host her own late-night talk show on Fox in the mid-1980s, *The Late Show Starring Joan Rivers*. She was most famously known for the line "Can we talk?" in her stand-up act, as if about to share some juicy gossip. She was asked to do the voice for Dot Matrix after Brooks decided in rehearsals that Lorene Yarnell's voice was not right for the character. She agreed to do the role after being let go from the movie *Hot to Trot*, which features John Candy's voice as a talking horse. Rivers would return to voice the role of Dot Matrix again in the subsequent animated series, *Spaceballs: The Animated Series*. She died in 2014 due to complications while having surgery on her throat.

Dom DeLuise as Pizza the Hutt

DeLuise performed only as the voice for this rather disgusting-looking character. He'll be back on-screen for Brooks in *Robin Hood: Men in Tights*.

Playing the on-screen role of Pizza the Hutt were actor Richard Karron (1934–2017), who had been one of the prehistoric men in *History of the World, Part I*, and Rick Lazzarini, a special effects artist on the film.

Also Appearing

- Sal Viscuso (born 1948) as Sergeant Ricco, the first Spaceball to feel the wrath of Dark Helmet in the movie. Viscuso may be recognizable to fans of the television series *Soap*, where he played the troubled Father Timothy Flotsky. He also popped up as various characters on *Barney Miller* and occasionally did the announcements heard on the television series *MASH*.
- Ronny Graham as minister at wedding. Cowriter of the script and previously seen as Sondheim in *To Be or Not to Be*. He'll do a voice in *Life Stinks* and appear briefly in *Robin Hood: Men in Tights*.
- Thomas Meehan as assistant to King Roland. Cowriter of the script. He appears for "ten seconds" in the film as a promise to Brooks to get him into the film somehow.
- Michael Winslow (born 1958) as Radar Operator on Spaceball One. Winslow is a comedian who gained fame by his ability to mimic various noises with his voice. He used this talent as Sgt. Jones in the *Police Academy* movies, which is the role for he is best remembered.
- Jim J. Bullock (born 1955) as Prince Vallium. Bullock was a regular on the Ted Knight sitcom *Too Close for Comfort* (1980–1987)
- Leslie Bevis (born 1954) as Commanderette Zircon. Playing the only female Spaceball that gets a speaking part in the movie, Bevis made her mark in guest roles on television. She would later appear in three episodes of *Star Trek: Deep Space Nine* (1993–1996).
- John Hurt as unfortunate diner patron. This was Hurt's second cameo in a Mel Brooks film, after appearing as Jesus in *History of the World, Part I*. In *Spaceballs*, Hurt's character has an alien burst out of his chest just as it had in the film *Alien* (1979).
- Rudy De Luca as Vinnie, Pizza the Hutt's henchman. Brooks's past and future cowriter appears briefly in *Spaceballs*. As many have noted, his metallic look is based on that of then-popular television character Max Headroom, and was done with makeup rather than any appliances.
- Tim Russ (born 1956) as the Spaceball who Ain't Found Shit. Tim Russ appeared with Bill Pullman in the play *Barabbas*, which Brooks had gone to see in order to judge if Pullman would be right for the role of Lone Starr. He would go on to play Tuvok, a Vulcan, on the series *Star Trek: Voyager* (1995–2001).
- Jack Riley as the newscaster announcing the death of Pizza the Hutt. This was the last film Riley would do for Brooks, having performed in each of his films since *Silent Movie*. Riley would continue to work in television and

films including as a voice actor on such shows as *Rugrats*, where he played Stu Pickles. He passed away in 2016 due to a bout of pneumonia.

In the Crew

- Harold Michelson, who did storyboarding for *High Anxiety* and *History of the World, Part I* returned to do the same for *Spaceballs*.
- Peter Albeiz was the supervisor on special effects in the film and will return on *Dracula: Dead and Loving It* to do some effects work.
- Richard Ratliff, who also helped with special effects on *Spaceballs*, will go on to coordinate the effects on both *Robin Hood: Men in Tights* and *Dracula: Dead and Loving It*.
- Ray Robinson, who also worked on effects, will return to do the effects on *Life Stinks*.
- Albert Whitlock supervised the matte paintings for effects use this time around, with Syd Dutton and Bill Taylor doing the paintings. Both Dutton and Taylor will do the matte painting work on *Life Stinks* and *Robin Hood: Men in Tights*.
- John Morris was once again the composer on this Brooks film, with Jack Hayes as the orchestrator and Eugene Marks as the music editor.
- The script supervisor, Julie Pitkanen, had previously had this position on *Blazing Saddles* and would perform a second duty on *Spaceballs* as the voice of the self-destruct system.
- Ezra Swerdlow was the coproducer with Brooks on the film. and had worked as a unit manager on several Woody Allen films before going on to be an executive producer on *Life Stinks*.
- Ben Nye Jr. did makeup and had been brought in at the suggestion of John Candy, who had worked with him on the movie *Armed and Dangerous* earlier in 1986. Nye would go on to do the makeup for Candy on many of his subsequent films.
- Terence Marsh worked as the production designer, having done the same role on *To Be or Not to Be*, and several of Gene Wilder's films starting with *The Adventure of Sherlock Holmes' Smarter Brother*. Marsh had worked as an assistant art designer on *Lawrence of Arabia* (1962) and later as production designer on such films as *The Shawshank Redemption*, *The Hunt for Red October*, and *The Green Mile*.
- Donfeld, sometimes listed as Don Feld, was the costume designer. Donfeld had worked in this capacity since 1961, on such films as *The Great Race* (1965), *The Cincinnati Kid* (1965), and *They Shoot Horses, Don't They?* (1969). Brooks would say in *Spaceballs: The Documentary* that the designs were so good he asked Donfeld to go ahead with what he initially created without any major changes, although Dark Helmet's helmet became much smaller than originally planned.

Production

Filming started out in Yuma, Arizona, for the daytime scenes on the planet Vega. The desert outside of Yuma was essential to give the film the look people remember from the first *Star Wars* movie, but it also meant the cast and crew having to work in sweltering conditions, with sand dunes that had to constantly be raked or blown to make it look like they had not been tread on by a cast and crew for additional takes. In fact, if you look even vaguely at the scene with the Spaceballs "combing" the planet, you can see that they've been combing the same tracts of land a few times by that point. For most of the cast, it was rough, but for Yarnell as Dot Matrix, it meant being stuck inside a suit that completely covered her body, a mask that limited her vision and breathing, and shoes that made walking in sand difficult. Thus, repeated breaks were needed for her as they filmed.

Shooting then moved to the MGM lot in Los Angeles for filming in November and into December. At least three sound stages were used: Stage 30 was used for the massive Spaceball One command post set seen throughout the film; Stage 27 was used for the Yogurt set; and Stage 15 was used for other sets, including the entrance to the prison area in Spaceball City. According to a *Los Angeles Times* article in November 1986, Stage 15 was where cast and crew found random samples of the Yellow Brick Road from the 1939 movie *The Wizard of Oz*. The wedding scenes were shot in January at St. Matthew's Episcopal Church in Pacific Palisades, California,

Brooks has always been known for his multiple takes when filming, usually asking for six to ten takes from his actors for a scene even after telling them that the latest take was "perfect." This created a dangerous situation during the filming of the Pizza the Hutt scene, as Brooks required the costume to look as grotesque as possible; spending a long time filming the scene with Richard Karron inside the costume. Bill Pullman in his ArcLight interview remembered seeing some of the testing for the creature, which involved real cheese and meat dripping from a costume that had heating wires inside of it to keep everything hot. "Mel was so serious as he stood in front of Pizza the Hutt. They got the steam going and it was cooking and everything, and they were all laughing to help sell the thing, the work that they'd done. But Brooks's not laughing. He goes, 'I want that bubble to like . . . pop.' Very serious." When it came to filming under the hot lights for numerous takes, it was discovered that the costume couldn't take the intense heat—much less what Richard Karron inside the suit was having to deal with. Rudy De Luca, who played Vinnie in the scene, at one point noted smoke coming from the costume and alerted Brooks to the situation. After alarms were raised and the smoke finally dissipated, Brooks asked if they could get one more take. Karron refused to get back into the costume, and the Pizza the Hutt scene was completed with Rick Lazzarini, one of the effects technicians, inside the costume instead.

To be fair, Brooks had his own issues with makeup during the film. The least being that the little mustache he wore as President Skroob kept sliding down as they filmed under the hot lights. In that case, it became in in-joke with the character, with Skroob's mustache changing positions throughout the film. Worse was the gold makeup used for Yogurt, which Brooks had been assured was nontoxic. "My eyes broke out because of the fumes of the gold paint," Brooks remembered in 2012 to the AV Club. "It was right in the middle of shooting it. I just kept taking Benadryl and all that stuff to fight the allergy. . . . I'm supposed to chalk it up to show business, but I nearly died." Between suffering from the fumes and having to walk around on his knees as the character, Brooks suddenly switched to being a very efficient, less demanding director, deciding shots were perfect after one or two takes, so he could get out of costume and makeup as soon as possible.

Speaking of makeup, John Candy worked with Ben Nye Jr. on the makeup for Barf, with the initial idea to wear latex appliances on his face so that he would look more like a dog. Brooks's reaction was, "If we're covering up his face, why even bother hiring John Candy to play the part when I can get someone cheaper?" A second attempt was made that would have put more of a dog-nose on Candy's face, but this was rejected as well. Instead, makeup was used to cover one eye and part of the nose, while a hairpiece was created to cover Candy's ears and put dog ears on the top of his head that were controlled off-camera by technicians and powered by a thirty-pound battery on Candy's back. Even this caused some minor issues, as the technicians became so involved with the movement of the ears that they were starting to upstage Candy's performance.

Brooks, who usually had little use for improvisations on the set, allowed Rick Moranis and John Candy more space to make changes than he typically would have allowed. As a matter of fact, neither attended rehearsals before filming, preferring to keep their performances fresh for the camera. Brooks's willingness to let his usually strict standards slacken a bit for the two actors led to Moranis improvising a scene where Dark Helmet is playing with a bunch of Spaceballs dolls. "What I remember," Moranis told The Hollywood Reporter, "is not feeling well that day. I think I had a fever. I wasn't at the top of my game, but somehow was able to come up with that. George [Wyner] was so fantastic in that scene." Candy's line of "Ooh, that's going to leave a mark!" when trying to get out of his chair while wearing his seatbelt, was also improvised on the set.

The one person on the set that Brooks gave little such flexibility was Pullman, who was usually told to stay with the script when offering suggestions. John Candy, however, attempted on occasion to help push through some of Pullman's ideas, including "Gimme paw," a line tossed in by Pullman that Brooks initially turned down but was fought for by Candy. Brooks would later say that he considered Moranis a "pain in the ass" during filming because Moranis would come up with new ideas after a shot and—to Brooks's consternation—would sometimes deliver something funnier than what was written. Both he and Candy were also known for intentionally trying to crack up the other actors just as they were beginning to film, with Wyner remembering Moranis getting to hide behind the Dark Helmet mask while Wyner would ruin a take laughing at something Moranis had said.

Postproduction effects—such as the shimmering effects of the Schwarts through the film, and the starfield going plaid—were done by Industrial Light and Magic, George Lucas's special effects team. Other effects done on camera—like Barf's ears, the little alien puppet that bursts out of John Hurt's stomach, and Lone Starr's ship—were done in-house by the production team on set. Greenscreens, a series of green walls or sheets that could then be filtered out and replaced with effects were everywhere on the sets, in particular on the Spaceball One set, which at the time featured the largest use of such screens in film history. At the time the film was made, there was a genuine fear that repeated exposure to the color of the screens could cause eye damage, and so everyone working on the film was given yellow sunglasses to wear between takes, a look that the cast and crew found funny and one that it was later discovered was unnecessary.

Filming was completed in January, leaving the composing, additional effects work, and editing to be done by April 1987. This was an incredibly fast turnaround for Brooks in the editing phase, which would typically take many months to complete. By May the film was ready to be previewed in theaters for paying audiences to see.

Backend

The first sneak preview for the film occurred in San Francisco the second weekend of May, with some subsequent sneak previews in the country before the film was released on June 24, 1987 (some parts of the country did not get it until that Friday, June 26, 1987, which is typically the date given for when the film finally made it to theaters). The movie poster artwork was once again by John Alvin, but this time it would not match what had been done in his previous posters for Brooks's films. Rather than a profile shot of Brooks taking up the majority of the frame, Alvin went with a look that was more designed to parody the *Star Wars* posters, with multiple characters looking off in various directions.

Brooks appeared in ads for the film, introducing the ads as himself. He also promoted the film by appearing as a guest host of Joan Rivers's *The Late Show*, along with most of the cast, which some television critics at the time complained about, although it was certainly not out of the ordinary for such talk shows to promote a film in such a manner (such as when Burt Reynolds guest-hosted on *The Tonight Show* with his fellow cast members from *Lady Luck*, as mentioned in chapter 12).

There is a novelization that is somewhat odd, as it was published by Scholastic Inc. and advertised to be sold to children. Quite a unique sales campaign for a movie with the word "fuck" in it. Such dialogue, as well as jokes about "I see your Schwartz is as big as mine," are missing for this reason, of course. The novelization was written by "Jovial" Bob Stine, who would later become quite well known for his series of *Goosebumps* novels, which are directed at young teenagers. The novelization for *Spaceballs* would be the last released for one of Brooks's films.

The film started off strong, making $20 million in its first two weeks, but critical response was very mixed, with a good number of reviewers feeling it was about ten years too late to be satirizing *Star Wars*. Many did praise certain moments in the film—in particular the use of a video of the movie being used by the villains before the film is even finished—as well as some of the performances, such as Moranis's, but some felt "Brooks seems stuck in the shtick of these parodies and more than anything you'd like him to free himself, try something different," as Michael Wilmington said in his review in the *Los Angeles Times*. Harper Barnes of the *St. Louis Post Dispatch* felt the film "has a few laughs in it, but not nearly enough." Even Rick Moranis would tell the *Chicago Tribune*, "It's uneven, but if you like Mel Brooks, you'll probably like it."

Jack Garner of *The Cincinnati Enquirer*, however, gave the film three stars and felt that Brooks "has rediscovered his creative juices" with *Spaceballs*. Ben Yagoda had the most striking comment in his positive review for *the Philadelphia Daily News*, however, calling it "Laughs for the Under-14 Set."

The film did well, but in a summer that saw a slew of solid hit movies, such as *Dragnet*, *The Untouchables*, *Predator*, *Roxanne*, *Robo-Cop*, and *Crocodile Dundee*, *Spaceballs* did not do as well as expected. With a budget of $22 million, it would eventually gross $38 million domestically, which would suggest a borderline success or even a flop depending on who was pushing the accounting pencil at the studio. Yet Ben Yagoda was pretty much on the mark about who liked the film: kids. The children who saw it went back for more, and eventually played the video over and over, making it much like *The Producers* in being a cult favorite. The stars would find people who had grown up on the film reciting lines back to them, and besides *Blazing Saddles* and *Young Frankenstein*, *Spaceballs* is one of Brooks's films that the general public can name without a thought. In the end, belief in the film overcame what looked to be its final destination. The Schwartz was really with this movie all along.

Reflections

One really had to be at the right age or in the right mood for *Spaceballs*. Me, I was twenty-two and remember laughing once—the little alien dancing in the diner.

Yet, having come back to the film for—okay, for this book, actually—I've got to admit now that it has grown on me. (Candy giving the finger and making the kissy sounds now makes me giggle just thinking about it, while in my youth I would have just groaned at the immaturity of it.) Performances in general are good, and—as always—Brooks does a fine job in his two roles. Granted, he has some of the funnier lines as well, but he's the writer-director, so you have to give him that.

Perhaps part of the problem at the time of release is that we already had comedies that played with such science-fiction ideas. *Airplane II* from 1982 had already parodied the opening scroll of the *Star Wars* film and—truthfully—in a funnier way, turning the narrative into a sex novel just as the ship smashes through the scroll. There had been *Flesh Gordon* to make fun of the old 1930s science-fiction adventures; *Dark Star* and *The Hitchhiker's Guide to the Galaxy* for more cerebral gags; *Morons from Outer Space, The Creature Wasn't Nice,* and *Galaxina* for more obvious visual jokes. It was an area that was already being mined by the time of *Spaceballs,* which probably hurt it at the time. And yet, which one of them is remembered the most?

Spaceballs does present us with some firsts for Brooks. As mentioned earlier in the chapter, it was the first film of his since *Young Frankenstein* where he was not the lead. It was the first to really bring in new actors to headline since that film as well. Perhaps most importantly, it was the first film he directed that featured a strong female character. We tend to concentrate on Lone Starr, but Vespa is the pro-active character. She's the one to leave behind a loveless marriage; the one that decides to "grow up" and do the responsible thing; the one that makes sure she gets what she wants in the end. Is it any wonder that she's the only one of the heroes who knows how to shoot straight when given a gun?

Perhaps having just come off of *To Be or Not to Be,* with its strong female lead character, influenced this, but whatever may have caused it, Brooks would continue to feature female characters in his movies that do more than an occasional punch line, such as in his next film, *Life Stinks* and to a lesser degree in his last two, *Robin Hood: Men in Tights* and *Dracula: Dead and Loving it.* Ironically, just as critics were beginning to say that Brooks was stuck in his ways, he was showing signs of developing as a writer who had been hiding behind all the jokes.

If Brooks really was maturing as an artist, it was about to be put to the test with his next film. A test that ultimately would lead him right back to the parody films he thought he was leaving behind.

17

A Bunch of Moments

Life Stinks

Release Date: July 26, 1991, distributed through MGM

Hitler References

None.

Musical Moments

One and a half. A full musical dance number with Brooks and Lesley Ann Warren dancing in the fabric shop to Cole Porter's "You'd Be So Easy to Love." Also, Brooks briefly scats while dancing for loose change early in the film.

Pre-production

In November 1977, Mel Brooks was asked by writer Gene Siskel what was next for him after completing *High Anxiety*. "I feel our real enemy is the economy and the people who construct it. I really want to nail some of those bastards. I mean their profit margins never go down. And without going too deeply into politics, I'd love to be able to say something about how absolutely corrupt I think all politicians are. So, what I'm looking for now is a story that says all that and still is very funny." It would take thirteen years and three movies before Brooks finally felt compelled to get back to that idea.

Brooks announced to *Variety* in August 1988 that his next film would be *Life Stinks*, with Ron Clark and Rudy De Luca, along with new writer Steve Haberman, writing it. In October of that year, however, Ron Clark had to drop out of production in order to concentrate on saving a new sitcom for Dick Van Dyke he was executive producer on called *The Van Dyke Show* on CBS (the extra effort didn't help; the show was cancelled by December).

Brooks and the others may have been writing, but it was March 1990 before MGM announced that *Life Stinks* was to move forward at the studio. Then in November 1990, financier Giancarlo Parretti took over MGM/UA and changed the name of the studio to Pathe, which was the company listed in *Variety* to release the film. The studio would then become MGM-Pathe, with distribution through MGM but television distribution through Warner Bros., which is why some later entries in newspapers and *Variety* list the film as "coming soon from Pathe or MGM or Warner Bros." It seems everyone was getting confused when it came to the studio, and it would get worse before it got better.

The poster for *Life Stinks*—a film that Brooks considers to be one of his three best. It would be a commercial disappointment and the last time Brooks starred as a lead in one of his films.

While the studio worked out their issues, the production team for Brooks's new film suggested the title be changed to *Life Sucks*. However, although today the term "sucks" has relatively little meaning besides another way to say something was bad, at the time it was still considered offensive, and many newspapers would have objected to advertising such a film, so *Life Stinks* is what it remained. While the title was tossed around a bit, the plot of the film stayed consistent from beginning to end, focusing on "the wretched social conditions of this country that have thrown so many normal people into homelessness," as Brooks said after filming was completed. He suggested their goal was to comment about homelessness the same way that *MASH* did about war: "They deal with their issue honestly and savagely and focused on interesting characters, while the guts and horror of the battlefield was kept on the periphery."

Rumors emerged in May 1990 of who would be cast in the film with an article in the *Chicago Tribune* stating that Brooks planned to play both Crasswell and Bolt; but if so, that quickly died with the hiring of Jeffrey Tambor for the villainous Crasswell. There were also rumors as to who Brooks was looking at to play Molly, the love interest. The story at the time was that Brooks had attempted to interest Madeline Kahn, who passed due to financial reasons. There were also reports that Jamie Lee Curtis was in consideration for the role, but more widespread was that Annie Potts (*Ghostbusters*) had been hired for the role. The Potts story led to Brooks publicly denying the rumor to Marilyn Beck, stating, "There is no leading lady set yet. We have many good choices, but I don't want to say who because we don't want to hurt the feelings of the ones who aren't selected." As it turns out, Lesley Ann Warren was announced to play the role of Molly before May was over.

The majority of the cast were performers who would appear in this one film for Brooks, although there were a few veterans of his earlier films that still popped up, although fairly unrecognizable from their earlier roles: Howard Morris, who is excellent as Sailor, and Rudy De Luca in his best role in a Brooks movie as "J. Paul Getty." Ronny Graham can also be heard as the priest refusing to let Bolt into the church, while Robert Ridgely, the hangman of *Blazing Saddles*, once again pops up for a couple of lines as Fergueson, the man putting the anklet on Bolt early in the film. Marilyn Beck also mentioned in her syndicated column in late June 1990 that Dick Van Patten had a role in *Life Stinks*, but if he did, his footage ended up on the cutting-room floor. However, his son, James Van Patten, does appear as the hospital worker who wants his wheelchair back late in the movie.

By April 1990, MGM announced that the film would begin production on June 11. That was then bumped to June 14, 1990, with the goal of completion in time for the Easter box-office weekend in 1991.

Cast

Mel Brooks as Goddard Bolt

Mel Brooks had this to say to Stephen Whitty about his experience with the actor: "I don't get along with him. We have big fights. I'm very patient as a director, but he's an arrogant, egotistical maniac."

Lesley Ann Warren (born 1946) as Molly the Bag Lady

Warren first came to national attention in the 1965 television production of the Rodgers and Hammerstein musical *Cinderella*, where she played the lead role. She had previously appeared in musicals on Broadway such as *110 in the Shade* (1963) and *Drat! The Cat!* (1965). She would later appear as Lois Lane in the 1975 television production of the musical *It's a Bird . . . It's a Plane . . . It's Superman!*, which featured music by former Brooks associate Charles Strouse and Kenneth Mars in a costarring role.

Lesley Ann Warren as Molly. Brooks once again tried to attract Madeline Kahn to one of his films, but when she passed, rumors abounded that both Jamie Lee Curtis and Annie Potts were being looked at for the role before it went to Warren.

Bolt (Mel Brooks) taking a seat in Molly's place while getting used to being homeless in *Life Stinks*.

She had done comedy roles in various films, including *Clue* (1985), and was nominated for an Academy Award for Best Supporting Actress for her role as the jilted girlfriend Norma in Blake Edwards's *Victor/Victoria* (1982). She continues to work in television and movies.

Jeffrey Tambor (born 1944) as Cresswell

Tambor had built a career in television playing weaselly characters, appearing on *Three's Company* several times, which led to him becoming a regular on *The Ropers* (1979–1980), where he played . . . another weasel, actually. His career grew as he got the role of Hank Kingsley on *The Larry Sanders Show* (1992–1998), which earned him four Emmy nominations. He was also a regular on the series *Arrested Development*. His work in the Amazon series *Transparent*, where his lead role is that of a transgender person, won him an Emmy Award for Outstanding Lead Actor in a Comedy Series.

Howard Morris as Sailor

Morris had last appeared in a Brooks film as the court spokesman in *History of the World, Part I*. Sailor would be his last role on any Brooks project.

Rudy De Luca as J. Paul Getty

De Luca had cowritten the script for *Life Stinks* and had appeared in Brooks's films since *Silent Movie*. He'll be back in *Robin Hood: Men in Tights*.

Teddy Wilson (1943–1991) as Fumes

A popular actor who appeared as a regular on many series, such as *That's My Mama* (1974–1975), and played Sweet Daddy Williams in multiple episodes of the sitcom *Good Times* (1974–1979). Wilson would die of a stroke on July 21, 1991, five days before the release of *Life Stinks* in theaters.

Stuart Pankin as Pritchard, the Attorney

Pankin has done a lot of television over the years, making his first big mark in the HBO comedy series *Not Necessarily the News* (1983–1990), where he typically played the role of head anchorman Bob Charles. He usually has played characters slightly full of themselves, and has appeared in such hits as *Fatal Attraction* (1987), *Arachnophobia* (1990), and *The Artist* (2011).

Also Appearing

- Sammy Shore as the minister officiating at the weddings. Shore had previously played one of the prehistoric men in *History of the World, Part I*. This was his second and last appearance in a Brooks film.

Bolt is hassled by J. Paul Getty (Rudy De Luca) in a posed shot not in the film. This would be De Luca's best performance in one of Brooks's films, going back to *Silent Movie* (1975).

- Billy Barty (1924–2000) as Willy. Barty had been in anything and everything that needed someone who was small, going back to working in Hollywood since the age of three in the silent movie days. For modern audiences, he is probably best remembered as High Aldwin in *Willow* (1988) and as Noodles, the cameraman, in *UHF* (1989).
- Robert Ridgely as Fergueson. His last appearance in a Brooks film was as the flasher in the bathroom in *High Anxiety*. He'll be back once more in Brooks's next film, *Robin Hood: Men in Tights*.
- Brad Grunberg, aka Johnny Cocktails, as burrito-eating bum. Grunberg later appears in *Robin Hood: Men in Tights* and *Dracula: Dead and Loving It*.

In the Crew

- John Morris wrote the music for the film. It would be his last with Brooks, after having worked with him since *The Producers* in 1967, and before that on other projects. Morris would later state that he was never asked to compose music for either of Brooks's last two films. "I admire him greatly," Morris said in a 1997 interview with *Film Score Monthly*, "but I did ten movies with him after all. First of all, in terms of the schedule, I am a morning person.

He is an evening person. I had an apartment in California and Mel would call up and tell me he's coming over at eight o'clock at night. But he doesn't come over at eight; he comes over at nine-thirty. I had to play things for him and people in the building would want to go to sleep. It just got to be nuts!"

- Jack Hayes as the orchestrator once again. This was his last time working for Brooks, after having orchestrated the music in his films since *High Anxiety*.
- Mitchell Bock as first assistant director. Bock had worked as a second assistant director on both *History of the World, Part I* and *Spaceballs*, which also featured him in small roles.
- Ezra Swerdlow as executive producer. Swerdlow had previously worked as a coproducer on *Spaceballs*.
- Kim Kurumada was an associate producer and production manager on the film.

Production

Filming began June 14 at Culver Studios in Culver City, California, for the interiors of Bolt's and Cresswell's offices. The lobby of Bolt's office building, seen in the opening credits, was that of the First Interstate World Center in Los Angeles. A couple of different mansions in Beverly Hills—one for the exterior, the other for the interior—were used for Bolt's home when he has his meltdown two-thirds of the way into the film. The homeless mission was the Chinese Congregational Church in Los Angeles. Everything else was in a section of Los Angeles that had the look needed for the film, and took up the majority of the filming between July and September 1990. "We were shooting in the heat of late summer in downtown alleys and buildings, with the heartbreak of the homeless all around us," Brooks told Marilyn Beck soon after filming was completed. The production team tried their best to avoid inconveniencing the homeless by the filming, paying some under the table—and against union rules—to do chores, while also making sure that the studio catering company had enough food to feed those around that asked when food was being served to the cast and crew.

"Every once in a while, someone who was on the street when he should have been in an institution would make things difficult," Brooks admitted, "but we tried to deal with the situation ourselves and keep the police out of it." There was also an issue with gang violence, and at one point in early September—just as the filming was about to wrap—two security guards watching over equipment were abducted at gun point by gang members around 3:00 a.m. One of the guards was beaten before the pair were released.

Filming was completed on September 14, 1990.

Backend

The film was planned to be released by the end of March 1991, but it was then promoted as coming out a couple of weeks later on April 17, 1991. Greg

Morrison, who was MGM's president of marketing at the time, admitted in October 1991 to the *Los Angeles Times* that the studio was in such a financial crisis they had to bump the release to July 26 because they "ran out of money for distribution." The film did at least preview at Cannes on May 15, 1991, in non-competition. The movie poster would be the first since *High Anxiety* to feature photo artwork rather than a painting, and this one has Brooks as Bolt after the breakdown, looking vacantly at the camera, with his hair a mess. A second poster was also used that shows Brooks in four different poses. One of those poses—Brooks standing in a trash can with his hands to his head in shock—would later be used for the cover of the DVD release.

Some of the films playing in theaters at the time of release were *Terminator 2: Judgment Day*, *Bill & Ted's Bogus Journey*, *City Slickers*, *Hot Shots*, and *Naked Gun 2½: The Smell of Fear*. Two of those films were parodies and two others were big comedies, with *City Slickers* in particular a huge comedy hit that summer. While Brooks had always faced some harsh reviews in the past, *Life Stinks* seemed to bring out a large number of hostile and not always very imaginative negative responses from the critics; in particular from those critics who thought themselves clever by saying variations of the line *"Life Stinks and so does this movie."* Some would even critique Warren as being a poor choice as she "isn't comfortable with comedy and shouldn't be in one," as critic Bill Von Maurer said in his review; seemingly forgetting that Warren had been appearing in comedies for years up to that point and was even nominated for her comedy work in *Victor/Victoria*. Dave Kehr of the *Chicago Tribune* at least credited Brooks for trying to address a serious topic in a comedic fashion, although he felt the film showed "a poverty without pain, set in a basically benign, protective world that everywhere contradicts the film's title."

But not all critics were negative, with some steering their reviews much like Kehr had, by giving Brooks kudos for at least trying something different, even if they did not agree it completely worked. Meanwhile, Jack Mathews in the *Los Angeles Times* called the film "a remarkably effective blend of slapstick and pathos . . . not only one of the summer's most entertaining films, but also one of its most relevant." Jack Mathews at *Newsday* called it "One of the year's most entertaining films, but also its most relevant." Roger Ebert gave the film three stars out of four, saying that Brooks pulled off the theme of the movie and calling it "warm and poignant."

Even so, the film was not helped by the low box-office returns. *Life Stinks* had cost $13 million to make and made less than $2 million after its first week out of 865 screens throughout the United States. The film supposedly only made $4 million domestically, although articles at the time put that at more like $17 million throughout North America by January 1992. Either way, it was enough to establish the film as a flop.

Brooks would later reflect to George Anderson on the film's box office take as being hit by two things in particular: "MGM needed money and threw out almost 1,000 prints and tried to compete with *Terminator 2* and all those other big films, which was crazy. It was a total mistake. They should've opened it in three theaters in three different cities. It could've gathered some steam and then they could've broken it in September or October." He also admitted that the title may have been wrong after all, but not because it didn't say "Life Sucks." "The biggest mistake I made was calling the film *Life Stinks*. I assumed that America understood irony, since it's an ironic title. I was wrong. Of course, now it's too late to change the title."

After the film was pulled in August, MGM reconsidered the way it had been released and attempted to reintroduce it in smaller theaters in selected cities on October 18, 1991. It did little business; ironically just as another comedy about the homeless, the Terry Gilliam–directed *The Fisher King*, was the number one comedy film in the country. On the bright side, the film was released in the fall of 1991 in such a smaller pattern overseas, where it did much better than in the United States. "In Italy," Brooks told Mike Cidoni in January 1992, "we're No. 1; in France, we're No. 2 for nine weeks; in Germany, we're No. 3 for 11 weeks; in Spain, we were No. 1 for four weeks and No. 2 for the next four weeks." At the time, Brooks said that international sales were about $28 million, which was "not bad for a low budget film." Even so, the legacy of its release in America would brand the film as a flop, both commercially and critically.

It would be his first noted flop since *The Twelve Chairs*, but at a time when Brooks was much more famous than when he had done the earlier film. And just like that film, Brooks would commonly rate *Life Stinks* as one of his top favorite films. Strangely enough, in both cases, Brooks would promote each film by mentioning that he was planning to make *She Stoops to Conquer* as his next, and in 1991 said that he was already eighty-five pages into a new revised script. Once again, a dream project would have to be pushed aside. "I spent two and a half years on my little tragic comedy, writing it, working on it," Brooks told Stephen Whitty as *Life Stinks* was designated a flop in August 1991. "I'm not going to do that again. Next time, I'm going to make two movies in that kind of time."

Brooks was going to return to what worked best for him in what would turn out to be his last two films. One would prove profitable; the other would mark the end of the line for Brooks's directorial career.

Reflections

With films like *Blazing Saddles* and *Young Frankenstein* in the early 1970s, Brooks, alongside the college humor of *National Lampoon*, Second City, and *Saturday Night Live*, would pioneer the idea that there really was nothing sacred when it came to comedy. Soon there would be films like *Kentucky Fried Movie* (from the same team that would later create *Airplane!* and the *Naked Gun* series) and *The Groove Tube*; and, yes, those were born out of earlier live-theater projects, but without Brooks making the studios a ton of money; and without his willingness to be silly for the sake of being silly, many such films probably would not have been made or released on a national level. And as the 1980s came along, the genre grew, with such films as *Airplane!*; the *Naked Gun* series; the films of Carl Reiner with Steve Martin, such as *The Jerk*, *The Man With Two Brains*, and *Dead Men Don't Wear Plaid*. Soon, there were comedies that went way beyond what Brooks had done when it came to crude humor, as well as perhaps falling into a more sophomoric attitude than some of the loftier goals that Brooks strived to achieve.

And just as the "anything for a laugh" parody film genre became hot, Brooks took leave of the field to do *To Be or Not to Be*, the somewhat whimsical parody of *Spaceballs* (which he had to get an okay on before filming), and then *Life Stinks*. To do that was to leave himself open to the critics who could not wrap their heads around an artist trying to do something beyond what was expected of him. Brooks wasn't filling in the cliché some critics and fans wanted, instead giving audiences a film about the homeless and perhaps a brief glimpse in the mirror of our own cruelty when "the audience was expecting another *Spaceballs*," as Brooks said in late 1991.

Granted, there is a somewhat sterile feeling to portions of the film. A feeling that, even with the setting correct, there's too much Hollywood around. The streets look too orderly and clean, the people all have the same layer of Hollywood dirt on them. Everyone is lovable around Bolt, making the world seem somewhat safe. Even the bad guys amongst the homeless are two drug abusers and they are so cartoonish that when boiling water is dumped on them at one point, they just run off in a silly manner instead of screaming in pain before being carted off to the hospital with severe burns; not to mention that they never reappear in the narrative. It is easy to see that Brooks held back just a tad too much, and perhaps more of a push could have made the comedy and the message a little deeper.

There are signs that the film was tampered with during editing as well. An obvious jump-cut comes when we see Bolt first being dropped off on the streets in clean clothes, and then a moment later appearing to have been wrestling in the dirt when trying to find a room for the night. This suggests that there were scenes cut between those two moments. It also seems like a fair jump from when Sailor dies—in what appears to be early in Bolt's confinement to the area—and Bolt having made it thirty days. What happened in the rest of those thirty days? Surely something, but we don't see it, and it makes Bolt's journey in this world seem like a cakewalk rather than the possibly scary, life-changing experience it could have been. (It makes one wonder if perhaps in this day and age the film would have worked better as a mini-series on Netflix or Amazon rather than a ninety-minute movie.)

Then there's the fantasy dance number that comes out of nowhere, everyone's teeth being too white, and of course, the fairy-tale ending where money wins happiness. (Let's face it, in reality, Cresswell's confession would have been deemed coerced, Bolt would have been sent to an asylum, and the homeless would have been pushed out to make way for Cresswell's dream city.) Many of the hard edges that probably should have been there amongst the comedy are

That was stitched in! Goddard Bolt suffers the first of many surprises in his contest to spend a month as a homeless person in *Life Stinks*.

missing. But while those are noticeable, it has to be expected that Brooks was never going to be able to tell a story without a happy ending, nor avoid a chance to lessen the pain by throwing in some music and laughs. Not to mention that Brooks has stated in interviews that a comedy should never try to go past ninety minutes in length. Something has to give, and perhaps what went was some of the darkness in order to include more of the light. There has to be some levity, even in the darkest times, and it is the movies after all—why should it have to end as reality too often dictates?

Brooks stated in an interview with the AV Club that he saw the film as his version of the Preston Sturges classic *Sullivan's Travels* (1941), about a movie director of comedies who joins a hobo camp in order to be able to make a drama about such life, only to discover that making comedies to help bring lightness into people's lives did more than showing them what they already knew. "I saw the movie and I loved the movie, and I wanted to make something like it about the current state of the world . . . and see whether there is any joy you could cling to, like a raft." As Brooks found out, "[The audience] they see the name Mel Brooks, they want something really funny. They don't want to be moved; they don't want to be taught any lessons."

Yet, at the same time, "I get more letters for *The Twelve Chairs* and *Life Stinks* than I get from any other movie, because people actually agree with the philosophy, or were moved, or they love the movie." In 1991, *Life Stinks* was considered a flop, but over time, just like *The Twelve Chairs* before it, people have come back to it and thought to themselves, "This isn't the bad movie that people keep saying it is." People are touched by it. In the end, Brooks wasn't trying to save the world by presenting a reality, but just to touch a part of us that knows no matter how poor we are, we are all just humans looking for what little happiness we can find. In that sense, Brooks succeeded with *Life Stinks,* and it really is a brief chance to see a part of him that he rarely allows to be seen.

18

It Worked in *Blazing Saddles*

Robin Hood: Men in Tights

Release Date: July 28, 1993 by 20th Century Fox

Hitler References

None.

Musical Moments

Four, with a reprise of one at the end of the film. The film kicks off with "Sherwood Forest Rap," written by Mel Brooks with Hummie Mann and sung by Kevin Dorsey. Maid Marian sings "Marian" in the tub, which was also written by Brooks and Mann, and has Debbie James singing, with Amy Yasbeck mouthing the words. This song is revised at the end of the film as a duet, with Cathy Dennis and Lance Ellington singing over the ending credits. "Men in Tights" comes two-thirds of the way through the film, written by Brooks, and is a rift off his earlier "Jews in Space" song heard in *History of the World, Part I*. It is sung by "The Merry Men Singers"—Steve Lively Randy Crenshaw, Kerry Katz, Geoff Koch, and Rick Logan. When Robin sings to Marian in Sherwood Forest, it is "The Night Is Young and You're So Beautiful," written by Billy Rose, Irving Kahal, and Dana Suesse, and sung by Arthur Rubin. Rubin had previously appeared as one of the auditioning Hitlers in *The Producers*.

Pre-production

Life Stinks had been Mel Brooks fulfilling a dream. With that project now out of his system, he was scouting around for a new movie to make. For a new studio, as well. Signing with MGM and reuniting with Alan Ladd Jr. seemed like a dream come true when *Spaceballs* was being put together, but the studio was still stabilizing after the financially rocky 1980s. The performance of *Life Stinks* at the American box office didn't help the studio, nor Brooks's plans. His long-planned adaptation of *She Stoops to Conquer* had stalled again, and after Gene

Wilder's 1991 movie with Richard Pryor, *Another You*, did poorly at the box office, it was becoming increasingly clear that the *Dr. Jekyll and Mr. Hyde* parody with Wilder that Brooks had pitched in interviews around this time was not going to happen either.

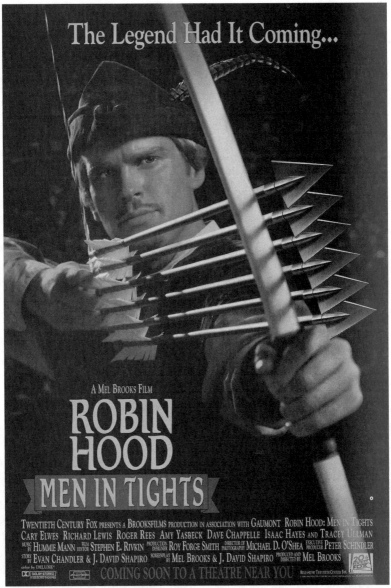

With the failure of *Life Stinks*, Brooks returns to the world of parody with *Robin Hood: Men in Tights*.

However, as mentioned in the previous chapter, *Life Stinks* did have a good run in foreign territories, including France, where Le Studio Canal—a motion picture distribution company that had invested in the film—was satisfied with the results. It was with this in mind that Brooks was able to arrange a deal with the French studio Gaumont, the oldest film studio in the world (started in 1895), to help with any new films he decided to make. Brooks just had to find the projects that were viable.

If *She Stoops to Conquer* was going to have to wait once again as not being commercial enough, Brooks could at least consider another long-delayed project that suddenly had studio interest again: Robin Hood. Brooks had been involved with the 1975 television series that parodied the character, *When Things Were Rotten* (see chapter 21), but that was short-lived, and his involvement was more as an executive producer rather than a writer and certainly not as a director. Thus, he would occasionally mention bringing the character back for a film, and in 1981 went so far as to say that he was in the early stages of doing exactly that with Marty Feldman starring; but other opportunities came up, and he would once again push the project aside.

Besides, for many years Robin Hood had become an increasingly minor hero in movies and television, and beyond the somewhat serious, introspective *Robin and Marian* (1976) with Sean Connery and Audrey Hepburn as older versions of the characters, Robin Hood had been treated as a joke; from Brooks's own *When Things Were Rotten*, to the idiot with good intentions seen in *Time Bandits* (1981), and the full-out, pre-Brooks parody film *The Zany Adventures of Robin Hood* (1984). It was only into the later 1980s when the UK's ITV series *Robin of Sherwood* (1984–1986) aired on Showtime in America that interest in a new, serious remake of the story began to blossom. By 1990, a script that would become the Kevin Costner movie *Robin Hood: Prince of Thieves* was bought by Morgan Creek and became so hot that 20th Century Fox and Tri-Star Pictures both announced competing versions in hopes of getting in on the potential gravy train (Tri-Star eventually abandoned their version, while Fox would air their version, starring Patrick Bergin, with Uma Thurman as Marian, on Fox TV in May 1991). With the fight in Hollywood to produce a new Robin Hood movie becoming so great, it seemed that the time had finally arrived for Brooks to get the interest needed to produce his own version.

Brooks felt an affectionate jab at the character was in order after all the pomposity of the Costner film, which he and the others on *Men in Tights* felt bloated the story and ruined what was a simple adventure. "When I read the script of *Prince of Thieves*," Cary Elwes, the actor who played Robin Hood in *Men in Tights*, remembered to Barry Koltnow, "I knew they weren't going to do it right. They were going to do a Hollywood version of what the Robin Hood legend was supposed to be. And sure enough, that's what happened. . . . They were trying to make another *Batman*." Brooks agreed with that sentiment to Barry Koltnow as well, adding, "I have been in love with the legend since I was a little boy playing with stick swords in the back alleys of Brooklyn. Because of that, I didn't want the last Robin Hood movie to be *Prince of Thieves*. I didn't want the legend to rest on that movie."

As it turns out, there was already a script floating around that was a parody of the Costner film, written by J. David Shapiro and Evan Chandler, and Brooks was one of the first to see it. The script came together when the eleven-year-old son of a Beverly Hills dentist, Evan Chandler, saw *Robin Hood: Prince of Thieves* and told his father that the movie was ripe for a spoof. A few days later, Dr. Chandler told J. David Shapiro, a patient of his that had recently moved to Los Angeles to become a scriptwriter, about his son's idea for the movie parody. Chandler and Shapiro decided to collaborate on a script and send it to various studios "on spec" (essentially, delivering it to studios, producers, anyone working in Hollywood in speculation someone will like it enough to buy it), whereupon a copy ended up in front of Brooks.

Although Gene Wilder had said when trying to get *Young Frankenstein* started, "Mel won't do anything he hadn't written himself," the Brooksfilms production company was now in full operation. Thus, it was no longer unusual for Brooks to be looking at scripts from other writers. Plus, he had been down this road before with *Tex X* for *Blazing Saddles* (see chapter 10)—a script handed to him that he could mold into his own. Brooks bought the script from Shapiro and Chandler in March 1992, and then began rewriting most of it with the help of Shapiro. By June 1992, He pitched the rewritten script to 20th Century Fox, having already obtained initial financial help from Le Studio Canal (which got European television rights) and Gaumont (which was granted overseas distribution) to make the film. Once Fox signed on, it was announced that Brooks's next film would be called *Robbin' the Hood*, which he said was a spoof "on all the Robin Hoods that have ever been and will probably ever be."

The final credits for the film, however, would also list Evan Chandler alongside Brooks and Shapiro for the screenplay. This was fought by Brooks in arbitration with the Writers Guild, as Brooks felt that so much had been changed from the initial script that Chandler should only be given a "story by" credit, and even went so far as to suggest that Chandler's son should be awarded a "story by" credit as well, since it was the eleven-year-old's idea in the first place. The guild did not agree, and when the film was released, the story was credited to J. David Shapiro and Evan Chandler alone, with Shapiro, Brooks, and Chandler sharing the screenplay credit.

The title of the movie was changed from *Robbin' the Hood* in September 1992 to *Robin Hood: Men in Tights*, as a parody of both the title of Costner's film and the fact that Costner laughed off the idea of wearing tights like how the role had traditionally been costumed in films for ages. "Kevin did a disservice to the legend when he said that," Brook stated during the filming of *Men in Tights*. "In a Robin Hood movie, they should wear tights and those pointy hats with the long feather sticking out of them."

Considering the long gestation of earlier films made by Brooks, *Robin Hood: Men in Tights* came together very quickly, with a script sold in March

1992, a production deal all set by June, and filming begun in January 1993 for a summer release. On his official website, Shapiro notes that "from concept to release, it was a little over a year," and at the time naively thought "it was always going to be this easy." As with other writers before him on a Brooks film, he discovered that Brooks "likes having the writer around, so I was involved in every aspect of the making of *Men in Tights*," helping with casting and even with some of the lyrics to the songs used in the film.

Production began on January 5, 1993, with 20th Century Fox hopeful that the film could be ready for a late summer release that year. Along with *Life Stinks*, most of the casting would be performers who were new to Brooks's films. However, this time around he did find a few roles to film with some of his old favorites.

Cast

Cary Elwes (born 1962) as Robin Hood

Born in England, which explains his native English accent, Elwes had already been seen in the United States in such films as *The Bride* (1985), a version of *Bride of Frankenstein*, starring Sting and Jennifer Beals, and *Lady Jane* (1986) before getting the role of Westley in Rob Reiner's *The Princess Bride* (1987). He would move on to roles in *Day of Thunder* (1990), *Glory* (1989), and even the *Top Gun* parody film *Hot Shots!* (1991) before being hired for *Robin Hood: Men in Tights*.

When Elwes got the call for the role from Brooks, he didn't believe it at first, as he told Jeff Baker. "He actually called me at home and I thought someone was pulling my leg, so I hung up on him. He called back and he said, 'Don't hang up, it's really me!'" Having seen Elwes in *The Princess Bride*, Brooks thought he would be perfect for the role of Robin, because of his looks and he knew that Elwes could play comedy. "Cary is a natural swashbuckling movie hero," Brooks remarked at the time of filming. "He's good-looking, his sword-fighting is great, he's romantically superb, and he has that twinkle in his eye that allows him to do comedy. . . . I wanted an actor who had a talent for comedy and that's what I got."

Elwes followed up *Men in Tights* with roles in *Twister* (1996), *The Cat's Meow* (2001), *Saw* (2004), and many other films since that time. This was his only film for Brooks.

Amy Yasbeck (born 1962) as Maid Marian

Working in television at that point, Yasbeck had her first starring role in the television movie sequel *Splash, Too* (1988). She would meet her future husband John Ritter while filming *Problem Child 2* in 1991, and later be cast as a regular in the series *Wings* (1994–1997), before returning in Brooks's last film, *Dracula: Dead and Loving It* in 1995.

Megan Cavanagh as Broomhilde and Amy Yasbeck as Maid Marian. The pair would appear together in Brooks's next and final film, *Dracula: Dead and Loving It.*

Richard Lewis (born 1947) as Prince John

Starting out as a stand-up comedian in the 1970s, Lewis had ventured into acting in 1977 with the television movie *Diary of a Young Comic*, which aired as a replacement for *Saturday Night Live* in the summer of 1979. He would have a regular role on the short-lived series *Harry* (1987), starring Alan Arkin, and eventually star in his own series, *Anything but Love* (1989–1992) with Jamie Lee Curtis. Brooks claims that the Prince John character was the only role in the film that he wrote with a particular actor in mind. "He's the only counter-casting," Brooks said to Marshall Fine at the time. "Everyone else is more or less true to their character." Brooks also admitted that he allowed Lewis to ad lib the role, with "one out of three times he could come up with something better than the script." Lewis agreed to the role under the stipulation that he would not have to get anywhere near a horse.

During filming, however, Lewis did run into a problem just before he had completed his role. With only one scene left to shoot, Lewis wound up with a 106-degree temperature thanks to a bout of Hepatitis A. As Lewis mentioned in the PBS documentary *Mel Brooks: Make a Noise*, while lying in the hospital, trying to recover, Brooks called him with a suggestion that Lewis hop out of bed and be driven to the set so they could them prop him up on a piece of wood. "You'll do your two lines, we'll carry you right back into the stretcher, you'll be back in twenty minutes." When Lewis told him no, Brooks called him several more times, trying to get him to commit to the idea.

Tracey Ullman as Latrine and Richard Lewis as Prince John in *Robin Hood: Men in Tights*. Brooks stated at the time of filming that he had written the role of Prince John with Lewis in mind. Brooks had performed with Ullman on her Fox comedy series, *The Tracey Ullman Show*, in 1990.

After *Men in Tights*, Lewis continued to guest-star on a variety of television shows, including a fictional version of himself in the series *Curb Your Enthusiasm* (2000–2011). This would be his only film for Brooks.

Roger Rees (1944–2015) as the Sheriff of Rottingham

Rees came to international attention with the lead Broadway role in *The Life and Adventures of Nicholas Nickleby*, which earned him a Tony Award for Best Actor in 1982, and which he would reprise in a television miniseries that same year. He would be a regular on the British sitcom *Singles* (1988–1989), and then move to America in 1989, where he started appearing periodically on the series *Cheers* as billionaire Robin Colcord from 1989 to 1993. After *Men in Tights*, Rees continued to work in television including the series *The West Wing* (2000–2005) and in theater, including replacing Nathan Lane in the Broadway production of *The Addams Family* in 2010. He died in 2015 from brain cancer.

David Chappelle (born 1973) as Ahchoo

A stand-up comic at the age of fourteen, Dave Chappelle was looking to get work as an actor when he auditioned for the role of Ahchoo. Both J. David Shapiro and Cary Elwes would say that they were in on the casting of Chappelle for the role, with Shapiro stating on his website that he convinced Brooks to hire Chappelle over another actor for the role, while Elwes would tell Den of Geek, "We actually cast Dave together. We saw a lot of actors and when Dave came in, he was just so amazing and we knew right then and there—this was a star."

Chappelle moved between television and movies while still doing stand-up over the next few years, including appearances in *The Nutty Professor* (1996), *Con Air* (1997), and *You've Got Mail* (1998), but it was really in 2003 when he got his own Comedy Central series, *Chappelle's Show*, that things really took off. Over the next few seasons, Chappelle became increasingly popular, but he found the show was subverting his stand-up and other aspects of his life. Audiences began to see Chappelle only through the characters and routines from the show instead of anything new he had to offer. He would turn down a $50 million contract with Viacom to continue the series and took time off before returning to stand-up, which he has concentrated on since.

Tracey Ullman (born 1959) as Latrine, the cook and sometimes witch

Tracey Ullman had already made a name for herself in comedy in the United Kingdom, thanks to shows like *A Kick Up the Eighties* and *Three of a Kind*, when she recorded a music album called *You Broke My Heart in 17 Places*, which featured the song "They Don't Know" that reached #8 on the U.S. charts and led to a music video that was on heavy rotation on MTV (and showed off her comic skills as well as her singing). By 1987, Ullman would have her own comedy series, *The Tracey Ullman Show* (1987–1990) on the Fox Network—a series where short animated pieces in between sketches would later become the long-running series *The Simpsons*.

Brooks was a fan of Ullman's television series and had appeared in a sketch on the program in 1990. Yet she was not the first choice for the role of Latrine. The biography *Madeline Kahn: Being the Music, A Life* by William Madison says that Brooks had first offered the role to Madeline Kahn, who turned it down when told what the salary would be, according to friends of hers. However, Brooks's take was that Kahn refused the role due to it being too small rather than because of the salary. When Kahn backed out, Brooks turned to Ullman.

After her series for Fox, Ullman had various appearances on other shows as well as film roles. She also has had other variety series over the years, including *Tracey Takes On . . .* (1996–1999) and *Tracey Ullman's Show* (2016–2017). *Men in Tights* was the only film she made for Brooks.

Mark Blankfield (born 1950) as Blinkin

Blankfield's first big success came by way of the comedy series *Fridays* (1980–1982), which had him playing a number of recurring roles. His first starring role came in the parody film *Jekyll and Hyde . . . Together Again* (1982). Blankfield

A young Dave Chappelle appears as Ahchoo in *Robin Hood: Men in Tights*. This press photo shows Ahchoo and Robin (Cary Elwes) in a brief dialogue scene cut from the film.

also appeared in the Amy Yasbeck–starring television film *Splash, Too*. He appeared as Freddy, the nearly blind elevator operator in the television series *The Nutt House*, which had been created by Mel Brooks with Alan Spencer (1989), which led directly to him being cast as the blind servant Blinkin in *Men in Tights*. He'll appear briefly in *Dracula: Dead and Loving It*.

Megan Cavanagh (born 1960) as Broomhilde

Cavanagh's first film was *A League of Their Own*, where she played the shy Marla Hooch. For the role of Broomhilde, Cavanagh had to wear a fat-suit to make her look the size Brooks wanted for the role. After *Men in Tights*, she would appear as a regular in the second season of Bob Newhart's series *Bob* (1993) and then reprise the role of Marla Hooch in the television series version of *A League of Their Own* the same year. She was also the voice of Judy Neutron in the *Jimmy Neutron* animated series, which ran on Nickelodeon. She will appear as the maid to Amy Yasbeck's character in the final Mel Brooks film, *Dracula: Dead and Loving It.*

Matthew Porretta (born 1965) as Will Scarlet O'Hara

Porretta also appeared briefly in the ballroom sequence of *Dracula: Dead and Loving It.* He would play Robin Hood in the first two seasons of the TNT cable network television series *The New Adventures of Robin Hood* (1997–1998).

Eric Allan Kramer (born 1962) as Little John

Kramer has appeared in various guest roles on television over the years, including a version of the Marvel superhero Thor in *The Incredible Hulk Returns.* He appeared alongside Megan Cavanagh as a regular in the second season of Bob Newhart's sitcom *Bob* (1993). In 2001, he played Alan Hale Jr. in the television movie, *Surviving Gilligan's Island: The Incredibly True Story of the Longest Three Hour Tour in History.* Alan Hale Sr. had played Little John in *The Adventures of Robin Hood* (1938). (Yes, that's a very minor, not-easily-navigated piece of trivia, but it is what it is.)

Also Appearing

- Isaac Hayes (1942–2008) as Asneeze. Musician and actor, Hayes is probably best remembered for composing the music for the film *Shaft* (1971), which won him an Oscar for Best Original Song. In 1974, he started starring in blaxploitation films, including *Truck Turner* (1974) and *Three Tough Guys*, and played the Duke in John Carpenter's *Escape from New York.* Later, he would become known as the voice of Cook on the animated series *South Park.* Hayes died from a stroke in 2008.
- Dom DeLuise as Don Giovanni. This was DeLuise's last role in a Brooks film after five previous appearances, going back to *The Twelve Chairs.*
- Dick Van Patten as The Abbot. This would be Van Patten's third and final role in a Brooks film.
- Robert Ridgely as The Hangman. As mentioned previously, Ridgely had popped up in Brooks films since he first appeared as the hangman in *Blazing Saddles*, and here he makes his last appearance in a Brooks film playing the same role.
- Mel Brooks as Rabbi Tuckman. Actor too busy to do more than cameo in this film.
- Patrick Stewart (born 1940) as Richard the Lionheart. This role was originally written for, of all people, Kevin Costner. According to Shapiro, Brooks decided against the idea because "Mel feared he would be turned down, and, well, you know, Costner's expensive." According to James Robert Parish's book *It's Good to Be the King*, Brooks did hear from the man who

Brooks directing while dressed as Rabbi Tuckman, the character he plays in the film.

played Richard in *Prince of Thieves*, Sean Connery, about reprising the role in *Men in Tights*, on the stipulation that he got to do the role dressed as a woman (which would have worked within the story line, actually) and that $1 million be donated to a Scottish charity. The production couldn't afford the price, however. Instead, Stewart, who had made a name for himself thanks to his role as Captain Picard in *Star Trek: The Next Generation* was offered the role and accepted.

- Avery Schreiber (1935–2002) as the tax assessor. Schreiber was a popular comedian and actor who worked for several years with Jack Burns as a comedy duo. He also did a series of well-remembered ads for Doritos chips. He'll be back as the villager in the coach with Renfield at the beginning of *Dracula: Dead and Loving It*.
- Chuck McCann as a villager learning to be a merry man. Last appeared as the studio guard in *Silent Movie*. He'll pop up as a villager near the beginning of *Dracula: Dead and Loving It*.
- Carol Arthur as Complaining Villager. First appearance in a Brooks film since she appeared as the pregnant woman picked up at the beginning of *Silent Movie*. She'll be back as a villager in *Dracula: Dead and Loving It*.
- Clive Revill (born 1930) as the Fire Marshall in the opening scene where the village is being burnt down. Revill has appeared in a variety of films and television, including an episode of the 1950 television series *The Adventures of Robin Hood* (1955–1960). He also appeared in *The Legend of Hell House* (1973) and was the voice of the Emperor in *The Empire Strikes Back* (1980),

as well as appearing as the killer in the last episode of the original *Columbo* series in 1978. He'll be back in *Dracula: Dead and Loving It* with a little more screen time than here.

In the Crew

Nearly all of the technical crew from *Robin Hood: Men in Tights* were new to the world of Brooks and his movies, and yet with the exception of the last four individuals listed here, nearly all will be back to do the same services on *Dracula: Dead and Loving It* in 1995:

- Hummie Mann (born 1955) composed the music, with Frank Bennett, Brad Dechter, and Don Nemitz as the orchestrators. Chris Ledesma was the music editor, with Gary Wasserman assisting.
- Michael D. O'Shea as director of photography. He previously did second-unit cinematography on *Spaceballs* for Brooks.
- Robert Lathan Brown as production manager. He also performed this function on *Spaceballs*.
- Lindsay Chag and Bill Shepard for casting.
- Roy Forge Smith for production design.
- Gregg Goldstone as first assistant director.
- Kenneth J. Silverstein as second assistant director.
- Peter Schindler as second unit director and executive producer. Schindler produced the television series *Anything but Love*, starring Richard Lewis, and was an executive producer of *The Tracey Ullman Show*.
- Michael Sarley as storyboard artist.
- Cindy Montoya-Picker did choreography for the film. This was the only film she did for Brooks, as Alan Johnson will be back to do choreography for *Dracula: Dead and Loving It*.
- Adam Weiss as editor.
- Bruce Robert Hill as art director.

Production

Production began January 5, 1993, at the Sable Ranch in Santa Clarita, California. The timing had been perfect thanks to the torrential rain and mudslides occurring before filming began, causing the land to look lush with greenery. "When we filmed last winter," Brooks told *Parade Magazine* as the film was being released in the summer of 1993, "all the mud slides and torrential rain turned us into Merrie Olde England. . . . It looks more like England. And it looks better than the Kevin Costner one." The downside of the rain was that it caused flooding in certain spots, forcing the production team to stick close to the paved parking lot for a lot of the scenes, and at one point requiring a crane to move the cast and crew to a location over a flood. Nature also contributed to the demise of the ranch in the summer of 2016 when it was destroyed by one of many wildfires that plagued Southern California that year. On this location the castle was built, which was 280 feet long and 50 feet high, and took four months to build by Roy Forge Smith and the art department. Some of the outdoor scenes—such as the archery training sequence—were shot at Lake Sherwood in Santa Monica, where *The Adventures of Robin Hood* (1938) and *Robin Hood* (1922) had also been filmed.

All interior scenes were shot at the Warner Hollywood Studio in West Hollywood, California (currently known as "The Lot"), where parts of Douglas Fairbanks's 1922 version of *Robin Hood* was filmed as well. Using just one studio lot was unusual for Brooks, who typically had been using multiple studios for interior scenes since *History of the World, Part I*. As filming began, many of the performers spent weekends training on how to stage-fight with swords, a skill that only Elwes and Rees had any experience in; Elwes having trained extensively at fencing for *The Princess Bride* and Rees from his years working with the Royal Shakespeare Company. For the most part, any archery on display in the film was done through effects work rather than skill, although Elwes was pressed by Brooks to shoot a bull's-eye on camera in the scene where he is showing the villagers how to use a bow and arrow, as he told the audience at the Motor City Comic Con in 2013. "I was quite proud of the fact that I got a bull's-eye shooting the bow and arrow because there was a lot of pressure from Mel to get that in a few takes. He said, "Okay, you've got three takes. Get a bull's-eye, let's go!' And I'm like 'Really, Mel? I've only got three? Really?' And I got it on the third one, thank god."

One notable incident occurred with the trained fox that was used near the end of the film where the Merry Men need to send a message quickly to the villagers to come and attack the castle. The trained fox was put in the special harness and then released. It never returned. Brooks at least got the needed shot of the fox running, however, so it did not throw off production by any means.

Production finished March 25, 1993, with Brooks locking himself away with the editing staff to trim the film down—a frustrating event for Brooks, who knew he did not have the luxury of six to nine months to edit the film like he had with most of his earlier ones for 20th Century Fox. This meant there was little time for the multiple screenings to secretaries on the studio lot, which had been helpful in finding what did and did not work in a film. "I don't know if it's any good," Brooks told Marilyn Beck at the end of April 1993. "I haven't got any taste. But I can tell you that I like this movie so much I'm finding it harder to trim than any movie I've made. And it's got to be trimmed by at least 15 or 20 minutes. I don't think any comedic film should be longer than 100 minutes. I'm finding it hard—very hard—to find the footage to lose."

Yet trim he did, and the film was cut down to 104 minutes. Many of the cuts came down to trimming scenes rather than discarding them all together. For example, we first see Prince John telling a gaggle of people around him in the castle to disperse, but the script has him talking to them for a time before the sheriff arrives. The trailer for the film shows additional footage of Prince John in his makeshift Jacuzzi ("More bubbles! More bubbles!"). The HBO documentary made to promote the movie shows an exchange between Robin and Ahchoo after Robin drops the chandelier on his own head that was cut from the final film. There were longer cuts as well: the press-kit mentions a jousting scene that takes place at the castle, but there is none in the film. There is a curious cut after the villagers are pulled off their horses by the wooden fake soldiers when training and Robin contemplates Ahchoo's joke that the "dummies" should be sent into battle instead of the villagers, but there is no payoff to this setup. (The HBO documentary does show the "dummies" standing outside of the castle, but it is not clear if this was the payoff to said gag.) Soon after in the film, the sheriff visits Prince John in the "Jacuzzi" to say that "Loxley has struck again," but there's no previous scene to show that Robin had done such a thing. There's also a photo of Robin screaming as he flies through mid-air at the castle—one used for some of the foreign movie posters for the film, with a large arrow superimposed under him—that is never seen in the film.

Backend

Fox had plans to release the film on August 13, 1993, but in May they decided to debut it earlier on July 28, 1993, instead. In theaters at the time were *Coneheads*, *Free Willy*, *Sleepless in Seattle*, *In the Line of Fire*, *Jurassic Park*, and *Dennis the Menace*. The film was promoted on HBO with the twenty-five-minute documentary called *Robin Hood: Men in Tights—The Legend Had It Coming*. This tagline was also used in the movie posters and trailers for the film. The movie poster seen in America featured Robin using the six arrows in his bow as shown when rescuing Ahchoo in the film. The teaser trailer—from which segments were used in subsequent trailers and even for a couple of visual shots in the film—has Robin shooting an arrow that goes on an extended journey around the forest with a mind of its own before finally missing the target and instead splitting the tree in half. This directly parodies *Robin Hood: Prince of Thieves*, which featured a visual of an arrow's journey to its target.

Critical reviews were mixed, although not quite as severe as what appeared for *Life Stinks*. Gene Siskel of the *Chicago Tribune* only gave the film half a star, feeling "Brooks has a long set-up for one joke in a scene" too often, leaving the audience bored, and would later list the film as one of the worst of 1993. Bob Fenster of the *Arizona Republic* thought the film so bad that he ends his review suggesting "Brooks needs to retire and take Lewis with him before the guy becomes convinced he can have a film career."

On the other hand, Peter Rainer of the *Los Angeles Times* felt the film connected when Brooks got past the Costner film–related material and went back to the earlier Hood of his childhood, finding this the reason the film nearly makes it but just "misses the bullseye." Vincent Canby of the *New York Times* is actually quite positive about the film, calling it "so frontally rude that only the terminally humorless might object." The best response, however, has been to the video, where the movie continues to sell well and—no surprise—as well as Brooks's other "first-disdained, now considered a cult-classic" *Spaceballs*.

But such success was still in the future for the film, as strong box office the first week quickly tapered off the following week; the film eventually making $36 million off a budget of $20 million. This, once again, gave Brooks a film that had only done marginally well and in some eyes in Hollywood one that couldn't be viewed as a success at essentially making back costs in production and promotion. Nor were there any awards for the film. It at least did do well overseas, as had *Life Stinks* before it. Thus, there was still interest in Brooks making films, even if that meant any future financial assistance was going to increasingly come from across the ocean.

At the time of release, Brooks told Marilyn Beck that he wanted to do a sequel. "I have always said no to 'twos' of pictures I've directed. I wouldn't do *Blazing Saddles II*. I wouldn't do *Young Frankenstein II*. But I've loved working with this cast so much I'd like to do it again." He was able to keep a handful of the cast and most of the crew together for his next film, but it would not be the sequel as planned. Instead, it would be a return to a genre he had already visited, the horror film.

Reflections

One problem with taking someone else's script and making it your own is that you can end up with a film that looks like two separate films jammed together, and while *Robin Hood: Men in Tights* is strictly a Robin Hood movie, it is one part *Robin Hood: Prince of Thieves* and one part *The Adventures of Robin Hood*. At times, the twains do not seem to meet, especially in the earlier part of the movie.

It is easy to see where the original Shapiro-Chandler script came from with the parodies of the Costner film, as they are very specific to both films and not to any traditional telling of the Robin Hood myth:

- Robin escapes from Jerusalem. (At least in *Men in Tights* he helps everyone escape.)
- His kissing the ground upon reaching England.
- The blind servant.
- Saving a young boy from the soldiers (usually it's a man, not a boy).
- A witch (okay a witch-cook in *Men in Tights*) who attempts to stop Robin (speaking of which, we never do see her actually trying to stop Robin in *Men in Tights*, do we?).
- Friar Tuck/Rabbi Tuckman arriving in the forest with a cart full of wine.
- Maid Marian agreeing to the wedding to the sheriff, "but you'll never have my mind. . . . ."
- The catapult used in both films as a means for someone to fly through the air (it is easy to suspect that the shot of Robin flying through the air that was not used in the film may have been related, as Costner's Robin uses a catapult at one point as a means of escape).

• The visual of using the arrow's point of view.

And then, forty-five minutes into the film, Brooks abandons that setup and goes directly into parodying Errol Flynn: having Robin throw a wild pig in front of Prince John and then fighting the guards alongside his men in the castle—all traditional aspects of the legend, but nowhere to be seen in the Costner film. Perhaps it is just as well. Brooks stated early on that the initial script was going to take the movie in a darker direction: "It'll show everybody was on the take. Robbin' the Hood robbed from everybody, and kept it all himself." That may be closer to what some assume the real Robin may have been like, but it would have been a hard sell in a light comedy for summer audience. Plus, as more time goes by, the further from the audience's mind is the connection between Brooks's parody and the Costner film, leading to some of the early gags being merely curious when the film being mocked is not a recent memory (e.g., the names of Ahchoo and Asneeze; Robin kissing the ground; Prince John's little jump in fright when he sees Latrine—Alan Rickman as the sheriff in the Costner film does the same action when he visits the witch; amongst other little in-jokes). More than two decades on, the second half of the film plays better than the first, because one doesn't have to have seen *Robin Hood: Prince of Thieves* to get the jokes. True, there's the "I can speak with an English accent" gag that is directed at Costner, but American actors not being able to do an accent has always been a common problem in movies, so it works even without that knowledge. In fact, in foreign prints of the film, the joke had to be changed in translation anyway; after all, a joke about accents would be little understood if both films had been translated to another language anyway (changing it to other things to make fun of, such as the probable cost of the actor to play the role, or the actor's willingness to wear tights).

Perhaps because of this switchover from one style of parody film to another, there seems an imbalance in the film, like things are missing that should be there. As mentioned earlier, we see Robin seemingly hatch a plan about the "dummies" to use in battle, but we never see a punch line to that setup. The sheriff starts the film off with every other line being a form of spoonerism (mixing up words in a sentence), only for the character to stop doing so halfway through the film. Ahchoo is set up in the first half of the film as a constant companion and even a second lead, only to fade away to simply the punch line for the "black sheriff" joke at the end. Even the acting at times feels off, as if the actors were unsure sometimes how broad to go—Elwes in particular seems to become almost immobile at times—which is too bad, as some of the performances are rather good, such as Mark Blankfield in essentially the Marty Feldman role (and a shame he didn't get more to do in his subsequent appearance in *Dracula: Dead and Loving It*) and Amy Yasbeck, given little to do in the script, but making up for it with her physical reactions in showing she has good comedic timing.

In retrospect, however, there is something in particular Brooks is saying in the film, although it is not the normal message about life. Rather, he had made a movie that is a homage to all his other films. As sure as any fan watching the film may have noticed, there are gags that directly wink at the audience about earlier comedies he has done. At first it seems like a case of lazy writing, but as the film goes along, it appears Brooks was looking at the film as perhaps a way to tie up all his other films into one big tribute to his earlier work. To demonstrate, here's a partial list of gags in the film that had appeared in earlier films:

- Sheriff's sword breaking off at the handle—*History of the World, Part I*
- Camera breaking window as it moves into Marian's bath—*High Anxiety*
- Camera being whacked by the abbot's staff when it gets too close—*Spaceballs*
- Sheriff's expression in portrait changing based on actions happening in front of it—*Young Frankenstein*
- Ahchoo telling Robin "Nice knowing you" when he's about to do something stupid that will probably get him killed—*Young Frankenstein*
- Robin giving Will a treat like a performing animal after succeeding at showing the villagers how to fight—*Young Frankenstein*
- Prince John's mole moving around—*Young Frankenstein*, and variation of such in *Life Stinks*
- "Men in Tights" is a variation of the song "Jews in Space"—*History of the World, Part I*
- Robin demanding that a song be sung in a certain key—*High Anxiety*
- Mime at party crossing his eyes and uncrossing them in an odd manner—*Silent Movie*
- Robin's arrow winning the contest by flying around the area and finally entering the target through the back, knocking the other arrows out—*When Things Were Rotten*
- Sheriff telling others to "walk this way" and then they all walk the silly way he does—*Young Frankenstein*
- The camera crew being attacked during the final sword fight—*Spaceballs*
- Rabbi Tuckman noting that "It's good to be the king"—*History of the World, Part I*
- Ahchoo's direct comment about *Blazing Saddles* when being named the new sheriff

Once you get to the hangman being the same actor playing the character the same way as in *Blazing Saddles*, it becomes pretty clear: *Robin Hood: Men in Tights* is *Mel Brooks: Life in Films*. Perhaps in some ways Brooks thought this may have been his last chance to make a film and wanted to close things out in a glorious fashion by giving multiple winks to his earlier films for the audience to appreciate if they noticed them. As it stands, the film works fine on its own, but much better with a little bit of the history behind it—be it the Costner and Flynn films or Mel Brooks's earlier movies.

And there is still one more movie to come from Brooks.

19

Would an Enema Help?

Dracula: Dead and Loving It

Release Date: December 22, 1995 by Castle Rock Entertainment and Columbia Pictures

Hitler References

None. Turns out there weren't as many references in his films as you thought, didn't it?

Musical Moments

Three dance numbers, two of which are by Dracula and Mina. "El Choclo" is played as they dance at Carfax Abbey. With others, the pair dance to "The Kaminsky Two-Step," written by Hummie Mann; Johann Strauss's "The Artist's Waltz"; and then to "Hungarian Rhapsody #5" by themselves as the mirror is presented.

Preproduction

Variety announced on January 12, 1995, that Brooks was working on a new "vampire spoof." The next day, the magazine listed the title as being *Dracula: Dead and Liking It*, which was corrected to being *Dracula: Dead and Loving It* in the February 3, 1995, issue.

The script was written by Brooks with his *Life Stinks* cowriters Steve Haberman and Rudy De Luca, going back to an idea he had been rolling around since the days of his first venture into horror, *Young Frankenstein*, creating a bookend to the first film. "It took me so many years," Brooks told Jenny Peters as *Dracula: Dead and Loving It* was being released. "My problem was I could not find a Dracula. I simply could not find Dracula. I didn't know who Dracula was. It's very difficult to find somebody who's very funny, and make the people laugh, and yet be arrogant, bold, scary and menacing." And eventually Brooks found that person to play the role—Kelsey Grammer.

The problem was that Grammer wasn't interested in the role, even when offered $3 million to star. In fact, his agents did not even return calls about the role. Thus, Brooks had to keep looking and eventually went with a man who had been a serious dramatic actor who found new life in the 1980s as a comedy star, Leslie Nielsen. Nielsen agreed to star in the film in early March 1995. Amy Yasbeck, who had worked for Brooks so well in *Robin Hood: Men in Tights*, happily

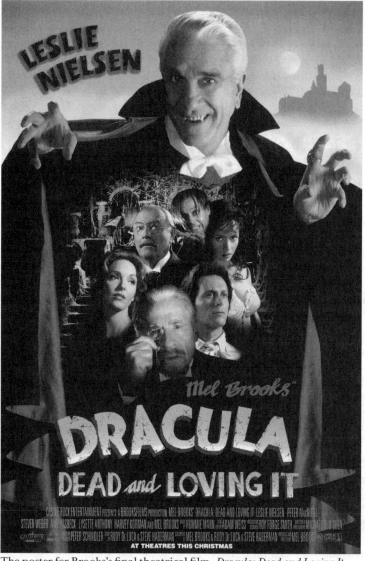

The poster for Brooks's final theatrical film, *Dracula: Dead and Loving It*.

signed on, after Brooks's attempt to find a blonde British actress for the role of Nina went nowhere. Yasbeck brought with her Steven Wright, who was her costar on the NBC comedy series *Wings* at the time.

With the French studio Gaumont once again supplying financial support, Brooks was able to get additional financing from Castle Rock Entertainment along with Columbia Pictures to make the film in time for a Christmas 1995 release. Initially the writers discussed whether the film should be in black and white like *Young Frankenstein* but eventually discarded the idea when it was agreed that some of the best vampire films had been made in color by the British studio Hammer in the 1960s and onward. Also, as the script was looking to parody some aspects of Francis Ford Coppola's *Bram Stocker's Dracula*—such as the weird hair of Dracula and Dracula's shadow moving on its own—it made sense that the film would be in color as that film had been.

Brooks managed to pull together most of the crew from *Robin Hood: Men in Tights*, allowing the film to begin production at Culver Studio in Culver City, California, on May 5, 1995.

Cast

Leslie Nielsen (1926–2010) as Count Dracula

Nielsen had started his career as a dramatic leading actor, beginning in live television in New York during the late 1940s and early 1950s (at the same time as Anne Bancroft, leading to the two reminiscing about those years while filming *Dracula: Dead and Loving It*). In 1956, he played the lead role of the captain in the classic science-fiction film *Forbidden Planet*. While occasionally getting a role in a comedy and at one point playing the lead in the Disney series *The Swamp Fox*, he typically was the handsome, somewhat bland, hero in a variety of films. By the 1970s, he was a standard go-to actor for guest-starring roles in television dramatic series where he would play both good and bad characters.

That status as a fixture in dramatic television roles led to him being cast in the disaster movie parody film *Airplane!* (1980) by David Zucker, Jim Abrahams, and Jerry Zucker. The film took the type of parody Brooks had been advancing through the 1970s one step further with a "joke a minute" approach. *Airplane!* would open up a second career for Nielsen as a comedic actor, following up with the successful *Naked Gun* films also done with Zucker, Abrahams, and Zucker. After a number of such roles in other parody films came *Dracula: Dead and Loving It*, which gave Nielsen a chance to do his Bela Lugosi impression. He continued to make similar movies into his eighties, passing away in 2010 at the age of eighty-four.

Brooks directing Leslie Nielsen as Dracula and Lysette Anthony as Lucy in *Dracula: Dead and Loving It*.

Peter MacNicol (born 1954) as Thomas Renfield

MacNicol started on off-Broadway in *Crimes of the Heart* in 1981, which led to him winning the lead role in the Disney film *Dragonslayer* (1981), followed by a strong dramatic role in *Sophie's Choice* (1982). MacNicol was also in *Ghostbusters II* (1989) and *Addams Family Values* (1992), and a regular on *Chicago Hope* (1994–1998). After *Dracula: Dead and Loving It*, which featured MacNicol doing a credible crazed Dwight Frye impression, he would move on to a feature role in the series *Ally McBeal* (1997–2002), for which he won an Emmy for Outstanding Supporting Actor in a Comedy Series in 2001. Since then, he has mostly worked as a voice actor, with occasional appearances on television.

Steve Weber (born 1961) as Jonathan Harker

Weber began appearing on television and in films in the 1980s, gradually winning one of the lead roles in the sitcom *Wings* (1990–1997). Most of his work since has been in television, including a miniseries version of *The Shining*

(1997), and in series such as *Once and Again* (2000–2002), and *NCIS: New Orleans* (2014–2017).

Amy Yasbeck as Mina

This was Yasbeck's second film for Brooks. She continues to make guest appearances in various television programs and has remained friends with Brooks, leading to him suggesting that she could play a part in the anticipated, but never made, *Spaceballs II*.

Harvey Korman as Dr. Seward

Korman makes a surprise return to the world of Brooks's films after having last appeared in *History of the World, Part I* back in 1981, although he had worked for Brooks in 1989 as one of the leads in the short-lived series *The Nutt House*. Korman stated at the time of filming that he based his performance of Dr. Seward on the mannerisms of Nigel Bruce, who played Watson in the Sherlock Holmes movies with Basil Rathbone.

Korman would continue to work in television as well as appearing with his former *Carol Burnett* costar Tim Conway in a series of stage shows where they would perform skits and other comedy routines. He died in 2008.

Lysette Anthony (born 1963) as Lucy

Anthony was no stranger to the world of the supernatural, having played the witch Angelique in the 1991 television remake of the horror soap opera *Dark Shadows*. She had previously appeared in Woody Allen's *Husbands and Wives* (1992) and would later play the only female speaking role in Quentin Tarantino's *Reservoir Dogs* (1992), although her one scene was cut from the film before release. She also was in the film *Krull* in 1983 and has been seen more recently in the series *Hollyoaks* (2016–2017).

Mel Brooks as Professor Van Helsing

This actor finally spreads his wings after numerous films with the same damn director and ends up creating a major Broadway hit just a few years after filming this movie.

Mark Blankfield as Martin

Blankfield had previously appeared in *Robin Hood; Men in Tights* in the much more substantial role of Blinkin, the blind servant. He played the more minor role of the orderly in *Dracula*. He continued working in television into the 2000s.

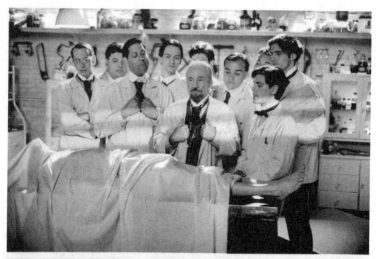

Brooks takes on an important secondary role in the film as Dr. Van Helsing.

Megan Cavanagh as Essie

This was Cavanagh's second appearance in a Brooks film and also the second time she played a servant to Amy Yasbeck's character in a Brooks film.

Also Appearing

- Anne Bancroft as Madame Ouspenskaya. The character's name is based on actress Maria Ouspenskaya, who played the foreshadowing gypsy woman in the original *The Wolfman* (1941). Bancroft would eventually work with

Brooks again in other programs and films, but this would be their last association in a film directed by him.

- Clive Revill as Syke, the unfortunate man Lucy kills in the crypt. He appeared briefly in *Robin Hood: Men in Tights* as the fire marshal directing efforts to stop the fire in the village.
- Chuck McCann as the innkeeper in the village who has a long mustache. McCann had previously appeared as the studio guard in *Silent Movie* and as the villager who bends his bow all out of shape in *Robin Hood: Men in Tights*.
- Avery Schreiber as Peasant in the Coach with Renfield. Schreiber previously had appeared as the man sending Robin's castle on its way in *Robin Hood: Men in Tights*.
- Matthew Porretta as Handsome Lieutenant at Ball. Porretta was Will Scarlett O'Hara in *Robin Hood: Men in Tights*.
- Rudy De Luca as a guard. Frequent cowriter and actor on Brooks's films, he had been working with Brooks since *Silent Movie*.
- Charlie Callas as the Man in the Straitjacket. He is listed in the credits, but appears to have not made it to the final cut of the film. The same fate seems to have fallen upon Phillip Connery as the Ship Captain and Tony Riffin, Casey King, and Nick Rempel as crew members of the *Demeter* who are never seen in the finished film.

In the Crew

As mentioned in the previous chapter, most of the crew remained the same between *Robin Hood: Men in Tights* and *Dracula: Dead and Loving It*. The main additions were:

- Alan Johnson returning to work with Brooks again for the choreography of the dances in the film.
- Leah Zappy, who had been an executive producer on *Robin Hood: Men in Tights*, is listed as an associate producer on *Dracula: Dead and Loving It*.
- Stephen E. Rivkin as editor.
- Stephen Myles Berg as art director.

Production

Production began without incident at the Culver Studio on May 5—some sources state May 8, but there was never any correction in *Variety* as to the starting date. It is the only film made by Brooks that is shot entirely indoors except for some establishing exterior shots. Two of those are actually clips from previous films: the shot of the *Demeter* sailing in dangerous weather was footage from the 1962 version of *Mutiny on the Bounty*, and Lucy's funeral procession is from the film *The Premature Burial* (1962), which explains why the shape of the coffin for Lucy does not match what is seen in the crypt later in the film.

Second to *Spaceballs, Dracula: Dead and Loving It* is one of the most effects-intensive of Brooks's films, even more so than *Young Frankenstein*, which restricted itself to makeup and some limited prop use. The scene where Dracula clings to the ceiling in Lucy's room was done with Leslie Nielsen lying in "a steel-reinforced carbon fiber pan made from a cast of the actor's body," according to the production information given with the press-kit. MacNicol and Nielsen also had to be suspended in trapeze bars with knee and ankle locks in order to perform the scene of them upside down in Renfield's cell. The most complex stunt work by one of the actors was left for Amy Yasbeck, who is seen in the film dancing and twirling in the air without support in the scene where Dracula dances with her at the ball. This involved Yasbeck being spun on a "Lazy Susan-like disc," while the airplane spins were done with wires supporting her in the air at speeds "up to twenty miles per hour." Additional effects work was done by Dream Quest Images and Optic Nerve Studios.

Of course, there was the big effect scene where Steven Weber stakes Lucy in her casket, forcing two vast eruptions of blood spraying him twice ("She just ate."). Although it has been written in various places that Weber was not aware of the spray of blood, it is clear from press photos and the script itself that he did know what was to occur. What was a surprise to him, however, was how much blood would be used when the cameras began to roll. Fortunately, Weber managed to stay in character after being almost completely covered in blood, leading to one of the more memorable scenes in a Brooks film and definitely a highlight in the level of gross-out humor Brooks used at times.

Filming was completed on July 26, 1995. Brooks then began the process of editing the film with Stephen E. Rivkin through August and September. Columbia hoped the film, rumored to cost close to $30 million to make, would be a blockbuster. It would be released on December 22, 1995, in most parts of the United States on over 1,000 screens.

Backend

As with *Robin Hood: Men in Tights* and *Life Stinks*, the movie poster created for U.S. audiences was photo art rather than an illustration as for earlier Brooks films. At least this time it was used in a manner to resemble a traditional action movie poster rather than the bland *Men in Tights* one, with a collage of faces and Brooks in front as Van Helsing, instead of the cape of Dracula.

Casino, Waiting to Exhale, Cutthroat Island, Ace Ventura: When Nature Calls, Heat, and *Toy Story* were in theaters when *Dracula: Dead and Loving It* was released. Once again, reviews were harsh, with a very negative one from Jack Garner of the Gannett News Service getting a lot of coverage in various newspapers around the country, calling it "Dracula: It's dead and I'm hating it." David Kroke at the *Los Angeles Times* lamented that "there are great, arid stretches of this film in which there aren't even any bad jokes to not laugh at." Even critics who gave some praise to Peter MacNicol's performance had little to say about the rest of the film, with Joe Leyden at *Variety* calling it "perilously close to blandness."

Yet, contrary to what people believe, there were a good number of positive reviews as well. Stephen Hunter of the *Baltimore Sun* gave the film three stars and said that while it would not be confused with *Young Frankenstein* or *The Producers*, "It's easily his best movie since then." Hunter also pointed out that, unlike many parody films in theaters at the time, Brooks seemed to have made a film "committed to being a total movie and not a joke platform." Michael Wilmington of the *Chicago Tribune* also gave the film three stars, saying that "at its best, *Dracula: Dead and Loving It* has the manic giddiness and controlled hysteria of Brooks's best stuff." Janet Maslin of the *New York Times* was positive as well, stating that although it felt at times "thin-blooded, its better moments redeem a lot of dead air."

The box office became the ultimate reviewer for the film, which took in very little in its first week, the biggest holiday week of the year. The second week was even worse, and in some quarters it was being pulled from theaters after only two weeks. Domestically, the film made close to $11 million, which on a budget of $30 million was hard to call anything other than a dud. Further, although it did solid business in some European countries, especially Italy, the film performed weakly in both the United Kingdom and Australia. There was no way to manipulate the numbers—*Dracula: Dead and Loving It* died at the box office.

In the summer of 1996, the film was released to video, where the numbers finally began to shift. People who didn't see it in the theaters were renting and buying it to watch at home. It was gaining fans, which provided some relief to Brooks. "Video is heaven," he told AP that summer after seeing how many cassettes of the film were selling. "Even lousy movies [get a second chance]. All dogs go to heaven. It's a great idea, this video. Because as a filmmaker you'd pray for a re-release of your film. And very few get re-releases."

Reflections

One problem with *Dracula: Dead and Loving It* is similar to that which affected *Spaceballs*—there had already been several decent parody films on the subject of vampires. Maybe not the horrible *Old Dracula* (1974), starring David Niven, but there was the earlier *The Fearless Vampire Killers* (1967), from which Brooks and company borrowed the large mirror in the ballroom gag (and which, admittedly, has a better payoff in the earlier film as well); the amusing *Love at First Bite* (1979) with Dick Shawn; and the tepid *Once Bitten* (1985) with Cleavon Little. Although Brooks may have had the idea hanging around for quite a while, it looked as if he was coming in behind the pack instead of being the front-runner as he had been in the past.

Yet the film does work as a comedy on its own terms. The main criticism of *Dracula: Dead and Loving It*, and of Mel Brooks's role in comedy at that point, is that he refused to follow a trend that he himself created. When a film like *Blazing Saddles* came along, with its irreverent attitude not only to the western genre but to Hollywood itself, it took a few years to even attempt to follow that lead. Yet, although Brooks's work demonstrated to the next generation of film-makers that comedies could be outrageous, there was a general feeling that anything over-the-top, gross, and outrageous superseded plot, message, and even general storytelling. In looking for a bombardment of jokes, the plot was getting lost along the way. There would end up being no message to the films because there wasn't even a story to wrap the message in anyway.

At first, those that tried such parodies, like the various "college comedies" that came in the 1970s such as *The Groove Tube* and *Kentucky Fried Movie*, only partially succeeded, with fragmented films that had as many or even more dud moments than funny ones, and never by a major studio. *The Big Bus* (1976), a parody of disaster movies dealing with a massive nuclear-powered bus that is out of control, came close, but it wasn't until *Airplane!* (1980)—ironically another disaster film parody—that it looked like the studios were finally getting the idea and letting the right people explore comedy the way Brooks had. Not in the manner of gross-out humor, although there certainly was some there, but in accepting that the audience knows more about moviemaking than Hollywood likes to think and that the process can be mocked within the confines of telling a story as well.

And that's where the problem came into play. From then on out, the emphasis became not one of telling a story within all these "meta" (self-referential) jokes, but simply joke, joke, joke. This is how we have come to a point where we have endless *Scary Movie Part 85* films and *Not Another Run of Poor Reference Gags* movies—movies that were just frothy, mindless filler, forgotten before the credits even ended. Brooks himself was swinging that way with *History of the World, Part I*, but then recovered with—surprisingly—*Spaceballs*, which does at least have a story to tell. And then went back to a strong story in *Life Stinks*, which got beaten up by the critics, followed by *Robin Hood: Men in Tights*, with its traditional folklore wrapped in funny gags, that was also ripped apart, and . . . well, you get the idea.

The critics had become conditioned to the rapid-fire pace of parody films by 1995. They expected Brooks to follow the crowd and give them more of the same, or perhaps a higher-class version of the same. Instead, Brooks made a traditional comedy based on the source material. This is still *Dracula* as we have always known it to be from the original movie. Place the plot of Brooks's film up against the Lugosi version or one of the Hammer films and it could still work once the jokes were removed.

It can't be said that the film defines Brooks's legacy. But it's still a Mel Brooks movie. Brooks himself has said that "only ten percent of anything is good." *Dracula: Dead and Loving It* may not be perfect, but it's not an embarrassment. The movie tells its story and gives us a few laughs along the way. And unlike too many of the parody films coming out at the time and even since, it works. Not a bad way to go out if it is the last one Brooks ever directs.

And besides, as mentioned earlier in the chapter, there were other things to do beyond directing films. Critics have always praised Brooks's acting skills in his films, and he would do some more in television into the 1980s and onward. He also had Brooksfilms and later would prove himself once again on Broadway with the musical version of *The Producers*. There was still life in the kid, as will be seen.

20

They're All Oddballs

The Films of Brooksfilms

In 1976, Anne Bancroft decided it was time to create a film herself. To those who knew her, this wasn't much of a surprise, having lived with a writer/director like Brooks for years, as well as being friends with many other iconic writers and directors. Her first attempt was a short film called *The August*. It was never released, but it gave her the motivation to attempt something more ambitious.

She then wrote a script called *Fatso*, with her and Brooks's friend Dom DeLuise in mind as the star and her directing. Soon after Bancroft began work on her project, Brooks was approached with a script about John Merrick, the famous "elephant man" of Victorian London. Brooks decided to produce both *Fatso* and the John Merrick film himself. Yet he also knew that putting his name on the films would present a problem: neither was like one of his own films, and having the "Mel Brooks" name anywhere near either one in the credits or on a poster could send the wrong message to ticket buyers. As he discussed with the Directors Guild in 2012, "I was always afraid that part of my baggage would be 'Oh, crazy Mel Brooks, funny Mel Brooks.' And if I were going to do the Frances Famer story, they wouldn't buy it. I'm sure they would see *The Elephant Man* and wait for the big laughs. 'Wait'll he shows his trunk,' you know?"

Brooks already had a production company, Crossbow Productions Inc., which he created and used since 1962 and up through 1978. Yet people within the industry associated the Crossbow name with Brooks, leading straight back to the problem of how to produce these serious films without people assuming they were going to be "Mel Brooks" comedies. Thus, even though early reports had *Fatso* and *The Elephant Man* slated as upcoming Crossbow Productions films, by August 1979 they were announced as coming from Brooks's new production company, Brooksfilms Ltd.

The kicker to this story about not wanting to commingle his own comedies with those made through his Brooksfilms Ltd. is that from 1979 onward, all Brooks-connected productions including his future comedy films would carry the production company's name. Brooksfilms would also be used for the two television series involving Brooks done in later years, *The Nutt House* (1989) and *Spaceballs: The Animated Series*, as well as a few television specials: *An Audience with Mel Brooks* (1983), *Mel Brooks and Dick Cavett Together Again* (2011), *Mel Brooks*

Strikes Back! (2012), and *Mel Brooks Live at the Geffen* (2015). Mainly, however, Brooksfilms was seen as a production company that made serious films by up-and-coming talents such as David Cronenberg (born 1943) and David Lynch (born 1946), as well as offbeat "smaller," more artistic endeavors like *84 Charing Cross Road* and even the comedy film *My Favorite Year.*

To Brooks's surprise, he found himself being seen as one of the few people in Hollywood willing to take a risk in making films that were not the next "summer blockbuster." "When I started Brooksfilms in 1979," he said to Desmond Ryan in 1985, "I didn't intend to be the only production company in Hollywood that made alternative films. When we're done, the world has a unique, bright film. It enriches anyone older than 14. [Other production companies] churn out mindless nonsense and instead of calling it 'mindless nonsense,' they call it 'youth-oriented." It's trash."

Brooks's stance as a producer of the Brooksfilms movies was to let the film-makers get on with it unless he was needed. "When I first initiated Brooksfilms, I really had a motto—Give talented people the room to express their talent." In doing so, he made a number of smaller films—some would probably call most of them "art films"—that are highly regarded. Brooks also noted in the PBS documentary *Make a Noise,* "Seems to be a running theme of Brooksfilms that all our characters are outside the normal mainstream of civilized activity. They're all oddballs, but incredibly human, incredibly gifted, all of them."

In 1990, he tried to take Brooksfilms public with a $15 million offering, right at a time when interest in independent production companies such as his was drying up, and four years after the company's last box-office success, *The Fly.* When only $6 million was raised, Brooks dropped the idea and instead set up a deal for co-financing through Le Studio Canal in 1991. By that point, it was becoming harder and harder to get financing for the films Brooks wanted to make beyond his own comedies, and when the 1992 Brooksfilm *The Vagrant* died at the box office, the only remaining films to be released through the production company were directly related to Brooks himself, such as *Robin Hood: Men in Tights* (1993), *Dracula: Dead and Loving It* (1995), and *The Producers* (2005).

Below is a list of films made by the Brooksfilms production company over the years besides Brooks's comedy films already listed in previous chapters. And one ringer that was promoted at one point as a Brooksfilms production that actually wasn't.

Coming Attractions, aka Loose Shoes (1977)

This sketch comedy film from 1977 was made two years before Brooksfilms was created and is listed on such websites as Wikipedia and imdb.com as a Brooksfilms, although it is not a Brooksfilms production.

The movie was directed and cowritten by Ira Miller—who appeared as an extra in several Brooks films (in *Blazing Saddles,* he played the baker in the commissary who asks who wants pies)—and appeared in theaters in 1977 and

1978 as *Coming Attractions*. Then two of the film's stars, Bill Murray and Howard Hesseman, achieved fame in the late 1970s from their work on *Saturday Night Live* and *WKRP in Cincinnati*, respectively, and the film was rereleased in theaters in 1980 under the new title of *Loose Shoes*. The U.S. movie poster created for the 1980 rerelease announced that it was a "Brooks Films Ltd. Production ("Brooks Films" rather than Brooksfilms, which is the proper name for the company). A look at the film itself shows no mention of Brooksfilms in the credits, and there is no mention of "Brooks Films" on the British version of the poster, although there is a quote supposedly from Brooks stating that he "laughed his socks off." Even if he did, *Coming Attractions* should not be considered part of the official catalogue of films made by Brooksfilms Productions Ltd., which commonly was listed as either Brooksfilms Ltd. or "A Brooksfilms Production" in the credits.

Fatso (1980), released February 1, 1980, by 20th Century-Fox

The first film released under the Brooksfilms name, dealing with a man struggling to control his weight as he finds true love for the first time. See chapter 7 for more details on the making of the movie. *Fatso* received a Best Actor award for Dom DeLuise at the Taormina International Film Festival in Italy. The film was not a hit at the box office, however.

The Elephant Man (1980), released October 10, 1980, by Paramount Pictures

Christopher De Vore and Eric Bergren had written a script based on two books: *The Elephant Man; A Study in Human Dignity* by Ashley Montagu and *The Elephant Man and Other Reminiscences* by Frederick Treves; both detailing the life of Joseph Merrick (named John Merrick in the script), a man with an extremely irregular physical appearance struggling to be accepted as a human being in Victorian England. De Vore and Bergren gave a copy of the script to a woman who babysat for Jonathan Sanger, an associate producer on *Fatso*. Sanger liked it enough to pass it on to Brooks, who decided to make it his second film for his production company.

Executive producer Stuart Cornfeld suggested to Brooks that David Lynch would be the perfect director for the project and urged him to see Lynch's 1977 cult film *Eraserhead*, a black-and-white film about an "everyday" man living in a nightmarish world where he attends to the needs of his monster-like baby. "I saw that Lynch could deal very primitively and surrealistically with human feelings," Brooks told *Rolling Stone* in 1982. "The outsides of things are critical to him, but not in any normal way."

When pitching the film to studios for money, Brooks ran into exactly what he feared—that he would not be taken seriously. As he commented to *Rolling*

Stone many years later about taking the script for *The Elephant Man* to studios, "Mel Brooks goes to all these studios, and the people there sit grinning. Frank Wells over at Warner Bros. really thought I was putting him on. He told me later, 'Mel, I thought this was one of your most grotesque jokes.'" Michael Eisner, who was working at Paramount at the time, liked the script and supported the film. Brooks also got a $4 million commitment from network executive Fred Silverman, along with additional funds from EMI.

The film starred John Hurt as John Merrick, with Anthony Hopkins and featuring Anne Bancroft. When it was announced, the production was soon hit by a lawsuit from the producers and writer of a Broadway play about Merrick with the same title who assumed that calling the movie *The Elephant Man* would confuse possible ticket buyers. Brooks scoffed when asked by the *New York Times* about the suit, "They appropriate something that is in the public domain and claim it as their own property. And what is this 'damages?' It could only help them [by making the play more widely known]." Brooks would countersue for slander and "restraint of trade." The case was settled in a pretrial agreement in June 1980, allowing for the film to be made.

The film was a box-office success, earning over $26 million in the United States alone from a budget of only $5 million. It was also a critical success and nominated for several awards, winning BAFTA Awards for Best Film, Stuart Craig for Best Production Design, and John Hurt as Best Actor. Freddie Francis won Best Cinematography Award from the British Society of Cinematographers and from the London Critics Circle as well as the National Society of Film Critics. It was also voted one of the top ten films for 1980 by the National Board of Review in the United States. Writers Christopher De Vore and Eric Bergren will go on to work on the script for *Frances*.

"I AM NOT AN ANIMAL!
I AM A HUMAN BEING!
I...AM...A MAN!"

Although *Fatso* (1980) was the first Brooksfilm production, it would be *The Elephant Man* the same year that would cement Brooksfilms as a promising new production company in Hollywood.

My Favorite Year (1982), released October 8, 1982, by MGM

Television writer Dennis Palumbo (born 1951) wrote a script about a young man's adventures as a comedy writer on a show very much like *Your Show of Shows* in the 1950s, where he had to chaperone a drunken has-been movie star. Brooks bought the script in 1980 and then added writer Norman Steinberg—who had cowritten *Blazing Saddles*—to beef it up. Steinberg later stated in the PBS *Make a Noise* documentary that Brooks wanted the main character to be himself as the young man, but Steinberg felt the character would be too strong and unsympathetic. Brooks has gone on record that the plot was similar to what happened to him once on *Your Show of Shows*. "I was locked in the Waldorf Towers with Errol Flynn and two red-headed Cuban sisters. For three days, I was trying to get them out of there and he was trying to get me drunk and in there. It was the craziest weekend of my life."

Brooks originally tried to get Albert Finney for the role of the movie star, Alan Swann, but when Finney declined, Peter O'Toole (1932–2013) got the part. Mark Linn-Baker (born 1954) had his first big role as Benjy, the young writer, and would go on to additional success as one of the stars of the sitcom *Perfect Strangers* (1986–1993). Lainie Kazan (born 1940), who plays Benjy's mother in the film, said in 1983 that she got the role thanks to Brooks remembering her from playing "a funny Jewish lady" in an episode of *When Things Were Rotten* back in 1975. The film was the first directed by actor Richard Benjamin (born 1938). Selma Diamond, who was a writer with Brooks on *Your Show of Shows*, appeared as the wardrobe lady. A musical version, starring Tim Curry as Alan Swann, appeared on Broadway in 1992, and only lasted a month. O'Toole would be nominated for an Academy Award for his role, although he would not win.

The film was another critical and commercial success for Brooksfilms, making over $20 million domestically from a budget of around $8 million.

Frances (1982), released December 3, 1982, by Universal Pictures

First reported by *Variety* in February 1980 as *The Frances Farmer Story*, the title was soon changed to *Frances*. The film starred Jessica Lange (born 1949) as Frances Farmer (1913–1970), a movie actress whose career was derailed due to an escalating psychological illness. It would end up being the second Brooksfilms production that faced a lawsuit, as writer William Arnold and co-plaintiff Noel Marshall sued for copyright infringement, feeling the film lifted its plot from Arnold's book about Farmer, *Shadowland*, which was revealed in the court trial as being a fictionalized account of Farmer's life. The courts found in favor of Brooksfilms in November 1983, stating "the two works are very different in style, structure, emphasis and treatment."

The script was written by Eric Bergren, Christopher De Vore, and Nicholas Kazan. The director was Graeme Clifford (born 1942). The film was released slowly across the United States and eventually grossed $5 million domestically, just about covering costs. Lange was nominated for an Academy Award for Best Actress, along with Kim Stanley (1925–2001) for Best Supporting Actress. Lange won second place as Best Actress from the New York Film Critics Circle Awards and the Los Angeles Film Critics Association Awards. She also won Best Actress at the Moscow International Film Festival in 1983.

The Doctor and the Devils (1985), released October 4, 1985, by 20th Century Fox

Freddie Francis (1917–2007) had received acclaim for his work as the cinematographer on *The Elephant Man*, but he was also famous for his work as a director on several later Hammer horror films in the 1960s. The film is a variation on the story of Burke and Hare, the two men in the early nineteenth century who murdered people in order to sell cadavers to a medical school. The film starred

Timothy Dalton (born 1946) as the doctor who bought the bodies, with Jonathan Pryce (born 1947) and Stephen Rea (born 1946) portraying renamed versions of Burke and Hare. The film was released slowly in the United States, mostly in art theaters, and did poorly, with a domestic box-office total of $147,070.

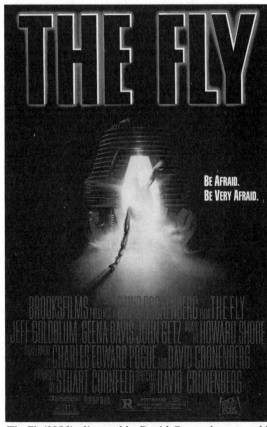

The Fly (1986), released August 15, 1986, by 20th Century Fox

First mentioned as being picked up by 20th Century Fox, in *Variety* in September 1985, this was a remake of a classic science-fiction/ horror film from the 1950s that starred Vincent Price and dealt with a scientist who accidentally exchanges parts of his body with that of a fly when attempting to teleport. This version features Jeff Goldblum (born 1952), who plays the scientist, with his then-girlfriend Geena Davis (born 1956) cast as his love interest.

The Fly (1986), directed by David Cronenberg, would become the biggest success of the films done for Brooksfilms.

Director Robert Bierman had intended to direct the film, following initial talk of Tim Burton possibly directing. Bierman, however, dropped out after a death in the family, and Brooks finally hired David Cronenberg, who reworked the script that Charles Edward Pogue had written for the remake. Cronenberg had been making films about biological and psychological horror since the 1970s and had achieved some box-office notice with the success of *Scanners* (1981) and *The Dead Zone* (1986).

The Fly was the biggest Brooksfilms success, earning over $40 million domestically, with an additional $20 million overseas. It also received strong critical reviews and won an Academy Award and BAFTA Award for Makeup.

Solarbabies (1986), released November 26, 1986, by MGM

The film came by way of D. A. Metrov, who had seen his friend Abel Ferrara's successful horror film *Driller Killer* that was done for $100,000, and Metrov thought he could do something similar. His idea was to do a small science-fiction film about "the Little Rascals of the future," and created a treatment and a short film with some local kids to show what his intentions were. The footage he filmed—never used in the movie—and the treatment interested Brooks, especially the way Metrov planned to make a futuristic film on a very modest budget.

Brooks paid for another writer to create a script based on Metrov's treatment, but rejected it and instead agreed to have Metrov try his hand at the script. Metrov worked with Walon Green (*The Wild Bunch*) on the script, which was then beefed up in an additional draft by Green and Brooks. Brooks was told by the producers, Irene Walzer and Jack Frost, that they could make the movie look bigger for only $5 million if they shot it in Spain, where it would be cheaper to make due to no union restrictions (something Brooks himself had done to cut costs when making *The Twelve Chairs*). Because of the boost in budget from the initial "modest little film" Metrov had planned, Brooks decided that a more seasoned director was needed and brought in Alan Johnson, who had directed Brooks's *To Be or Not to Be* in 1982. The cast featured Jason Patric, Jami Gertz, Richard Jordan, Lukas Haas, and Charlie Durning.

Production in Spain soon ran into problems with constant rain slowing filming, and arguments between the cast and the director leading to delays that ate up the budget. As the cost spread to $8 million, Brooks went overseas to the film location to "lay down the law" to the cast, telling them to listen to their director. (Brooks would later joke to an interviewer after the film bombed, "Maybe they shouldn't have listened to him.") Needing to borrow more money to finish the film, Brooks went as far as getting a second mortgage on his house in order to pay for it, the cost spiraling to $23 million for a film originally intended to be made for $100,000.

"I'm practically ready to jump off a roof . . . I mean a roof like the Empire State Building, I'm ready to go. Because I am legally broke and in debt

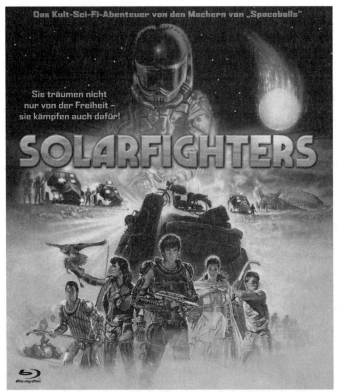

Solarbabies (1986), shown here with the Blu-ray cover for the film in Germany as *Solarfighters*, was a little art film that grew into a money-draining project that nearly personally bankrupted Mel Brooks.

for the first time in my life," Brooks reflected to Blake Harris on his mental state at the time when interviewed about the film's history several years later. Hoping for the best, he took what footage he had and made a ten-minute trailer to sell the film to a studio and hopefully get some of the cash back. "I make a phony baloney trailer so it looks like *Star Wars*. It looks like the greatest thing—it looks like it's going to be the greatest sci-fi picture ever made—a fairy tale in space." He took the trailer to Paramount, which nearly picked up the film, but ultimately turned it down. Brooks then showed it to Alan Ladd Jr., who was the new head of MGM. Ladd gave in to Brooks and gave him $14 million for distribution of the film. It was just enough to get him out of hock, although he still lost about $9 million when all was said and done. "When I wrote [the Broadway musical of] *The Producers*," Brooks said, "I put the line in: 'There are two things a Broadway producer must know. It's the rule of being a Broadway producer.' Leo Bloom says to Max Bialystock, 'And what are those two rules, Mr. Bialystock?' 'One: never put your own money in the show. And two . . . NEVER PUT YOUR

OWN MONEY IN THE SHOW!'" The film, which cost $23 million to make, according to Brooks, made only $1.5 million at the box office.

In 2016, Brooks reported that thanks to cable and video sales, the film did eventually make its money back, although it would take nearly twenty-five years to do so. "It was a great lesson," Brooks said after many years. "It was an incredible lesson in diligence. You must pay attention to the finances of what you're doing. Not just the artistic. Because, until then, I was only focused on the art of the film—making sure that worked—I didn't give a shit about the money."

84 Charing Cross Road (1987), released February 13, 1987, by Columbia Pictures

Discussed in more detail in chapter 7, this film starred Anne Bancroft and Anthony Hopkins, and was released as an art film to selected theaters. It would eventually gross just a little over $1 million. Anne Bancroft would win for Best Actress at the BAFTA Awards, while Anthony Hopkins won for Best Actor at the Moscow International Film Festival.

The Fly II (1989), released February 10, 1989, by 20th Century Fox

A sequel was just bound to happen with the success of *The Fly*, although Cronenberg and most of the cast were long gone by the time a script was finally put together for the film. The script was written by a variety of people: Mick Garris, Jim Wheat, Ken Wheat, and Frank Darabont (later the writer-director of *The Green Mile* and *Shawshank Redemption*).

The film starred Eric Stoltz (born 1961) as the son of the protagonists in the first film, with the sequel killing off Geena Davis's character in childbirth offscreen. Daphne Zuniga of *Spaceballs* played the main love interest. The plot has Stoltz's character slowly discovering his shocking heritage as a possible fly-hybrid, while a corporate leader aims to profit from his mutation.

The film, which never had its budget disclosed, made $20 million domestically and an additional $18 million overseas, thus likely making at least a small profit. It received mostly poor reviews, while ticket sales dropped off quickly after its opening weekend.

The Vagrant (1992), released May 15, 1992, by MGM

Studio Canal helped with the financial side of this MGM picture. This horror-comedy was directed by Chris Walas (born 1955), written by Richard Jefferies, and starred Bill Paxton (1955–2017) as a man who buys a home only to be quickly victimized by a homeless person (Marshall Bell) who actually turns out to be the ghost of a former resident with the intention of driving Paxton's character out. The film played at a paltry eight theaters for a week before being pulled, making less than $6,000 at the box office.

Although Brooksfilms planned to make future films, with the low box-office returns on *The Vagrant*, and Brooks's wish to dedicate himself to making his last two movies in 1993 and 1995, future movies produced by the company were put on hold. Even so, Brooks continued to buy certain projects over time that he planned to eventually see be made under the Brooksfilms name. Below is a list of projects he mentioned as being in development at Brooksfilms that, in most cases, never came to fruition:

Grand Mall (1980)

Listed by Brooks in an interview with the *New York Times*, as a comedy no doubt inspired by the 1932 movie *Grand Hotel*, and centering "on a shopping center as a metaphor for the world," it was to feature several actors from previous comedies done by Brooks (much like how *Grand Hotel* used many famous movie stars of the time). The film was in development at Universal in September 1980, but nothing further came of the project.

Great Aspirations (1980)

Another comedy mentioned at the same time as *Grand Mall* that concerned "the wish-fulfillment of a desperately poor boy who is able to pass himself off as one of the richest men in the world." In 1980, it was announced the film was to star Tim Matheson, who would go on to costar in *To Be or Not to Be*. The script was written by Marshall Efron and Alfa-Betty Olsen, who had worked together on the television series *The Great American Dream Machine* for PBS. Olsen had also helped write *The Producers* and *The Twelve Chairs* with Brooks.

Low Doings in High Places (1981)

Variety in April 1981 wrote that Brooks was planning a new project for producer Jonathan Sanger called *Low Doings in High Places*, with Anne Bancroft starring. The film was to be a "1920s detective story set during the scandal-ridden Harding administration," with a script by Lee Hudson, with Jack Clayton (who had directed Anne Bancroft in the 1964 film *The Pumpkin Eater*) directing.

Sanger would instead produce *Frances* in 1982 for Brooksfilm, while Clayton would direct Ray Bradbury's *Something Wicked This Way Comes* in 1983.

Filthy Rich (1982)

This was a movie project to be done for Brooksfilm with Richard Benjamin directing. The project, about which no other details are available, made the rounds until May 1982, when it disappeared. Benjamin's next film as a director would be that of *Racing with the Moon* in 1984 for Paramount.

Tar Baby (1984)

Based on Toni Morrison's 1981 novel about a young African American woman from a wealthy society falling in love with a young man from the Caribbean and the struggles they have as they try to commit to life together in the United States. A possible film produced by Jonathan Sanger was discussed in 1984, but never went any further.

Helene Mayer Biography (1985)

A biographical film about Helene Mayer, a Jewish fencer who competed for Germany in the 1936 Olympics. Brooks hyped the story for a few months in 1985 in interviews leading up to *Spaceballs*, but it never came to fruition.

Paul Verhoeven Project (1988)

In 1988, Mel Brooks became involved with writer-director Paul Verhoeven (*RoboCop*, *Starship Troopers*, *Showgirls*) on a project dealing with the story of Jesus Christ. The concept, which was extensively researched by Verhoeven, involved telling the story of Jesus not from the standpoint of miracles and religious symbolism, but rather how Jesus would have been perceived in the political climate of the time and how he presented "a new set of ethics, an openness towards the world," as Verhoeven stated in 2011 to Mike Fleming Jr.

Brooks told Marilyn Beck of the *Chicago Tribune* in September 1988 that he had already conversed with Verhoeven several times about the project and, "If it turns out to be wonderfully exciting and uplifting, we would want to make it for my Brooksfilms company." When asked about the controversy that surrounded Martin Scorsese's *Last Temptation of Christ*, Brooks shrugged it off, saying, "Our project, if we proceed, is at least two years away from release; by that time all the furor about *The Last Temptation of Christ* should have died down."

The project was still on the slate for Brooksfilm up through 1991, but as things began to wind down for the company, so too did interest in the project. Instead, Verhoeven would release his study as a book in 2011 called *Jesus of Nazareth*, while still looking to someday produce it as a theatrical film.

Ask the Dust (1988)

In 1988, Brooks optioned the rights to the 1939 John Fante novel *Ask the Dust*, and had scripts prepared for it, when Robert Towne (*Chinatown*) was brought in to write and direct it in 1993. The project, about a young writer and his relationship with a Mexican waitress in 1933, would continue to be on the Brooksfilm slate up until it went to Warner in 1993. It would be another twelve years before Towne was able to make the film, which was distributed by Paramount and starred Colin Farrell and Salma Hayek.

My Traitor's Heart (1992)

Based on Rian Malan's 1990 best-selling nonfiction book about a journalist whose great-great uncle founded apartheid.

Homma (1992)

Dramatization of a real-life war-crimes trial against Japanese General Homma, who was tried for his leadership in the 1942 Bataan Death March, which killed over 10,000 soldiers. The script was by Tom Wright, with Chris Carlson and Mark Jean producing another draft in 1999 that Mark Jean was to direct under the title of *The Beast of Bataan*. In 2005, Paul Verhoeven was announced as the director, but he eventually dropped out. Fred Schepisi (*Roxanne, The Russia House, Plenty*) was listed in 2007 as directing, and *Variety* reported that the film was about to go into production, but it was never pushed forward and was abandoned that year.

Flies (1993)

A second sequel to *The Fly*. Brooks told Marilyn Beck that the script was written by Richard Jefferies, based on a concept by Geena Davis and her then-husband Renny Harlin. Brooksfilms was negotiating at the time with Geena Davis to star in as well as produce the film. Writer Mick Garris in an interview on a podcast called *Shock Waves* in June 2016 said that all he knew was that the film would act as if *The Fly II* had never happened. There were rumors that the story line dealt with Davis's character giving birth to twins, leading to multiple fly creatures in the film. Although proposed as a big film, the production never came together, and Davis and Harlin went on to make *Cutthroat Island* (1995) instead.

Sunrise at Hasting (2000)

Brooks optioned a spec script by Dan Witt about William the Conqueror and the battle to create a "unified England near the end of the 11th century" in hopes of reviving dramatic offerings from the production company, which had not done a film outside of Brooks's directed comedies since 1992. Brooks proclaimed to *Variety* at the time, "The project unites two of my great passions: conquering England and making movies."

The script had been in development at Longbow Productions, which was run by Ronnie Clemmer and Bill Pace, and which Jonathan Sanger had picked up while working for C/W Productions, a company owned by Tom Cruise and

Paula Wagner. In May 2001, Brooks was still hopeful that a "$100 million epic" would begin filming later that year. It was the last mention of the project in *Variety*.

Sam (2015), released April 21, 2015, by Sony Pictures

This low-budget fantasy-comedy was written and directed by Nicholas Brooks, one of Brooks's sons from his first marriage. The movie is a traditional "body-switch" comedy like *Switch* and *Goodbye Charlie*, where a misogynist businessman is transformed into a woman (played by Natalie Knepp) and learns to deal with living his life now as the opposite sex. The film was originally listed in some publications as coming from Brooksfilms, but instead Mel Brooks is listed as executive producer only.

Blazing Samurai (2017), released August 4, 2017, by Sony Pictures

This animated film has been in the works since early 2015, with Brooksfilms being listed as one of several productions companies involved, but more in a figurehead role than actually doing much as a production company. The film is a loose adaptation of *Blazing Saddles*, with a dog becoming the samurai of a town inhabited only by cats. Mel Brooks did a voice in the production, which was directed by Chris Bailey from a script by Ed Stone and Nate Hooper. The film is by Mass Animation, and the main production company behind the project is Flying Tigers Entertainment.

While Brooksfilms remains active in name, it has not produced a film since the movie adaptation of the Broadway adaptation of the movie *The Producers* in 2005. The promise of a continuing company thriving on making smaller, intelligent films only truly existed for a little over a dozen years and then petered out, ironically depending on the comedies Brooks directed, which was never intended to be the focus of the production company. Still, within those years came a handful of films that have been critically acclaimed and that Brooks can proudly look to as not only prestigious but successful as well, which was more than many expected from the man who studios thought could do nothing but fart jokes and silly gags.

21

Talking in a Closet Under a Naked Lightbulb

The Later Television Series

Thre was some surprise when Mel Brooks had two blockbuster movie comedies in 1974. There was even more shock when he announced in February 1975 that he was to be the executive producer on a new television series for ABC called *When Things Were Rotten*. When asked in June that year why he was doing it, Brooks said, "My wife, what's-her-name, told me not to forget about TV just because I'm a big moviemaker now, because TV paid the rent when I was getting started."

Of course, there was the money he made while working for Sid Caesar in the 1950s, but the checks that came in for having developed *Get Smart* and personal appearances as the 2000 Year Old Man in the 1960s kept him going during a creative dry spell in the later 1960s.

After *Get Smart*, Brooks would be involved with three separate television series, each only lasting a handful of episodes before being cancelled. Maybe they never turned out as popular as *Get Smart*, but two of the three have been released on DVD in the years since, proving that there were fans for the shows even if the networks never quite got it.

When Things Were Rotten—Aired weekly September 10–December 3, 1975, on ABC

Brooks's involvement with the series began when he received a call from Norman Steinberg in late 1974. "One of the writers on *Blazing Saddles* got a big job in TV development at Paramount and he called me and said . . . 'HELP,'" Brooks joked when discussing the development of the show in May 1975 with the *Baltimore Sun*. The two collaborated on what would work for a television series and finally landed on the idea of doing a spoof of Robin Hood, which excited Brooks. "The first night the idea came out, I didn't sleep. I had nothing but ideas. Friar Tuck likes to eat, so I have him with a sword in one hand, a chicken in the other." After that, Brooks worked with writers John Boni and Norman Stiles to write the pilot script while he helped as an executive producer on the program in helping firm up the cast.

Dick Gautier (1931–2017) was hired for the role of Robin Hood. Gautier had previously played the semi-regular role of Hymie the Robot in *Get Smart*, but Brooks was not associated with that hire. However, he had seen Gautier on the program and felt he had great timing, and when deciding on who would play the role, agreed to Gautier being selected. That would change over time, however, as Gautier told Kliph Nesteroff in an interview in 2015: "I heard he wanted to fire me. . . . He thought that I was difficult on *When Things Were Rotten*—and I was. They wrote me a little vain and egotistical in the pilot, but they didn't know how to write me so that it was funny. Everyone else was funny and my character wasn't." Feeling the writers could not get a handle on the character, Gautier attempted to rally support to do more with Robin, but instead merely made himself look "problematic."

Certainly, the show's writers were more focused on Richard Dimitri (born 1942), who played two roles in the series thanks to the characters being identical twins: Bertram, an assistant to the Sheriff of Nottingham, and Renaldo, one of Robin Hood's merry men. Many episodes highlighted the two characters, and thus gave the actor good exposure on the program, even if it felt at times that the show focused on them more than on Robin Hood. Dimitri had previously appeared in ads Brooks had done for Bic ballpoint pens, and Brooks was proud to be able to find another showcase for the actor. "I also have the opportunity to launch an astonishing new, young actor name Rick Dimitri," Brooks stated in May 1975, "who has done nothing in films, yet." Dimitri went on to play a role in *Johnny Dangerously* and has also achieved the status of being a minor footnote in the career of Robin Williams, as Dimitri was originally hired to play the character Mork on an episode of *Happy Days*, but was replaced by Robin Williams

New Show. The comedy is wild and the gags fly like arrows in this madcap version of Robin Hood. Dick Gautier is the leader of the far-out gang in Sherwood Forest.

WHEN THINGS WERE ROTTEN
ⓐⓑⓒ **8:00PM** ⑦ ⑬

Ad for *When Things Were Rotten*, the 1975 series produced by Brooks, started off well, but slowly sinking ratings and higher-than-normal productions costs for a comedy series led to it being cancelled after only thirteen episodes were filmed.

before the episode aired due to mutual agreement between Dimitri and the program's producers.

Rounding out the cast was Misty Rowe (born 1950), who had been a regular on *Hee Haw* for four years by that time and had just completed the lead role of Marilyn Monroe in Larry Buchanan's questionable biopic *Goodbye, Norma Jean* (1975). A photograph of Rowe—one she stated in an AP interview in 1975 was "a horrible picture of me"—from the film appeared in a national magazine, which Norman Steinberg saw and asked her to come in to audition for the role of Maid Marion for Brooks, who agreed she would be good for the role.

Also in the cast were Bernie Kopell as Alan-a-Dale, Kopell having been a semi-regular on *Get Smart* in the role of the villain Siegfried; Dick Van Patten in his first role in a Brooks production as Friar Tuck; Henry Polic II (1945–2013) as the Sheriff of Nottingham, and who would later appear in Marty Feldman's *The Last Remake of Beau Geste*; David Sabin as Little John; and Ron Rifkin as Prince John. Special guest appearances were by Dudley Moore, Sid Caesar, Paul Williams, Steve Landesberg. and in the final episode, a brief cameo from Ron Glass of *Barney Miller* fame. Mel Brooks also made a brief appearance in the first episode as a guard in a suit of armor being manhandled by Little John at the party, while Marty Feldman directed one episode as well ("Those Wedding Bell Blues" with Dudley Moore). The catchy theme song to the program was done by Charles Strouse, with lyrics surprisingly not by Mel Brooks, but by Lee Adams.

Brooks had a vision for the show that would make it different from other situation comedies then airing on the networks (and still today in many ways). He described the show to Barbara Holsopple of the *Pittsburgh Press*. "The TV people's idea of a situation comedy would be to have two people talking in a closet under a naked lightbulb. You notice how most sitcoms never leave the living room and how they have one vocal explosion after another instead of physical movement? Wait until you see *When Things Were Rotten*. We'll have dozens of actors and at least six sets, including a dungeon just to bring people in and break bones. How often do you see that?" When asked how he could fit in time to work on the series with his movies happening, Brooks thought he could do it, "It won't be too much if I allocate my time right. I will devote two hours a day to examining the scripts and I have some very capable people to help me."

The first episode, which aired on September 3, 1975, at 8:00 EST, placed at #20 in the ratings for the week, which may not have been fantastic, but was deemed a good start for a new series. Unfortunately, from there, the ratings began to slip with the show at 36 by the second week, then 43 by the fourth. Michael Eisner, who was vice president in charge of programming at ABC at the time, was hinting in interviews by the fourth week of the series that the network was eyeing the show for cancellation, and by the ninth week, the show was at 55 out of 65 programs. On November 26, 1975, ABC announced it was cancelling the show, along with the program that aired after it, *That's My Momma!*, which was in its second season. (Ironically, Bernie Kopell would soon join Ted Lange from *That's My Momma!* on the successful series *The Love Boat* in 1977, while

Teddy Wilson from *That's My Momma!* went on to play Fumes in *Life Stinks* for Mel Brooks.)

Brooks would later claim that ABC cancelled the show because it was too expensive. "The ratings weren't bad," Brooks said in 2013 to the *New York Times* when the DVD collection of all thirteen episodes was being released. "We were on our way to doing 36 episodes and then someone at Paramount called and said, 'Mel, could you do it as a three-camera show?' I said, 'You mean like *I Love Lucy*? Are you crazy? Everybody said, 'I'm sorry it didn't work.' I said: 'It did work. It was just too expensive.'" Nevertheless, it is clear that ratings were very low for the program, and critical reviews were not helping, with many reviewers pointing out that that the plots were already stale after just two weeks on the air, with Robin and his men disguising themselves to mess with the sheriff, or vice versa. Oddly enough, the last few episodes began to pick up a bit as the writer started steering away from that plotline, but it was too late. In early 1976, the show was replaced by *The Bionic Woman*, giving ABC's Wednesday night lineup three action programs, with *Starsky and Hutch* and *Baretta* following *The Bionic Woman*, which led to a solid ratings lineup for the network.

The Nutt House—Aired weekly September 20–October 25, 1989, on NBC

In early 1989, Brooks contacted Alan Spencer, who as a kid had sneaked onto the set of *Young Frankenstein*, and became friends with Marty Feldman and Mel. Spencer had kept in touch with Brooks as the young man worked his way through writing for various series while in high school. Eventually he would create the crime-drama spoof series *Sledge Hammer!*, which ran from 1986 to 1988, and which many noted shared a heritage with *Get Smart*. Brooks knew Spencer was scouting around for something as a follow-up and invited him to see the sets Disney still had standing.

The main set Disney wanted to try to use was that of a costly, elegant New York hotel seen in the movie *Big Business* before tearing it down. Discussing their options, the pair came up with a goofy sitcom set within a once elegant, but now rapidly falling apart New York hotel. Soon after, they knew that inviting Harvey Korman and Cloris Leachman to star would help the project as well. "When Mel called and said he wanted to do a TV series with Harvey and me," Leachman recalled in an interview just a month before the show began to air, "he didn't have a script or a complete idea of what it was going to be about. Usually in this business you don't say yes to anything without a script, not in a million years. But this was Mel and Harvey and me; it was us. I didn't have to think once, never mind twice."

Korman was also anxious to work with Leachman and Brooks again. "The show feels right," Korman told the *Chicago Tribune*, "and we have a strong lead-in [*Night Court* had been moved from its traditional Thursday night spot in the lineup to Wednesdays that season]. If we blow the lead-in and I'm wrong about the show, then that's it—definitely. I have my four Emmys and I have my place in *Who's Who*, and that should be enough, but to tell you the truth, I need the activity."

Korman played Reginald Tarkington, the manager of the hotel, while Leachman played the head housekeeper, Ms. Frick, who was a somewhat gentler, more feminine version of her Nurse Diesel. Also on the case was Brian McNamara as Charles Nutt III, the grandson of the owner, Edwina Nutt; Molly Hagan as Sally Lonnaneck, a business representative for the hotel; Mark Blankfield as the nearly blind elevator operator; and Gregory Itzin as Dennis, the assistant manager

Brooks wrote the pilot with Spencer and then took a backseat to the proceedings, while Spencer and others tried to write in terms of how Brooks would do it. "Mel brings an ethereal presence to the set," Korman explained in an interview with the *Chicago Tribune* just as the series was beginning to air. "He is here in spirit as a shepherd. The show is part of the Mel Brooks world, which means it's crazy, unexpected and fun. Before every scene, people around here think: 'What would Mel do in this situation' and the results are crazy."

The pilot also starred Jeanette Nolan as Edwina Nutt, the owner of the hotel. However, a disastrous showing of the pilot episode that summer found the critics not even raising a chuckle, while Korman in the Q&A afterwards was repeatedly asked what it was like to be in projects with Ian Hammer that bombed. The dismal reaction led to the pilot being partially redone, and Nolan to be replaced by Cloris Leachman in aged makeup to play the same role in a more comedic fashion. The character of Edwina Nutt only appeared in the first episode and then disappeared from the series.

The revised pilot was the first episode shown and placed at #24 in the ratings, which wasn't that far from where *When Things Were Rotten* had started back in 1975, but the ratings game had changed a lot since then, and even numbers in the lower 20s could set network programmers into a panic by the late 1980s. The second episode dropped to 43 the following week, and a week's break until the third

Harvey Korman and Cloris Leachman appear together again in the short-lived 1989 series *The Nutt House*, which had its pilot episode reshot after a disastrous summer preview for critics and was cancelled by NBC before all episodes filmed were aired.

episode didn't help, with the show finally placing at 58. A jump did occur the following week, with the show reaching a high of 31 on October 18, but then it dropped again for its fifth episode on October 25, landing at 46.

On October 31, NBC announced they were cancelling the series, and they made no bones about wanting to see the show gone from their schedule. Five more episodes were still to run, but NBC simply stopped airing the program. The remaining episodes did eventually air overseas, where in the United Kingdom the show gained success, but it has never been repeated in the United States, or been made available in syndication or video as *When Things Were Rotten* and *Spaceballs: The Animated Series* had. The only way it has been seen since has been via "grey market" editions where fans had recorded the episodes off-the-air and then traded or sold them to other fans.

Fortunately, Harvey Korman was not as good as his word about the show being "it" for him if it failed. He would continue to work in television and onstage for the rest of his life, including his role in Brooks's *Dracula: Dead and Loving It*. Such an attitude reflected all involved with *The Nutt House*—working to put 100 percent of their effort into the show, but when it bombed, everyone moved on with their lives.

Spaceballs: The Animated Series—Aired November 21, 2008– March 1, 2009

Back in 1998, MGM approached Brooks with an idea to finally do *Spaceballs 2* as an animated feature. Brooks replied with a resounding "no," and that seemed to be the end of the story. However, by 2005, Brooks had agreed to create more stories within the Spaceballs universe, and in animated form. The series was first announced in *Variety* in January 2005, with Brooksfilms, MGM, and a German animation company called Berliner Films Companie (BFC), to be ready by the fall of 2006. Then it became by the fall of 2007. Finally, the series of thirteen episodes and a pilot were completed and set to air in the fall of 2008 on the cable network G4. G4 was known as a channel with programming for fans of video games, but began airing more general programming aimed at men in the 18–24 bracket.

The two-part pilot was written by Brooks with Thomas Meehan, who had worked together on the original film. The pilot was a shortened "alternate universe" retelling of the original film, with enough changes to open up the story line so a series could be made. Changes included renaming Planet Spaceballs to Planet Moron and Lone Star not being found to be a prince, while Princess Vespa decides to stay single. Subsequent episodes were parodies of various other movies, games, and television, including *Grand Theft Auto*, *Lord of the Rings*, *Jurassic Park*, *Harry Potter*, and *Spider-Man*. None of these episodes, however, were written by Brooks.

Brooks did the voices of President Skroob and Yogurt, while Daphne Zuniga and Joan Rivers reprised their roles of Vespa and Dot Matrix. No other member of the original cast was involved. Animation was a flash-style that was popular for many of the "mature audience" animated shows that were appearing on the Cartoon Network, and the writing was obviously geared to that style as well, with bizarre plot twists, long stretches of dead air, and abrupt endings to the stories. All episodes were eventually released on DVD in 2004, while the repeats of the program stopped airing on G4 in 2009.

Brooks's attempts to get back into television as a producer did not lead to the success he had hoped. Yet, strangely enough, he would soon find success in another manner—as an actor. This opened up a revue for his work just as it appeared his movie and producing career was about to end, as will be seen in the next chapter.

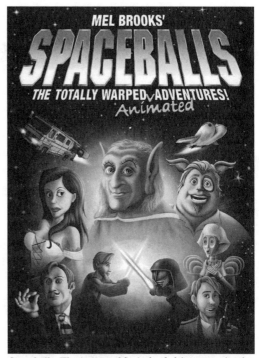

Spaceballs: The Animated Series had thirteen episodes and a pilot made and aired on the G4 cable network in 2008–2009. The series featured the voices of Mel Brooks, Joan Rivers, and Daphne Zuniga, and the pilot was written by Brooks with *Spaceballs* cowriter Thomas Meehan.

22

You Be What's-His-Face

Guest Appearances

A s we can see, Mel Brooks is obviously a performer as well as a writer, director, and producer. It's how he started in the Catskills, and it's part of how he made his living in the 1960s with appearances on talk shows as well as in performance as the 2000 Year Old Man. When he began appearing in his films, at first out of necessity, and then . . . well, because it made sense, many critical reviews mentioned that Brooks was surprisingly good as an actor, which meant that you couldn't keep him away from getting in front of a camera if you tried. Below is a list of appearances outside of his own films over the years.

On-Screen Appearances

When Things Were Rotten: "The Capture of Robin Hood": Aired September 10, 1975, on ABC

Brooks appears in an uncredited cameo as a guard at Prince John's party who is manhandled by Little John.

Peeping Times: Aired January 25, 1978, on NBC

Brooks appeared in this pilot written and directed by Rudy De Luca and Barry Levinson, who were his cowriters on *Silent Movie* and *High Anxiety*. The program was a parody of television news shows, and featured fellow Brooks alumni Ron Carey. Brooks appears as Hitler in "home movies" supposedly just discovered. Instead of gritty details of the madman, as one would expect, the footage shows a goofy Hitler dancing and doing as many of us do when being filmed in such home movies. The segment is undoubtedly the longest sketch featuring Brooks as Hitler outside of the "Hitler Rap" video he did for *To Be or Not to Be*. The portions of the sketch with Brooks are featured on the Shout! Factory DVD boxset, *The Incredible Mel Brooks*.

The Muppet Movie: Released June 22, 1979, by Associated Film Distribution

Brooks has a brief role in the film as a mad scientist, Professor Max Krassman, who gets beaten up by Miss Piggy. Also featured in the film were some Brooks associates: Dom DeLuise, Madeline Kahn, Cloris Leachman, Charles Durning, and Richard Pryor.

The Tracey Ullman Show: "Due Diligence": Aired February 4, 1990, on Fox

Brooks plays Buzz Schlanger in this sketch from Tracey Ullman's first variety series in the United States. The sketch can be found on the Shout! Factory *The Incredible Mel Brooks* boxset.

Mickey's Audition: Released 1992 by Disney

A five-minute film made for the Disney-MGM Studios. Brooks appears as a movie director.

The Silence of the Hams: Released March 11, 1994, by October Films

Brooks appears about midway through this Italian-American production that parodies both *Silence of the Lambs* and *Psycho*. The film was written and directed by Italian comedian Ezio Greggio, who appears briefly in *Dracula: Dead and Loving It* as the coach driver, and would give Brooks a starring role in his film *Screw Loose*. Other Brooks alumni in this film were Dom DeLuise and Stuart Pankin.

The Little Rascals: Released August 5, 1994, by Universal Pictures

Brooks appears as Mr. Welling, a bank teller who instantly sees through the disguise of the kids when trying to get a loan.

Mad About You: "The Grant," "The Penis," "Uncle Phil and the Coupons," and "Uncle Phil Goes Back to High School"

This sitcom lasted for seven seasons on NBC (1992–1999) and centered around the romance of two people, played by Paul Reiser and Helen Hunt. Brooks appeared in four episodes as Uncle Phil, beginning in 1996 with the episode "The Grant," which aired on September 24, 1996. Uncle Phil is cantankerous and a bit crazed, with his hair seemingly always out of place.

The appearance went over so well, with strong critical praise for his performance, that Brooks was invited back the same season to appear in the episode "The Penis," which aired on February 11, 1997. His performance in that episode won him an Emmy for Outstanding Guest Actor in a Comedy Series, making it the first Emmy Award he had won for acting rather than writing (he had won previously for his writing on *The Sid Caesar, Imogene Coca, Carl Reiner, Howard Morris Special* in 1967).

Brooks returned in the following season in the episode "Uncle Phil and the Coupons," which aired on November 4, 1997, and won him a second Emmy. He appeared one last time, and won one final Emmy Award in 1999 for the role of Uncle Phil in the episode "Uncle Phil Goes Back to High School."

Screw Loose: Released February 19, 1999, in Italy through Wolf Pictures. Distributed on video in the United States by Columbia TriStar Home Video

This comedy, written by Rudy De Luca and Steve Haberman, was made in both Italy and America and directed by Ezio Greggio. Greggio stars as a man who is instructed by his rich, dying industrialist father to find the American who saved his life during World War II, Jake Gordon (Mel Brooks). Gordon, it turns out, has been in a sanitarium for decades. Greggio manages to break Gordon out of the asylum, but then loses him on the way back to Milan, where his father is. The film deals with Greggio's character trying to track down Gordon, while also being followed by the woman head of the sanitarium who wants Gordon back.

Brooks is not the lead, but does get plenty of screen time, allowing him to simply act for the second time in a film (after *To Be or Not to Be*). Little seen in the United States, *Screw Loose* is not up to the level of a Brooks film, but still of interest to fans of his.

Up at the Villa: Released May 5, 2000, by October Films

This movie, based on W. Somerset Maugham's 1941 novella of the same name, featured Anne Bancroft in a major role. Brooks cameos as the Train Station Man.

Sex, Lies and Video Violence: Released on video May 5, 2000, in Sweden. Never released in the United States.

This low-budget homage to violent movies features Brooks in a cameo as a "stressed old man." The movie is known for being the last appearance of Brandon Lee on film before his death while filming *The Crow*.

Curb Your Enthusiasm: "Brooks's Offer," "The Blind Date," "The Surrogate," and "Opening Night": Aired January 4–March 14, 2004

This HBO comedy series is a "fly on the wall" look at the life of a character who is a writer and actor named Larry David, played by writer-actor Larry David. In the fourth season opener, "Brooks's Offer," David signs on to replace Nathan

Lane in the Broadway production of *The Producers*. The season has various story lines running through the episodes, but the main thread is that of David getting ready to appear on Broadway.

As it turns out, he is horrible in the role, but the audience thinks it is planned that way and enjoys the show, saying that *The Producers* will run for years to come thanks to David. Mel Brooks and Anne Bancroft play themselves, and the season finale ends with them looking miserable about the news of David's success, as they had hoped David would be a flop and thus end the production that had trapped them in New York for so many years. It would be the last appearance of Brooks and Bancroft together before her death in 2005.

The Comedians, "Celebrity Guest": Aired April 30, 2015, on FX cable network

Brooks makes an appearance as himself in this situation comedy starring Billy Crystal and Josh Gad, where he attempts to give some guidance to Billy as to what needs to be done with the television show he is making with Josh.

Voice Actor

Brooks has also done voice work in several television shows and movies over the years:

- *Free to Be . . . You & Me* (1974)—Voice of newborn boy
- *The Adventure of Sherlock Holmes' Smarter Brother* (1975)—Offscreen voice of Bruner
- *The Electric Company* (1971–1977)—Voice of the Blond-Haired Cartoon Man, looking at words and sentence structure
- *Looks Who's Talking Too* (1990)—Voice of Mr. Toilet Man
- *Frasier* (1993)—Voice of Tom, in the episode "Miracle on Third or Fourth Street"
- *The Simpsons* (1995)—Voice of himself in the episode "Homer vs. Patty and Selma"
- *The Prince of Egypt* (1998)—Uncredited voice work
- *The Kids from Room 402* (2000)—Voice of Mr. Miller in the episode "Squeezed Out"
- *It's a Very Merry Muppet Christmas Movie* (2002)—Voice of Joe Snow
- *The Adventures of Jimmy Neutron: Boy Genius* (2003)—Voice of Santa Claus in the episode "Holly Jolly Jimmy"
- *Robots* (2005)—Voice of Bigweld in this computer-animated feature film
- *The Producers* (2005)—Voice of Hilda the Pigeon and Tom the Cat
- *Jakers! The Adventures of Piggley Winks* (2003–2007)—Voice of Wiley the Sheep
- *Spaceballs: The Animated Series* (2008–2009)—Voice of President Skroob and Yogurt
- *Ruby's Studio: The Feelings Show* (2010)—Voice of Sally Simon Simmons

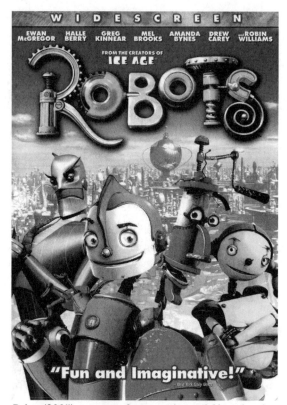

Robots (2005) was one of many animated films that features the vocal talents of Mel Brooks.

- *Glen Martin DDS* (2010)—Voice of Canine in the episode "A very Martin Christmas"
- *Special Agent Oso* (2011)—Voice of Grandpa Mel in the episode "On Old MacDonald's Special Song"
- *The Paul Reiser Show* (2011)—Voice of the Angry Cat in the episode "The Playdate"
- *Mr. Peabody & Sherman* (2014)—Voice of Albert Einstein
- *Dora the Explorer* (2014)—Voice of the Mad Hatter in the episode "Dora in Wonderland"
- *Hotel Transylvania 2* (2015)—Voice of Vlad
- *The Guardian Brothers* (2016)—Voice of Rogman in English version of the film
- *Leap!* (2016)—Voice of character in film
- *Blazing Samurai* (2017)—Voice of Shogun

23

King of Broadway

M el Brooks was inspired as a nine-year-old when he sat in the cheap seats and saw Ethel Merman in *Anything Goes*. It made him what he would become—all of his films are musicals in disguise, with characters bursting into song and/or dancing, as shown in the previous chapters of this book. Even his silent movie couldn't avoid three dance numbers in it, as well as a chance for him to dance with his wife on camera.

When Brooks had the opportunity to write the books for Broadway shows in the 1950s and early 1960s, it no doubt felt like a fulfillment of a dream: here he was on Broadway, helping to create musical-comedy magic. Yet in each case, something would occur that led to the productions not lasting long or bombing. As anyone would do, once you beat your head against a door that doesn't open enough times, you realize it is time to find one that will open for you elsewhere. Movies became that outlet and gave Brooks the opportunity to do musical theater in a fashion. By doing so, there was no need to ever look back. In 1975, Brooks had washed his hands of Broadway, as he told the *New York Times*: "If I wanted to do something unexpected, I'd do it so it wouldn't cost anything. If I write a somber comedy—not 'don't like this joke, wait ten seconds'—I'd do it as an experiment, off-Broadway, so it wouldn't have to have yoks."

Then the movie culture changed, and Brooks found by the mid-1990s that the type of films he wanted to make, even the serious ones he wanted to produce through Brooksfilms, were not what the studios and even the audiences were wanting, as seen in previous chapters. More frustrating was that Brooks never was short of new ideas and promising movie options, but the ticket buyers, or rather the studios feeding the ticket buyers, didn't want what he was selling.

Then Broadway suddenly came knocking again.

The Producers (2001–2007) at the St. James Theatre, April 19, 2001–April 22, 2007

It was easy to see why people would want to turn *The Producers* into a Broadway musical. People in show business love nothing better than to tell audiences why they love show business, even if it means doing a show that mocks that business. And since the 1967 movie already featured some musical numbers, as well as becoming a cult film that many potential audience members have seen at some point, who wouldn't want to try to bring it to the Great White Way?

Well, Mel Brooks was one person that didn't want to do it. Previous attempts to talk him into turning it into a musical had gone nowhere. The first attempt was by drummer Keith Moon of the Who, who had tried through Marty, only for Brooks to shrug it off. Brooks stated in the "making of" book about the musical, *The Producers: The Book, Lyrics, and Story Behind the Biggest Hit in Broadway History!—How We Did It*, that he was also once approached by producer Alexander Cohen (*Hellzapoppin'* with Jerry Lewis, *I Remember Mama* with Liv Ullmann) about making it into a musical. He ignored that suggestion as well.

In the spring of 1998, Brooks received several calls from David Geffen, a businessman who has worked in film and music, along with producing such Broadway blockbusters as *Cats* and *Dreamgirls*. Brooks was still adamant that it would make for a terrible musical, but Geffen persisted and Brooks began to buckle. Brooks suggested that he would consider the project if he could write the score. Geffen, however, told him that he already had been in contact with songwriter Jerry Herman (*Hello, Dolly!*, *Mame*, *La Cage aux Folles*), and Brooks agreed to at least hear Herman out on what he thought would work for the show.

Herman, on the other hand, didn't agree with Geffen; to him, the show already had two songs that would transfer from the movie, "Springtime for Hitler" and "Prisoners of Love," and audiences would be disappointed if those two songs didn't appear in the new show. Both had been written by Brooks for the 1967 film, and Herman felt that if Brooks could come up with a handful more, there was no need for him to be there. Geffen was hesitant, but felt if Herman thought Brooks could do it, then he was willing to at least give him a try.

The Broadway Cast album cover for *The Producers*, using a shot of Nathan Lane and Matthew Broderick that also appeared on the *Playbill* for the Broadway show. The show was considered a risk but would end up winning twelve Tony Awards.

Later that summer, Brooks met up with Tom Meehan, who had cowritten *To Be or Not to Be* and *Spaceballs*, as well as penning the book for the Broadway smash *Annie* back in the 1970s. They actually met to discuss *Spaceballs 2*, but when that project quickly fizzled out, Brooks asked Meehan if he would help write the book for the proposed *Producers* musical. Meehan agreed, and he soon suggested that Brooks talk to Mike Ockrent (1946–1999) as a possible director for the show. Ockrent in 1992 had directed the popular backstage musical comedy *Crazy for You*, based on several George Gershwin songs, and met choreographer Susan Stroman on the show. They began to date and would marry in 1996. Stroman, who had been working as a choreographer on Broadway for a few years, had also begun directing, doing a revival of *The Music Man* in 2000. As both Ockrent and Stroman were considered two of the biggest talents in Broadway musicals at the time, getting them for *The Producers* was a coup in many ways.

Ockrent also helped by suggesting they bring in Glen Kelly, who had been a musical arranger on the Broadway version of *Beauty and the Beast*. After *The Producers*, he would perform the same duties on *Spamalot* and *Book of Mormon*, amongst others. Kelly would listen to Brooks's ideas for songs along with his lyrics, and then transform them into the finished score. The songs used in *The Producers* were:

- "Opening Night"—Sung by audience leaving Max's latest show, *Funny Boy* (his musical comedy version of *Hamlet*). Originally, *The Producers* was to open with the staging of a musical number from Max's latest show called *Hey, Nebraska!* The song, a parody of "Oklahoma!," was deemed too much like something from an off-Broadway revue, and instead Brooks wrote "Opening Night," which better demonstrates how Max is a laughingstock of Broadway.
- "The King of Broadway"—Sung by Max after seeing the terrible reviews for *Funny Boy*. This production number was filmed but then cut from the 2005 movie adaption. It appears as an extra on the DVD.
- "We Can Do It"—Sung by Max and Leo, with Max trying to convince Leo to join him in the scheme to defraud the little old ladies. The film adaptation opens the number so that most of it occurs out in the streets and the park, and is reprised after the next number.
- "I Wanna Be a Producer"—Sung by Leo at the accounting firm.
- "In Old Bavaria"—Franz's first song, with a choir of pigeons. This too was filmed for the movie, but then edited out. It is included in the extras on the DVD.
- "Der Guten Tag Hop Clop"—Franz, with Max and Leo. This production number created some initial concerns, as covered in Jeffry Denman's book *A Year with The Producers*, as some in the cast and crew felt the number slowed the show down. It was retooled a bit and never left the show, however.
- "Keep It Gay"—Sung by Roger, Carmen, and ensemble in Roger's living room when discussing how to make the show a hit.
- "When You Got It, Flaunt It"—Sung by Ulla as she visits the office of Max and Leo. It is her introduction in the show and evidence that the musical will give her more to do than in the 1967 movie.
- "Along Came Bialy"—Sung by the ensemble as little old ladies. There was much more to this number, which was trimmed several times as the musical began running in previews. The version in the film adaptation is shorter than in the Broadway show as well, losing moments between verses where Max is playing up to some of the women. Some of these antics can be found in the deleted scenes on the DVD as well.

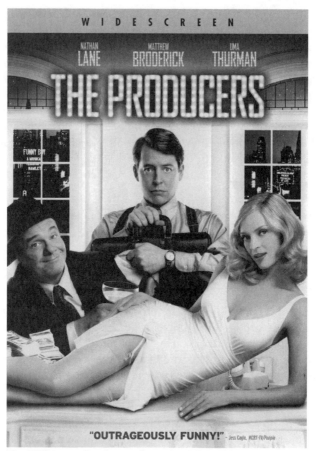

The DVD cover for the movie version of the Broadway version of the movie, *The Producers*. The film was an attempt to bring the Broadway show to the screen intact, and comes close to achieving that feat.

- "Act One Finale"—Typical first act mash-up of several songs before the intermission sung by nearly the whole cast. This number is missing from the movie adaptation.
- "That Face"—The first number in the second act, sung by Leo about Ulla.
- "Haben Sie Gehoert das Deutsche Band?"—It's "Have You Heard the German Band?" and was briefly featured in the 1967 movie. In the Broadway show (and later film adaptation), it is done to completion by Franz, which leads to him being signed to play Hitler.
- "You Never Say 'Good Luck' on Opening Night"—Sung by Franz, Roger, Carmen, and Leo when Leo accidentally wishes everyone "Good Luck" on opening night.

- "Springtime for Hitler"—The song, of course, originates from the 1967 film, but has been extended to include Roger as Hitler singing a song within the song ("Heil Myself!") before it goes back to a final portion of "Springtime for Hitler." The Broadway musical also included a segment where Hitler has a dance-off against Stalin, Churchill, and Roosevelt, which never quite came off and at one point was dropped from the show. The dance-off is missing from the film adaptation.
- "Where Did We Go Right?"—Sung by Max and Leo after the reviews start to come in praising the show. It is missing from the film adaptation.
- "Betrayed"—Sung by Max in jail. Brooks had originally written a song called "Goodbye to Broadway," but Stroman and Lane both felt the song was too downbeat. Brooks wrote "Betrayed" to replace it. In the film adaptation, there is also a bit of a song called "You'll Find Your Happiness in Rio" while Leo and Ulla are dancing in Rio. This song was originally to appear in the Broadway show, but was deemed to be taking too much time near the end of the show and did not add anything.
- "Til Him"—Sung by Leo, Max, and the ensemble at the trial.
- "Prisoners of Love"—Song by all as the new show by Max and Leo moves to Broadway.
- "Leo and Max"—Sung by Max and Leo.
- "Goodbye!"—Sung by all after the bows are taken for *The Producers*, effectively telling the audience that the show is over and they need to "get out!"

Things were going smoothly for the production, but then Mike Ockrent died in December 1999 from leukemia. At first, it appeared the production was going to have to go on without Susan Stroman, who didn't think she could continue with the show and felt if she dropped out, the production could find someone else and move ahead. Brooks and the other principals involved disagreed, however, feeling that the best thing for her would be to not only choreograph the show, but also direct. After a time thinking it over, she decided to stay on.

None of this was happening in secret by this point—Brooks had been talking up the production since April 1999, at first referring to the proposed musical by its original title of *Springtime for Hitler*, but quickly switching back to the movie's title, which is how most people knew the work. In May 1999, rumors were filtering through news reports that Nathan Lane was being wined and dined for the role of Max Bialystock. Lane had seen success on Broadway for quite a while by that point, having played "Max Prince" (the Sid Caesar role) in Neil Simon's *Laughter on the 23rd Floor* in 1993 and picking up a Tony Award for the role of Pseudolus (the same role Zero Mostel had played) in a 1995 Broadway revival of *A Funny Thing Happened on the Way to the Forum*. Yet, as the rumor continued on for month, Lane refused to publicly commit to the role.

On March 2, 2000, Nathan Lane was guest-hosting *The Late Show with David Letterman* (Letterman was recovering from a heart attack at the time), and Mel Brooks was a guest on the program. At one point in the interview, Brooks pulled out a contract from his pants (much like how Bart pulled out paperwork in *Blazing Saddles*) and told the audience that it was a contract for Lane to sign to commit him to *The Producers*. Lane laughed it off, but the on-air prank pretty much put to rest that Lane would be part of the show. In the interview, Brooks stated that he couldn't wait for the show to get started with Lane as Max and Martin Short as Leo Bloom.

Yes, about that whole Martin Short thing. Short was of course a known performer at the time and had been on Broadway a few times in the past, including a starring role in the musical version of Neil Simon's *The Goodbye Girl* with Bernadette Peters in 1993. Short, however, bowed out due to not wanting to commit to the length of time needed for the show, although he would go on to play the role in the Los Angeles production that ran from May 2003 through January 2004 and costarred Jason Alexander as Max. Instead, with Short out of the picture, Matthew Broderick (born 1962), who had already won two Tony Awards—for *Brighton Beach Memoirs* (1983) and *How to Succeed in Business Without Really Trying* (1995)—agreed to take on the role.

Joining the cast was Gary Beach (born 1947), who had played Lumiere in the original Broadway production of *Beauty and the Beast*, as director Roger De Bris (born 1962); Roger Bart, who would later play the Leo Bloom role after Matthew Broderick left the show and would eventually play Frederick Frankenstein in the Broadway production of *Young Frankenstein*, as Carmen Ghia; Cady Huffman (born 1965) as Ulla; and Brad Oscar (born 1964) as Franz Liebkind, after Ron Orbach had to leave the production due to a knee injury while rehearsing the role. Brad Oscar would eventually take over the role of Max on Broadway for a time after Nathan Lane left as well.

The musical version of the story is very similar to that of the movie, with a few exceptions:

- The musical is set in 1959, whereas the movie was set in the "present year" of 1967.
- The amount of money to be raised is $2 million in the musical, instead of only $1 million in the movie.
- Ulla is one of the main characters in the movie, whereas in the movie she is just the punch line to a couple of gags.
- De Bris does not live with a group of men in the movie.
- The tryouts for Hitler in the musical ends with Franz being picked to play Hitler. In the film, a whacked-out hippie-type named LSD gets the role.
- In the musical, De Bris ends up playing Hitler and wins over the audience with his camp version. In the movie, LSD wins over the audience by playing Hitler as a silly, but hip, beatnik.
- In the musical, Leo and Ulla head to Rio, while Max goes on trial. In the movie, Max and Leo go on trial together after a botched attempt to blow up the theater.

- The musical plays out *Prisoners of Love* as being a Broadway smash. In the film, it is just a dinky little production being put together for the prison.

The musical also has many homages to Brooks's other films besides *The Producers*:

- One character in "The King of Broadway" number states "It's good to be the king"—*History of the World, Part I*
- Franz saying, "What nice guys" at the door—*Blazing Saddles*
- Carmen saying "Yesssssssssssss."—*The Producers* as well as *Blazing Saddles*
- Max asking the jailer, "Why am I asking you?" (only in the film version of the musical)—*Blazing Saddles*
- "Yes, it's nece!"—*High Anxiety* (and based on a bit in *Blazing Saddles*)
- "Break a leg" leading to Franz actually breaking a leg—*To Be or Not to Be*
- "Heil myself."—*To Be or Not to Be*
- "Walk this way"—*Young Frankenstein* and *Robin Hood: Men in Tights*
- "What Booth did to Lincoln" in "Opening Night"—a variation of a line in *To Be or Not to Be*
- Franz demanding a "key change!"—*High Anxiety*
- "Death of a Salesman on Ice" on a marquee—a variation of "Hitler on Ice" from *History of the World, Part I*

Tryouts for the show were done at the Cadillac Palace in Chicago from February 1 through 25, 2001, with the cast then moved to the St. James Theatre in New York, with the first preview on March 21, 2001. The show would have its official opening night on April 19, 2001, and continue at the St. James until April 22, 2007, a full six-year run for the musical and a total of 2,502 performances.

The Producers was nominated for fifteen Tony Awards that year, and won in twelve categories—a record number of wins for a production on Broadway. The awards were for:

- Best Musical
- Best Book of a Musical—Mel Brooks and Thomas Meehan
- Best Original Score—Mel Brooks
- Best Performance by a Leading Actor in a Musical—Nathan Lane, with Matthew Broderick being nominated
- Best Performance by a Featured Actor in a Musical—Gary Beach, with Roger Bart and Brad Oscar also being nominated.
- Best Performance by a Featured Actress in a Musical—Cady Huffman
- Best Direction of a Musical—Susan Stroman
- Best Choreography—Susan Stroman
- Best Orchestrations—Doug Besterman
- Best Scene Design—Robin Wagner
- Best Costume Design—William Ivey Long
- Best Lighting Design—Peter Kaczorowski

The musical also won ten Drama Desk Awards for many of the same catego-ries, and later would win three Laurence Olivier Awards for the 2005 London production: Best New Musical, Best Actor in a Musical for Nathan Lane, and Best Performance in a Supporting Role in a Musical for Conieth Hill in the role of Roger De Bris.

Lane and Broderick would remain with the production until March 17, 2002, when they were replaced by British actor Henry Goodman as Max and Steve Weber (who had been in Brooks's *Dracula: Dead and Loving It*) as Leo. In a surprising move, Goodman was released from the show after four weeks and thirty performances and Brad Oscar was moved up from the role of Franz to that of Max. Oscar would also play Max in a subsequent U.S. tour in 2003. When sales began to lag in 2003, Lane and Broderick returned from December 2003 through April 2004 in their roles.

The show moved to the West End in London on November 2004 and con-tinued until January 6, 2007, with 920 performances. The show was originally to feature Richard Dreyfuss as Max, but he left the production four days before the first previews, and Nathan Lane agreed to step in to save the show from having to delay its opening. Lane was eventually replaced by Brad Oscar and others after him.

Other productions were done around the United States, with two national tours between 2002 and 2005, as well as the Los Angeles production in May 2003 through January 2004 starring Jason Alexander as Max and Martin Short as Leo. There was also an abridged version of the musical that played in Las Vegas from 2007 through 2008 with Brad Oscar as Max, Larry Raben as Leo, and David Hasselhoff as Roger De Bris (Oscar later left the production and was replaced by Tony Danza).

Since that time there have been various professional and amateur pro-ductions of *The Producers* up to the present date, proving the longevity of the material. In 2005, a movie adaptation of the Broadway musical was done with Susan Stroman directing most of the original cast, with exception of two, Brad Oscar and Cady Huffman. Brad Oscar was unavailable, although he appears briefly in one scene as a taxi driver, and was replaced by Will Ferrell as Franz. Cady Huffman was replaced by Uma Thurman in the role of Ulla after Nicole Kidman turned down the role.

As stated in the documentary on the DVD, Brooks requested that the movie look as much like the Broadway show as possible, and for the most part everyone on the film gave him exactly what he wanted there. Except for a couple of edits listed above with the songs, and one additional scene of Max and Leo singing a brief bit of a song about Rio in a bar that was cut from the film, audiences watching the movie got a 100-proof version of the show. Which may explain why many critics and audience members had issues with the film adaptation, as none of the performances are toned down from the stage—where you're vocally and physically projecting to the back wall of the theater—for the big screen—where everyone is a couple of stories tall. Nearly everyone gives an over-the-top performance in the film, with Lane almost like a live-action cartoon character at times. Fortunately for him, Max is an over-the-top character anyway, so he gets away with it . . . barely, but he gets away with it. That same factor saves Gary Beach as Roger De Bris, while Uma Thurman is more toned down for the camera anyway. It is really only Broderick's performance that seems a bit off at first, but once the show gets away from him having to play "Matthew Broderick as Gene Wilder as Leo Bloom"—especially in the first scene—Broderick settles nicely into the role for the film.

Yet, although the performances are a bit too strong at times, fans of the Broadway production will no doubt feel Brooks was right in wanting what is essentially the Broadway show on film, and if you can step back a bit from the screen—as most people can when watching on video—the film plays better than in a movie theater. Sure, a couple of the jokes don't quite play as well—Ulla painting the office during the Intermission is a much better gag for the show than her having done it during her lunch break in the film, for example; and it's a shame to lose "King of Broadway"—but most of the gags with minor variations do work.

Brooks was to have taken a more active role in helping with the film, but with the death of Anne Bancroft, left most of the work to Stroman, who did a good job in visualizing the look of a Broadway show on film. Perhaps the film did not do well at the box office, but the end result of a big movie was never the initial intentions of the musical anyway, so most who worked on it were satisfied with the results. If nothing else, as the signs in 2006 were showing that *The Producers* was soon to end its run on Broadway, Mel Brooks was beginning to think that perhaps there was a chance to do another.

Young Frankenstein (2007–2009) at the Hilton Theatre from November 8, 2007, through January 4, 2009

Although Brooks began discussing the idea of turning *Young Frankenstein* into a Broadway musical in earnest in 2006, he was already pushing the idea of doing it back in June 2001, with Susan Stroman confirming they were discussing the prospects of such a production. Brooks didn't see a reason to change anything, and began working with Tom Meehan on the book for the show as well as creating new music. By March 2004, Meehan reported to *Variety* that the first act of the musical for *Young Frankenstein* had been completed, although there was no word at the time when such a production would be ready to roll.

In February 2007, Stroman was signed on to direct and choreograph the musical, which at first was to even be in the same theater immediately after *The Producers* closed in April that year, but it instead was moved over to the Hilton Theatre (today known as the Lyric Theatre) when expectations for the show were downsided after a so-so response to the production in tryouts. A table

Mel Brooks's follow-up on Broadway was a musical adaptation of *Young Frankenstein*. It would struggle on Broadway, but continues to be restaged in community productions throughout the world.

reading of the completed book in October 2006 featured Cloris Leachman as Frau Blücher (neigh!), along with Brian d'Arcy James as Frederick Frankenstein, Kristin Chenoweth as Elizabeth, Sutton Foster as Inga, Marc Kudisch as Inspector Kemp, Shuler Hensley as the Monster, and Roger Bart, a holdover from *The Producers*, as Igor.

Leachman for a time thought she would reprise her role from the film in the new Broadway musical, but in January 2007 was told that the producers had decided to keep the movie and the musical separate in people's minds, as well as Brooks being concerned if Leachman at her age could handle the rigors of a Broadway show (her later appearance on *Dancing with the Stars*, displaying her agility and strength, proved them wrong, and she was later asked to join the cast in the role, but the show ended its run before she could do so).

Tryouts were performed between August 7 (originally to have started August 4) and September 1 at the Paramount Theater in Seattle, Washington. The cast for opening night featured Roger Bart moving up to the role of Frederick Frankenstein, with Megan Mullally as Elizabeth, Christopher Fitzgerald as Igor, Sutton Foster as Inga, Shuler Hensley as the Monster, Fred Applegate as Inspector Kemp, and Andrea Martin as Blücher (neigh!). The plot of the musical is much like that of the film it is based on, with some exceptions, although much of it is song, making *Young Frankenstein* at times play more like an opera than a musical.

There are some minor changes to the plot between the film and the musical:

- The audience is first introduced to the villagers after the death of Von Frankenstein instead of later as in the film.
- Frederick finds out about Frau Blücher (neigh!) and his grandfather being an item much earlier in the musical than in the film.
- No digging of a grave for a body in the musical as in the film.
- When Inspector Kemp arrives to talk to Frederick, he arrives with a group of villagers with him in the musical, instead of alone as in the film.
- Elizabeth arrives unexpectedly at the castle in the film. She arrives with an entourage in the musical.
- Frederick and the others capture the Monster at the Hermit's hut in the musical.
- The Monster takes off with Elizabeth at the theater where he has just performed "Puttin' on the Ritz."
- Elizabeth is assumed dead, as is the Monster when it appears the transference has not worked. The villagers take Frederick away and execute him, only for the Monster to arrive and save Frederick. Elizabeth then arrives and the Monster admits his love for Elizabeth to Frederick and Frederick and Inga pair off as well.
- The musical ends with a surprise appearance of another character who wants to buy a castle, but Frederick refuses, as he plans to go into the family business instead.

As mentioned, the production has many, many songs:

- "The Happiest Town in Town"—by the Villagers after the elder Frankenstein's death
- "(There is Nothing Like) The Brain"—Frederick and his medical students
- "Please Don't Touch Me"—Elizabeth and ensemble as she sees Frederick off on his trip
- "Together Again"—Igor and a reluctant Frederick discuss going into the family business together when they meet
- "Roll in the Hay"—Inga, Igor, and Frederick on their way to the castle
- "Join the Family Business"—Frederick's nightmare
- "He Vas My Boyfriend"—Frau Blücher (neigh!)

- "Life, Life"—Frederick, Inga, Igor, Frau Blücher (neigh!), and ensemble
- "The Law"—The Villagers deciding to check in on Frederick
- "Welcome to Transylvania"—Kemp and Villagers
- "Transylvania Mania"—Igor, Monster, Frederick, Inga, and Villagers.
- "He's Loose"—Villagers, Igor, and Kemp
- "Listen to Your Heart"—Inga
- "Surprise"—Elizabeth, Frau Blücher (neigh!), Igor, and Entourage
- "Please Send Me Someone"—Hermit
- "Man About Town"—Frederick to the Monster
- "Puttin' On the Ritz"—Monster, Frederick, Igor, and Inga
- "Sweet Mystery of Life"—Elizabeth
- "Deep Love"—Elizabeth
- "Hang the Doctor"—Villagers and Kemp
- "Finale Ultimo"—All
- "Together Again" (Reprise)—All, ending the show by sending the audience on their way, along with a hint that "maybe next year *Blazing Saddles!*"

Critical reviews of the show were mixed, with some reviewers saying the score felt rushed and the story not as entertaining for a Broadway audience as *The Producers* had been. Audience response was also lower than for *The Producers*, which was not helped by having huge cross-over stars opening the show as it had with the earlier production. No doubt as well that Brooks and company deciding not to report box-office returns gave the impression of a show knowing it was in trouble rather than a show trying to be frank about its finances. The show was nominated for three Tony Awards in 2008—Christopher Fitzgerald for Best Featured Actor in a Musical, Andrea Martin for Best Featured Actress in a Musical, and Robin Wagner for Best Scenic Design of a Musical—but did not win in any categories. The show moved along with some minor tinkering on the book, and did last over a year on Broadway, but soon petered out. A national tour followed in 2009, and then another in 2011, and then began to make the rounds to community theater.

The show was not a failure, but in comparison to the massive success of *The Producers* it was hard to not feel that things did not gel as they should have with the show. Brooks has admitted that more fixing was needed on the show and in 2017 announced that he and Tom Meehan had been tinkering with the book and reworking some of the music with Glen Kelly for a West End production of the show initially slated for August 2017. With Susan Stroman returning to direct and choreograph, the revised version of the musical debuted on October 10, 2017 at the Garrick Theatre, with Hadley Fraser as Frederick Frankenstein, Summer Strallen as Inga, Ross Noble as Igor, Lesley Joseph as Frau Blucher, and Shuler Hensley returning from the earlier Broadway production as the monster. Four songs were cut from the show and two new songs, "It Could Work" and "Hang Him Till He's Dead" were added. The revised version of the musical would receive glowing response from the critics, proving that Brooks still could produce new material.

Once it is in your blood it is hard to give it up, especially as the success of *The Producers* helped revive the state of musical comedy on Broadway. "I think I'm the father of *Spamalot* and *Book of Mormon* [on Broadway]," Brooks reflected in a 2013 interview with CNN. "Because for twenty years Broadway was serious. . . . So when David Geffen bothered me morning, noon and night to make a musical of *The Producers*, 'I said, 'No, no, no, no, yes.' And I did it and part of why I did it was my duty to bring back the musical comedy."

As for the idea of *Blazing Saddles*? "I like the music in *Blazing Saddles*, and I think it would make a good musical. It already has two or three musical numbers, so I'm thinking, maybe."

And with a revised *Young Frankenstein* being warmly received after Mel Brooks has reached the age of ninety-one. Just goes to show that creativity can never be stopped when you've got something to say.

24

To Be or Not to Be

Projects Abandoned

E veryone at one time or another has a project planned at their work that is cancelled for one reason or another, and the same holds true for people in the entertainment business. Usually, it's an announcement in one of the entertainment papers, like *Variety*, stating "this actor" or "that director" is going to be in a film or star in a television series and it just doesn't happen. For example, in 1974, the pages of *Variety* announced over a period of weeks that Dan Dailey was to costar in *Blazing Saddles* . . . then Gig Young . . . and finally Gene Wilder—that's just how it goes sometimes in Hollywood.

This is true of Mel Brooks as well. More importantly, with Brooks being interviewed often through the years, he has shown an impulse to sometimes blurt out ideas, concepts, and even ongoing negotiations for projects that simply never were done. Listed in this chapter are some of the more well-known projects that had been mentioned either to be done by Brooks or to have had the participation of Brooks in some fashion beyond that of Brooksfilms, which is covered in chapter 20.

Marriage Is a Dirty Rotten Fraud (1962–1966)

Brooks discussed *Marriage Is a Dirty Rotten Fraud* for many years in the 1960s, having finished the script around 1962. *Variety* announced on August 27, 1965, that a film was set to be made as a "joint venture of Blackhill and Brooks's company." Although he would heavily push the script, little was known about the plot beyond being based on his own concerns over alimony payments to his first wife. In December 1965, Brooks did go so far as to say in an interview with the *Montreal Gazette*, "It's a comedy which says, whether you know it or not, you marry for societycal reasons," which is not only nonsensical; as there is no such word as societycal; but doesn't really tell much about the script's plot. It is known that a copy of Brooks's script resides in the Terry Southern archive at the New York Public Library, so there is proof of a script being written and not just Brooks feeling his way through the plot when interviewed about it. Brooks finally gave more details about it in 2013 to CNN: "It's about a guy who gets divorced and the only way out of his big alimony payments is if his ex-wife gets married again. But she hasn't met anybody and it's been two years; all he's got left in his life is a grapefruit plant. He has no money. Every penny he makes goes to the alimony. So he decides to make a fictitious character—he knows what she likes—and wear a beard and marry her and then disappear in a drowning accident and be off the hook."

The *Detroit Free Press* on October 14, 1966, ran an article saying that Robert Vaughn had been signed to star, while Brooks would mention in his HBO special *Mel Brooks Strikes Back!* (2012) that he had at one time met with Cary Grant about being in the film. Brooks himself would keep promoting the script through most of 1966, but although he would always look at the script as one he loved, he eventually conceded it was never going to happen. Instead he would abandon the project for his *Springtime for Hitler* concept, which he had been working on even before *Marriage Is a Dirty Rotten Fraud*, and would be on its way to becoming a movie in late 1966.

Triplets (1964)

Variety on August 19, 1964, announced that *Get Smart* was being looked at by ABC as a possible series, mentioning also that Brooks had sold through Talent Associates a pilot script to ABC for a show called *Triplets*. According to David Susskind at Talent Associates, the show was to be "about three children born to a father who goes to law school, while his wife works." Susskind went on to state in an interview with Harold Stern that *Triplets* was "70 percent home" on being sold. Alas, it never made up the 30 percent difference.

Carl Reiner–Directed Movie (1965)

Carl Reiner planned to direct a "low budget comedy for Columbia to star Mel in his first feature," according to an article in the October 28, 1965, edition of *Variety*. This fell through once Reiner was set to move on to *Enter Laughing* and Brooks was hearing promising words of *Marriage Is a Dirty Rotten Fraud* finally going in front of the camera in 1966.

Have You Heard, Bronsky Is Dying (1966)

While trying to get *Springtime for Hitler* and *Marriage Is a Dirty Rotten Fraud* off the ground, Brooks worked on a stage play called *Have You Heard, Bronsky Is Dying*, for which he envisioned Zero Mostel as the lead.

Brooks would dig into the plot of the play for an article with Herbert Gold for the *New York Times* in 1975: "I have this character called Bronsky who realizes he's gonna die, so he visits the tombstones of all his friends. . . . Bronsky owns some property in Larchmont [a suburb of New York City], and he knows it takes a few years to build a pyramid, and he starts to build . . . a monument, he wants to stay around, like a pharaoh. . . ." Brooks would expand on the idea a bit more in an interview with Paul H. Zimmerman the same year: "Poor Bronsky, he's a little more than halfway finished with building his pyramid. But I don't think he'll ever finish it all the way to the top. You see, the more successful he is, the bigger he wants to build the bottom of the pyramid. And the bigger he builds the bottom, the farther it is to the top. Frankly, if he ever felt he could reach the top of it, he'd never start building it in the first place."

And just like Bronsky, as Brooks continued to layer more on the story, the play never was completed.

America, You're Beautiful (1970)

Norman Panama (writer-director of *The Court Jester* and *The Road to Hong Kong*, amongst others) and Digby Wofe (*Laugh-In*) had written a script that they planned to produce with Panama directing to be called *America, You're Beautiful*. The script was "a la *Mad, Mad, Mad, Mad World*" and they hoped to get such stars as "Jackie Gleason, Angela Lansbury, George C. Scott, Donald Sutherland, Jane Fonda, Anne Bancroft, Mel Brooks, and Elliott Gould." Obviously a wish list of actors, but the project never went any further than a write-up in *Variety*, yet it does show that people were thinking that Bancroft and Brooks were a team, an idea Brooks himself would eventually put to good use in both *Silent Movie* and *To Be or Not To Be*.

Spy Film for Stanley Chase at Universal (1970)

Stanley Chase, off-Broadway producer (*The Three-Penny Opera*) and film and television producer (*Colossus: The Forbin Project*), was featured in a *Variety* article on March 24, 1970, as working on an untitled "spy epic." Mel Brooks was to direct the film from a script penned by Noel Behn. Chase had cowritten the pilot *Inside Danny Baker* with Brooks in 1962.

Behn's novel *The Kremlin Letter* had just been adapted into a movie by 20th Century Fox in February of that year. Behn would not see another of his scripts filmed until *The Brink's Job* in 1978. Brooks, instead, would concentrate on getting a dream project up on the screen. One that, sadly enough, never happened.

She Stoops to Conquer (1971–1995)

As seen through the previous chapters, for years Brooks had attempted to bring an adaptation of Oliver Goldsmith's famous comedy *She Stoops to Conquer* to the screen.

The play from 1773 was essentially a "comedy of manners," dealing with a woman who hopes to marry a rich man who disliked women of his own social class, whom he found stuffy and dull. Thus, the woman decides to act as a maid for the man in hopes of attracting him; in other words, she "stoops" by lowering herself in order to make him fall in love with her and marry her.

The film nearly got made in 1971 with UMC, and then twenty years later in 1991 with MGM, but in both cases, Brooks found himself having to follow films that did not do well at the box office. He would attempt to bring the project back one more time in 1995, stating that he planned to make it in 1996 with an English cast. Like a type of bad luck charm, the mention of doing the adaptation came just as his latest film, at that point his last, *Dracula: Dead and Loving It*, did poorly at the box office. Although the project would be one of Brooks's goals as a director, it would end up remaining a dream.

Dom DeLuise Television Pilot (1971)

Dom DeLuise was in talks with CBS to star in a pilot for "Mel Brooks's new series in which he'd play a spoof detective," according to an article in the November 14, 1971, issue of *Variety*. No further developments appear to have occurred after this, however.

Every Little Crook and Nanny (1972)

In her syndicated entertainment column from July 1971, Joyce Haber interviewed Cy Howard (creator of *My Friend Irma* and the director of *Lovers and Other Strangers*, 1971) about his upcoming movie *Every Little Crook and Nanny*. The comedy, based on a novel by Ed McBain, who wrote *Blackboard Jungle* and the *87th Street* novel series, is about a nanny taking care of the brattish son of a mob boss who decides to fake the child's kidnapping in order to get a $50,000 ransom. In the Haber interview, Howard says that he was hoping to get Gene Wilder and Mel Brooks for roles in the film, most probably to play two American lawyers who work for the mob boss (who were played by Dom DeLuise and John Astin in the film).

As with *America, You're Beautiful*, it was obviously a case of dream-casting a picture, as Howard mentioned wanting to sign Marcello Mastroianni in the same article and instead ended up with Victor Mature. Just the ways of Hollywood when it comes to promoting upcoming film projects. Speaking of which. . . .

Oh, God! (1974)

Oh, God! was a novel written by Avery Corman and published in 1971. The plot is about a grocery store clerk who become a modern-day messenger for God. Producer/talk show host David Susskind got the movie rights for the novel and then approached Larry Gelbart about adapting it into a script. Gelbart told Jurgen Wolff and Kerry Cox in 1988 that he envisioned cowriting the script with Mel Brooks, who he had worked with while writing for Caesar years before.

Gelbart, in an interview with Jurgen Wolff and Kerry Cox, also thought Brooks would be perfect for the role of God: "Mel to me was always the obvious

Oh, God!, the Carl Reiner–directed film, and written by former Brooks cowriter Larry Gelbart. Gelbart initially was in talks with Mel Brooks to play the role of God and Woody Allen to play the grocery store clerk who talks to God, but both bowed out quickly.

choice for God because the book smacked of the '2000 Year Old Man' routines that Mel used to do with Carl Reiner." Further, Gelbart thought another former writer for Caesar, Woody Allen, would be perfect in the role of the grocery store manager who becomes God's messenger.

The discussion between Gelbart and Brooks made it to the pages of *Variety* in 1974, but eventually the deal fell through, as 20th Century-Fox felt the script was "too gentle." Allen almost immediately turned down the idea of playing the clerk, while Brooks cooled to it after second-guessing if the idea would even work. Instead, the script would end up at Warner Bros., with another Caesar alumnus, Carl Reiner, directing, John Denver as the clerk, and George Burns as God. It should be noted that Burns had told Reiner and Brooks to record the "2000 Year Old Man" routine back in the early 1960s, or else he would steal it. As Gelbart envisioned the role to be like Brooks's character, in a way Burns ended up doing exactly as he promised years before by taking the role.

Hollywood Musicals Parody (1975)

Brooks hoped to make a parody of Hollywood musicals for his next "spoof subject," when asked by *Variety* in January 1975. Instead, within the month, he announced his next film would be a parody of silent movies, which eventually became *Silent Movie*.

Bombs Away (1977)

Brooks and fellow writers Ron Clark, Rudy De Luca, and Barry Levinson announced in the June 2, 1977, edition of *Variety* that they were working on a movie about World War II air corps pilots called *Bombs Away*, which they would begin to write after the release of *High Anxiety*. Brooks would later comment that this idea would evolve into *The Follies of 1979* in 1977, which then became *History of the World, Part I* by 1978. Oddly enough, that movie has nothing to do with World War II air corps pilots.

The Return of the Grandson of the Hunchback of Notre Dame (1979)

Brooks was to have produced this comedy film "under his Crossbow" banner, according to *Variety* on March 8, 1979, with Dom DeLuise directing from a script by Jay Burton and Gene Wood. Burton had written a story used on *When Things Were Rotten* and had brought the script to Brooks in 1977. Wood had worked with Burton on comedy material since the 1960s and would go on to becoming a well-known announcer on game shows in the United States. Although Brooks states the script was "fabulous," the project was never completed.

Brookscable (1982)

In the spring of 1982, Brooks pursued the idea of starting a production company in conjunction with HBO and/or Showtime. The objective would be to produce programming that was "more intelligent than network television and less expensive than feature films." While this was very forward thinking of Brooks and shows signs of the direction HBO and Showtime would go within the past twenty years with original programming, nothing further was heard of the project.

Dr. Jekyll & Mr. Hyde (1986)

Rumors abounded for ages that Brooks would team up with Gene Wilder on a project of some type, and Army Archerd in the March 12, 1986, edition of *Variety* has Brooks stating, "I would like to do a classic update of *Dr. Jekyll & Mr. Hyde* with Gene Wilder." Wilder, in the same article, hinted that he would be interested in working on such a script with Brooks, but on the condition that either Brooks star and Wilder direct or vice versa, as Wilder felt their acting styles were too similar to work in a film together. Even so, Brooks would mention the project again to *Variety* in January 1991, saying that he was not only reteaming with Wilder, but "looking for a new Marty Feldman" for the proposed film. In March 1991, he would tell Marilyn Beck that the two were still going over the idea, "trying to decide if it should be a modern piece or not." In the interview, Brooks mentioned he had hopes to do the project after *Life Stinks* came out, but when that film did not do well at the box office, he moved back to other parody topics.

Money, Money, Money and Bimbo (1987)

In an interview with William Russell at the time of *Spaceballs'* release in 1987, Brooks mentioned a possible upcoming movie called *Money, Money, Money*. The project, born out of seeing the Caryl Churchill play *Serious Money*, would have been a *The Producers* take on Wall Street. Brooks said in the article that he was working on the script with Rick Moranis and that in one sight gag, "the floor of the Stock Exchange would be occupied by animals in suits and ties."

He also mentioned in the article a concept called *Bimbo*, a parody of the *Rambo* series and other action films popular at the time made by Chuck Norris and Arnold Schwarzenegger. "About a guy with a red sock tied 'round his head who goes into Chinese restaurants and shoots everyone who is yellow. I would be completely oiled up as Bimbo." The *Bimbo* project appeared to be an improvised joke in the interview, but it is obvious that *Money, Money, Money* would eventually evolve into his next realized project, *Life Stinks* (1991).

Hotel Mel (1989)

In the 1980s, Disney was trying to recover from years of management issues dealing with both the film studio and their amusement parks. Former president and CEO of Paramount Pictures Michael Eisner had been hired to be the CEO at The Walt Disney Company, and with his appointment came a number of changes within the company, including the idea of a new amusement park that would also function as a movie, television, and animation studio for productions in the Orlando, Florida, area. Such a concept would serve two functions—to have a new park for people to pay to see and to entice creative people in Hollywood to work for the studio. The park would be done in collaboration with MGM and would be known as the Disney-MGM Studio. The park opened on May 1, 1989, with everything in place, but a major problem—there really wasn't that much for ticket-holders to do, and lines for what was there had waits of up to five hours. Something needed to be done, or else the park was soon going to lose business once everyone realized there was not much to see and do there.

One of the first concepts considered was to do a "dark ride" (i.e., a thrill ride that would put an amusing scare into people as they rode it), as Disney had found success with the Haunted Mansion at both Disneyland and Disney World. The thing was, how to tie it into the concept of a movie studio? As Jim Hill points out in his history of the ride to come on his website, the studio began looking at possible horror movie properties that could support a ride, yet were always having to pull back due to the concepts being too adult and humorless to attach the Disney name to. (For example, would families really want to ride the Disney *Dawn of the Dead* coaster; and vice versa, would fans of *Dawn of the Dead* really want to see a Disney-fied version of the film in a ride for the whole family?)

In the meantime, Eisner was working to entice Mel Brooks to do projects at the studio. This wasn't as far-fetched as it sounds: in 1987, Brooks had filmed *Spaceballs* for MGM, who were collaborating with Disney on the amusement park. Brooks was also working on the (albeit short-lived) television series *Nutt House* for Disney's Touchstone Pictures during the spring and summer of 1989 (see chapter 21 for more details on this series). With Brooks in mind, not to mention that the earlier "dark rides" at the parks had been heavily invested with humor, it made sense to bring the writer-director in to discuss his take on such a ride.

The first concept was a spin on *Young Frankenstein*, with a village that would lead to a castle that would feature the ride. This quickly changed into the concept of "Mel Brooks's Hollywood Horror Hotel," more widely remembered as "Hotel Mel." The idea of the place was that it would appear to be part of a real hotel on the premises that was built to resemble a hotel from the 1930s (in fact, in some ways similar to the hotel sets that Brooks was using for *Nutt House*). The ride part would be a portion of the hotel that supposedly was "rundown and condemned" because of a horrible incident that happened there many years before. In a filmed portion shown to the riders, Brooks would appear to tell them that they are auditioning for a new movie of his being filmed in the condemned hotel. When Brooks yells "Cut!" the riders would plunge downward for the start of the ride, where they would see a variety of gags involving various Hollywood monsters, such as Dracula shaving himself in a mirror where his reflection cannot be seen, and Frankenstein accidentally using some of the Mummy's wrap as toilet paper when using a stall in the men's room.

After a few conversations with the Disney people about the ride, however, Brooks eventually lost interest, just as the Disney people were beginning to see the ride in other ways as well; instead they went with the concept of Rod Serling's *The Twilight Zone*, and the ride that became the *Tower of Terror* would open in 1994. With bigger concerns going on for Brooks—including a misfired attempt to have Brooksfilms go public, as well as beginning work on *Life Stinks*— he would step away from this and other projects, deciding instead to stick with ventures directly related to his writing and directing.

S.N.A.F.U. (1996)

In an interview with Kate Meyers in 1996, Brooks stated that he was working on a World War II comedy called *S.N.A.F.U.* "It's [based on] my adventures as a combat engineer. If anything went wrong in World War II, they could blame it on me."

Space Jam 2 (1997)

Space Jam (1996) was a mix of animated cartoon and live-action in a comedy film featuring Warner Bros.' Looney Tunes characters like Bugs Bunny and Daffy Duck playing basketball alongside basketball star Michael Jordan. It was also a huge success, leading to hundreds of millions of dollars in ticket sales and merchandise. Thus, a sequel was quickly devised in 1997 to cash in on the film's success.

Initially, there was talk of having Mel Brooks voice the villain in the sequel, and animator Bill Camp went so far as to design some shots of the villain looking much like a caricature of Brooks. However, it soon turned out that Michael Jordan had not agreed to do the film, and Warner abandoned the project before negotiations with Brooks even started.

Spaceballs II (?)

As with *History of the World, Part I*, rumors have circulated for years of a sequel to *Spaceballs*. In the case of *History*, the idea of further installments was part of the joke: no further films were to be made or it would ruin the joke, although Brooks hinted at the time that he could always go ahead and do one if he ever felt like it. The same is true in *Spaceballs*; there's a brief gag later in the film to suggest that all the characters would meet up again in *Spaceballs II: The Search for More Money*. Of course, the *Star Wars* series, which *Spaceballs* targets the most, is renowned for its many sequels, so the idea of a sequel to the parody was always enticing to fans.

Yet, realistically, the idea never went much further. *Spaceballs* had respectable results at the box office, but not remarkable enough to make MGM—a studio that was having its own financial difficulties to deal with at the time— want to pursue anything. As the years went by, several of the cast members had passed away, leaving only some of the main leads, and thus making a direct sequel was simply impossible. Further, for many, the various real *Star Wars* sequels that occurred in the 1990s were seen sometimes as parodies themselves, therefore lessening the need for anything else.

On the flip side of that, the movie did remarkably well on video and has gained a cult status among fans of both Brooks and *Star Wars*. On top of that, the eventual *Star Wars* sequels, especially those that came with the new cycle of films, starting with the 2015 *Star Wars: The Force Awakens*, has shown that even a handful of original character can be brought back to help introduce new characters into that cinematic world and be accepted by the fans. Thus, it is not unreasonable that the same could be done with a *Spaceballs 2*.

There had been earlier attempts to get something started, as well. In 2013, Rick Moranis spoke of such an offer to Brian Abrams, saying that once the film became a hit on video, both Brooks and MGM began discussing such a venture in the late 1980s. Moranis's concept was to call the film *Spaceballs III: The Search for Spaceballs II*, but after some negotiations, Moranis felt a deal would be unworkable for him. "It would have been something I would have wanted to do. But that ship has sailed," said Moranis.

There was also an attempt in the late 1990s by the studio. Tom Meehan, cowriter of the film, stated in *The Producers: The Book, Lyrics, and Story Behind the Biggest Hit in Broadway History! How We Did It*, that he had gone to California in the late summer of 1998 to discuss a *Spaceballs 2* with MGM, Brooks, and fellow writer Ronny Graham. That fell through when MGM suggested they make the sequel an animated film rather than live action, and Brooks told MGM, "We don't do cartoons." As it turns out, animation was the form used to bring the characters back in the 2000s (see chapter 21), but Brooks was proven right in the long run as that cartoon series only lasted a few episodes before being cancelled.

Brooks still hints that he would like to do such a sequel. In February 2015, he told Adam Corolla in his podcast *Take a Knee* that he had thought about it, saying, "I still have Daphne Zuniga and I still have Rick Moranis if he'd do it, and I've still got me." However, Brooks also made clear that the safest fashion to do such a movie would be "If I did a movie that came out right after [the new] *Star Wars* comes out—maybe a couple of months later—I'd have a big weekend, you know? Even if it fell on its ass and didn't get its money back . . . but that first weekend; the anticipation of seeing *Spaceballs 2*. . . ." From this, it is clear that there was essentially a window for such a film to come out, and with nothing occurring before *The Force Awakens*, it looks like that window has closed and Brooks knew it would be nearly impossible to make such a deadline back in February 2015.

That doesn't kill fans' interest, however. In February 2016, with *The Force Awakens* in theaters, posters appeared in the New York City subway that showed the damaged helmet of Dark Helmet with the legend, "The Schwartz awakens with an even greater helmet," and advertising *Mel Brooks's Spaceballs: The Search for More Money* as "The Teaser Poster." For a brief moment, fans were hopeful that something was actually going to happen on a sequel. Brooks, when asked about it a few days later, would say that he had nothing to do with it and no such movie was currently planned, although he was thrilled that fans would want to go through that much trouble.

Just wishful thinking. Shared by fans and Brooks alike.

Mortality

One thing that you can't avoid in examining the life of someone, even someone who has outlived nearly all of his critics like Mel Brooks has, is seeing how many remarkable people who contributed to the laughter Brooks brought us over the years are now gone: Gene Wilder, Madeline Kahn, Sid Caesar, Harvey Korman, Dom DeLuise, Zero Mostel, Ron Carey, Richard Pryor, Cleavon Little, Marty Feldman, John Candy, Anne Bancroft, just to name a few.

Yet there they are on the wide screen, on the television set, in our memories. Through his films and shows, Mel Brooks has given us the opportunity to see these special people live once again and for many years to come. We'll always cherish the friendship we see in Max and Leo, as well as Bart and Jim. The laughs of Igor (or should I say Eye-gor?). The insane personalities of Frau Blücher (neigh!) and Nurse Diesel. The French royalty who knew how good it was to be the king. Lone Starr proving his Schwartz is better than Dark Helmet. Even that English-accented Robin Hood, and the klutzy Dracula. And the actors playing them with such freshness even as more and more years go by.

Mel Brooks certainly has made some commentary on our lives over time, disguised as it were through his comedy. Although the previous chapters show that Brooks didn't spend quite as much of his career obsessed with Hitler as we sometimes tend to believe, he certainly knew how to knock down the darkness, the fear, the hatred that Hitler brought and unfortunately continues to bring into our world. "By using the medium of comedy, we can try to rob Hitler of his posthumous power and myths." Brooks told *Der Spiegel* in 2006. "We take away from him the holy seriousness that always surrounded him and protected him like a cordon." And denouncement of what corners us and makes us less than human is at the core of so much in Brooks's work. Corporate greed, power obsession, the numerous ways to lose our humanity—they all face attack in his movies, dressed up in comedy, only to knock down the villains in our heads and hearts and perhaps allow us to see more clearly that laugher can defeat them.

Over time, Brooks's attitude about his work changed little, although he finally admitted that he wishes to be remembered as being as good a director as he was and remains as a writer. When in 2013 the American Film Institute gave him a Lifetime Achievement Award for his work as a writer and director, Brooks proudly boasted to Reuters at the time, "They're finally recognizing that I'm a pretty good director. They say, 'Comedy force, good writer, funny actor.' Nobody ever, in the press or anywhere, said I was a good director." And of course, perhaps we tend to not notice because we can readily see it on the screen. It is obvious that Brooks could tone Zero Mostel down to a human-like performance in *The Producers* just as he could get other actors who sometimes could overpower their directors (and even themselves when directing) to stay within the framework of believability for the screen. Comedy—even the broadest kind—always plays better when grounded by reality.

Perhaps at times we have felt overwhelmed by Mel Brooks. He does like to draw attention, just as he always has. But we never could stop him from doing the work he was born to do, nor really every wanted him to stop. The popular story always told is one Brooks noted about himself to *Newsweek* in 1975: "Look at Jewish history. Unrelieved lamenting would be intolerable. So, for every ten Jews beating their breasts, God designated one to be crazy and amuse the breast-beaters. By the time I was five, I knew I was that one!" But that's selling himself short. He has played that role for all of us. Maybe once in a while with a Yiddish word or two that a kid out in the middle of America didn't get, but the emphasis was always the same—calling someone a schmuck was easy to figure out, as well as when someone was called a mensch. Being Jewish was only a part of being human, and we all got that message along the way.

Mortality? Well, it comes for us all in the end. Best you can do is "make some noise" and laugh in the face of the hatred and sorrow that life sometimes brings. Brooks has given so many millions of people through the years an invitation to do exactly that. And through his shows, his albums, his interviews, and, most especially, through the films he created and those that he contributed to, his guide to laugh the darkness out of the room will be with us for generations to come. And for that, he is loved. There is no greater gift in life than that.

Appendix

The Awards

EGOT—As of 2017, Mel Brooks is one of only twelve individuals that have won the four main competitive entertainment awards in the United States—the Emmy, the Grammy, the Oscar, and the Tony.

Academy Award—Best Original Screenplay for *The Producers* (1969)

American Comedy Award—Lifetime Achievement Award in Comedy (1987)

American Comedy Award—Funniest Male Guest Appearance in a TV Series for *Mad About You* (1997 and 2000)

American Film Institute—Lifetime Achievement Award (2013)

BAFTA Fellowship (2017)

CINE Competition Award—CINE Golden Eagle for *The Critic* (1963)

Drama Desk Award—Outstanding Lyrics for *The Producers* (2001)

Drama Desk Award—Outstanding Musical for *The Producers* (2001)

Drama Desk Award—Outstanding Book of a Musical for *The Producers* (2001)

Emmy Award—Outstanding Writing for a Variety Series for *The Sid Caesar, Imogene Coca, Carl Reiner, Howard Morris Special* (1967)

Emmy Award—Outstanding Guest Actor in a Comedy Series for "Uncle Phil" in *Mad About You* (1997, 1998, and 1999)

Ernst Lubitsch Award—Honorary Award for *The Producers* (2009)

Grammy Award—Best Long Form Music Video for *Recording The Producers: A Musical Romp with Mel Brooks* (2002)

Grammy Award—Hall of Fame Award for *Carl Reiner & Mel Books: 2000 and Thirteen* (1999)

Grammy Award—Best Spoken Comedy Album for *The 2000 Year Old Man in the Year 2000* (1999)

Grammy Award—Best Musical Theater Album for *The Producers* (2002)

Hollywood Walk of Fame—Star on the Walk of Fame (2010)

Hugo Award—Best Dramatic Presentation for *Young Frankenstein* (1975)

Kennedy Center Honors (2009)

Laurence Olivier Award—Best New Musical for *The Producers* (2005)

National Medal of the Arts (2015)

Nebula Award—Best Script for *Young Frankenstein* (1976)

Outer Critics Circle Award—Outstanding Broadway Musical for *The Producers* (2001)

Outer Critics Circle Award—Outstanding New Broadway Musical for *Young Frankenstein* (2008)

Saturn Award—Best Director for *Young Frankenstein* (1976)

Tony Award—Best Musical for *The Producers* (2001)

Tony Award—Best Original Score for *The Producers* (2001)

Tony Award—Best Book of a Musical for *The Producers* (2001)

TV Land Legend Award (2010)

Writers Guild of America Award—Best Variety Series or Special for *The Sid Caesar, Imogene Coca, Carl Reiner, Howard Morris Special* (1968)

Writers Guild of America Award—Best Original Screenplay for *The Producers* (1969)

Writers Guild of America Award—Best Original Comedy for *Blazing Saddles* (1975)

Writers Guild of America—Laurel Award for Screen Writing Achievement (2003)

Mel Brooks as Frederick Bronski in *To Be or Not to Be*. Bronski may never had gotten the acceptance he thought he deserved, but Mel Brooks certainly has the awards and accolades to prove his importance in the world of comedy and in the motion picture industry.

Bibliography

Abrams, Brian. "You Don't Do Liner Notes with the Dead Sea Scrolls: Rick Moranis in Conversation." *Heeb Magazine.* June 23, 2013.

Anthony, Michael. "What's Doing? Entertainment News," *Minneapolis Tribune,* April 14, 1974.

Associated Press. "Mel Brooks Enjoys Writers," *Ocala Star-Banner,* July 22, 1977.

Baker, Danny. *Going Off Alarming: The Autobiography—Volume 2,* Weidenfeld & Nicolson, London, 2014.

Baltake, Joe. "Film Silence IS Golden," *Philadelphia Daily News,* July 1, 1976.

Battaglio, Stephen. *David Susskind: A Televised Life,* St. Martin's Press, New York. 2010.

Beck, Marilyn. "Cher, Connery Paired for Show," *The Journal News,* White Plains, NY, June 22, 1990.

———. "The Film Script Temptation of Mel Brooks." *Chicago Tribune.* http://articles.chicagotribune.com/1988-09-21/features/8802010264_1_dutch-filmmaker-temptation-inspirational-story. September 21, 1988.

———. "Janet Jackson Virgin Deal Is One for the Records," *The Courier-Journal,* Louisville, KY, March 21, 1991.

———. "*Life Stinks* Filming Was Tough on Crew," *Honolulu Advertiser,* October 14, 1990.

———. "Mel Brooks Can't Find Any Slack in *Robin,*" *The Journal News,* White Plains, NY, April 30, 1983.

———. "Mel Brooks Will Have Two Roles in Latest Comedy," *Spaceballs,*" *The Courier Journal,* Louisville, KY, October 31, 1985.

———. "Neil Diamond Predicts a Second Son," *Ithaca Journal,* January 4, 1978.

———. "Schlatter Denies Reports of MDA Rift with Lewis," *Reno Gazette Journal,* May 11, 1990.

Beier, Lars-Olav. "With Comedy, We Can Rob Hitler of His Posthumous Power," *Der Spiegel,* March 16, 2006.

Berger, Phil. *The Last Laugh: The World of Stand-Up Comics.* Ballantine Books, New York, 1976.

Blank, Ed. "Cleavon Little Finds Success Again in N.Y.," *Pittsburgh Press,* January 28, 1986.

Blau, Eleanor. "Brooks Sued by *Elephant Man* Producers," *The News Journal,* Wilmington, August 15, 1979.

Bouls, Jean-Claude. "Gene Wilder Does Everything in His Own Way," *Ottawa Journal,* January 7, 1978.

Brady, James. "In Step with Mel Brooks," *Parade Magazine,* August 1, 1993.

Brooks, Mel. "Springtime for the Music Man in Me," *New York Times*. April 15, 2001.

———. "Williamsburg Days: Being Poor Was Good!" *Brooklyn: A State of Mind*, Workman Publishing Company, New York City,1998.

Brooks, Mel, and Tom Meehan. *The Producers: The Book, Lyrics, and Story Behind the Biggest Hit in Broadway History—How We Did It!*, Roundtable Press Book, New York, 2001.

Brown, Phil. *In the Catskills: A Century of the Jewish Experience in "The Mountains."* Columbia University Press, New York, 2002.

Caesar, Sid, and Bill Davidson. *Where Have I Been?*, Crown Publishers, New York, 1982.

Caesar, Sid, and Eddy Friedfeld. *Caesar's Hours*, Perseus Books Group, Cambridge, 2003.

Champlin, Charles. *"Silent Movie*—a Joy for Summer," *Rochester Democrat and Chronicle*, June 30, 1976.

Chen, Julie. "Honoring Funnyman Mel Brooks," *CBS News*, www.cbsnews.com/news/honoring-funnyman-mel-brooks/, December 23, 2009.

"A Conversation with Gerald Hirschfeld, ASC," *The American Society of Cinematographers*, www.theasc.com/asc_news/News_Articles/News_79.php, October 25, 2006.

Cox, Kerry, and Jurgen M. Wolff. *Successful Scriptwriting*. Writer's Digest Books, Cincinnati, 1988.

Daly, Sean. "Mel Brooks Finally Opens Up About Depression, Anne Bancroft," http://thetvpage.com/2013/05/10/mel-brooks-finally-opens-up-about-depression-anne-bancroft/, May 10, 2013.

Daly, Steve. "You've Got Mel," *Entertainment Weekly*, March 2000.

David, Ivor. "A Conversation with Mel Brooks," *Tablet*, June 28, 2016.

Dawidziak, Mark. "Mel Brooks Talks About Life, Laughter, and Performing Live for HBO Special," *Plain Dealer*, Cleveland, January 29, 2015.

DeCaro, Frank. "Borscht Belt Sherwood Forest," *New York Times*, July 19, 2013.

Demster, Chas. *"Blazing Saddles," Filming Locations of Chicago and Los Angeles*, www.itsfilmedthere.com/2015/05/blazing-saddles.html, May 2015.

Denman, Jeffry. *A Year with The Producers*, A Theatre Arts Book, New York, 2002.

Deusner, Stephen. "Mel Brooks: 'The Only Weapon I've Got Is Comedy," www.salon.com/2012/11/14/mel_brooks_the_only_weapon_ive_got_is_comedy/, November 14, 2012.

Dick Cavett Show, January 21, 1972.

Doan, Richard. "Mel Brooks's Wit Is a Television Rarity," *Montreal Gazette*, December 29, 1965.

Dodge, Shyam. "Mel Brooks Reminisces About Late Wife Anne Bancroft in Touching Interview," *Daily Mail*, London, April 30, 2013.

Ebert, Robert. "Brooks Back in the Saddle Again," *Los Angeles Times*, November 15, 1977.

———. "Here's to Anne Bancroft (1931–2005)," www.rogerebert.com/interviews/heres-to-anne-bancroft-1931-2005, June 7, 2005.

———. "Mel Brooks Still Dares to Be Daring," *Poughkeepsie Journal*, December 9, 1983.

———. "The Movie's Silent, but Mel Brooks Isn't," www.rogerebert.com/interviews/the-movies-silent-but-mel-brooks-isnt, July 22, 1976.

Erlanson, Amanda A. "On Writing *Blazing Saddles*," http://flickeryflicks. blogspot.com/2008/01/on-writing-blazing-saddles.html, January 17, 2008.

Estrin, Eric. "Young Mel-enstein: How Brooks Crashed Showbiz," www.thewrap. com/young-mel-enstein-how-brooks-crashed-showbiz-4462/, July 21, 2009.

Flatley, Guy. "Screams Come from Korman," *New York Times*, May 28, 1977.

Fleming, Marka B. "Labor Strikes in the Entertainment Industry: Essential to Preserving the Collective Bargaining Process," *Southern Law Journal*, June 2008.

Fleming Mike, Jr. "Hollywood & Religion: More Controversy to Come if New Films Anger the Faithful." *Deadline: Hollywood*. http://deadline.com/2011/04/ hollywood-religion-more-controversy-to-come-if-new-films-anger-the-faithful-125006/. April 24, 2011.

Fox, Margalit. "Lucille Kallen, 76, Writer for Show of Shows, Dies," *New York Times*, January 21, 1999.

Friedfeld, Eddy. "Mel Brooks: Exclusive *Cinema Retro* Interview," *Cinema Retro*, May 17, 2013.

Fussman, Cal. "Woody Allen: What I've Learned," *Esquire*, September 2013.

Gaghan, Jerry. "World Premiere Gets Cold Shoulder," *Philadelphia Daily News*, December 19, 1967.

Galbraith, Jane. "Toothy Tales of Hollywood . . . Script Dentist!" *Los Angeles Times*, June 13, 1993.

Garr, Teri. *Speedbumps: Flooring It Through Hollywood*, Hudson Street Press, New York, 2005.

Gilchrist, Todd. "Interview: Dom DeLuise," www.ign.com/articles/2006/04/01/ interview-dom-deluise, March 31, 2006.

Gold, Herbert. "Funny Is Money," *New York Times*, www.nytimes.com/1975/03/30/ archives/funny-is-money-2000yearold-48yearold-mel-brooks-comedy-is-not. html?_r=0 , March 30, 1975.

Graham, Sheilah. "I Am Wonderful—and Modest Too," *The Gastonia Gazette*, North Carolina, November 26, 1970.

Gregory, Mollie. *Women Who Run the Show: How a Brilliant and Creative New Generation of Women Stormed Hollywood*, St. Martin's Press, New York, 2002.

Haas, Al. "Peter Boyle Likes Being a Monster," *Philadelphia Inquirer*, December 16, 1974.

Haber, Joyce. "*Little Crook and Nanny* Film Has Italian Locale," *Sarasota Journal*, July 1, 1971.

———. "N.Y. Showman Mel Brooks Arrives in Hollywood," *Los Angeles Times*, November 1, 1970.

Hadleigh, Boze. *Celebrity Diss & Tell: Stars Talk About Each Other.* Andrews McMell Publishing, Kansas City, 2005.

Haithman, Diane. "Can *Nutt House* Crack the Ratings?" *Los Angeles Times*, October 4, 1989.

Harmer, Ian. "*Nutt House*: Mel Brooks Reunites Comic Duo," *Reading Eagle*, August 20, 1989.

Harmetz, Aljean. "Mel Brooks to Film Own Version of *Elephant Man*," *New York Times*, May 1, 1979.

Harris, Blake. "How Did This Get Made: A Conversation with Mel Brooks, Executive Producer of *Solarbabies*," www.slashfilm.com/mel-brooks-interview/, May 26, 2016.

———. "How Did This Get Made: A Conversation with Metrov, Writer of *Solarbabies*," www.slashfilm.com/solarbabies-oral-history/2/, May 2, 2016.

Harris, Will. "Mel Brooks," *A.V. Club*, www.avclub.com/article/mel-brooks-61517, September 9, 2011.

Heisler, Steve. "Mel Brooks and Carl Reiner," *A.V. Club*, www.avclub.com/article/mel-brooks-and-carl-reiner-35829, December 1, 2009.

———. "Mel Brooks on How to Play Hitler, and How He Almost Died Making Spaceballs," *A.V. Club*, December 13, 2012.

Heuck, Marc Edward. "'It's Good to Be the King': Mel Brooks' 1981 Single Made Him the First White Artist to Land a Rap Song on the R&B Charts!," http://nightflight.com/mel-brooks-1981-hit-made-him-the-first-white-artist-to-land-a-rap-song-on-the-rb-charts/, August 17, 2016.

Hill, Jim, "Why For?—Hotel Mel, Where's My Mummy, and Who Broke Tik Tok?", http://jimhillmedia.com/editor_in_chief1/b/jim_hill/archive/2003/10/02/why-for-hotel-mel-where-s-my-mummy-and-who-broke-tik-tok.aspx, October 2, 2003.

"Historical Vignette 109—Mel Brooks Was a Combat Engineer in World War II," www.usace.army.mil/About/History/Historical-Vignettes/Sports-Entertainment/109-Mel-Brooks/, August 2007.

Howard, Jeffrey K. "John Morris Interview," *Film Score Monthly*, August 2001.

———. "Lost Issue Wednesday: Mel Brooks Interview," *Film Score Monthly*, www.filmscoremonthly.com/articles/2001/15_aug---lost_issue_mel_brooks_interview.asp, 1997.

Hyatt, Wesley. *Emmy Award Winning Nighttime Television Shows*, 1948–2004, McFarland & Company, North Carolina, 2006.

Jewish Humor Central.com. "Found at Last! Mel Brooks's Lost Five Commandments," www.jewishhumorcentral.com/2013/05/found-at-last-mel-brooks-lost-five.html, May 22, 2013.

Karpel, Ari. "A Shtick with a Thousand Lives," *New York Times*, November 12, 2009.

Kashner, Sam. "The Making of The Producers," *Vanity Fair*, January 2004.

Kauffman, Jeffrey Michael. "Frances Farmer: Shedding Light on *Shadowland*," http://jeffreymichaelkauffman.com/frances-farmer/shedding-light-on-shadowland/, 1999.

King, Larry. "Hail Sid Caesar," *CNN Larry King Live*, September 7, 2001, http://transcripts.cnn.com/TRANSCRIPTS/0109/07/lkl.00.html.

Koltnow, Barry. "Will *Nutt House* be Harvey Korman's Ticket to Genuine Stardom?," *Chicago Tribune*, September 27, 1989.

"Laugh Tracks," *Philadelphia Daily News*, November 23, 1977.

Lea, Becky. "Cary Elwes Interview: The Princess Bride, as You Wish," *Den of Geek!*, www.denofgeek.com/books-comics/cary-elwes/32780/cary-elwes-interview-the-princess-bride-as-you-wish, November 11, 2014.

Leachman, Cloris, with George Englund. *Cloris: My Autobiography*, Kensington Books, New York, 2009.

Lewis, Dan. "Mel Brooks's Latest Madness: A Noisy *Silent Movie*," *Baltimore Sun*, May 4, 1975.

Liebenson, Donald. "Finding Long-Lost Treasure Among *The Twelve Chairs*," *Los Angeles Times*, July 6, 1997.

Lipton, James. "Neil Simon, The Art of Theater No. 10," *Paris Review*, Winter 1992.

"Look for Fox to Re-release Silent Movie," *Philadelphia Daily News*, August 15, 1978.

Lundegaard, Bob. "Henny Youngman . . . ," *Star Tribune*, Minneapolis, April 10, 1977.

Lybarger, Dan. "Believing in Make Believe: An Interview with Mel Brooks," *The Keaton Chronicle*, Autumn 1997.

Madison, William. *Madeline Kahn: Being the Music, A Life*, University Press of Mississippi, Jackson, 2015.

Mancini, Mark. "11 Dashing Facts About Robin Hood: Men in Tights," *Mental Floss*, December 2, 2016.

Mandelbaum, Ken. *Not Since Carrie: 40 Years of Broadway Musical Flops*. St. Martin's Press, New York. 1991.

Mann, Roderick. "Charles Durning Is Driven by Doubts," *Los Angeles Times*, September 9, 1983.

McLellan, Dennis. "Dom DeLuise Dies at 75; Actor Was a 'Naturally Funny Man,'" *Los Angeles Times*, May 6, 2009.

———. "Television Comedy Writer for Sid Caesar and Others," *Los Angeles Times*, November 27, 2007.

McWeeny, Drew. "Mel Brooks Discusses *Blazing Saddles*, Brooksfilms, and the Best Screening Ever," http://uproxx.com/hitfix/mel-brooks-discusses-blazing-saddles-brooksfilms-and-the-best-screening-ever/, May 12, 1914.

Meehan, Thomas. "To Write or Not to Write Was One of the Questions," *Sydney Morning Herald*, April 6, 1984.

"Mel Brooks: 'I'm an EGOT; I Don't Need Any More,'" *Fresh Air*, www.npr. org/2013/12/27/256597762/mel-brooks-im-an-egot-i-dont-need-any-more, December 27, 2013.

"Mel Brooks: Second Interview, 1975," *The Playboy Interviews*. Playboy Press, New York, 1981.

Meyers, Kate. "10 Smart Questions for Mel Brooks," *Entertainment Weekly*. www. ew.com/article/1996/06/28/10-smart-questions-mel-brooks, June 28, 1996.

Mills, Nancy. "Comedy Remake Features Actor Who Believes War Can Be Funny," *Asbury Park Press*, New Jersey, December 18, 1983.

"NBC Testing Agency Reaction on Sat. Night Program Plan," *Billboard*, January 28, 1950.

Nesteroff, Kliph. *The Comedians: Drunks, Thieves, Scoundrels and the History of American Comedy*, Grove Press, New York, 2015.

———. "An Interview with Dick Gautier—Part Three," http://classicshowbiz. blogspot.com/2015/12/an-interview-with-dick-gautier-part.html, December 1, 2015.

———. "Red Buttons and the Acrimony of Hilarity," http://blog.wfmu.org/ freeform/2015/03/acrimony-not-hilarity-the-contentious-story-of-the-red-buttons-show-by-kliph-nesteroff.html, March 26, 2015.

O'Brian, Jack. "Voice of Broadway," *Monroe News-Star*, Louisiana, May 9, 1973.

Parker, Jerry. "Brooks: 'Patron Saint of Going Too Far' Near Edge in New Movie," *Clarion-Ledger*, Jackson, MS, June 18, 1981.

Pearce, Garth. "Behind-the-Scenes Trouble During Robin Hood," *Entertainment Weekly*, June 21, 1991.

Pearson, Ben. "Q&A with Actor Bill Pullman—*Spaceballs*, an *Independence Day* Sequel, and Much More," http://geektyrant.com/news/2011/1/13/qa-with-actor-bill-pullman-spaceballs-an-independence-day-se.html, January 13, 2011.

Peters, Jenny. "History of Mel, Part I," *Kokomo Tribune*, Indiana, January 8, 1996.

Plume, Ken. "Dom DeLuise Interview," http://asitecalledfred.com/2010/10/18/ dom-deluise-interview-ken-plume/, 2003.

Pockross, Adam. "Mel Brooks on Blazing New Comedic Trails in *Blazing Saddles*," www.yahoo.com/movies/mel-brooks-on-blazing-new-comedic-trails-in-blazing-85066818302.html, May 14, 2014.

Richards, Tad. www.tadrichards.com/pubs.html.

Rohan, Virginia. "Mel Brooks Reveals the Stories Behind Blazing Saddles," *USA Today*, August 22, 2016.

Rose, Charlie. "Anne Bancroft," *The Charlie Rose Show*, PBS, April 25, 2000.

———. "Carl Reiner and Mel Brooks," *The Charlie Rose Show*, October 9, 1997.

———. "Interview with Madeline Kahn," *The Charlie Rose Show*, December 16, 1996.

Rosen, Lisa. "Where Did He Go Right?" *WGAQ Written By*. Writers Guild of America West, Los Angeles, January 2016.

Ross, Robert. *Marty Feldman: The Biography of a Comedy Legend*, Titan Books, London, 2011.

Rowe, Douglas. "Video Breathes New Life into *Dracula: Dead and Loving It*," *Asheville Citizen Times*, North Carolina, June 28, 1996.

Rushfield, Richard. "The Yahoo Movies Q&A: Mel Brooks on the 40th Anniversary of His Monster Hit *Young Frankenstein*," www.yahoo.com/movies/the-yahoo-movies-q-a-mel-brooks-on-the-40th-97315076687.html, September 12, 2014.

Russell, William. "The Parody King Who Boldly Goes Where Others Fear to Tread," *Glasgow Herald*, December 12, 1987.

Ryan, Desmond. "The Antic Mel Brooks in Back," *Philadelphia Inquirer*, December 11, 1983.

———. "Mel Brooks Shows His Serious Side," *Poughkeepsie Journal*, November 8, 1985.

———. "Peerless Parodist Shows His Serious Side," *Ottawa Citizen*, November 13, 1985

Sack, Mike. *Poking a Dead Frog: Conversations with Today's Top Comedy Writers*, Penguin Books, New York, 2014.

Sarno, Art. "Mel Brooks: Producer-Director-Actor Would Rather Be Writing," *Valley News*, Van Nuys, CA, July 12, 1977.

Saul, Scott. *Becoming Richard Pryor*. HarperCollins Publishers, New York. 2014.

Schaap, Dick. "A Man Who Makes Us Laugh," *Parade Magazine*, January 22, 1984.

Sepinwall, Alan. "Mel Brooks Looks Back on Sid Caesar, *Blazing Saddles* and More," http://Uproxx.com, December 10, 2012.

Shapiro, J. David. www.jdshapiro.com.

Sharbutt, Jay. "Actress' First Trip to NYC Turns into Memorable Visit," *Odessa American*, October 14, 1975.

Sikov, Ed. *Mr. Strangelove: A Biography of Peter Sellers*. Hyperion Books, New York, 2002.

Silverman, Stephen M. "Mel Brooks and Anne Bancroft Shared Love and Laughs," *People Magazine*, May 19, 2013.

Silverman, Stephen M., and Joan Micklin Silver. *The Catskills: Its History and How It Changed America*. Knopf, Borzoi Books, New York. 2015.

Simon, Scott. "Brooks and Reiner's 2,000-Year-Old Man Turns 50," www.npr.org/templates/story/story.php?storyId=120909130, November 28, 2009.

Siskel, Gene. "Mel Brooks: He's Worth a Million . . . Laughs, That Is," *Chicago Tribune*, August 1, 1976.

———. "No Kidding, Mel Brooks Is a Serious Filmmaker." *Chicago Tribune*, November 6, 1977.

———. "On the Next Frontier," *Chicago Tribune*, January 1987.

———. "Stars Go Pell-MEL for Silent Movie," *Chicago Tribune*, August 2, 1976.

———. "Words from 'Chief Brooks,'" *Chicago Tribune*, March 1, 1974.

Smith, Liz. "Mel Turns Serious to Deny Riff," *Detroit Free Press*, February 24, 1978.

———. "Newhouse Seeks Murdoch Magazine," *The Palm Beach Post*, May 22, 1984.

Spaceballs: The Documentary, MGM, 2005.

Stanley, Susan. "Mel Brooks Tells What His Films Are All About." *Tallahassee Democrat*, March 12, 1978.

Stern, Harold. "David Susskind," *Indianapolis Star*, December 20, 1964.

Stewart, Jocelyn Y. "Artist Created Many Famous Film Posters," *Los Angeles Times*, February 10, 2008.

Suskin, Steven. *Second Act Trouble: Behind the Scenes at Broadway's Big Musical Bombs*. Applause Books, New York. 2006.

Terry, Clifford. "Mel Brooks: Funny, He Doesn't Look Apache," *Chicago Tribune Magazine*, November 11, 1973.

Tessel, Harry. "Mel Brooks's *Silent Movie* Says It with Physical Humor," *Independent Press Telegram*, June 19, 1976.

Themal, Harry F. "3 in *Greatest Lover* Talk About What's Next," *Morning News*, Wilmington, December 18, 1977.

Thomas, Bob. "If *History of World* Flops, Blame Mel Brooks," *News Press Sun*, May 24, 1981.

———. "Mel Brooks: The Magic of the 10,000th Lunch Invitation," *Observer-Reporter*, Washington, PA, July 16, 1976.

———. *"To Be or Not to Be*: A New Side of Mel Brooks," *Iowa City Press Citizen*, December 15, 1983.

Thomas, Bob. *"Young Frankenstein* Is Takeoff on 1930's Horror Movies Style," *The Index-Journal*, Greenwood, SC, May 20, 1974.

UPI, "Cloris Leachman—'a Finer Madness,'" *Morning Herald*, Hagerstown, MD, November 3, 1976.

Vincent, Mal. "Mel Brooks Sang for Mal Vincent. It Wasn't Swell," *Virginian-Pilot*, Los Angeles, July 31, 2015.

Wakeman, John. *World Film Directors, Volume II 1945–1985*, H. W. Wilson Co., New York, 1988.

Weide, Robert. "Quiet on the Set!" www.dga.org/Craft/DGAQ/All-Articles/1203-Summer-2012/DGA-Interview-Mel-Brooks.aspx, Summer 2012.

Weiler, A.H. "New Twist on the Old West," *Baltimore Sun*, November 26, 1972.

White, Timothy. "Producers' Producer: The Man Behind a Classic," *Billboard*, April 26, 1997.

Whitty, Stephen. "Does *Life Stink*? Ask Mel Brooks," *Knight-Ridder Newspapers*, August 20, 1991.

Wilder, Gene. *Kiss Me Like a Stranger*, St. Martin's Griffin, New York, 2005.

Wise, Damon. "The Making of *The Producers*," *The Guardian*, August 15, 2008.

WLRN, "Mel Brooks—'Unhinged' and Loving It," http://wlrn.org/post/mel-brooks-unhinged-and-loving-it, January 23, 2013.

Woerner, Meredith, "R.L. Stine Reveals His Most Gruesome Scene Ever," *Los Angeles Times*, October 14, 2015.

Yacowar, Maurice. *Method of Madness: The Comic Art of Mel Brooks*, St. Martin's Press, New York, 1981.

Young, Charles M. "Seven Revelations About Mel Brooks," *Rolling Stone*, February 9, 1978.

"You've Got Mel," *The New Yorker*, November 13, 2012.

Zemler, Emily. "Mel Brooks: A Comedic Torch to Light the Way," www.cnn.com/2013/05/20/showbiz/mel-brooks-qa/, May 20, 2013.

Zimmerman, Paul D. "The Mad Mad Mel Brooks," *Newsweek*, New York. February 17, 1975.

Index

84 Charing Cross Road, 85, 311, 318
"The 2500 Year Old Brewmaster," 60
2000 and One Years with Carl Reiner and Mel Brooks (album), 58
2000 and Thirteen (album), 60–61
2000 Year Old Man (character), 3, 31, 50, 54–64, 71, 87, 88, 91, 226, 238, 323, 330, 352–53, 361
2000 Year Old Man (television special), 61–62, 117, 125
2000 Year Old Man Goes to School, The (book), 63
2000 Year Old Man in Year 2000, The (album), 63
2000 Year Old Man in Year 2000, The (book), 63
2000 Year Old Man; The Complete History, The (album), 63–64
2000 Years with Carl Reiner and Mel Brooks (album), 56–58

ABC, 27, 31, 32, 35, 42, 43, 46, 47, 48, 52–53, 81, 82, 145, 171, 181, 323–26, 330, 349,
Academy Awards (Oscars), ix, 59, 80, 91, 92, 107, 143, 152, 182, 219, 220, 244–45, 274, 314, 315, 316, 361
Adams, Lee, 41, 48, 70–72, 325
Admiral Broadway Revue, 20–24, 25, 29, 30, 46
Airplane!, ix, 278, 301, 308
All American, 58, 70–73, 76, 77, 79, 90, 91, 104
Allen, Stanford C., 176, 200, 201
Allen, Steve, 50, 56, 58, 63
Allen, Woody, 15, 35, 45, 95–96, 99, 127, 140, 189, 197, 264, 303, 352
Alvin, John, 129, 150–51, 158, 181, 188, 203, 224, 236, 267

Animal House, ix, 244
Anything Goes, 4–5, 114, 335
Appell, Don, 7–8, 13, 17–19
Arthur, Bea, 46, 103, 231, 237
Arthur, Carol, 146, 199, 292
As Caesar Sees It, 46

Bancroft, Anne, 2, 45, 50, 77–87, 91, 96–97, 99, 101, 107, 118, 119, 120–121, 123, 131, 157, 176, 187, 192, 195, 197, 201–3, 219, 226, 233, 240–43, 245–47, 249–52, 301, 304–5, 310, 313, 318, 319, 332, 333, 343, 350, 358
Bart, Roger, 340–41, 344–45
Beach, Gary, 340–41, 343
Belkin, Gary, 41, 53
Bergman, Andrew, 47,131–32, 137, 138, 143, 152, 153, 244
Big Bus, The, 213, 308
Blankfield, Mark, 289–90, 297, 303, 327
Blazing Saddles, ix, 4, 27, 45, 47, 61, 82, 87, 104, 121, 122, 126, 127, 128–56, 158, 159–60, 173, 175–76, 178, 180-82, 184, 185, 187, 190, 199, 205, 206, 209, 213–15, 220, 222, 226, 231, 233, 236, 238, 244, 264, 268, 272, 278, 285, 291, 296, 298, 308, 311, 314, 322, 323, 340, 341, 346, 347, 348, 362
Bologna, Joseph, 103, 128
Boyle, Peter, 125, 158–60, 169–70, 174, 176, 179, 181, 186
Broderick, Matthew, 137, 336, 340–43
Brooks, Mel (on education), 3–4
Brooks, Mel (on family), 2–4, 7, 12, 13, 15, 80–81, 130, 171

Brooksfilms, 48, 84–85, 103–5, 125, 137, 226, 241, 243, 247, 256, 258, 285, 309, 310–22, 328, 335, 348, 356

Caesar, Sid, 17–33, 35–36, 38–42, 43, 45, 46, 50, 54, 65, 69, 70, 71, 72, 91, 95, 101, 103, 133, 161, 169, 191, 197, 198, 201, 202, 212, 226, 227, 233, 323, 325, 339, 351, 352, 358
Caesar's Hour, 36, 39–42, 45, 46, 53, 231
Caesar's Hours (book), 19, 27, 28,
Callas, Charlie, 198, 212, 213, 231, 305
Carey, Ron, 84, 197, 210, 212, 213, 217, 227, 330, 358
Carl Reiner and Mel Brooks at the Cannes Film Festival (album), 58–59
Carney, Art, 40–41, 42, 45, 46
Carter, Jack, 24, 233
Catskills, ix, 7–9, 12, 13, 14–16, 17–20, 36, 44, 65, 66, 330
Cavanagh, Megan, 287, 290–91, 304
Cavett, Dick, 34–35, 60, 132
Champion, Gower, 18, 20, 22, 34, 41, 45
Chaplin, Charlie, 6, 88, 110, 189
Chappell, Dave, 288–289, 290
Chase, Stanley, 47, 350
Clark, Ron, 187–91, 207, 210, 213, 225, 232, 270, 353
Coca, Imogene, 26–28, 30–33, 35–36, 39, 41, 43, 46, 66
Complete 2000 Year Old Man, The (album), 62
Critic, The (short film), 59
Cronenberg, David, x, 311, 315–16, 318
Crossbow Production, 48, 310, 353
Curb Your Enthusiasm, 86, 146, 288, 332–33
Curtain Going Up, 17, 65–66

De Luca, Rudy, 44, 84, 190, 191, 199, 207, 213, 217, 219, 225, 226, 229, 257, 263, 265, 270, 272, 274–75, 299, 305, 330, 332, 353
DeLuise, Dom, 46, 84, 118, 120–26, 130, 146, 167, 190–93, 195, 199, 201–3, 210, 225, 229, 253, 257, 263, 291, 310, 312, 331, 351, 353, 358
Dennis, John, 175
Diamond, Selma, 40–41, 314
Dick Van Dyke Show, The, 25, 40, 46, 58
Dracula: Dead and Loving It, 86, 103, 104, 142, 146, 176, 198, 199, 213, 229, 243, 247, 264, 269, 275, 286, 287, 290, 291–93, 297, 299– 309, 311, 328, 331, 342, 351
Dunn, Liam, 145, 175, 199

Ebert, Roger, 80, 84, 112, 125, 152, 182, 189, 204, 220, 225, 251, 277
Elephant Man, The, x, 85, 104, 226, 232, 233, 310, 312–13, 315
Elwes, Cary, 284, 286, 288–90, 294, 297
Emmy Awards, ix, 31, 32, 35, 40, 41–42, 46, 140, 167, 246, 274, 302, 327, 331–32, 361

Fatso, 84–85, 121, 195, 197, 233, 310, 312, 313
Feldman, Marty, 83, 104, 158–59, 162–65, 167, 168–70, 173, 179–82, 184, 190–91, 193–95, 201–4, 225, 230, 243, 284, 297, 325, 326, 354, 358
Finney, Albert, 118, 129, 314
Fly, The, x, 311, 315–316, 318, 321

Garr, Teri, 167, 171–175, 178, 180, 184
Gelbart, Larry, 38, 40, 41, 43, 73, 95, 169, 172, 187, 351–53
Get Smart, 25, 34, 41, 46, 48, 49–53, 70, 74–76, 80, 87, 91, 132, 140, 212, 323–26, 349
Gibson, William, 79, 81, 82
Glazier, Sidney, 92–93, 95, 98–99, 104, 105, 107–9, 111, 113, 116, 122, 124, 126, 128, 147

Goodman, Hannah Grad, 34
Graham, Ronny, 45, 66–67, 232, 239,
    242–243, 247, 251, 253, 254,
    256, 257, 263, 272, 357
Grammy Awards, ix, 57, 63, 361

Haberman, Steve, 270, 299, 332
Henry, Buck, 50–53, 98, 99, 125, 143,
    228
Hertzberg, Michael, 104, 106–8, 121,
    122, 147, 149
High Anxiety, 25, 84, 103, 142, 146,
    147, 174–76, 197–200, 204,
    207–22, 224–25, 228, 229,
    231–33, 236, 251, 253, 262,
    264, 270, 275–77, 298, 330,
    341, 353
Hillerman, John, 82, 145–46, 233
Hirschfeld, Gerald, 176, 178
History of the World, Part I, 58, 66, 84,
    98, 101, 103, 104, 121, 137,
    142, 146, 147, 176, 184, 195,
    197–99, 211–15, 223–38, 239,
    248, 251–53, 263, 264, 274,
    276, 282, 294, 298, 303, 308,
    341, 353, 356
Hitchcock, Alfred, 69, 176, 206–11,
    214–17, 219–22, 254
Hitler, Adolf, ix, 77, 88–90, 92–93,
    100, 103, 105, 106, 108, 110,
    112, 113, 116, 128, 157, 187,
    205, 207, 223, 225, 226, 238,
    239–41, 248–50. 253, 254, 270,
    282, 299, 330, 339–41, 358
Howard, John C., 147, 152, 174, 200,
    201, 214, 233
Huddleston, David, 146
Hurt, John, 226, 232, 260, 267, 313

*Incomplete Works of Carl Reiner and Mel
    Brooks, The* (album), 61
Inside Danny Baker, 47–48, 58, 91, 142,
    350

Jerry Lewis Show, The, 43–45
Johnson, Alan, 104–105, 109, 147, 233,
    241–242, 244, 250, 253, 293,
    305, 316

Jordan, Will, 14, 89–90

Kahn, Madeline, 66, 100, 142–44, 145,
    151, 152, 167, 170, 172, 173–74,
    175, 184, 185, 191, 196, 198,
    210, 211, 212, 228, 244, 272,
    273, 289, 331, 358
Kallen, Lucille, 20–27, 29–31, 34, 36,
    39, 40, 80
Karras, Alex, 133, 145
Keaton, Buster, 6, 104, 191, 202
Keller, Sheldon, 40–41
Kelly, 50, 74–75, 76, 93
Kitt, Eartha, 67, 69
Korman, Harvey, 141–42, 210, 212,
    217, 226–27, 229, 230, 238,
    253, 303, 326–28, 358
Kutcher, Benjamin, 13–14, 65, 90

Ladies' Man, The, 44–45
Laine, Frankie, 150–151
Lane, Nathan, 288, 332–33, 336,
    339–43
Langella, Frank, 81, 118, 119–20, 123,
    124–27
Leachman, Cloris, 46, 100, 142, 145,
    163, 170–72, 174, 179, 210–12,
    217, 229, 238, 326–28, 331,
    344–45
Leonard Sillman's New Faces of 1952,
    66–68, 69, 82, 142
Levine, Joseph E., 74, 93–94, 105,
    107–109, 111–13
Levinson, Barry, 44, 190–91, 199, 200,
    207, 213, 217, 225, 226, 232,
    330, 353
Lewis, Jerry, 20, 43–45, 198, 212, 235,
    336
Lewis, Richard, 287–88, 293, 295,
Liebman, Max, 18–24, 26–27, 29–31,
    33, 34–37, 40
Life Stinks, ix, 66, 104, 127, 176, 214,
    225, 228, 229, 231, 232, 263,
    264, 269, 270–81, 282–84, 286,
    295, 296, 298, 299, 306, 308,
    326, 354, 356
Little, Cleavon, 133, 138–40, 307, 358

Lubitsch, Ernst, 81, 88, 240–41, 243,
    252–53, 361
Lynch, David, x, 85, 311–13

Make Mine Manhattan, 18, 19
Marriage Is a Dirty Rotten Fraud, 91,
    348–49,
Mars, Kenneth, 76, 99–100, 166, 170,
    174, 273
Martinez, Jimmy, 146
Marty Feldman Comedy Machine, The,
    159, 169, 190, 230
Mazursky, Paul, 111, 146, 231
McCann, Chuck, 199, 292, 305
Meehan, Thomas, 241–43, 252–54,
    256, 263, 328, 329, 336, 341,
    343, 346, 357
*Mel Brooks & Carl Reiner Present the
    2000 Year Old Man* (album), 62
Melnick, David, 49–50, 74–75
Merman, Ethel, 4–5, 114, 335
Moody, Ron, 72, 118–19, 120, 125–27
Morris, Howard, 25, 28–30, 35, 46,
    210, 212, 229, 272, 274
Morris, John, 104, 109, 121, 122, 147,
    152, 176, 194, 200, 214, 219,
    220, 233, 248, 264, 275–76
Mostel, Zero, 34, 46, 72, 73, 89,
    94–96, 98–100, 105, 107, 108,
    110, 112–14, 340, 349, 358,
    359
My Favorite Year, 103–104, 129, 137,
    176, 226, 243, 247, 311, 314
My Son, The Hero, 59-60

NBC, 18, 20, 24, 29, 32, 34, 35–36,
    38–40, 42–43, 45, 46, 52, 53,
    54, 258, 261, 301, 326–28, 330,
    331
Nichols, Mike, 45, 50, 98, 99
Nutt House, The, 66, 142, 180, 212,
    229, 290, 303, 310, 326–28,
    355

Oh, God!, 172–173, 351–53
Olson, Alfa-Betty, 91, 93, 94, 100, 103,
    105, 109, 113, 122, 319

Padula, Edward, 70–71, 90,
Parish, James Robert, 27, 178, 180,
    291
Peters, Bernadette, 187, 191, 195–97,
    202, 204, 340
Pickens, Slim, 142, 144
Polly Bergen Show, The, 42–43, 93
Porretta, Matthew, 291, 305
Poston, Tom, 51–52, 70
Producers, The (film musical), 32, 246,
    311, 322, 333, 338, 343–44
Producers, The (film), ix, 2, 14, 45, 46,
    71, 74, 76, 81, 88–115, 116, 121,
    122, 124, 125, 126, 127, 130,
    146, 153, 154, 159, 174, 184,
    205, 230, 241, 268, 275, 282,
    307, 319, 336, 340–41, 354,
    359, 361
Producers, The (musical), 86, 87, 168,
    247, 309, 317–18, 333, 335–43,
    344, 346–47, 361–62
Pryor, Richard, 47, 132–35, 137–39,
    154–55, 167, 219, 227, 228, 231,
    235, 236, 261, 283, 331, 358

Reiner, Carl, ix, 25, 28–30, 34, 35, 38,
    40–42, 43, 46, 54–64, 72, 76,
    82–84, 87, 88, 125, 151, 173,
    192, 196, 202, 226, 229, 247,
    258, 279, 286, 332, 349, 352,
    353, 361, 362
Rich, Buddy, 7, 8
Richmond, Bill, 44–45
Ridgely, Robert, 213–14, 272, 275, 291
Riley, Jack, 199, 213, 232, 247, 264
Robin Hood; Men in Tights, ix, 55, 56,
    66, 103, 120, 121, 146, 176,
    190, 199, 213, 214, 228, 242,
    243, 262–264, 269, 274–75,
    282–298, 300, 301, 303, 305,
    306, 308, 311, 341
Ruben, Aaron, 38, 40

Schrieber, Avery, 47, 292, 305
Sellers, Peter, 49, 96, 97–99, 104,
    111–12, 118, 121, 144, 230
Shaw, Artie, 7

Shawn, Dick, 59, 81, 82, 100–101, 106, 107, 110, 111, 114, 212, 307
She Stoops to Conquer, 206, 278, 282, 284, 350–51
Shinbone Alley, 66, 68–70, 72, 104
Sid Caesar Invites You, 43
Sid Caesar, Imogene Coca, Carl Reiner, Howard Morris Special, The, 46, 332, 361, 362
Silent Movie, 82–84, 85, 112, 121, 145–47, 166, 169, 175–76, 187–206, 207, 210, 211, 213, 214, 220, 225, 227, 231–33, 236, 242, 264, 274–75, 292, 298, 305, 330, 335, 350, 353
Simon, Danny, 35, 38, 43
Simon, Neil, 35, 38, 41, 43, 47, 102, 110, 197, 204, 219, 228, 340
Solarbabies, 105, 244, 256, 316–18
Spaceballs II, 328, 337, 356–58
Spaceballs, ix, x, 66, 87, 121, 147, 153, 176, 199, 213–15, 225, 229, 231, 232, 247, 254–69, 276, 279, 282, 293, 296, 298, 303, 306, 307, 308, 318, 320, 328–329, 336, 355, 356–58
Spaceballs: The Animated Series, 310, 328–29, 333
Spencer, Alan, 180, 290, 326–27
Stein, Joe, 34, 38, 40, 95
Steinberg, Norman, 132, 134, 137, 140, 314, 323–26
Stern, Leonard, 34, 52–53, 75
Stewart, Michael, 41, 43, 70
Straw Hat Revue, The, 18, 20
Stroman, Susan, 337–339, 341–343, 346
Strouse, Charles, 41, 48, 70–73, 77, 79, 273, 325
Susskind, David, 3, 15, 36, 48, 49–50, 70, 74–75, 82, 96, 98, 130, 349, 351

Talent Associates, 48, 49–50, 52, 65, 74, 75, 96, 98, 349
Tars and Spars, 18–19, 29
To Be or Not to Be, ix, 2, 66, 81, 82, 85–86, 88, 104, 105, 130, 166,

176, 185, 199, 223, 232, 233, 239–253, 254, 256, 262, 263, 264, 269, 279, 316, 319, 330, 332, 336, 341, 350, 362
Tolkin, Mel, 20–23, 25–27, 30–31, 36, 38–41, 43, 45–46
Tony Awards, ix, 46 47, 63, 70, 73, 77, 79, 94, 95, 104, 118, 120, 138, 146, 174, 241, 244, 288, 336, 340, 341, 346, 361, 362
Tunick, Jonathan, 122, 147, 176
Twelve Chairs, The, ix, 81, 82, 92, 101, 104, 116–27, 128–30, 146, 154, 159, 179, 205, 206, 222, 230, 278, 280–81, 291, 316, 319

Uger, Alan, 132, 137
Ullman, Tracey, 288–89, 293, 331

Van Patten, Dick, 207, 212, 213, 217, 257, 262, 272, 291, 325
Voutsinas, Andreas, 101–2, 107, 121, 230, 238

Weaver, Jr., Sylvester "Pat," 24, 30
Webster, Tony, 34, 38, 40
When Things Were Rotten, 130, 137, 146, 177, 190, 213, 214, 242, 284, 298, 314, 323–28, 330, 353
Where Have I Been?, 22, 23, 29, 30, 39
Whitelock, Albert J., 214, 215, 232, 264
Wilder, Gene, 47, 49, 81, 82–83, 93, 95, 96–99, 100, 103–5, 107–8, 111–14, 121, 124, 137, 139, 140–42, 144, 146, 157–69, 171, 173–86, 190–91, 195, 200, 210, 219, 229, 230, 241, 264, 283, 285, 343, 348, 351, 354, 358
World War II, 10–12, 40, 55, 88, 90, 116, 197, 225, 229, 332, 353, 356
Writers Guild of America, 113, 126, 148, 152, 183, 204, 236, 252, 285, 362

Yasbeck, Amy, 282, 286–87, 289, 291, 297, 300–301, 303, 304, 306

Young Frankenstein (film), 32, 61, 76,
    83, 103, 112, 122, 145, 147, 150,
    157–86, 187, 190, 194, 199, 200,
    203, 205, 208, 211, 219, 220,
    248, 252, 256, 257, 268, 269,
    278, 285, 296, 298, 299, 301,
    306, 307, 326, 355, 361
Young Frankenstein (musical), 340, 341,
    343–47, 361, 362

Youngman, Henny, 198–99, 217, 232
Your Show of Shows, 21, 22, 24–27,
    28–37, 38, 39, 40, 42, 45, 46,
    54, 77, 78, 93, 227, 233, 314

Zuniga, Daphne, 258–59, 318,
    328–329, 357

THE FAQ SERIES

AC/DC FAQ
by Susan Masino
Backbeat Books
9781480394506...$24.99

Armageddon Films FAQ
by Dale Sherman
Applause Books
9781617131196.........$24.99

The Band FAQ
by Peter Aaron
Backbeat Books
9781617136139 ....$19.99

Baseball FAQ
by Tom DeMichael
Backbeat Books
9781617136061........$24.99

The Beach Boys FAQ
by Jon Stebbins
Backbeat Books
9780879309879..$22.99

The Beat Generation FAQ
by Rich Weidman
Backbeat Books
9781617136016 ....$19.99

Beer FAQ
by Jeff Cioletti
Backbeat Books
9781617136115 ....$24.99

Black Sabbath FAQ
by Martin Popoff
Backbeat Books
9780879309572....$19.99

Bob Dylan FAQ
by Bruce Pollock
Backbeat Books
9781617136078 ....$19.99

Britcoms FAQ
by Dave Thompson
Applause Books
9781495018992 ....$19.99

Bruce Springsteen FAQ
by John D. Luerssen
Backbeat Books
9781617130939.......$22.99

Buffy the Vampire Slayer FAQ
by David Bushman and Arthur Smith
Applause Books
9781495064722.....$19.99

Cabaret FAQ
by June Sawyers
Applause Books
9781495051449......$19.99

A Chorus Line FAQ
by Tom Rowan
Applause Books
9781480367548 ...$19.99

The Clash FAQ
by Gary J. Jucha
Backbeat Books
9781480364509 ..$19.99

Doctor Who Faq
by Dave Thompson
Applause Books
9781557838544 ....$22.99

The Doors FAQ
by Rich Weidman
Backbeat Books
9781617130175........$24.99

Dracula FAQ
by Bruce Scivally
Backbeat Books
9781617136009 .....$19.99

The Eagles FAQ
by Andrew Vaughan
Backbeat Books
9781480385412.....$24.99

Elvis Films FAQ
by Paul Simpson
Applause Books
9781557838582.....$24.99

Elvis Music FAQ
by Mike Eder
Backbeat Books
9781617130496......$22.99

Eric Clapton FAQ
by David Bowling
Backbeat Books
9781617134548 ......$22.99

Fab Four FAQ
by Stuart Shea and Robert Rodriguez
Hal Leonard Books
9781423421382.......$19.99

Fab Four FAQ 2.0
by Robert Rodriguez
Backbeat Books
9780879309688...$19.99

Film Noir FAQ
by David J. Hogan
Applause Books
9781557838551......$22.99

Football FAQ
by Dave Thompson
Backbeat Books
9781495007484...$24.99

Frank Zappa FAQ
by John Corcelli
Backbeat Books
9781617136030 ....$19.99

Godzilla FAQ
by Brian Solomon
Applause Books
9781495045684 $19.99

The Grateful Dead FAQ
by Tony Sclafani
Backbeat Books
9781617130861........$24.99

Guns N' Roses FAQ
by Rich Weidman
Backbeat Books
9781495025884 ..$19.99

Haunted America FAQ
by Dave Thompson
Backbeat Books
9781480392625.....$19.99

Horror Films FAQ
by John Kenneth Muir
Applause Books
9781557839503 ....$22.99

Jack the Ripper FAQ
by Dave Thompson
Applause Books
9781495063084....$19.99

James Bond FAQ
by Tom DeMichael
Backbeat Books
9781557838568.....$22.99

Jimi Hendrix FAQ
by Gary J. Jucha
Backbeat Books
9781617130953.......$22.99

Johnny Cash FAQ
by C. Eric Banister
Backbeat Books
9781480385405.. $24.99

KISS FAQ
by Dale Sherman
Backbeat Books
9781617130915........$24.99

Led Zeppelin FAQ
by George Case
Backbeat Books
9781617130250 ......$22.99

Lucille Ball FAQ
by James Sheridan and Barry Monush
Applause Books
9781617740824.......$19.99

MASH FAQ
by Dale Sherman
Applause Books
9781480355897.....$19.99

HAL•LEONARD®
PERFORMING ARTS
PUBLISHING GROUP

Prices, contents, and availability subject to change without notice.

FAQ.halleonardbooks.com